Connections

Effective Reading and Writing

William Van Nest

Prentice-Hall Canada Inc.,
Scarborough, Ontario

For My Mother and Father

Canadian Cataloguing in Publication Data

Van Nest, William
    Connections: effective reading and writing

ISBN 0-13-168097-8

1. Exposition (Rhetoric). 2. English language –
Composition and exercises.   3. College readers. I. Title

PE1429.V36 1987   808'.042   C87-094853-9

Prentice-Hall Inc., Englewood Cliffs, New Jersey
Prentice-Hall International, Inc., London
Prentice-Hall of Australia, Pty., Sydney
Prentice-Hall of India Pvt., Ltd., New Delhi
Prentice-Hall of Japan, Inc., Tokyo
Prentice-Hall of Southeast Asia (Pte.) Ltd., Singapore
Prentice-Hall do Brasil Ltda., Rio de Janeiro
Prentice-Hall Hispanoamericana, S.A., Mexico

ISBN 0-13-168097-8

Production Editor: John Metford
Cover: "Linkages" by Canadian Artist Antonio E Costa
    Courtesy Del Bello Gallery, Toronto
Designer: Lorraine Le Camp

Typesetter: ISIS Communications Limited

Printed and bound in Canada

1 2 3 4 5   92 91 90 89 88

Contents

Thematic Table of Contents   vi
Preface   ix

General Introduction – Connections   *1*

Reading and Vocabulary   2
Fast Reading and Slow Reading   3
Making Connections   4

Chapter One – Description   *8*

Introduction   8
The *Patna* at Sea, *Joseph Conrad*   11
Signs of Spring in the Valley? *Michael Harris*   14
Sophie, *Emily Carr*   16
Morocco, *Anaïs Nin*   22
Marrakech, *George Orwell*   30
The Acquisitors' Roost, *Peter C. Newman*   36
Writing Descriptions   42

Chapter Two – Narration   *44*

Introduction   44
Little Red Riding-Hood, *Traditional*   46
The Little Girl and the Wolf, *James Thurber*   48
The Coppermine Massacre, *Samuel Hearne*   50
A Gentleman of the Old School, *Nellie McClung*   54
The Halifax Explosion, *Hugh MacLennan*   62
The Diary of One Now Dead, *George C. Hodge*   69
Mr. Toad, *Kenneth Grahame*   76
Writing Narration   85

Chapter Three – Comparison and Contrast   *87*

Introduction   87
Deduction and Induction, *Irving Copi*   89
The Next Depression, *Michael Bliss*   93
Pronunciation, *Mark Orkin*   101

Erotica vs. Pornography, *Gloria Steinem*   107
The Death of the Moth, *Virginia Woolf*   113
Writing Comparisons   116

Chapter Four – Classification   *118*

Introduction   118
Distance in Man, *Edward T. Hall*   121
Giving Things Names, *S.I. Hayakawa*   131
Sheldon's Scale of Temperament, *Calvin S. Hall* and *Gardner Lindzey*   136
Winning and Losing at Work, *Michael Maccoby*   140
The Flames of Youth, *Wayne S. Wooden*   148
Writing Classifications   153

Chapter Five – Examples   *156*

Introduction   156
The Peter Principle, *Laurence J. Peter* and *Raymond Hull*   158
It Shouldn't Happen to a Vet, *James Herriot*   164
A Place in the Sun, *Debra Black*   170
The Painful Realities of the New Technology, *Rod McQueen*   175
Motorcycle Maintenance, *Robert Pirsig*   187
Canada's Forgotten Poor, *Leonard Shifrin*   193
Writing Examples   203

Chapter Six – Cause and Effect   *205*

Introduction   205
Being a Man, *Paul Theroux*   207
Guilty Verdict, *Kirk Makin*   211
Why Are Movies So Bad? *Pauline Kael*   216
Ice and Light, *Barry Lopez*   226
The Ladies Converse, *Robert Sommer*   235
Writing about Causes and Effects   244

Chapter Seven – Processes   *246*

Introduction   246
The Oxford English Dictionary, *Paul Roberts*   249
How to Weave a Basket, *Susan Sargent*   251
Secrets of the Squash King, *J.L. Welch*   258
The Basque Connection, *Harry Thurston*   263
A Day's Fishing, *Tiny Bennett*   277
Writing about Processes   286

Chapter Eight – *Definition*   *288*

Introduction   288
The Meaning of Cliché, *Bergen Evans* and *Cornelia Evans*   291
Profits, *John Kyle*   293
The Female System, *Anne Wilson Schaef*   303
Arrest, *Aleksandr Solzhenitsyn*   321
Writing Extended Definitions   337

Authors and Sources   339

Thematic Table of Contents

Business and Economics

The Acquisitors' Roost, *Peter C. Newman*   36
The Next Depression, *Michael Bliss*   93
Winning and Losing at Work, *Michael Maccoby*   140
The Peter Principle, *Laurence J. Peter* and *Raymond Hull*   158
A Place in the Sun, *Debra Black*   170
The Painful Realities of the New Technology, *Rod McQueen*   175
Profits, *John Kyle*   293

Canadiana

Signs of Spring in the Valley? *Michael Harris*   14
Sophie, *Emily Carr*   16
The Acquisitors' Roost, *Peter C. Newman*   36
The Coppermine Massacre, *Samuel Hearne*   50
A Gentleman of the Old School, *Nellie McClung*   54
The Halifax Explosion, *Hugh MacLennan*   62
The Diary of One Now Dead, *George C. Hodge*   69
The Next Depression, *Michael Bliss*   93
Pronunciation, *Mark Orkin*   101
A Place in the Sun, *Debra Black*   170
The Painful Realities of the New Technology, *Rod McQueen*   175
Canada's Forgotten Poor, *Leonard Shifrin*   193
Guilty Verdict, *Kirk Makin*   211
Ice and Light, *Barry Lopez*   226
Secrets of the Squash King, *J.L. Welch*   258
The Basque Connection, *Harry Thurston*   263
A Day's Fishing, *Tiny Bennett*   277

History and Politics

Marrakech, *George Orwell*   30
The Coppermine Massacre, *Samuel Hearne*   50
A Gentleman of the Old School, *Nellie McClung*   54
The Halifax Explosion, *Hugh MacLennan*   62

The Diary of One Now Dead, *George C. Hodge* 69
The Next Depression, *Michael Bliss* 93
Canada's Forgotten Poor, *Leonard Shifrin* 193
The Basque Connection, *Harry Thurston* 263
Arrest, *Aleksandr Solzhenitsyn* 321

Humour

The Little Girl and the Wolf, *James Thurber* 48
A Gentleman of the Old School, *Nellie McClung* 54
Mr. Toad, *Kenneth Grahame* 76
The Peter Principle, *Laurence J. Peter* and *Raymond Hull* 158
It Shouldn't Happen to a Vet, *James Herriot* 164
The Ladies Converse, *Robert Sommer* 235

Language

Pronunciation, *Mark Orkin* 101
Erotica vs. Pornography, *Gloria Steinem* 107
Distance in Man, *Edward T. Hall* 121
Giving Things Names, *S.I. Hayakawa* 131
The Ladies Converse, *Robert Sommer* 235
The Oxford English Dictionary, *Paul Roberts* 249
The Meaning of Cliché, *Bergen Evans* and *Cornelia Evans* 291
The Female System, *Anne Wilson Schaef* 303

Literature

The *Patna* at Sea, *Joseph Conrad* 11
Signs of Spring in the Valley? *Michael Harris* 14
Morocco, *Anaïs Nin* 22
Little Red Riding-Hood, *Traditional* 46
The Little Girl and the Wolf, *James Thurber* 48
The Halifax Explosion, *Hugh MacLennan* 62
Mr. Toad, *Kenneth Grahame* 76
The Death of the Moth, *Virginia Woolf* 113

Morality and Ethics

Marrakech, *George Orwell* 30
Erotica vs. Pornography, *Gloria Steinem* 107
Giving Things Names, *S.I. Hayakawa* 131
Being a Man, *Paul Theroux* 207
Guilty Verdict, *Kirk Makin* 211
Arrest, *Aleksandr Solzhenitsyn* 321

Personalities

Sophie, *Emily Carr*   16
Morocco, *Anaïs Nin*   22
The Acquisitors' Roost, *Peter C. Newman*   36
A Gentleman of the Old School, *Nellie McClung*   54
The Diary of One Now Dead, *George C. Hodge*   69
Sheldon's Scale of Temperament, *Calvin S. Hall* and *Gardner Lindzey*   136
Winning and Losing at Work, *Michael Maccoby*   140
The Flames of Youth, *Wayne S. Wooden*   148
Being a Man, *Paul Theroux*   207
Guilty Verdict, *Kirk Makin*   211
The Female System, *Anne Wilson Schaef*   303

Society and Culture

Morocco, *Anaïs Nin*   22
Marrakech, *George Orwell*   30
The Acquisitors' Roost, *Peter C. Newman*   36
Pronunciation, *Mark Orkin*   101
Erotica vs. Pornography, *Gloria Steinem*   107
Distance in Man, *Edward T. Hall*   121
Being a Man, *Paul Theroux*   207
Why Are Movies So Bad? *Pauline Kael*   216
How to Weave a Basket, *Susan Sargent*   251
Secrets of the Squash King, *J.L. Welch*   258
A Day's Fishing, *Tiny Bennett*   277
The Female System, *Anne Wilson Schaef*   303

Thinking

Deduction and Induction, *Irving Copi*   89
Erotica vs. Pornography, *Gloria Steinem*   107
The Death of the Moth, *Virginia Woolf*   113
Giving Things Names, *S.I. Hayakawa*   131
Motorcycle Maintenance, *Robert Pirsig*   187

Women and Men

Sophie, *Emily Carr*   16
Morocco, *Anaïs Nin*   22
The Little Girl and the Wolf, *James Thurber*   48
A Gentleman of the Old School, *Nellie McClung*   54
Erotica vs. Pornography, *Gloria Steinem*   107
Being a Man, *Paul Theroux*   207
The Female System, *Anne Wilson Schaef*   303

PREFACE

Connections is a book of selections illustrating traditional patterns of development in expository writing. The forty or so reading selections, largely from Canadian sources, include essays, diary entries, journalistic pieces, and literary fare. Each has been chosen for its intrinsic interest and for its relevance as an example of such expository techniques as comparison, classification, and process analysis. Students will find accompanying each selection questions which direct attention to reading comprehension and to special features of language and logic. Throughout the text, new words and expressions are introduced by exercises designed to develop students' reading vocabulary.

Connections is also a book for writers and furnishes writers of exposition with suggestions for their own work. Each of the eight chapters includes a discussion of the management, from the writer's point of view, of a particular expository technique and some suggested topics for practice which, taken together with the work on reading, get the writer off to a good start.

The book asks, really, that students learn to wear two hats. They are asked to be readers, to look and see what is actually going on, and then they are asked to be writers, to try their own hand at things. *Connections* is for readers and writers of practical expository prose. It pays attention to clarity, to logic, and to audience. It asks readers to look closely at what is on the page, and it asks writers to plan and take care when they put something on a page.

A number of friends and colleagues have contributed to the preparation of this book. I gratefully acknowledge the support of Frances Aspinall, John Flatt, Pamela Gilchrist, Katherine Hooke, George Tompkins, and Judith Wikman. In addition, I would like to thank the reviewers provided by the publisher: Dan Gaze, Jim Payne, Don Precosky, and Robert Watson. The project would not have been completed without the encouragement, patience, and skill of the editorial staff at Prentice-Hall Canada. To them, too, my thanks.

William Van Nest

GENERAL
INTRODUCTION
CONNECTIONS

Read not to contradict and confute, nor to believe and take for granted, not to find talk and discourse, but to weigh and consider. Some books are to be tasted, others to be swallowed, and some few to be chewed and digested; that is, some books are to be read only in parts; others to be read, but only curiously; and some few to be read wholly, and with diligence and attention.

Francis Bacon, "Of Studies"

This book works on the assumption that reading is a form of thinking, that, in particular, reading amounts to thinking along with a writer. An implication of this assumption is that readers can think and read more effectively if they practise an awareness of the patterns and signals writers ordinarily provide for them to follow.

The patterns represented in the more than forty readings in this book illustrate the principal approaches to presenting facts and ideas (description, comparison, classification, narration, examples, causality, processes, and definition). The selections are not models. They are meant to serve as samples which show how these methods work and to give readers practice in attuning themselves to the patterns of a writer's thinking.

This book samples writing which sets out to add to the reader's store of information and to the reader's understanding. When writers set out to present things to readers, they treat the world of experience as though it were composed of objects and events. The world is made to stand still and its objects are described, or it is set in motion and events are narrated. Descriptions treat the world of objects, structures, and

1

static relationships and answer questions like *who, what,* and *where.* Descriptions are concerned with sensory data (appearances, smells, sounds), measurements (size, magnitude), meanings, and logical relations. Narratives, on the other hand, treat a world of events, functions, and dynamic relations. They answer questions like *how, why,* and *when* and are concerned with the connections between events, with the manner in which things are done, and with outcomes.

In order to give readers practice in following the patterns and recognizing the signals in a writer's explanation, an array of questions accompanies each selection. The questions aim at directing the reader's attention to significant features of the writer's thinking, pointing out important connections, developments, and transitions, and suggesting how they work. At the beginning of each section the reader will find a discussion of the pattern represented. Narratives do not work like descriptions, and a reader needs to recognize the differences. A reader needs to know what to look for, say, in a comparison or a definition, and how causal connections are made.

Reading and Vocabulary

Each of us has four vocabularies, not one: a speaking vocabulary, a listening vocabulary, a writing vocabulary, and a reading vocabulary. While these vocabularies overlap one another and most common expressions can be found in all four, a word or expression first enters a vocabulary when it is heard or read. When people are very young, they acquire a beginning vocabulary by asking the names of designated common objects and by pronouncing the names. The expressions enter the hearing vocabulary and migrate very quickly to the speaking vocabulary. Later in life, a word or expression may stick in the reading vocabulary and not find use or expression in any of the others. Everyone can think of a word which is familiar enough when read but which, for one reason or another, is not ordinarily written or spoken and is seldom heard. Most later vocabulary growth occurs as a natural part of reading, and most new expressions first enter our vocabularies by this route (where many stick rather than migrate to any of the other three vocabularies).

Some approaches to reading are particularly suited to the acquisition of new words and readily admit them into reading vocabularies. An example of such a useful practice might be called the "Underlining and Dictionary Method." It simply requires the reader to use a pen and a dictionary to "capture" new or unusual words in the following way:

1. Whenever a new word is encountered, it is underlined or circled.
2. The meaning of the new word is ascertained by consulting a standard dictionary, and an appropriate note is made in the margin.

If this procedure is followed systematically, a reader naturally will begin to acquire new words. At its first occurrence the word "factitious" may be only a curiosity, but a reader will encounter this stranger several times: when it is first discovered on the page, when it is marked or underlined, when it is located in the dictionary, and when a marginal note is entered. When the word "factitious" appears a second time, a careful reader will have encountered it quite a few times already and likely will find it familiar.

This procedure is encouraged in the exercises and comments which accompany the selections: words and expressions which a reader may encounter for the first time are singled out and are meant to be marked and investigated with pen and dictionary as a natural way of admitting them to vocabularies.

Fast Reading and Slow Reading

As the "Underlining and Dictionary Method" of vocabulary acquisition suggests, efficient reading is often slow reading (slow enough to underline a new word, consult a dictionary, and make a marginal note), but this sort of efficiency may not be recognized by those who associate efficiency with speed. The popularity of speed-reading courses and the emphasis on reading rates which would have readers develop a capacity for gulping down six or eight hundred words per minute have tended to obscure the wisdom of Bacon's remark about tasting, swallowing, chewing, and digesting reading fare. When the objective is to find specific ideas and bits of information, an efficient reader *does* need to be able to read quickly, leaping over and ignoring irrelevant material or skimming content to get acquainted with the drift. But just as surely an efficient reader must be able to go slowly along a writer's path, to read "wholly and with diligence and attention."

The selections in this book are meant to be read twice: the first time to get a notion of the writer's route and intent and the second time to follow the writer's thinking in detail. The reader should pay attention to the first and last paragraphs and to the first sentence or two of each middle paragraph, because most writers announce their intentions at the beginning and restate their main ideas at the end. A quick look at the middle paragraphs will yield an impression, but an impression only, of the writer's route. This way a reader gets acquainted with the general drift of things. This first reading, a form of skimming, is meant to acquaint a reader with the map of the writer's territory. The second reading invites a reader to move along the writer's actual path through the territory. One asks: "What's this?" "What's going on here?" "What does this mean?" "Why are we going this way?" Good slow readers ask these questions. Good writers provide answers, and the mutual enterprise goes ahead.

Making Connections

The writer is a connecting link between the reader and the reality of the writer's world. The writer must know the territory through which a reader is invited to travel and accept the responsibility of guiding a reader through it. Therefore the writer must be faithful to the facts and helpful to the reader.

A WRITER NEEDS TO KNOW THE FACTS AND THEREFORE SHOULD WRITE ABOUT THE FAMILIAR.

This is the most common advice given to writers. Often, however, "the familiar" is taken to mean "the ordinary," that with which everyone is presumably familiar. But the familiarity here is the writer's, not the reader's, for there is little point in guiding a reader through common-places unless there is some special corner which few know about and fewer still have explored.

A WRITER NEEDS TO KNOW HOW THE FACTS ARRANGE THEMSELVES.

Many people who are familiar with, say, automobiles and how they work can disassemble an engine, leaving piles of parts here and there on the garage floor, and then reassemble the parts into something that works more or less the way it should. However very often this is rote work. The worker knows one way things go together, but if asked why or how they go together, the rote worker will say, "It just goes that way." Someone who tries to learn from a rote worker will be invited to imitate the rote worker: "Watch me and do what I do." The writer cannot ask the reader to imitate; the writer needs to be able to say why something is done, what the alternatives are, how a job should be approached. The writer needs to know the form of the work – how it is similar to other jobs, what the connections are, and the different ways in which the facts arrange themselves.

THE WRITER MUST DECIDE WHO THE READER IS.

Even though the writer is the reader's servant, the writer invents a reader to whom the work is addressed. The writer decides what a reader already knows and begins from there; the writer decides what the reader wants to know and sticks to that. If the writer decides that a comparison of oil-based and latex paints is meant to help a householder make decisions about decorating the kitchen, then a discussion of obsolete paints and mixing procedures wastes that reader's time and will not hold his or her attention. If the writer's reader, though, is a neophyte paint-seller, then an understanding of the ease with which modern paints can be used by a semi-skilled householder (without the highly-developed skills of old-time painters, who were part chemist and part alchemist) very well may be important. The writer needs to ask, "Who is this for?" "Who will read this?" "What will the reader want from my writing?"

THE WRITER'S PURPOSE NEEDS TO BE CLEAR TO THE READER.

Certainly the general aim of any writing is to inform a reader or to help a reader understand, but the writer must have a more specific aim. Through what particular aspects of a subject should a reader be led in order for the reader to acquire a more thorough understanding? What will a reader be able to do, having read the writer's explanations? The reader needs to know why the writer is writing, and the writer must say how the message will profit the reader.

THE WRITER'S LANGUAGE SHOULD KEEP THE CONNECTION WITHIN REACH.

The writer needs to decide what sort of language will work for the reader. This decision is implicit in the larger decision about who the reader is. A chemical engineer writing for other chemical engineers must know that technically precise expression is expected. That same engineer, writing for a technician who needs to be told how a particular metering device is to be calibrated, will adopt the language of the expert addressing an assistant. Should the engineer need to write for the general public or certain management people, the level of technical expertise reflected in the language will be suitably modest. Only those who choose not be understood refuse to modify their language and take refuge in obfuscation.

THE WRITER SHOULD CONFIDE IN THE READER.

Sometimes everything is not perfectly clear or certain; the ground may be soft or the path a bit tricky; a reader should be told this. It is not required that the writer know everything with perfect certainty any more than it is required that a guide be clairvoyant. A writer who sets out to explain why it is that the leaves of deciduous trees turn colours in the fall may fairly acknowledge that the mechanisms of plant sugars are a mystery and yet produce a useful explanation which features the effects of the shortened photoperiod of autumn. By taking the reader into his or her confidence, the writer gives the reader confidence.

THE WRITER SHOULD FOLLOW THE MAXIM, "TELL YOUR READER WHAT YOU ARE GOING TO SAY, SAY IT, AND THEN TELL YOUR READER WHAT YOU'VE SAID."

No matter what specific approach the writer takes, no matter what connecting device is used, the overall organization should (to cite an older formula) have a beginning, a middle, and an end. In the beginning the reader is told what is going to happen, in the middle the main work gets done, and at the end the result is identified.

THE WRITER NEEDS TO HELP THE READER GET READY.

The writer is a guide to the reader and, like any good guide, needs to explain to his or her companion, before they set out, the route they will follow, where they are going, and how they are going to get there. It is exactly like any other journey. If the traveller has had a look at the map first, can anticipate the stops along the way, and knows what the territory will look like – where it will be most interesting and where it is likely to be a bit dull – then the journey has a shape, seems shorter, and more readily engages the traveller. Otherwise, for the reader, as for the traveller, it is too much like riding the night-train with no landmarks to be seen, mysterious stops along isolated sidings, the conductor muttering the names of obscure stations ahead.

THE WRITER SHOULD SIGNAL INTENTIONS.

The connections between the parts of the discussion need to be clearly indicated so that the reader can anticipate the order of the writer's presentation. If the writer works with three examples, each of which illustrates a different aspect of a topic, then the fact that three examples are about to be presented should be announced. The writer should not leave it to the reader to puzzle out what is happening. The traffic rule applies.

THE WRITER SHOULD REMIND THE READER OF WHAT HAS HAPPENED.

When the writer has finished explaining the route they have taken, its result should be identified or summarized so that the reader can more easily assimilate, or "process," the information. In summarizing, the writer packages the final product so that the reader can more easily carry it away.

Making connections is one of the most important jobs writers do because an understanding of the facts of experience is fundamental to our working together, whatever the situation. It is even fundamental to constructive disagreements, for unless the parties to a dispute have a shared understanding of the facts, what should be done about them is impossible to settle, and people remain forever at loggerheads. Writing and reading are two aspects of the single process of reaching mutual understanding and comprise two sets of mutual responsibilities: writers need to work to help readers, and readers need to know how to help themselves.

CHAPTER

ONE

DESCRIPTION

*Your sheep that were wont to be so meek and tame, and so
small eaters, now ... become so great devourers and so wild,
that they eat up and swallow down the very men themselves.
They consume, destroy and devour whole fields, houses and
cities.*

Thomas More, *Utopia*

INTRODUCTION

Descriptions serve to give the reader an awareness of the sensory reality
of experience, and therefore the writer of a description aims to summon
up for the reader the sensory qualities of objects and events – how they
look, smell, taste, sound. Almost any approach, any device or technique,
may be appropriate. The writer may seek to convey the qualities of an
experience in images (words for pictures), through the sound of language, in the choice of words, or by an emphasis on significant details.
The best, the most effective, and the most telling descriptions present
the reader with sensory specifics, with details which appeal ultimately
to the senses. Impoverished descriptions lack attention to such details.
Thomas More's description of the enclosure of common lands which
depopulated the English countryside in the fifteenth and sixteenth centuries retains its force, despite the centuries, from the image of flocks of
wild sheep swallowing the country and its people whole and from vivid
phrases such as "consume, destroy and devour" and "eat up and swallow down."

Emily Carr's account in *Klee Wyck* of her discovery of a totem, a
"great wooden image," has a vividness of detail, enforced by the plain-

8

ness of her language, which brings almost the same "Oh's" from the reader as Carr says were "jerked" out of her:

> Her head and trunk were carved out of, or rather into, the bole of a great red cedar. She seemed to be part of the tree itself, as if she had grown there at its heart, and the carver had only chipped away the outer wood so you could see her. Her arms were spliced and socketed to the trunk, and were flung wide in a circling compelling movement. Her breasts were two eagle heads, fiercely carved. That much, and the column of her great neck, and her strong chin, I had seen when I slithered to the ground beneath her. Now I saw her face.[1]

And here is the description of that face:

> The eyes were two rounds of black, set in wider rounds of white, and placed in deep sockets under wide, black eyebrows. Their fixed stare bored into me as if the very life of the old cedar looked out, and it seemed that the voice of the cedar itself might have burst from that great round cavity, with projecting lips, that was her mouth. Her ears were round, and stuck out to catch all sounds. The salt air had not dimmed the heavy red of her trunk and arms and thighs. Her hands were black, with blunt finger-tips painted a dazzling white. I stood looking at her for a long, long time.[2]

In this description there is a sense of climax and suspense ("Now I saw her face") as the writer leads the reader through the experience of a dramatic discovery, and the plainness of the language helps make the experience available to everyone.

In direct contrast to Carr's force and simplicity, a writer sometimes may strive with elaborate, decorative language to orchestrate or to heighten the effect of the description. This excerpt from *Saunterings* by Sarah Jeanette Duncan describes a July night in the countryside around Picton, Prince Edward County, Ontario (1886):

> It is ten o'clock when we puff into Picton, and at eleven we are driving through the soft radiance of a July moon, that shows us on one side of the road symmetrical maples ... on the other, glimmering whitely through the dark cedars and wild undergrowth, the sandbanks.... Silhouetted against the

[1]Emily Carr, *Klee Wyck* (Toronto: Irwin Publishing Inc., 1941), p. 33.
[2]*Ibid.*

sky, the dead cedars stretch pathetic arms above us, and
every now and then a plash from Lake Ontario, quiet tonight,
sounds from behind them.[3]

The writer's "pretty" language and the images which it calls up seem as
soft and alluring as the experience itself: "Dead cedars stretch pathetic
arms above us" and "the soft radiance of a July moon." The words
"plash" and "puff" would be out of place in Carr's description, and
Duncan's cedars are not Carr's. The two descriptions serve to illustrate
the writer's choices between the simplicity and the sophistication with
which experience can be portrayed for the reader.

Sometimes the writer, it seems, withdraws entirely from the writing, appears to want the object or the experience to stand alone, by
itself, with little help from the language, in what might be called an
"objective" description. Police officers are trained to gather the facts of a
situation (height, weight, time of day, colour of hair), doctors record
symptoms of illness, and engineers specify measurements and render
accurate drawings of mechanisms. These objective or technical descriptions are meant to serve the special interests of those who would
identify criminals and diseases, build devices, or reproduce results for
testing. Here is a typical example of this kind of description:

> [It is] a continuous sound from about half a second to eleven
> seconds in length. It consists of a fundamental frequency
> which may lie between 150 and 780 cycles per second, and
> up to 12 harmonically related overtones. Most of the time,
> the pitch remains constant or varies smoothly, and may
> change direction as many as four or five times. Total intensity
> does not greatly vary throughout.[4]

This description of a wolf howl uses information derived from applying
"spectographic and auditory analysis techniques to seven hundred howls
of three adult male wolves" and aims at accurately identifying the
features and components of a wolf's howl. Compare this technical description with one derived from an old trapper's account of the
experience:

> Take a dozen railroad whistles, braid them together and then
> let one strand after another drop off, the last peal so frightfully
> piercing as to go through your heart and soul.[5]

[3]Sarah J. Duncan, "Saunterings," *The Week* (1886).
[4]J. B. Theberge and J. B. Falls, "Howling as a Means of Communication in Timber Wolves,"
The American Zoologist, 7(1967), 334. Quoted in L. David Mech, *The Wolf* (Published for
the American Museum of Natural History by the Natural History Press, 1970), p. 97.
[5]H.W. Shoemaker, *Extinct Pennsylvania Animals* (2 volumes) (Altoona, Pa., 1917-19).
Quoted in Mech, *The Wolf*.

Here the wolf's howl is described in terms of the effect it has on a human listener, but we can be sure that the researchers, having heard seven hundred wolf howls during the course of their investigations, experienced no such excitement. They were no doubt busy adjusting meters and gathering up graphic print-outs.

It should be clear then that a reader needs to be aware of the writer's apparent intention in producing the description, as well as of the effect which the description calls forth. The reader needs to ask what the description sets out to do and needs to know what to do with it. Reading with these kinds of questions in mind helps readers understand writers; conversely, writing with these kinds of questions in mind helps writers understand readers. A description of the effect of an event (how the trapper felt) does not have the same purpose as, say, a spectographic analysis of a wolf howl and needs to be understood on its own terms.

The *Patna* at Sea
Joseph Conrad

This brief sketch from Conrad's novel Lord Jim *captures Nature's indifference to human affairs as well as the serenity of a night on the Arabian Sea.*

A marvellous stillness pervaded the world, and the stars, together   *1*
with the serenity of their rays, seemed to shed upon the earth the assurance of everlasting security. The young moon recurved, and shining low in the west, was like a slender shaving thrown up from a bar of gold, and the Arabian Sea, smooth and cool to the eye like a sheet of ice, extended its perfect level to the perfect circle of a dark horizon. The propeller turned without a check, as though its beat had been part of the scheme of a safe universe; and on each side of the *Patna* two deep folds of water, permanent and sombre on the unwrinkled shimmer, enclosed within their straight and diverging ridges a few white swirls of foam bursting in a low hiss, a few wavelets, a few ripples, a few undulations that, left behind, agitated the surface of the sea for an instant after the passage of the ship, subsided splashing gently, calmed down at last into the circular stillness of water and sky with the black speck of the moving hull remaining everlastingly in its centre.

Jim on the bridge was penetrated by the great certitude of   *2* unbounded safety and peace that could be read on the silent aspect of nature like the certitude of fostering love upon the placid tenderness of a mother's face. Below the roof of awnings, surrendered to the wisdom of white men and to their courage, trusting the power of their unbelief and the iron shell of their fire-ship, the pilgrims of an exacting faith slept on mats, on blankets, on bare planks, on every deck, in all the dark corners, wrapped in dyed cloths, muffled in soiled rags, with their heads resting on small bundles, with their faces pressed to bent forearms: the men, the women, the children; the old with the young, the decrepit with the lusty – all equal before sleep, death's brother.

3   A draught of air, fanned from forward by the speed of the ship, passed steadily through the long gloom between the high bulwarks, swept over the rows of prone bodies; a few dim flames in globe-lamps were hung short here and there under the ridge-poles, and in the blurred circles of light thrown down and trembling slightly to the unceasing vibration of the ship appeared a chin upturned, two closed eyelids, a dark hand with silver rings, a meagre limb draped in a torn covering, a head bent back, a naked foot, a throat bared and stretched as if offering itself to the knife. The well-to-do had made for their families shelters with heavy boxes and dusty mats; the poor reposed side by side with all they had on earth tied up in a rag under their heads; the lone old men slept, with drawn-up legs, upon their prayer-carpets, with their hands over their ears and one elbow on each side of the face; a father, his shoulders up and his knees under his forehead, dozed dejectedly by a boy who slept on his back with tousled hair and one arm commandingly extended; a woman covered from head to foot, like a corpse, with a piece of white sheeting, had a naked child in the hollow of each arm; the Arab's belongings, piled right aft, made a heavy mound of broken outlines, with a cargo-lamp swung above, and a great confusion of vague forms behind: gleams of paunchy brass pots, the foot-rest of a deck-chair, blades of spears, the straight scabbard of an old sword leaning against a heap of pillows, the spout of a tin coffee-pot. The patent log on the taffrail periodically rang a single tinkling stroke for every mile traversed on an errand of faith. Above the mass of sleepers a faint and patient sigh at times floated, the exhalation of a troubled dream; and short metallic clangs bursting out suddenly in the depths of the ship, the harsh scrape of a shovel, the violent slam of a furnace-door, exploded brutally, as if the men handling the mysterious things below had their breasts full of fierce anger: while the slim high hull of the steamer went on evenly ahead, without a sway of her bare masts, cleaving continuously the great calm of the waters under the inaccessible serenity of the sky.

QUESTIONS

Language and Style

1. What aspects of this description resemble a seascape painting?

2. This description of a passenger vessel loaded with pilgrims comes immediately before the account of the vessel's shipwreck in the Arabian Sea. How would you expect the language to change when the vessel runs into trouble?

3. Consider the writer's choice of language. What particular words and expressions contribute to the general effect of the description?

4. These three paragraphs contain only nine sentences. Why should the sentences be so long?

5. Notice the final sentence of paragraph 3. To what sense does the description most obviously appeal? Is this true of the description as a whole?

6. What sort of music would you suggest to accompany the description?

7. Can you identify lists and repetitions similar to those which close out the first paragraph? Why should they be appropriate? What is their effect?

Organization

1. How is the scene along the deck lit for the reader?

2. Each of the three paragraphs deals with a different aspect of the scene. What are the aspects?

Content

1. In what ways is Conrad's description not a literal description? What would such a literal description miss?

Vocabulary

undulations   paunchy
patent log

Signs of Spring in the Valley?

Michael Harris

Like some landscape paintings, Harris's seasonal newspaper piece puts a Spring figure in a Spring scene.

1   Spectral in the uncertain light, a lone figure climbs the long slope, following the line of the fence. Behind him, the farm buildings and the bleak limbs of an apple orchard have yet to emerge from the gloom of early morning. When the figure, now recognizable as that of a man, reaches the crest of the hill, it turns and looks back.

2   The Annapolis Valley, Nova Scotia's richest farmland, stretches before him – snowless patchwork fields ringed by a low range of mountains and cut by the pale, broad expanse of the Avon River. It is the first clear morning after days of rain and everything looks gently swollen.

3   But work is on the mind of Watson McNeil this morning. Having risen before first light to feed his hundred head of cattle, he must now walk the fence-lines, marking the places where new stakes are needed. Whittled to pencil-point sharpness, the replacements lay stacked in the farmyard, the winter work of Wat, 65, and his 66-year-old brother, Graham.

4   Continuing his reconnaissance, Wat looks for signs of true spring and a possible early start of the farm's operation. Normally, the land would be too wet to work until May, but the winter has been mild, nearly without snow, and the farm's two ponds are ice-free. So is the Avon River where the first flock of Canada geese is already at swim. Winter-frozen earth smells, released by the March sun, ride the mild air.

5   As he begins his descent on a path that leads to the dykeland abutting the river, the man in the green coveralls and rubber boots stops to pick up a snare hidden in the wheat-colored stubble. Intended for pheasant, it can also catch cats and dogs, as Wat has discovered. Snapping its lethal loop in his hands, he looks briefly toward the town suburbs spreading toward the farmland, then resumes his walk. It is not one of his favorite vistas.

6   In bygone days, he might have returned to the farmhouse by way of the limestone quarry, a horseshoe-shaped canyon near the river from which his father and brothers used to blast limestone for

"Signs of Spring in the Valley?", by Michael Harris. The Globe and Mail, *Toronto (March 25, 1983).*

fertilizing the fields. But the limestone, as Wat wryly advises, is as heavy as ever. So he doesn't bother to inspect the quarry's curious outcroppings of rusty, yellowish rocks. Instead, when he reaches the line of pine forest bordering the dykeland, he follows the barbed wire fence back in the direction from which he has come. From my bedroom window, I wonder if he will stop by for coffee and "the news."

As if debating the same proposition, he lingers for a moment,   *7* then begins down the sloping cornfield towards his own farmhouse. When he reaches the yard, a cat curls around his ankles, arching its back. Graham McNeil emerges from the woodshed with a chainsaw, on his way to trim and burn alder bushes. After a short conference with his brother, Wat disappears into the barn. I remember they are expecting a calf to be born.

Two days later, he appears at my door, as he does every second   *8* Sunday, with a bag of apples and a gunny sack of bailing twine. The bailing twine, I have learned, is excellent kindling. Sitting in front of a fire, he tells me with a shy grin that Graham has taken to practicing with their workhorse for the annual ploughing match. "Last year he came in third and won a bunch of strawberry plants. This year he means for things to be different."

The conversation shifts to the weather, which we both agree is   *9* unpredictable. "They say partridge berries are a sign of heavy snow," Wat says, his blue eyes shining, "but this year there was lots of berries and no snow. You just can't tell."

An hour later I watch him make his way through the line of giant   *10* elms which form a windbreak for the house. Caught in the afternoon sunlight, he looks younger than his years, an impression reinforced when he drops to one knee and picks up a handful of soil. Letting it escape between his fingers, I see him smile and, with that, it is easier to believe in the returning spring.

QUESTIONS

Language and Style

1. Consider how the writer makes language work, especially at the beginning of the essay. Why should Harris have chosen to write "at swim" rather than "is swimming"? Why should everything look "gently swollen"?

2. Compare the different tones of paragraphs 4, 5, 8, and 9. What connection does there seem to be between subject and tone?

3. Why is the relatively simple language of the essay appropriate?

Organization

1. There is a sense in which this description works like a series of photographs. What is the focus of the first seven paragraphs? Paragraphs 8 and 9? Paragraph 10? Who is the "camera"? Why is Wat not the camera?

Content

1. Not a great deal happens in Harris's descriptive essay, and it may be easy to think of it as a sort of landscape painting. But, on closer inspection, could the intention to be describe a relationship? Why might this be? Can you identify and explain the relationship?

2. In paragraph 5, two unpleasant matters are mentioned. What are they? How might they go together?

Vocabulary

spectral	abutting
reconnaissance	vistas
dykeland	gunny sack

Sophie
Emily Carr

In this chapter of her book Klee Wyck, *Emily Carr gives a very personal account of her friend Sophie, to whom the book is dedicated.*

1   Sophie's house was bare but clean. It had three rooms. Later when it got cold Sophie's Frank would cut out all the partition walls. Sophie said, "Thlee 'loom, thlee stobe. One 'loom, one stobe." The floor of the house was clean scrubbed. It was chair, table, and bed for the family. There was one chair; the coal-oil lamp sat on that. Sophie pushed the babies into corners, spread my old clothes on the floor to appraise them, and was satisfied. So, having tested each other's trade-straightedness, we began a long, long friendship – forty years. I have seen Sophie glad, sad, sick, and drunk. I have asked her why she did this or that thing – Indian ways that I did not understand – her answer was invariably, "Nice ladies always do." That was Sophie's ideal – being nice.

From Klee Wyck *by Emily Carr. Copyright © 1941 by Irwin Publishing Inc. Reprinted by permission of the Publishers.*

Every year Sophie had a new baby. Almost every year she buried   *2*
one. Her little graves were dotted all over the cemetery. I never
knew more than three of her twenty-one children to be alive at one
time. By the time she was in her early fifties every child was dead
and Sophie had cried her eyes dry. Then she took to drink.

"I got a new baby! I got a new baby!"   *3*
Sophie, seated on the floor of her house, saw me coming through   *4*
the open door and waved the papoose cradle. Two little girls rolled
round on the floor; the new baby was near her in a basket-cradle.
Sophie took off the cloth tented over the basket and exhibited the
baby, a lean, poor thing.
Sophie herself was small and spare. Her black hair sprang thick   *5*
and strong on each side of the clean, straight parting and hung in
twin braids across her shoulders. Her eyes were sad and heavy-
lidded. Between prominent rounded cheekbones her nose lay rather
flat, broadening and snubby at the tip. Her wide upper lip pouted. It
was sharp-edged, puckering over a row of poor teeth — the sooth-
ing pucker of lips trying to ease an aching tooth or to hush a
crying child. She had a soft little body, a back straight as honesty
itself, and the small hands and feet of an Indian.
Sophie's English was good enough, but when Frank, her husband,   *6*
was there she became dumb as a plate.
"Why won't you talk before Frank, Sophie?"   *7*
"Frank he learn school English. Me, no. Frank laugh my English   *8*
words."
When we were alone she chattered to me like a sparrow.   *9*

In May, when the village was white with cherry blossom and the   *10*
blue water of Burrard Inlet crept almost to Sophie's door — just a
streak of grey sand and a plank walk between — and when Vancouver city was more beautiful to look at across the water than to
be in — it was then I loved to take the ferry to the North Shore and
to Sophie's.
Behind the village stood mountains topped by the grand old   *11*
"Lions," twin peaks, very white and blue. The nearer mountains
were every shade of young foliage, tender grey-green, getting greener
and greener till, when they were close, you saw that the village
grass outgreened them all. Hens strutted their broods, papooses
and pups and kittens rolled everywhere — it was good indeed to
spend a day on the Reserve in spring.
Sophie and I went to see her babies' graves first. Sophie took her   *12*
best plaid skirt, the one that had three rows of velvet ribbon round
the hem, from a nail on the wall, and bound a yellow silk handkerchief round her head. No matter what the weather, she always wore
her great shawl, clamping it down with her arms, the fringe trick-
ling over her fingers. Sophie wore her shoes when she walked with
me, if she remembered.

13   Across the water we could see the city. The Indian Reserve was a different world — no hurry, no business.

14   We walked over the twisty, up-and-down road to the cemetery. Casamin, Tommy, George, Rosie, Maria, Emily, and all the rest were there under a tangle of vines. We rambled, seeking out Sophie's graves. Some had little wooden crosses, some had stones. Two babies lay outside the cemetery fence: they had not faced life long enough for baptism.

15   "See! Me got stone for Rosie now."

16   "It looks very nice. It must have cost lots of money, Sophie."

17   "Grave man make cheap for me. He say, 'You got lots, lots stone from me, Sophie. Maybe bymby you get some more died baby, then you want more stone. So I make cheap for you.' "

18   Sophie's kitchen was crammed with excited women. They had come to see Sophie's brand-new twins. Sophie was on a mattress beside the cook stove. The twin girls were in small basket papoose cradles, woven by Sophie herself. The babies were wrapped in cotton wool which made their dark little faces look darker; they were laced into their baskets and stuck up at the edge of Sophie's mattress beside the kitchen stove. Their brown, wrinkled faces were like potatoes baked in their jackets, their hands no bigger than brown spiders.

19   They were thrilling, those very, very tiny babies. Everybody was excited over them. I sat down on the floor close to Sophie.

20   "Sophie, if the baby was a girl it was to have my name. There are two babies and I have only one name. What are we going to do about it?"

21   "The biggest and the best is yours," said Sophie.

22   My Em'ly lived three months. Sophie's Maria lived three weeks. I bought Em'ly's tombstone. Sophie bought Maria's.

23   Sophie's "mad" rampaged inside her like a lion roaring in the breast of a dove.

24   "Look see," she said, holding a red and yellow handkerchief, caught together at the corners and chinking with broken glass and bits of plaster of Paris. "Bad boy bloke my grave flower! Cost five dollar one, and now boy all bloke fo' me. Bad, bad boy! You come talk me fo' p'liceman?"

25   At the City Hall she spread the handkerchief on the table and held half a plaster of Paris lily and a dove's tail up to the eyes of the law, while I talked.

26   "My mad fo' boy bloke my plitty glave flower," she said, forgetting, in her fury, to be shy of the "English words."

27   The big man of the law was kind. He said, "It's too bad, Sophie. What do you want me to do about it?"

"You make boy buy more this plitty kind for my glave." *28*

"The boy has no money but I can make his old grandmother pay *29*
a little every week."

Sophie looked long at the broken pieces and shook her head. *30*

"That ole, ole woman got no money." Sophie's anger was dying, *31*
soothed by sympathy like a child, the woman in her tender towards
old Granny. "My bloke no matter for ole woman," said Sophie,
gathering up the pieces. "You scold boy big, Policeman? No make
glanny pay."

"I sure will, Sophie." *32*

There was a black skirt spread over the top of the packing case *33*
in the centre of Sophie's room. On it stood the small white coffin. A
lighted candle was at the head, another at the foot. The little dead
girl in the coffin held a doll in her arms. It had hardly been out of
them since I had taken it to her a week before. The glassy eyes of
the doll stared out of the coffin, up past the closed eyelids of the
child.

Though Sophie had been through this nineteen times before, the *34*
twentieth time was no easier. Her two friends, Susan and Sara, were
there by the coffin, crying for her.

The outer door opened and a half dozen women came in, their *35*
shawls drawn low across their foreheads, their faces grim. They
stepped over to the coffin and looked in. Then they sat around it on
the floor and began to cry, first with baby whimpers, softly, then
louder, louder still – with violence and strong howling: torrents of
tears burst from their eyes and rolled down their cheeks. Sophie
and Sara and Susan did it too. It sounded horrible – like tortured
dogs.

Suddenly they stopped. Sophie went to the bucket and got water *36*
in a tin basin. She took a towel in her hand and went to each of the
guests in turn holding the basin while they washed their faces and
dried them on the towel. Then the women all went out except
Sophie, Sara and Susan. This crying had gone on at intervals for
three days – ever since the child had died. Sophie was worn out.
There had been too all the long weeks of Rosie's tubercular dying
to go through.

"Sophie, couldn't you lie down and rest?" *37*

She shook her head. "Nobody sleep in Injun house till dead *38*
people go to cemet'ry."

The beds had all been taken away. *39*

"When is the funeral?" *40*

"I dunno, Pliest go Vancouver. He not come two more day. 'Spose *41*
I gots lots money he come quick. No hully up, except fo' money."

She laid her hand on the corner of the little coffin. *42*

"See! Coffin-man think box fo' Injun baby no matter." *43*

44   The seams of the cheap little coffin had burst.

45   Sophie's other neighbour, Susan, produced and buried babies almost as fast as Sophie herself. The two women laughed for each other and cried for each other. With babies on their backs and baskets on their arms they crossed over on the ferry to Vancouver and sold their baskets from door to door. When they came to my studio they rested and drank tea with me. My parrot, sheep dog, the white rats, and the totem pole pictures all interested them. "An' you got Injun flowers too," said Susan.

46   "Indian flowers?"

47   She pointed to ferns and wild things I had brought in from the woods.

48   Sophie's house was shut up. There was a chain and padlock on the gate. I went to Susan.

49   "Where is Sophie?"

50   "Sophie in sick house. Got sick eye."

51   I went to the hospital. The little Indian ward had four beds. I took ice cream and the nurse divided it into four portions.

52   A homesick little Indian girl cried in the bed in one corner, an old woman grumbled in another. In a third there was a young mother with a baby, and in the fourth bed was Sophie.

53   There were flowers. The room was bright. It seemed to me that the four brown faces on the four white pillows should be happier and far more comfortable here than lying on mattresses on the hard floors in the village, with all the family muddle going on about them.

54   "How nice it is here, Sophie."

55   "Not much good of hospital, Em'ly."

56   "Oh! What is the matter with it?"

57   "Bad bed."

58   "What is wrong with the beds?"

59   "Move, move, all time shake. 'Spose me move, bed move too."

60   She rolled herself to show me how the springs worked. "Me ole'-fashioned, Em'ly. Me like kitchen floor fo' sick."

61   Susan and Sophie were in my kitchen, rocking their sorrows back and forth and alternately wagging their heads and giggling with shut eyes at some small joke.

62   "You go live Victoria now, Em'ly," wailed Sophie, "and we never see those babies, never!"

63   Neither woman had a baby on her back these days. But each had a little new grave in the cemetery. I had told them about a friend's twin babies. I went to the telephone.

64   "Mrs. Dingle, you said I might bring Sophie to see the twins?"

65   "Surely, any time," came the ready reply.

66   "Come, Sophie and Susan, we can go and see the babies now."

The mothers of all those little cemetery mounds stood looking   *67*
and looking at the thriving white babies, kicking and sprawling on
their bed. The women said, "Oh my! Oh my!" over and over.

Susan's hand crept from beneath her shawl to touch a baby's leg.   *68*
Sophie's hand shot out and slapped Susan's.

The mother of the babies said, "It's all right, Susan; you may   *69*
touch my baby."

Sophie's eyes burned Susan for daring to do what she so longed   *70*
to do herself. She folded her hands resolutely under her shawl and
whispered to me:

"Nice ladies don' touch, Em'ly."   *71*

QUESTIONS

Language and Style

1. Carr's choice of language seems especially well-suited to the subject. In what ways do the subject and the language most obviously complement one another?

2. Consider some of the comparisons in this sketch. See paragraphs 6, 9, and 18 for example. How does this sort of comparison fit the language of the sketch?

3. Carr uses some of Sophie's own words to suggest features of her situation and personality. One phrase in particular comes up several times. What is it and what is suggested by it?

4. Notice the length of the sentences. Compare paragraph 2 of Carr's description with paragraph 1 of Conrad's.

5. Compare also paragraphs 10 and 11 in Carr with paragraph 2 in Conrad.

6. Can you characterize Carr's attitude toward her subject? Is it a usual attitude?

Content

1. Carr's striking paintings are well-known to Canadians. Consider the possibility that her painting and her writing may have some things in common. Find some examples of Carr's painting and attempt a comparison with her writing.

Vocabulary

trade-straightedness   appraise

Morocco
Anaïs Nin

The diary kept by Anaïs Nin during her visit to North Africa in the 1930s includes this fascinating sketch of internal landscapes.

1   A trip to Morocco. A short but vivid one. I fell in love with Fez. Peace, Dignity. Humility. I have just left the balcony where I stood listening to the evening prayer rising over the white city. A religious emotion roused by the Arabs' lives, by the simplicity of it, the fundamental beauty. Stepping into the labyrinth of their streets, streets like intestines, two yards wide, into the abyss of their dark eyes, into peace. The rhythm affects one first of all. The slowness. Many people on the streets. You touch elbows. They breathe into your face, but with a silence, a gravity, a dreaminess. Only the children cry and laugh and run. The Arabs are silent. The little square room open on the street in which they sit on the ground, on the mud, with their merchandise around them. They are weaving, they are sewing, baking bread, chiseling jewels, repairing knives, making guns for the Berbers in the mountains. They are dyeing wool in vast cauldrons, big cauldrons full of dye emerald green, violet, Orient blue. They are making sienna earth pottery, weaving rugs, shaving, shampooing and writing legal documents right there, under your eyes. One Arab is asleep over his bag of saffron. Another is praying with his beads while selling herbs. Further, a big tintamarre, the street of copperwork. Little boys are beating copper trays with small hammers, beating a design into them, beating copper lamps, Aladdin's lamps. Little boys and old men do the work. They hold the tray between their legs. The younger men walk down the street in their burnouses, going I know not where, some so beautiful one thinks they are women. The women are veiled. They are going to the mosque, probably. At a certain hour all selling, all work ceases and they all go to the mosque. But first of all they wash their faces, their feet, their sore eyes, their leprous noses, their pock-marked skins at the fountain. They shed their sandals. Some of the old men and old women never leave the mosque. They squat there forever until death overtakes them. Women have their own entrance. They kiss the wall of the mosque as they pass. To make way for a donkey loaded with kindling wood, I step into a dark doorway. A choking stench overwhelms me. This stench is everywhere. It takes a day to get used to it. It makes you feel nauseated at first. It is the smell of excrement, saffron, leather being cured, sandalwood, olive oil being used for frying, nut oil on the bodies, incense, muskrat, so strong that at first you cannot swallow food. There is mud on the white burnous, on the Arab legs. Children's heads shaved, with one tuft of hair left. The women with faces uncovered and tattooed are the primitive Berbers from the mountains, wives of warriors, not civilized. I saw the wives of one Arab, five of them sitting on a divan, like mountains of flesh, enormous, with several chins and several stomachs, and diamonds set in their foreheads.

The streets and houses are inextricably woven, intricately inter-   *2*
woven, by bridges from one house to another, passageways covered with lattice, creating shadows on the ground. They seem to be crossing within a house, you never know when you are out in a street or in a patio, or a passageway, as half of the houses are open on the street, you get lost immediately. Mosques run into a merchant's home, shops into mosques, now you are under a trellised roof covered with rose vines, now walking in utter darkness through a tunnel, behind a donkey raw and bleeding from being beaten, and now you are on a bridge built by the Portuguese. Now admire lacy trelliswork done by the Andalusians, and now look at the square next to the mosque where the poor are allowed to sleep on mats.

Everywhere the Arab squats and waits. Anywhere. An old Arab is   *3*
teaching a young one a religious chant. Another is defecating carefully, conscientiously. Another is begging, showing all his open sores, standing near the baker baking bread in ovens built in the earth.

The atmosphere is so clear, so white and blue, you feel you can   *4*
see the whole world as clearly as you see Fez. The birds do not chatter as they do in Paris, they chant, trill with operatic and tropical fervor. The poor are dressed in sackcloths, the semi-poor in sheets and bathtowels, the well-to-do women in silks and muslins. The Jews wear a black burnous. In the streets and in the houses of the poor the floor is of stamped earth. Houses are built of sienna-red earth, sometimes whitewashed. The olive oil is pressed out in the street too, under large wooden wheels.

I had letters of introduction. First I visited Si Boubekertazi. He sat   *5*
in his patio, on pillows. A beautiful Negro woman, a concubine, brought a copper tray full of delicacies. And tea served in tiny cups without handles.

At the house of Driss Mokri Montasseb I was allowed to visit the   *6*
harem. Seven wives of various ages, but all of them fat, sat around a low table eating candy and dates. We discussed nail polish. They wanted some of mine, which was pearly. They told me how they made up their eyes. They bought kohl dust at the market, filled their eyes with it. The eyes smart and cry, and so the black kohl marks the edges and gives that heavily accented effect.

Pasha El Glaoui de Marrakesh offered me a military escort to   *7* visit the city. He said it was absolutely necessary. He signaled to a soldier standing at his door, who never left me from then on except when I went to my hotel room to sleep.

8   De Sidi Hassan Benanai received me under the fine spun-gold colonnades. But he had just begun a forty-day fast and prayer, so he sat in silence, counting his beads, and tea was served in silence, and he continued to pray, occasionally smiling at me, and bowing his head, until I left.

9   From outside, the houses are uniformly plain, with high walls covered with flowers. One cannot tell when one is entering a luxurious abode. The door may be of beautiful ironwork. There may be two, or four, or six guards at the door. But inside, the walls are all mosaics, or painted, and the stucco worked like lace, the ceilings painted in gold. The pillows are of silk. The Negro women are simply dressed but always beautiful. One does not see the children or the wives.

10   The white burnous is called a *jelabba*.

11   Mystery and labyrinth. Complex streets. Anonymous walls. Secret luxury. Secrecy of these houses without windows on the streets. The windows and door open on the patio. The patio has a fountain and lovely plants. There is a labyrinth design in the arrangement of the gardens. Bushes are placed to form a puzzle so you might get lost. They love the feeling of being lost. It has been interpreted as a desire to reproduce the infinite.

12   Fez. One always, sooner or later, comes upon a city which is an image of one's inner cities. Fez is an image of my inner self. This may explain my fascination for it. Wearing a veil, full and inexhaustible labyrinthian, so rich and variable I myself get lost. Passion for mystery, the unknown, and for the infinite, the uncharted.

13   With my guide I visited the Quartier Réservé. It lay within medieval walls, guarded at each gate by a French soldier. The houses were full of prostitutes. Only the poor Arabs go there because the others have enough wives to satisfy their need of variety. Dark, dramatic, tortuous streets. Bare cellars which have become cafés. Arabs slinking in and out. Negroes. Beggars. Arab music heard now and then. The walls, ceilings covered with shabby rugs and potteries. *Thé à menthe* served, or beer. No wine drinking but much drug traffic. Bare, cellarlike rooms. Doors covered by muslin curtains, or beaded curtains. Front room is the bar or café where the men sit and the musicians play. Back room is for the prostitutes. The muslin curtain was parted and I found myself before Fatima, the queen of the prostitutes.

14   Fatima had a beautiful face, straight patrician nose, enormous black velvet eyes, tawny smooth skin, full but firm, and the usual Arabian attributes of several folds of stomach, several chins. She could only move with difficulty on her enormous legs. She was both queenly and magnificent, opulent, and voluptuous. She was

dressed in a wedding costume, a pink chiffon dress embroidered with gold sequins laid over several layers of other chiffon petticoats. Heavy gold belt, bracelets, rings, a gold band across her forehead, enormous dangling gold earrings. Over her glistening black hair she wore a colored silk turban placed on the back of her head exposing the black curls. She had four gold teeth, considered beautiful by Arab women. The coal-black rim around her eyes exaggerated their size, as in Egyptian paintings.

She sat among pillows in a room shaped like many bedrooms in   *15* Fez, long and narrow. At each end of the room she had a brass bed, a sign of luxury and success. They are not used as beds, they are only a symbol of wealth. In between the two brass beds lay all the pillows, rugs, and low divans. (In rich homes the floors are tiled but the brass beds are displayed there too.) Fatima not only collected brass beds but also cuckoo clocks from Switzerland. One wall was covered with them, each one telling a different time. The other walls were covered with flowered cretonne. The atmosphere was heavy with perfume, enclosed and voluptuous, the womb itself. A young girl came in with an atomizer and lifting up my skirt gently atomized my underclothes with rose water. She came once more to throw rose petals around my feet. Then she came carrying a tray with glass tea containers sheathed in copper holders with handles. We sat cross-legged on vast pillows, Fatima in the center. She never made a vulgar gesture. Two blind, crippled musicians were invited in and played monotonously, but with such a beat that my excitement grew as if I had taken wine. Fatima began to prepare tea on the tray. Then she passed around a bottle of rose water and we perfumed our hands. Then she lit a sandalwood brazier and placed it at my feet. I was duly and thoroughly perfumed and the air grew heavier and richer. The Arab soldier lay back on the pillows. The handsome bodyguard in his white burnous, white turban and blue military costume conversed with Fatima, who could not speak French. He translated my compliments on her beauty. She asked him to translate a question about my nail polish. I promised to send her some. While we sat there dreaming between each phrase, there was a fight outside. A young Arab burst in, his face bleeding. "Aii, Aii, Aiii," he cried. Fatima sent her maid to see what could be done for the young Arab. She never lost her composure. The musicians played louder and faster so I would not notice the commotion and my pleasure would not be spoiled. I spent two hours with Fatima, as it is impolite to hurry here. It is a mortal insult to leave too soon or to seem hurried. It offends them deeply. Relationship does not depend so much on conversation or exchange as in the creation of a propitious, dreamy, meditative, contemplative atmosphere, a mood. Finally, when I was ready to leave, my escort made a parting speech.

It was after midnight. The city, so crowded during the day that I   *16* could hardly move in it, was silent and empty. The night watchman sleeps on the doorsteps. There are gates between different quarters. Six gates had to be opened for us with enormous keys. You are not allowed to circulate at night except by special permission and with a pass which the soldier showed to each watchman.

17   The frogs were croaking in the garden pools behind the walls, the crickets were announcing tomorrow's heat. The smell of roses won the battle of smells. A window was suddenly opened above me, an old woman stuck her head out and threw out a big rat she had just caught, with many curses. It fell at my feet.

18   Fez is a drug. It enmeshes you. The life of the senses, of poetry (even the poor Arabs who visit a prostitute will find a woman dressed in a wedding dress like a virgin), of illusion and dream. It made me passionate, just to sit there on pillows, with music, the birds, the fountains, the infinite beauty of the mosaic designs, the teakettle singing, the many copper trays shining, the twelve bottles of rose perfume and the sandalwood smoking in the brazier, and the cuckoo clocks chiming in disunion, as they pleased.

19   The layers of the city of Fez are like the layers and secrecies of the inner life. One needs a guide.

20   I loved the racial nobility of the Arabs, the pride, the love of sweets instead of alcohol, the gentleness, the peace, the hospitality, the reserve, pride, love of turquoise and coral colors, dignity of bearing, their silences. I love the way the men embrace in the street, proudly and nobly. I love the expression in their eyes, brooding, or fiery, but deep.

21   The river under the bridge was foul. Men held hands while talking on the street. A dead Arab was carried on a stretcher, covered with narrow white bandages like an Egyptian mummy. Over his feet they had thrown a red rug. Silence and quietism. Contemplation and chanting. Music. Tea served on copper trays with a samovar kettle. Glasses have colored tops. On another tray a big silver box with big rough pieces of rock sugar. Trays with perfume bottles. Trays with almond cakes covered by a silk handkerchief or copper painted lids.

22   I met the Arab women walking to their baths. They went there always in groups, and carrying a change of clothes in a basket over their heads. They walked veiled and laughing, showing only their eyes and the hennaed tips of their hands holding their veils. Their full white skirts and heavily embroidered belts made them heavy and full-looking, like the pillows they liked to sit on. It was heavy flesh moving in white robes, nourished on sweets and inertia, on passive watches behind grilled windows. This was one of their few moments of liberty, one of the few times they appeared in the street. They walked in groups with their servants, children, and bundles of fresh clothes, laughing and talking, and dragging their feet in embroidered mules.

I followed them. When they entered at the mosaic-covered build-　*23*
ing near the mosque, I entered with them. The first room was very
large and square, all of stone, with stone benches, and rugs on the
floor. Here the women laid down their bundles and began undressing. This was a long ceremony, for they wore so many skirts,
and several blouses, and belts which looked like bandages, so
much white muslin, linen, cotton to unroll, unfold, and fold again
on the bench. Then there were bracelets to take off, earrings,
anklets, and then the long black hair to unwind from the ribbons
tressed into the hair. So much white cotton fallen on the floor, a
field of white petals, leaves, lace, shed by the full-fleshed women,
and as I looked at them I felt they could never be really naked, that
all this they wore must cling to them forever, grow with their
bodies. I was already undressed and waiting, standing, as I would
not sit naked on the stone bench. They were waiting for the
children to be undressed by the African maids, waiting for the
maids to get undressed.

An old woman was waiting for us, a completely shriveled old　*24*
woman with only one eye. Her breasts were two long empty gourds
hanging almost to the middle of her stomach. She wore a sackcloth
around her waist. She gave me a little approving tap on the shoulder and smiled. She pointed to my finger nails and talked but I
could not understand, and I smiled.

She opened the door to the steam room, another very large　*25*
square room all of grey stone. But here there were no benches. All
the women were sitting on the floor. The old woman filled pails of
water from one of the fountains and occasionally poured one over
their heads, after they had finished soaping themselves. The steam
filled the room. The women sat on the floor, took their children
between their knees and scrubbed them. Then the old woman
threw a pail of water over them. This water flowed all around us,
and it was dirty. We sat in rivulets of soapy, dirty water. The women
did not hurry. They used the soap, then a piece of pumice stone,
and then they began to use depilatories with great care and concentration. All of them were enormous. The flesh billowed, curved,
folded in tremendous heavy waves. They seemed to be sitting on
pillows of flesh of all colors, from the pale Northern Arab skin to
the African. I was amazed that they could lift such heavy arms to
comb their long hair. I had come to look at them, because the
beauty of their faces was legendary, and proved not at all exaggerated. They had absolutely beautiful faces, enormous, jeweled eyes,
straight noble noses with wide spaces between the eyes, full and
voluptuous mouths, flawless skins, and always a royal bearing. The
faces had a quality of statuary rather than painting, because the
lines were so pure and clear. I sat in admiration of their faces, and
then I noticed that they looked at me. They sat in groups, looking
at me and smiling. They mimicked that I should wash my hair and

face. I could not explain that I was hurrying through the ritual because I did not like sitting in the darkening waters. They offered me the pumice stone after using it thoroughly all over their ponderous bodies. I tried it but it scratched my face. The Arab women's skin was tougher. The women chatted in circles while washing themselves and their children. I could not bring myself to wash my face with the soap they all used for their feet and armpits. They laughed at what they must have thought was a European woman who did not know the rules of cleanliness.

26   They wanted me also to pull out superfluous eyebrows, hair under the arms, and to shave my pubic hair. I finally slipped away to the next room and where pails of cooler water were thrown over me.

27   I wanted to see the Arab women clothed again, concealed in yards of white cotton. Such beautiful heads had risen out of these mountains of flesh, heads of incredible perfection, dazzling eyes heavily fringed, sensual features. Sometimes moss-green eyes in dark sienna skins, sometimes coal-black eyes in pale moonlit skins, and always the long heavy black hair, the undulating tresses. But these heads rose from formless masses of flesh, heaving like plants in the sea, swelling, swaying, falling, the breasts like sea anemones, floating, the stomachs of perpetually pregnant women, the legs like pillows, the backs like cushions, the hips with furrows like a mattress.

28   They were all watching me, with friendly nodding of their heads, commenting on my figure. By counting on their fingers they asked was I adolescent? I had no fat on me. I must be a girl. They came around me and we compared skin colors. They seemed amazed by my waist. They could enclose it in their two hands. They wanted to wash my hair. They soaped my face with tenderness. They touched me and talked with volubility. The old woman came with two pails and threw them over me. I was ready to leave, but the Arab women transmitted messages of all kinds with their eyes, smiles, talk. The old woman led me to the third room, which was cooler, and threw cold water over me, and then led me back to the dressing room.

QUESTIONS

Language and Style

1. What features of this description contribute to its vividness? What appeals to sensory experience are apparent? Can you explain the connection between the sensory appeal and the vividness?

2. Why should the patches of short sentences, the fragments of sentences, and the loosely linked lists be appropriate? See, for example, paragraph 1.

3. How would you describe the attitude of the writer towards the circumstances and the people in this sketch? Is there a sense in which the writer seems disconnected? In what way, by contrast, is the writer evidently connected to things? *Para 12 connected –* *disconnected – nail polish*

4. Explain the dreamlike (not "dreamy") quality of Nin's description.

Organization

1. What two scenes help to focus the reader's awareness? How do they achieve this result? *at Fatima's House Para. 14* *- Bathroom*

Content

1. Sometimes in Nin's account observations are combined in unusual ways. What she reports as a "fundamental beauty" includes "streets like intestines" and Arab shopkeepers who "sit on the mud." What are some other instances? How might the "beautiful" not be pretty? *Bath using dirty watery women.*

2. What do you make of Nin's observation in paragraph 12, "One always, sooner or later, comes upon a city which is an image of one's inner cities"? What light does this remark shed on the writer's treatment of her subject? *optimistic -*

3. Compare Nin's description with George Orwell's description in "Marrakech" – which was written about the same time. You might notice, for example, the donkeys.

Vocabulary

labyrinth	Berbers
Fez	sienna
saffron	tintamarre
burnouses	leprous
inextricably	lattice
trellised	Andalusians
colonnades	cretonne
propitious	brazier
samovar	hennaed
mules	pumice
depilatories	anemones

Marrakech
George Orwell

The British writer George Orwell, well-known for his political works 1984 *and* Animal Farm, *visited North Africa at about the same time as Anaïs Nin and produced quite a different account of his experiences.*

1   As the corpse went past the flies left the restaurant table in a cloud and rushed after it, but they came back a few minutes later.

2   The little crowd of mourners – all men and boys, no women – threaded their way across the market-place between the piles of pomegranates and the taxis and the camels, wailing a short chant over and over again. What really appeals to the flies is that the corpses here are never put into coffins, they are merely wrapped in a piece of rag and carried on a rough wooden bier on the shoulders of four friends. When the friends get to the burying-ground they hack an oblong hole a foot or two deep, dump the body in it and fling over it a little of the dried-up, lumpy earth, which is like broken brick. No gravestone, no name, no identifying mark of any kind. The burying-ground is merely a huge waste of hummocky earth, like a derelict building-lot. After a month or two no one can even be certain where his own relatives are buried.

3   When you walk through a town like this – two hundred thousand inhabitants, of whom at least twenty thousand own literally nothing except the rags they stand up in – when you see how people live, and still more how easily they die, it is always difficult to believe that you are walking among human beings. All colonial empires are in reality founded upon that fact. The people have brown faces – besides, there are so many of them! Are they really the same flesh as yourself? Do they even have names? Or are they merely a kind of undifferentiated brown stuff, about as individual as bees or coral insects? They rise out of the earth, they sweat and starve for a few years, and then they sink back into the nameless mounds of the graveyard and nobody notices that they are gone. And even the graves themselves soon fade back into the soil. Sometimes, out for a walk, as you break your way through the prickly pear, you notice that it is rather bumpy underfoot, and only a certain regularity in the bumps tells you that you are walking over skeletons.

4   I was feeding one of the gazelles in the public gardens.

5   Gazelles are almost the only animals that look good to eat when they are still alive, in fact, one can hardly look at their hindquarters

without thinking of mint sauce. The gazelle I was feeding seemed to know that this thought was in my mind, for though it took the piece of bread I was holding out it obviously did not like me. It nibbled rapidly at the bread, then lowered its head and tried to butt me, then took another nibble and then butted again. Probably its idea was that if it could drive me away the bread would somehow remain hanging in mid-air.

An Arab navvy working on the path nearby lowered his heavy   6
hoe and sidled towards us. He looked from the gazelle to the bread and from the bread to the gazelle, with a sort of quiet amazement, as though he had never seen anything quite like this before. Finally he said shyly in French:

"*I* could eat some of that bread."   7

I tore off a piece and he stowed it gratefully in some secret place   8
under his rags. This man is an employee of the Municipality.

When you go through the Jewish quarters you gather some idea   9
of what the medieval ghettoes were probably like. Under their Moorish rulers the Jews were only allowed to own land in certain restricted areas, and after centuries of this kind of treatment they have ceased to bother about overcrowding. Many of the streets are a good deal less than six feet wide, the houses are completely windowless, and sore-eyed children cluster everywhere in unbelievable numbers, like clouds of flies. Down the centre of the street there is generally running a little river of urine.

In the bazaar huge families of Jews, all dressed in the long black   10
robe and little black skull-cap, are working in a dark fly-infested booths that look like caves. A carpenter sits cross-legged at a prehistoric lathe, turning chair-legs at lightning speed. He works the lathe with a bow in his right hand and guides the chisel with his left foot, and thanks to a lifetime of sitting in this position his left leg is warped out of shape. At his side his grandson, aged six, is already starting on the simpler parts of the job.

I was just passing the coppersmiths' booths when somebody   11
noticed that I was lighting a cigarette. Instantly, from the dark holes all round, there was a frenzied rush of Jews, many of them old grandfathers with flowing grey beards, all clamouring for a cigarette. Even a blind man somewhere at the back of one of the booths heard a rumour of cigarettes and came crawling out, groping in the air with his hand. In about a minute I had used up the whole packet. None of these people, I suppose, works less than twelve hours a day, and every one of them looks on a cigarette as a more or less impossible luxury.

As the Jews live in self-contained communities they follow the   12
same trades as the Arabs, except for agriculture. Fruit-sellers, potters, silversmiths, blacksmiths, butchers, leather-workers, tailors, water-carriers, beggars, porters – whichever way you look you see nothing but Jews. As a matter of fact there are thirteen

thousand of them, all living in the space of a few acres. A good job Hitler isn't here. Perhaps he is on his way, however. You hear the usual dark rumours about the Jews, not only from the Arabs but from the poorer Europeans.

13   "Yes, *mon vieux*, they took my job away from me and gave it to a Jew. The Jews! They're the real rulers of this country, you know. They've got all the money. They control the banks, finance – everything."

14   "But," I said, "isn't it a fact that the average Jew is a labourer working for about a penny an hour?"

15   "Ah, that's only for show! They're all moneylenders really. They're cunning, the Jews."

16   In just the same way, a couple of hundred years ago, poor old women used to be burned for witchcraft when they could not even work enough magic to get themselves a square meal.

17   All people who work with their hands are partly invisible, and the more important the work they do, the less visible they are. Still, a white skin is always fairly conspicuous. In northern Europe, when you see a labourer ploughing a field, you probably give him a second glance. In a hot country, anywhere south of Gibraltar or east of Suez, the chances are that you don't even see him. I have noticed this again and again. In a tropical landscape one's eye takes in everything except the human beings. It takes in the dried-up soil, the prickly pear, the palm-tree and the distant mountain, but it always misses the peasant hoeing at his patch. He is the same colour as the earth and a great deal less interesting to look at.

18   It is only because of this that the starved countries of Asia and Africa are accepted as tourist resorts. No one would think of running cheap trips to the Distressed Areas. But where the human beings have brown skins their poverty is simply not noticed. What does Morocco mean to a Frenchman? An orange-grove or a job in government service. Or to an Englishman? Camels, castles, palm-trees, Foreign Legionnaires, brass trays and bandits. One could probably live here for years without noticing that for nine-tenths of the people the reality of life is an endless, back-breaking struggle to wring a little food out of an eroded soil.

19   Most of Morocco is so desolate that no wild animal bigger than a hare can live on it. Huge areas which were once covered with forest have turned into a treeless waste where the soil is exactly like broken-up brick. Nevertheless a good deal of it is cultivated, with frightful labour. Everything is done by hand. Long lines of women, bent double like inverted capital Ls, work their way slowly across the fields, tearing up the prickly weeds with their hands, and the peasant gathering lucerne for fodder pulls it up stalk by stalk instead of reaping it, thus saving an inch or two on each stalk. The plough is a wretched wooden thing, so frail that one can easily

carry it on one's shoulder, and fitted underneath with a rough iron spike which stirs the soil to a depth of about four inches. This is as much as the strength of the animals is equal to. It is usual to plough with a cow and a donkey yoked together. Two donkeys would not be quite strong enough, but on the other hand two cows would cost a little more to feed. The peasants possess no harrows, they merely plough the soil several times over in different directions, finally leaving it in rough furrows, after which the whole field has to be shaped with hoes into small oblong patches, to conserve water. Except for a day or two after the rare rainstorms there is never enough water. Along the edges of the fields channels are hacked out to a depth of thirty or forty feet to get at the tiny trickles which run through the subsoil.

Every afternoon a file of very old women passes down the road   *20*
outside my house, each carrying a load of firewood. All of them are mummified with age and the sun, and all of them are tiny. It seems to be generally the case in primitive communities that the women, when they get beyond a certain age, shrink to the size of children. One day a poor old creature who could not have been more than four feet tall crept past me under a vast load of wood. I stopped her and put a five-sou piece (a little more than a farthing) into her hand. She answered with a shrill wail, almost a scream, which was partly gratitude but mainly surprise. I suppose that from her point of view, by taking any notice of her, I seemed almost to be violating a law of nature. She accepted her status as an old woman, that is to say as a beast of burden. When a family is travelling it is quite usual to see a father and a grown-up son riding ahead on donkeys, and an old woman following on foot, carrying the baggage.

But what is strange about these people is their invisibility. For   *21*
several weeks, always at about the same time of day, the file of old women had hobbled past the house with their firewood, and though they had registered themselves on my eyeballs I cannot truly say that I had seen them. Firewood was passing – that was how I saw it. It was only that one day I happened to be walking behind them, and the curious up-and-down motion of a load of wood drew my attention to the human being underneath it. Then for the first time I noticed the poor old earth-coloured bodies, bodies reduced to bones and leathery skin, bent double under the crushing weight. Yet I suppose I had not been five minutes on Moroccan soil before I noticed the overloading of the donkeys and was infuriated by it. There is no question that the donkeys are damnably treated. The Moroccan donkey is hardly bigger than a St. Bernard dog, it carries a load which in the British army would be considered too much for a fifteen-hands mule, and very often its pack-saddle is not taken off its back for weeks together. But what is peculiarly pitiful is that it is the most willing creature on earth, it follows its master like a dog

and does not need either bridle or halter. After a dozen years of devoted work it suddenly drops dead, whereupon its master tips it into the ditch and the village dogs have torn its guts out before it is cold.

22   This kind of thing makes one's blood boil, whereas – on the whole – the plight of the human beings does not. I am not commenting, merely pointing to a fact. People with brown skins are next door to invisible. Anyone can be sorry for the donkey with its galled back, but it is generally owing to some kind of accident if one even notices the old woman under her load of sticks.

23   As the storks flew northward the Negroes were marching southward – a long, dusty column, infantry, screw-gun batteries and then more infantry, four or five thousand men in all, winding up the road with a clumping of boots and a clatter of iron wheels.

24   They were Senegalese, the blackest Negroes in Africa, so black that sometimes it is difficult to see whereabouts on their necks the hair begins. Their splendid bodies were hidden in reach-me-down khaki uniforms, their feet squashed into boots that looked like blocks of wood, and every tin hat seemed to be a couple of sizes too small. It was very hot and the men had marched a long way. They slumped under the weight of their packs and the curiously sensitive black faces were glistening with sweat.

25   As they went past a tall, very young Negro turned and caught my eye. But the look he gave me was not in the least the kind of look you might expect. Not hostile, not contemptuous, not sullen, not even inquisitive. It was the shy, wide-eyed Negro look, which actually is a look of profound respect. I saw how it was. This wretched boy, who is a French citizen and has therefore been dragged from the forest to scrub floors and catch syphilis in garrison towns, actually has feelings of reverence before a white skin. He has been taught that the white race are his masters, and he still believes it.

26   But there is one thought which every white man (and in this connection it doesn't matter twopence if he calls himself a Socialist) thinks when he sees a black army marching past. "How much longer can we go on kidding these people? How long before they turn their guns in the other direction?"

27   It was curious, really. Every white man there has this thought stowed somewhere or other in his mind. I had it, so had the other onlookers, so had the officers on their sweating chargers and the white NCOs marching in the ranks. It was a kind of secret which we all knew and were too clever to tell; only the Negroes didn't know it. And really it was almost like watching a flock of cattle to see the long column, a mile or two miles of armed men, flowing peacefully up the road, while the great white birds drifted over them in the opposite direction, glittering like scraps of paper.

QUESTIONS

Language and Style

1. Can you locate places where Orwell's description steps aside and while not lecturing the reader, clearly wants the reader to "see"? Para 22, 8, 1, 4

2. How, generally, would you characterize the writer's attitude? Can you identify instances of apparent amazement? Of indignation?

3. How does the language change from place to place? Why should it change?

4. At its best, Orwell's language is simple and concrete. Can you identify examples? See paragraph 2 among others.

Organization

1. Can you locate examples of Orwell's interest in interpreting events for the reader? Consider, for instance, paragraphs 4 and 5. Are there other instances?

Content

1. What apparent political purpose or understanding resides behind Orwell's descriptions? How might it influence the description?

2. To what extent are the humans in Orwell's account portrayed as nameless victims?

3. If this description is written for the people back home, where is "back home"? See the discussion of invisibility. What, by implication, might be some of the values of the reader?

Vocabulary

pomegranates	undifferentiated
ghettoes	Moorish
lathe	lucerne
screw-guns	

This story is negative.

vs.

morroco - positive. ugly things are made into beutifull

The Acquisitors' Roost
Peter C. Newman

If restaurants are known for their clientele, then Winston's must have been one of the most famous eating places in Canada when Peter C. Newman, chronicler of Canada's upper crust, described it in his book The Canadian Establishment.

1   They assemble just after high noon in the burgundy plush of Winston's Restaurant on Adelaide Street in Toronto to share Canada's most ostentatious lunch. In they flock, most of the city's (and many of the country's) high rollers who order, or like to think they order, Canada's economic universe. They come here – as they do to the Savoy Grill in London, Lasserre in Paris, Harry's Bar in Venice, the Polo Lounge in Beverly Hills, and the Four Seasons in New York – to compare fiscal exploits and match cash flows, to share the confidences and make the deals that will spread their money and their talent, their self-confidence and their sense of destiny, across the country and the continent.

2   At twenty-three tables in a seating arrangement choreographed with the exquisite care of a Sadler's Wells ballet, the power-lunchers arrive for their daily fix, well aware that Winston's is much more than a fancy watering hole. This is the place where the Acquisitors gather to be seen and overheard; the Canadian Establishment's day-care centre.

3   The standard Winston's two-hour lunch is a daily convention of the Establishment's current *illuminati* (not a high-tech microchip carver in the bunch) who want to remain within frequent sight and range of those who make the decisions that count – in other words, one another. They constitute a formidable gathering of bankers, former premiers, tax-shelter architects, ex-finance ministers, superlawyers, conglomerateurs, chief executive officers, corporate matchmakers, and millionaire proprietors. Nodding their heads sagaciously like wise turtles, they sip their Meursault, aware that for them fame and fortune is not a one-night stand. They have chosen this restaurant as a stage on which to parade themselves and their egos.

4   The room is dotted with Establishment monuments. A glitter of Eatons and Bassetts is in regular attendance. Peter Lougheed and Pierre Trudeau drop in whenever they're in town (not together), as do most of the leading Acquisitors from Vancouver, Calgary, Edmonton, and Montreal arriving to negotiate their head office bank credits. The *Toronto Sun*, whose publisher, Doug Creighton

(at Table One), spends an average of $3,416 a month at Winston's, claims that Darcy McKeough (Table Five for lunch, Table Sixteen for dinner), the president of Union Gas, got his bald spot "from years of rubbing his head against the burgundy banquette seats at Winston's." Hugh Housser Aird (Table Two), only son of Ontario's lieutenant-governor, paid Winston's a very personal compliment by getting married there. Conrad Black alternates between Winston's, the Toronto Club, and Chiaro's at the new King Edward, being granted the best table in each locale.

The chief reason Black and his fellow Establishmentarians pick   5
Winston's over Toronto's many other good restaurants is the character and personality of its owner, Giovanni Arena, known to everybody as John. "John is very astute and certainly takes good care of his clients if he's of the view that they have some prominence," says Black, who held his pre-wedding dinner at Winston's. "One evening my wife and I took the Duke of Wellington there and even though he had very little notice, Arena was at the door to greet us. His every third word was 'Your Grace.' Wine was served in decanters by him personally. I have to hand it to the guy."

"The most important thing about John," maintained the late   6
Preston Gilbride, who helped finance John's acquisition of Winston's, "is that he really loves people and gets himself involved with them. He's got a terrific memory, so he can discuss their families and business with them. His warmth comes through. They in turn feel at home and keep wanting to come back to his restaurant. Also, he never betrays any of the many confidences placed in him."

"There is no person in Toronto who can lay claim to such   7
exquisite confidentiality as John Giuseppe Arena," says his friend Colonel Ray Munro. "He probably holds more business and state secrets than anyone in Canada."

Munroe's comment is no exaggeration. Part of Arena's stock-in-   8
trade, like that of most other successful owners of luxury restaurants, is knowing how to make his patrons feel important. This he achieves superbly, remembering not only names but professional affiliations. His imperiously arched right eyebrow brings a waiter scurrying with a bottle of Pouilly Fumé, compliments of the house, to toast anniversaries, birthdays, and promotions. In addition to such niceties, Arena is something of a lay therapist, able to draw out people's personal and business problems without appearing to pry. Even the most petty-minded among the Establishment's power-wielders seem to feel little compunction about pouring out their most intimate secrets, as though he were their father confessor. His ebullience is infectious; supremely subtle messages left with him are passed on with the discretion worthy of a papal nuncio. If he is not exactly a power broker, he certainly acts as a highly charged go-between.

"I'd describe John as a person who gets up very early every   9
morning and goes down the street shaking trees because no god-

damn bird's going to sleep while he's awake," says Munroe. "He rides every day into the ground at full bloody gallop. He doesn't have problems for more than a very brief span of time because he faces them, tackles them head on — he's not afraid of anything. He analyses the bloody thing and embarks on a course to defeat whatever is bothering him, as if the problem were the enemy and the solution the friend. That's the way he approaches things."

10   John Arena's artistry and the roots of his power are demonstrated in the daily dance he performs allocating the tables available on the restaurant's main floor. This is not a matter of filling them. Winston's hasn't had an empty seat in nine years. Each lunch and dinner is staged like a theatrical production (with John Arena in the starring role) to produce the desired dramatic effect. "It's a very complicated process," he admits. "I personally supervise every table seating using the method, for example, that you never place two bankers next to one another. Over the years I've learned of the little intrigues that go on between people, which is very normal. One particular lady, for example, comes here and doesn't want to be seated next to another lady who also happens to be here quite often, because they've had their differences. So you have to be extremely careful. Now that we have a regular crowd of people, the new faces are very few, so that it's not a great problem any more. Recently it happened that a very well-known family in Toronto came in to dinner and at the next table there was someone that they had known for many years. It was quite embarrassing for me as soon as I realized what was really happening. They had said hello from one table to the other, but I'd recognized that there was a little bit of tension — enough for me to come back and say, loud enough that the second table could hear me, that 'the remainder of the party' was seated at another table, would they mind if I moved them? Of course, there was no 'remainder,' and whether the first table realized what was going on I don't know.

11   "That happens very rarely, but it's awkward."

12   The subtleties of Winston's seating plan have about them the byzantine quality of the pecking order of Louis XIV's court at Versailles. The dining room's west side, for instance, inexplicably has more prestige than its eastern exposure, even though they are identical. "One doesn't detract from the other," Arena patiently explains, "but it's true that one area has developed much more strongly than the other — the reason being, perhaps, that when we first opened we were operating only the west side of the restaurant.

13   "I assign certain tables for very specific reasons. There are people who come here and wish to be seen, while others desire maximum privacy. Conrad Black and John Robarts, for instance, always sit with their backs to the public — not that they don't want to be recognized, but they prefer to be left alone. I usually walk

through the room three or more times during every meal to make certain that every patron feels very secure in his seat." Tables One, Four, Six, Twenty, and Twenty-three are closest to heaven. Anyone shown to Tables Seventeen or Nineteen should quietly order hemlock on the rocks.

The moment of truth comes whenever a prospective patron   14
telephones for a reservation. A flick of Arena's pen will determine the caller's fate. Thirteen of the restaurant's twenty-three street-floor tables are permanently booked. Their proud possessors (or their secretaries) must telephone each day by 11:30 a.m. if they're *not* planning to be there. Otherwise, their spots stay reserved for them. (It's such an important ritual that even though Arena bills full fare to those who have forgotten to telephone, the total charges for no-shows amount to less than $2,000 a year.) Many of these lessees eat at Winston's five days a week and Arena could easily pre-book the entire restaurant, but he feels this would detract from its mood. Next to these permanent clients are the Regulars, who are allocated tables, though not always the same ones. Finally, there are the potluckers, who just telephone and hold their breath. Arena turns away an average of fifty requests a day, referring them to other high-ticket restaurants.

"Some days," he confesses, "when all our permanent table hold-   15
ers and most of our Regulars come in and we have very little room for manoeuvering, I have to say, 'Might we place you Downstairs?' "

Downstairs. It's called the Game Room, as in partridge and quail,   16
and it seats forty-five. This is the Establishment's gastronomic purgatory, reserved for clubwomen, faceless out-of-towners, and shopping-centre developers who wear triple-knits thick enough to stop bullets. It has a different décor, a different menu, and even though two of Winston's directors (Bill Andrews and Peter Brieger) actually eat there, Downstairs is not a place you ever admit enjoying. "I wouldn't want to infer that only the rejects are sent Downstairs," says Arena, "but if I were to receive people I felt didn't belong to the upstairs room, I would immediately send them Downstairs. That room was designed for those we feel don't like the upstairs environment. A few people, of course, like it down there because there is a sort of hum that exists as the stock market is discussed by the young up-and-comers. That hum can be very interesting to the ears of an ambitious young businessman."

Unlike most maîtres d' (who are all teeth and obsequiousness),   17
every noon hour John Arena stands at the door of his restaurant friendly but never patronizing, supremely confident that his masterly orchestration of the day's seating will produce yet another successful Establishment happening.

At night, Winston's becomes a very different place. The retinue   18
of Establishment types is still there, mainly in family groupings,

anxious to introduce their daughters to Toronto society. Here too are the refugees from the marital wars who use Winston's as a nocturnal life-support system. They are often accompanied by odd women, distinctly resembling debauched gazelles, whose eyelids don't quite close.

19　Mixed in with emissaries from the city's gastronomic intelligentsia (who visit Winston's simply to sample the splendid menu and long wine list) are some bona fide international celebrities. Here dine also the Establishment's picadors – the lance carriers, professional consultants, and dancing masters. They're guys with not quite enough chin and too much cuff whose eyes keep darting nervously around the room, like pilot-fish looking for sharks. Harmless but not very interesting, they keep asking the pianist-in-residence, Franz Loesgen, to play "Send in the Clowns." (Little do they know.)

20　Members of a sub-species that doesn't really belong at Winston's occasionally appear. They are vulpine men in barathea jackets and ruffled blue silk shirts who refer to martinis as silver bullets and order "vino" by the litre. They give each other the big smile, passing along the name of some guy on Water Street in Curaçao who's a real sweetheart and can set up offshore companies to hide the profits from acreage transfers in Hamilton. Their women tend to be *zaftig*, bold-nippled chicks who wear Diane von Furstenberg sunglasses and walk as if they were Las Vegas showgirls following imaginary chalk marks on the floor. They seldom come back.

21　Winston's is Toronto's seventh most expensive restaurant, with lunch tabs running about twenty-five dollars and dinner forty-five. Arena serves three hundred meals a day and because his rate of occupancy is so high grosses $25,000 for each upstairs restaurant seat, the highest return in North America. Winston's sales in 1980 topped $2 million, producing a 20-per-cent profit. He also owns the Terra Cotta Inn, forty-five minutes northwest of downtown Toronto, operates restaurants at the O'Keefe Centre and Ontario Place, leases a pheasant and quail farm near Flesherton, Ontario, and owns a huge tract of land between the former George Drew estate and the Eaton property at Caledon, Ontario. His catering business is the most lucrative in the country, netting a 34-per-cent return. There is hardly an Establishment function (including Preston Gilbride's funeral) that he hasn't been asked to handle. "Get John to cater it," is a common cry of embattled hostesses.

22　Nothing at Winston's is left to chance. Lighting is monitored with dimmers notched for the precise lunch and dinner levels of brightness, but any businessman who pulls papers out of his briefcase will find the lights above his table growing imperceptibly brighter. Arena always looks fresh in his Jean-Paul suits, changing his complete attire twice a day. He visits each table at least twice during each meal and reserves all of his tough language for his suppliers.

"You hear him on the phone calling up a meat broker," says his friend Ray Munro. "He buys only the best, but he may find that Bradley's is charging two cents a pound more than he thinks they should. That would amount to $200 a week, so he gets on the phone and blows them right out of their socks. You'd have to refer to the *Classical Dictionary of the Vulgar Tongue* to understand what he's saying, and that's even before he lets loose in Italian. It's something else, but he never apologizes. You're sitting there listening to him, and he won't say, 'I'm sorry you heard that.' He just tells you, 'That's the way I do business.'"

QUESTIONS

Language and Style

1. At what places is Newman's vocabulary obviously "fancy"? At what places "plain"? Is there an apparent reason for the variation?

2. At one point Arena is quoted as saying, "I wouldn't want to *infer* that only the rejects are sent downstairs. . . . " At another his conversation with a supplier is described. What apparently does Arena's use of language suggest about Winston's?

3. Can you characterize the attitude of the writer? You might consider the passage beginning, "Members of a sub-species that doesn't really belong to Winston's. . . . " Are there others?

4. Several images, many suggesting animal comparisons, contribute to the description's effectiveness. What are they? Why should they be effective?

5. The writer makes frequent reference to exotic places and mentions many well-known names. Why should he do this?

6. Newman occasionally wants to associate his subject with something grand or important. In paragraph 12, for example, Winston's seating plan is described as having the "byzantine quality" of "Louis XIV's court," and in paragraph 13 reference is made to "hemlock on the rocks." Can you explain these references? Are they warranted?

Organization

1. How does the account of Arena's personality focus the description? In what way could a description of a person serve to give a sense of place?

2. Compare Newman's treatment of Arena with the treatment of his customers.

Content

1. In what ways are the manipulators themselves manipulated?

Vocabulary

ostentatious	fiscal
acquisitor	illuminati
conglomerateurs	sagaciously
Meursault	banquette
byzantine	Versailles
inexplicably	hemlock
gastronomic	purgatory
obsequiousness	patronizing
debauched	vulpine
choreographed	

WRITING DESCRIPTIONS

One of the difficulties people encounter in writing successful descriptions is the selection of appropriate, telling details which will cause in a reader a sort of "second-hand" sensory awareness of the object or experience the writer is concerned with. This is partly a matter of the writer's concentration and attention to details. A glass of beer, for example, has certain sensory qualities which most readers can appreciate. Beer has colour and the dark beers are usually associated with stronger tastes than light-coloured beers. Beer has a particular liquid quality making it usually, but not always, thicker than water, and this characteristic causes it to cling to the sides of the glass. It does not pour like other liquids; it "heads up" in foam and little bubbles. A writer may be tempted to leave the beer itself behind, to expand on its taste, working like an advertising copy-writer with the associations and connections to "the good life." But attention had best be focussed on the beer itself, for it has its own interest, a special smell and a taste which seem to change with the weather, the temperature of the liquid itself, and, some people claim, the brand. A writer should not draw all the conclusions and tell a reader what the details show. It is better to let the wrinkles and lines in a face speak for someone's life and character, and therefore the writer needs to attend to selected sensory details.

The writer's choice of language depends in part on who the writer decides the reader is and the relationship with the reader into which the writer wishes to enter. The writer may decide to take the reader along and to direct the reader's attention to one or another aspect of an experience, or the writer may decide to bring the experience home to the reader in the way travellers do when they return with stories of their experiences away. The writer may be instructive and organized or intimate and impressionistic, or the writer can assume that a reader is familiar with the matter and only needs reminding of certain half-forgotten particulars. The writer needs to decide what a reader knows and would like to know. Will the writer introduce the reader to a new beverage at the end of a long, thirsty day? Or will the writer describe an exotic concoction discovered by happy accident last summer while on a visit to the Magdalen Islands? Perhaps the writer chooses to recall for the reader how different the same drink tasted served in a plastic cup at the ballgame.

The writer's choice of language is also a function of the language's expressive capacity, its ability to carry sensory impressions and detail. "Smooth" is a smooth word, and "bubbly" seems to bubble. Longer sentences and certain repetitions may contribute a long, languorous effect, while short sentences seem to chop things up. But there are so many choices of words and constructions that a writer who wants a recipe for descriptions must be disappointed or if handed one, will produce only a frustrating mechanical imitation. So the writer needs to experiment, to explore and sample, while attending to and noting the details and particulars.

SUGGESTIONS FOR WRITING

All the topics suggested here are small in scale to help the writer focus on particulars. They are familiar topics because the writer needs to know enough to be able to throw out more than is kept in the finished work. Approach these topics like studies or still lifes if you like, and pay attention to the light and dark patches on the fruit, the way the light strikes a surface....

1. The front door of an old house
2. A frog or a toad
3. A glass of milk
4. A grandparent's face
5. A tennis racket
6. An egg
7. A favourite item of clothing
8. A pair of skates
9. A cat's paw
10. A baseball glove
11. The palm of your hand
12. A house plant.

CHAPTER
TWO
NARRATION

INTRODUCTION

Narration is an account of function and action just as description is an account of structure and appearance. A successful narrative sorts the significant action from the background and arranges the action into a story.

Consider the following narrative:

> On Saturday we rose early and packed the car. We drove to the campground and ate lunch. We paddled across the lake and hiked over the ridge. There was an eagle's nest in a tall, white pine. It grew dark and we paddled back to camp. That night it rained, and by morning everything was soaking wet. We decided to stay another day. . . .

Nothing in this account is made more important than anything else, and the events are connected to one another only by virtue of succession: one thing happens, another thing happens, and another thing happens. The result is that very little is communicated about the camping trip, and the effect on the reader, if the "story" were to go on much longer, is boredom. All the work is left to the reader, and there is no apparent reason the reader should begin to do it.

Even the simplest narrative emphasizes some actions more than others and connects those actions in a meaningful way. "Little Red Riding-Hood" is an example: there is a scheme of development from the less important actions (packing a basket of goodies) to the more important ones (the conversation with the wolf), and the important actions are connected to each other (though of course no one knows why Little Red Riding-Hood chose the shortcut through the forest or how it happened that a woodcutter happened to be in the neighbourhood). More complex narratives provide an account of significant actions, suggest the reasons, motives, or causes of the events, and build to a conclusion or climax. A narrative can begin with a complicated set of circumstances and follow implications to their respective conclusions, or a narrative can begin somewhere in the middle of things, backtrack to their beginnings to show how things got started, and then drive the account to its conclusion.

Every story has a narrator, but the narrator is not the writer. The narrator is an invention of the writer and therefore can be given "powers" which people (writers) ordinarily do not command. A writer can choose from several kinds of narrators: the omniscient narrator, the intimate narrator, the innocent narrator, and the interested narrator. The omniscient narrator (like the one in "Mr. Toad") knows what is going on in several places at once, what a character is thinking, what the outcome will be, and the real reason things turn out as they do. The intimate narrator can give an "internal" account of hopes, feelings, and reactions to events which are revealed only by implication in the action of the story itself. The innocent narrator, often a participant in the story, tells the reader what is happening but is unaware of the entire significance of the events at hand. (Samuel Hearne's account of the incident on the Coppermine River furnishes an example of this sort of narrator.) The interested narrator is a participant in action, is implicated in it, and therefore has a stake not only in the telling of the story but in its outcome as well (see "A Gentleman of the Old School"). The writer's choice of narrator determines in large part what can and cannot be told. For instance, the choice determines the extent to which events are presented objectively or subjectively – whether observed behaviour alone will count or whether motives, reactions, and feelings are to be considered.

The reputed distinction between fiction and non-fiction has an attraction for those who claim a certain hard-headed attachment to facts, but it is a superficial difference. The actual difference between factual accounts and fictional accounts is not the difference between the true and the false or the real and the unreal. It is, rather, the difference between actions which in principle are part of the historical record (and actually happened and were observable at 3:15 P.M.) and those which are not part of that record (although, as possible events, they could have been part of that record). There is moreover an element of non-fiction in every fictional account (witness the behaviour of Mr. Toad) and an element of the fictional in every factual account (the account of the Halifax explosion is an example). The truth is that there are hundreds of ways to tell a story or compose a narrative, even given the constraints of coherence and plausibility.

The writer of narrative makes the same sort of choices any writer of fiction or non-fiction makes: to include or to omit, to tell the story one way rather than another, to present one set of facts and to ignore other facts.

The point of a story is always its outcome and its effect. No one will seriously claim that the story of Mr. Toad is "true," but the effect and the outcome are true enough. No sensible person would expect to encounter a toad in charge of a speeding automobile, but the effect of the story is real enough, and that is what matters.

Little Red Riding-Hood
Traditional

Here is a traditional version of the popular children's story from England, probably dating from the last century. It differs in interesting ways from accounts most people are familiar with.

1   Once upon a time there lived in a certain village a little country girl, the prettiest creature was ever seen. Her mother was excessively fond of her; and her grandmother doted on her still more. This good woman got made for her a little red riding-hood; which became the girl so extremely well that everybody called her Little Red Riding-Hood.

2   One day her mother, having made some custards, said to her:

3   "Go, my dear, and see how thy grandmamma does, for I hear she has been very ill; carry her a custard, and this little pot of butter."

4   Little Red Riding-Hood set out immediately to go to her grandmother, who lived in another village.

5   As she was going through the wood, she met with Gaffer Wolf, who had a very great mind to eat her up, but he durst not, because of some faggot-makers hard by in the forest. He asked her whither she was going. The poor child, who did not know that it was dangerous to stay and hear a wolf talk, said to him:

6   "I am going to see my grandmamma and carry her a custard and a little pot of butter from my mamma."

7   "Does she live far off?" said the Wolf.

8   "Oh! ay," answered Little Red Riding-Hood; "it is beyond that mill you see there, at the first house in the village."

9   "Well," said the Wolf, "and I'll go and see her too. I'll go this way and go you that, and we shall see who will be there soonest."

10   The Wolf began to run as fast as he could, taking the nearest way,

From The Blue Fairy Book, *edited by Andrew Lang (NY: Dover Press, 1965). Reprinted by permission.*

and the little girl went by that farthest about, diverting herself in gathering nuts, running after butterflies, and making nosegays of such little flowers as she met with. The Wolf was not long before he got to the old woman's house. He knocked at the door — tap, tap.

"Who's there?"   *11*

"Your grandchild, Little Red Riding-Hood," replied the Wolf,   *12* counterfeiting her voice; "who has brought you a custard and a little pot of butter sent you by mamma."

The good grandmother, who was in bed, because she was some-   *13* what ill, cried out:

"Pull the bobbin, and the latch will go up."   *14*

The Wolf pulled the bobbin, and the door opened, and then   *15* presently he fell upon the good woman and ate her up in a moment, for it was above three days that he had not touched a bit. He then shut the door and went into the grandmother's bed, expecting Little Red Riding-Hood, who came some time afterwards and knocked at the door — tap, tap.

"Who's there?"   *16*

Little Red Riding-Hood, hearing the big voice of the Wolf, was at   *17* first afraid; but believing her grandmother had got a cold and was hoarse, answered:

" 'Tis your grandchild. Little Red Riding-Hood, who has brought   *18* you a custard and a little pot of butter mamma sends you."

The Wolf cried out to her, softening his voice as much as he   *19* could:

"Pull the bobbin, and the latch will go up."   *20*

Little Red Riding-Hood pulled the bobbin, and the door opened.   *21*

The Wolf, seeing her come in, said to her, hiding himself under   *22* the bed-clothes:

"Put the custard and the little pot of butter upon the stool, and   *23* come and lie down with me."

Little Red Riding-Hood undressed herself and went into bed,   *24* where, being greatly amazed to see how her grandmother looked in her night-clothes, she said to her:

"Grandmamma, what great arms you have got!"   *25*

"That is the better to hug thee, my dear."   *26*

"Grandmamma, what great legs you have got!"   *27*

"That is to run the better, my child."   *28*

"Grandmamma, what great ears you have got!"   *29*

"That is to hear the better, my child."   *30*

"Grandmamma, what great eyes you have got!"   *31*

"It is to see the better, my child."   *32*

"Grandmamma, what great teeth you have got!"   *33*

"That is to eat thee up."   *34*

And, saying these words, this wicked wolf fell upon Little Red   *35* Riding-Hood, and ate her all up.

QUESTIONS

Language and Style

1. Naturally, some of the language in this story is old-fashioned, even archaic. Can you cite examples? What is the effect of the language on the reader?

Organization

1. Can you identify reasons for the outcome of the story? What have the human characters done to "deserve" their fate?

Content

1. Unlike the story which follows, "Little Red Riding-Hood" has no moral. What is the point of "Little Red Riding-Hood"? Can you supply your own moral?

2. This traditional version of the story would probably prove frightening to many small children. On what grounds might one justify telling it to a child?

Vocabulary

gaffer	faggot-maker
nosegays	bobbin

The Little Girl and the Wolf
James Thurber

The American humorist and cartoonist James Thurber puts the traditional story to very different purposes in his "modern" account.

1   One afternoon a big wolf waited in a dark forest for a little girl to come along carrying a basket of food to her grandmother. Finally a little girl did come along and she was carrying a basket of food. "Are you carrying that basket to your grandmother?" asked the wolf. The little girl said yes, she was. So the wolf asked her where

her grandmother lived and the little girl told him and he disappeared into the wood.

When the little girl opened the door of her grandmother's house she saw that there was somebody in bed with a nightcap and nightgown on. She had approached no nearer than twenty-five feet from the bed when she saw that it was not her grandmother but the wolf, for even in a nightcap a wolf does not look any more like your grandmother than the Metro-Goldwyn lion looks like Calvin Coolidge. So the little girl took an automatic out of her basket and shot the wolf dead.   *2*

Moral: It is not so easy to fool little girls nowadays as it used to be.   *3*

QUESTIONS

Language and Style

1. Compare the tone of the narrator in this story with that of the narrator in "Little Red Riding-Hood."

2. What is the effect of the narrator's straight-faced assertions in this story?

Organization

1. Compare the ways in which the events are presented in the two stories.

Content

1. In what sense might the moral of this story be somewhat wistful? What suggestion seems to be made about modern attitudes?

2. What has been left out of Thurber's version of this story? Why?

3. Why does Thurber's story need the earlier version of the story?

Vocabulary

Calvin Coolidge

The Coppermine Massacre
Samuel Hearne

Canadian Farley Mowat, author of Never Cry Wolf *(among others), is the editor of the* Journals of Samuel Hearne. *In this selection, Hearne, an early northern explorer, records the events of July 1771 on the Coppermine River near the Arctic coast.*

[*July 16, 1771*]

1   Early in the morning of the sixteenth, the weather being fine and pleasant, I again proceeded with my survey, and continued it for ten miles farther down the river; but still found it the same as before, being everywhere full of falls and shoals. At this time (it being about noon) the three men who had been sent as spies met us on their return, and informed my companions that five tents of Esquimaux were on the west side of the river. The situation, they said, was very convenient for surprising them; and, according to their account, I judged it to be about twelve miles from the place we met the spies. When the Indians received this intelligence, no farther attendance or attention was paid to my survey, but their whole thoughts were immediately engaged in planning the best method of attack, and how they might steal on the poor Esquimaux the ensuing night, and kill them all while asleep. To accomplish this bloody design more effectually, the Indians thought it necessary to cross the river as soon as possible; and, by the account of the spies, it appeared that no part was more convenient for the purpose than that where we had met them, it being there very smooth, and at a considerable distance from any fall. Accordingly, after the Indians had put all their guns, spears, targets, etc. in good order, we crossed the river, which took up some time.

2   When we arrived on the West side of the river, each painted the front of his target or shield; some with the figure of the Sun, others with that of the Moon, several with different kinds of birds and beasts of prey, and many with the images of imaginary beings, which, according to their silly notions, are the inhabitants of the different elements, Earth, Sea, Air, etc.

3   On enquiring the reason of their doing so, I learned that each man painted his shield with the image of that being on which he relied most for success in the intended engagement. Some were contented with a single representation; while others, doubtful, as I suppose, of the quality and power of any single being, had their shields covered to the very margin with a group of hieroglyphics,

From The Journals of Samuel Hearne *by Farley Mowat, 1958. Reprinted by permission of the Canadian Publishers, McClelland and Stewart.*

quite unintelligible to everyone except the painter. Indeed, from the hurry in which this business was necessarily done, the want of every colour but red and black, and the deficiency of skill in the artist, most of those paintings had more the appearance of a number of accidental blotches, than "of anything that is on the earth, or in the water under the earth"; and though some few of them conveyed a tolerable idea of the thing intended, yet even these were many degrees worse than our country sign-paintings in England.

When this piece of superstition was completed, we began to advance toward the Esquimaux tents; but were very careful to avoid crossing any hills, or talking loud, for fear of being seen or overheard by the inhabitants; by which means the distance was not only much greater than it otherwise would have been, but, for the sake of keeping in the lowest grounds, we were obliged to walk through entire swamps of stiff marly clay, sometimes up to the knees. Our course, however, on this occasion, though very serpentine, was not altogether so remote from the river as entirely to exclude me from a view of it the whole way: on the contrary, several times (according to the situation of the ground) we advanced so near it, as to give me an opportunity of convincing myself that it was as unnavigable as it was in those parts which I had surveyed before, and which entirely corresponded with the accounts given of it by the spies.   4

It is perhaps worth remarking, that my crew, though an undisciplined rabble, and by no means accustomed to war or command, seemingly acted on this horrid occasion with the utmost uniformity of sentiment. There was not among them the least altercation or separate opinion; all were united in the general cause, and as ready to follow where Matonabbee led, as he appeared to be ready to lead, according to the advice of an old Copper Indian, who had joined us on our first arrival at the river where this bloody business was first proposed.   5

Never was reciprocity of interest more generally regarded among a number of people, than it was on the present occasion by my crew, for not one was a moment in want of any thing that another could spare; and if ever the spirit of disinterested friendship expanded the heart of a Northern Indian, it was here exhibited in the most extensive meaning of the word. Property of every kind that could be of general use now ceased to be private, and every one who had any thing which came under that description, seemed proud of an opportunity of giving it, or lending it to those who had none, or were most in want of it.   6

The number of my crew was so much greater than that which five tents could contain, and the warlike manner in which they were equipped so greatly superior to what could be expected of the poor Esquimaux, that no less than a total massacre of every   7 one of them was likely to be the case, unless Providence should work a miracle for their deliverance.

8   The land was so situated that we walked under cover of the rocks and hills till we were within two hundred yards of the tents. There we lay in ambush for some time, watching the motions of the Esquimaux; and here the Indians would have advised me to stay till the fight was over, but to this I could by no means consent; for I considered that when the Esquimaux came to be surprised, they would try every way to escape, and if they found me alone, not knowing me from an enemy, they would probably proceed to violence against me when no person was near to assist. For this reason I determined to accompany them, telling them at the same time, that I would not have any hand in the murder they were about to commit, unless I found it necessary for my own safety. The Indians were not displeased at this proposal; one of them immediately fixed me a spear, and another lent me a broad bayonet for my protection, but at that time I could not be provided with a target; nor did I want to be encumbered with such an unnecessary piece of lumber.

9   While we lay in ambush, the Indians performed the last ceremonies which were thought necessary before the engagement. These chiefly consisted in painting their faces; some all black, some all red, and others with a mixture of the two; and to prevent their hair from blowing into their eyes, it was either tied before and behind, and on both sides, or else cut short all round. The next thing they considered was to make themselves as light as possible for running: which they did, by pulling off their stockings, and either cutting off the sleeves of their jackets, or rolling them up close to their armpits; and though the mosquitoes at that time were so numerous as to surpass all credibility, yet some of the Indians actually pulled off their jackets and entered the lists quite naked, except their breech-cloths and shoes. Fearing I might have occasion to run with the rest, I thought it also advisable to pull off my stockings and cap, and to tie my hair as close up as possible.

10   By the time the Indians had made themselves thus completely frightful, it was near one o'clock in the morning of the seventeenth; when finding all the Esquimaux quiet in their tents, they rushed forth from their ambuscade, and fell on the poor unsuspecting creatures, unperceived till close at the very eaves of their tents, when they soon began the bloody massacre, while I stood neuter in the rear.

11   In a few seconds the horrible scene commenced; it was shocking beyond description; the poor unhappy victims were surprised in the midst of their sleep, and had neither time nor power to make any resistance; men, women, and children, in all upward of twenty, ran out of their tents stark naked, and endeavoured to make their escape; but the Indians having possession of all the landside, to no

place could they fly for shelter. One alternative only remained, that of jumping into the river; but, as none of them attempted it, they all fell a sacrifice to Indian barbarity!

The shrieks and groans of the poor expiring wretches were truly *12* dreadful; and my horror was much increased at seeing a young girl, seemingly about eighteen years of age, killed so near me, that when the first spear was stuck into her side she fell down at my feet, and twisted round my legs, so that it was with difficulty that I could disengage myself from her dying grasps. As two Indian men pursued this unfortunate victim, I solicited very hard for her life; but the murderers made no reply till they had stuck both their spears through her body, and transfixed her to the ground. They then looked me sternly in the face, and began to ridicule me, by asking if I wanted an Esquimaux wife; and paid not the smallest regard to the shrieks and agony of the poor wretch, who was twining round their spears like an eel! Indeed, after receiving much abusive language from them on the occasion, I was at length obliged to desire that they would be more expeditious in dispatching their victim out of her misery, otherwise I should be obliged, out of pity, to assist in the friendly office of putting an end to the existence of a fellow-creature who was so cruelly wounded. On this request being made, one of the Indians hastily drew his spear from the place where it was first lodged, and pierced it through her breast near the heart. The love of life, however, even in this most miserable state, was so predominant, that though this might justly be called the most merciful act that could be done for the poor creature, it seemed to be unwelcome, for though much exhausted by pain and loss of blood, she made several efforts to ward off the friendly blow. My situation and the terror of my mind at beholding this butchery, cannot easily be conceived, much less described; though I summed up all the fortitude I was master of on the occasion, it was with difficulty that I could refrain from tears; and I am confident that my features must have feelingly expressed how sincerely I was affected at the barbarous scene I then witnessed; even at this hour I cannot reflect on the transactions of that horrid day without shedding tears.

QUESTIONS

Language and Style

1. How would you characterize the narrator's attitude toward the events of the story? Toward the other actors in the story? What connection is there to the narrator's tone?

2. What assumptions does the writer seem to make about the reader of this narrative? Who is the reader? How do you know?

3. How does the language work to distance the narrator from the people and the events of the story? What do you make of the language in the last paragraph ("I was at length obliged to desire. . . . ")? At what point does the distancing effect of the language fail?

4. Can you identify passages where the story is told in general language? In specific language? Why should this be? Are there similar differences in the vocabulary?

Organization

1. The account of the actual massacre occupies only the last two or three paragraphs. How does Hearne's personal experience in the last paragraph suggest everything that must have happened that night?

Content

1. What role would the narrator have the reader believe he played in the events of that day in July? How do you know? How convincing is he?

Vocabulary

shoals	target
hieroglyphics	marly
serpentine	altercation
reciprocity	ambuscade

A Gentleman of the Old School
Nellie McClung

An ardent campaigner for women's rights, Nellie McClung gives us this account of her dealings with the political establishment of her day.

1   The big city gathered us in when the pleasant summer at the beach was over. Mark, our youngest child, was born on October of that year, and quickly became the idol of the family, with his blonde

From The Streams Run Fast *by Nellie McClung, 1965. Published by Thomas Allen and Son Ltd. Reprinted by permission.*

curls, blue eyes and quaint wisdom. The other children were all at school and Jack had started at Wesley College. Every day was full of interest. I enjoyed my association with the Canadian Women's Press Club, when we met once a week for tea in our own comfortable quarters. There great problems were discussed and the seed germ of the suffrage association was planted. It was not enough for us to meet and talk and eat chicken sandwiches and olives. We felt we should organize and create a public sentiment in favor of women's suffrage.

The visit of Mrs. Emmeline Pankhurst and of Miss Barbara Wiley,   *2* also one of the British Militant Suffragettes, created a profound impression. The immediate cause of our desire to organize was the plight of women workers in small factories. Some of our members had visited these and we were greatly stirred over the question of long hours, small wages and distressing working conditions.

Mrs. Claude Nash spoke one day on this subject at a Local   *3* Council meeting, and as a result of this meeting she and I were deputed to bring pressure to bear on the government for the appointment of a woman factory inspector. We decided to go to see Sir Rodmond Roblin, the Premier, and if possible, get him to come with us to see some of the factories. She knew him quite well and I had often listened to him in the Legislative Assembly from the visitors' gallery. He was a florid, rather good-looking man in his early sixties, somewhat pompous in manner but very popular with his party and firmly seated on the political throne by what was known as the "Machine." He believed in the patronage system and distributed governmental favors to the faithful in each riding. However, even in all the exposures which followed his defeat in 1914, there was no proof that he had ever enriched himself at the country's expense.

Mrs. Nash must have had some political standing, for I certainly   *4* had not, and we got an interview. We found Sir Rodmond in a very genial mood, and he expressed his delight at our coming. Mrs. Nash was a very handsome young woman, dressed that day in a grey lamb coat and crimson velvet hat. I wasn't looking so poorly myself for I, too, had youth on my side, and we could see that the old man was impressed favorably. I told him I had just come to live in the City from Manitou and I mentioned the name of W. H. Sharpe (afterwards Senator Sharpe) and I think that Sir Rodmond took it for granted that I, too, was a good Conservative, or, as he expressed it, was of the "household of faith." Sir Rodmond had once been a lay preacher in the Methodist Church, and scriptural references came natural to him. He balked a bit when we asked him if he would come with us to see some of the factories and tried to get us to be satisfied with one of his deputies, but Mrs. Nash and I held firm, and much to our surprise, he consented. He called his car and we set out. He looked very well in his beaver coat, and his car was the most pretentious I had ever ridden in. The cut glass vase filled with real carnations impressed my country eyes.

5   On the way to the first factory, the Premier, who sat between us, with his plump hands resting on a gold-headed cane, gave us his views on women working in factories. He believed in work, especially for young women. There was too much idleness now, with electricity and short cuts in labor. As a boy he had worked from sunrise, and before, until the shadows of evening fell, and enjoyed it. Happiest days of his life . . . running barefoot under the apple trees. Perhaps we were oversentimental about factory conditions. . . . Women's hearts were often too kind . . . but he liked kind women – and hoped they would never change. And these young girls in the factories whom we thought were underpaid, no doubt they lived at home, and really worked because they wanted pin-money. Anyway, working wouldn't hurt them, it would keep them off the streets . . .

6   Knowing what we did, we let the monologue go on. He advised us not to allow our kind hearts to run away with us. Most of the women in the factories, he understood, were from foreign countries, where life was strenuous (that word was in the first flush of its popularity then). They did not expect to be carried to the skies on a flowery bed of ease! It doesn't do women any harm to learn how money comes. . . . Extravagant women are the curse of this age.

7   We conducted the Premier down dark, slippery stairs to an airless basement where light in mid-day came from gaunt light bulbs, hanging from smoky ceilings. The floor was littered with refuse of apple peelings and discarded clothing. There was no ventilation and no heat. The room was full of untidy women, operating sewing machines, and equally unattractive men cutting out garments on long tables. We urged Sir Rodmond to speak to some of the workers, but he was willing to call it a day at the first glance. He was shocked at the filth of the place, and asked one of the women if anybody ever swept the floor? He had to shout to drown the sound of the machines. The woman shook her head and kept on working. Then we reminded him that all these people were on piece work.

8   We led the Premier through a side door into the foul passage where a queue had formed before a door marked "Toilet." We could see that Sir Rodmond was deeply shocked that we should know about such things but Mrs. Nash led the way, and I pushed him along from behind. We drew his attention to the fact that there was no separate accommodation for the women, and we did not need to mention that the plumbing had evidently gone wrong. We knew that he was soon going to bolt away from us, so we didn't spare him anything.

9   "For God's sake, let me out of here," he cried at last. "I'm

choking! I never knew such hell holes existed!"

"These people work from 8:30 to 6:00, Sir Rodmond. Six days a   *10*
week," Mrs. Nash told him sweetly. "But no doubt they get used to
it." I am afraid her sarcasm was lost on Sir Rodmond.

When we got him up on the street again, he remembered an   *11*
important interview he had promised, but we coaxed him to come
to one more factory where men's shirts were being made, and all
the workers were young women, and by promising him that this
would be the last one, he came with us. This workroom was in
rather a better building and some daylight came in from the
windows. We wanted him particularly to see these young girls who
were being "kept off the streets." At one machine a girl worked
with a bandaged hand, a badly hurt hand and a very dirty bandage.
At another one a girl coughed almost continuously. I asked her
how long she had had her cold and she said she had no cold, it was
just a bit of bronchitis she had every winter, but she daren't stop
work for there were plenty more to take her place, and someone
had to earn some money in their family, as their father was out of
work. She said she had been lucky to get the job. The manager
came over to speak to us, anxious to show us the fine product they
were turning out. Mrs. Nash asked him how often the factory
inspector came around, but he didn't seem to know anything about
factory inspectors. "In fact," he said, "we hardly need one. All the
girls are glad of the work. I have no trouble with them."

"How about the girl who coughs so much?" I asked. "Couldn't   *12*
she be given a few days off with pay to get built up a bit?"

The manager regarded me sternly.   *13*

"The company is not a charitable institution," he said, "and   *14*
makes no provision for anything like that. If the girl is sick, she can
always quit!" He threw out his hands expressively in a fine gesture
of freedom.

Sir Rodmond was moving towards the door, and we followed.   *15*
When we got back into the car we could see that the fine old
gentleman of the old school was really shocked at what he had
seen.

"Now, Sir Rodmond," we said, "do you still think that these   *16*
women are pleasurably employed in this rich land of wide spaces
and great opportunities?"

Sir Rodmond let down one of the windows of the car and said: *17*

"I still can't see why two women like you should ferret out such   *18*
utterly disgusting things."

"Your factory inspector knows about these places," we told him.   *19*
"We mailed him a list of them and described them, but he has done
nothing. He takes your attitude: Why should women interfere with
what does not concern them? But we are not discouraged and have
no intention of allowing these conditions to continue. We would

like you to appoint a woman factory inspector, a real, trained social worker."

20   Sir Rodmond grew impatient at that. "I tell you it's no job for a woman. I have too much respect for women to give any of them a job like this. . . . But I don't mind admitting that I'm greatly disturbed over all this, greatly disturbed," he repeated. "I'll admit I didn't know that such places existed and I promise you that I will speak to Fletcher about it."

21   With this understanding we parted, thanking Sir Rodmond for giving us so much of his time.

22   Our investigations went on. We were only amateurs but we did find out a few things about how the "other half" lived. We made some other discoveries too. We found out that the Local Council of Women could not be our medium. There were too many women in it who were afraid to be associated with any controversial subject. Their husbands would not let them "go active." It might imperil their jobs. The long tentacles of the political octopus reached far. So one night at Jane Hample's house on Wolsley Avenue we organized the Political Equality League, with a membership of about fifteen. We believed that fifteen good women who were not afraid to challenge public opinion could lay the foundations better than a thousand. Some good work had been already done by the Icelandic women of the city, who had organized the first suffrage society many years before, and the W.C.T.U. women could always be counted on and the same was true of the Labor women.

23   We wanted to get first-hand information on the status of women in Manitoba, and, of course, the whole Dominion. Then it was our purpose to train public speakers and proceed to arouse public sentiment. We would be ready for the next election and hoped to make our influence felt. We had all the courage of youth and inexperience with a fine underpinning of simplicity that bordered on ignorance, but anything we lacked in knowledge we made up in enthusiasm.

24   On a sudden impulse one day I phoned to the Premier's office when the House was in session and asked for an interview with Sir Rodmond Roblin, and to my surprise I found myself speaking to the gentleman himself, who in his most gracious manner assured me he would be pleased to see me and I could come at once, which I did. There in his private office with its red plush hangings and heavy leather furniture, I told the head of the government what we were doing and what we hoped to do. He listened with amused tolerance, but I was grateful to him for listening.

25   "Sir Rodmond," I said, "the women of Manitoba are going to be given the vote, either by you or someone else, and as you are the present Premier, it can be your proud privilege to have this piece of progressive legislation to your credit. I know what you're thinking; you're not impressed with the importance of this matter but that's

because you never thought of it and you really should begin to think about it. You can no longer afford to take this attitude of indifference, and that's why I came to see you."

He looked up at me then and said: *26*

"What in the world do women want to vote for? Why do women   *27* want to mix in the hurly-burly of politics? My mother was the best woman in the world, and she certainly never wanted to vote! I respect women," he went on, "I honor and reverence women, I lift my hat when I meet a woman."

"That's all very nice to hear," I said, "but unfortunately that's not   *28* enough. The women of Manitoba believe that the time has come to make an effort to obtain political equality. The laws are very unfair to women. I would like to tell you about some of them, for I don't believe you know, and what I would really like to do this afternoon is to have a chance to talk to you and your cabinet. It wouldn't take me long; I think fifteen minutes would be enough, and if you and the cabinet could be convinced that it is the right thing to do, it would certainly be easier, more dignified and less disturbing than if we are compelled to make a fight for it. But that is what we are prepared to do, if that is the way you want it. I wish you would call them in, Sir Rodmond, there's plenty of room here in your office."

Sir Rodmond removed the dead cigar from his mouth and his   *29* eyes hardened.

"The cabinet wouldn't listen to you," he said.   *30*

"You'd be surprised," I answered, "I'm really not hard to listen to,   *31* and I don't believe the cabinet would mind at all. In fact," I said brazenly, "I think they'd like it. It would be a welcome change in the middle of a dull day."

He could scarcely find words to express his astonishment and   *32* disapproval.

"You surprise me," he said slowly. "Now who do you think you   *33* are?"

"At this moment," I said, "I'm one of the best advisers you ever   *34* had in all your life. I'm not asking you for a favor, I'm really offering you help."

"What if I tell you that I don't need your help?" he said severely.   *35* "And that I think you're rather a conceited young woman, who has perhaps had some success at Friday afternoon entertainments at country school houses, and so are laboring under the delusion that you have the gift of oratory. What would you say to that?"

"I wouldn't mind," I answered. "I wouldn't even resent it. But I   *36* wish to tell you again, Sir Rodmond, as clearly as I can make it, that we are going to create public sentiment in this province, which will work against you at the next election. Did you ever hear that quotation about there being a tide in the affairs of men, which taken at the flood leads on to fortune?"

We looked at each other across the wide space of his mahogany   *37* desk and the silence was eloquent. Then Sir Rodmond's mood changed. His self-confidence came back; for a moment a doubt had assailed him. But the absurdity of the situation gave him courage. After all, what had he to be afraid of? His party was firmly entrenched, having 29 of the 42 members. He grew jocular.

38   "It would never do to let you speak to the cabinet," he said in the tone that one uses to a naughty child. "Even if they listened to you, which I doubt, you would only upset them, and I don't want that to happen. They are good fellows — they do what they are told to do, now. Every government has to have a head, and I'm the head of this one; and I don't want dissension and arguments. I believe in leaving well enough alone. Take the Indians, for example, they were far happier eating muskrats and the bark of trees before the white man came with education and disturbing ideas. Now they've lost all their good old-fashioned ways. No, you can't come in here and make trouble with my boys, just when I have them trotting easy and eating out of my hand. Now you forget all this nonsense about women voting," he went on in his suavest tones. "You're a fine, smart young woman, I can see that. And take it from me, nice women don't want the vote."

39   His voice dripped fatness.

40   "By nice women," I said, "you probably mean selfish women who have no more thought for the underpaid, overworked women than a pussycat in a sunny window has for the starving kitten on the street. Now in that sense I am not a nice woman, for I do care. I care about those factory women, working in ill-smelling holes, and we intend to do something about it, and when I say 'we' I'm talking for a great many women, of whom you will hear more as the days go on."

41   I stood to go. Then he smiled good-humoredly at me and said:

42   "Now don't go away mad. You know you amuse me. Come any time, I'll always be glad to see you." My smile was just as good-natured as his when I said:

43   "I'll not be back, Sir Rodmond; not in your time. I hadn't much hope of doing any good by coming, but I thought it only fair to give you the chance. I'll not be back, but it's just possible that you will hear from me, not directly, but still you'll hear; and you may not like what you hear, either."

44   "Is this a threat?" he laughed.

45   "No," I said, "it's a prophecy."

QUESTIONS

Language and Style

1. By what means does the writer convey a sense of the personality of Sir Rodmond? See "florid" in paragraph 3.

2. How, generally, does the narrator want the reader to regard her? Why is our sense of the narrator important to the story?

Organization

1. How many scenes make up the story? Compare the scenes in which Sir Rodmond appears. How is his behaviour different? Why?

2. Why should a story featuring Sir Rodmond be more effective than a simple description?

Content

1. How are Sir Rodmond's words used against him? What does the narrator assume about the reader here?

2. Why should the reader share the narrator's apparent delight at Sir Rodmond's discomfort at the end of the first scene?

3. Can you explain the reference to "Icelandic women in the city"? Why should they have organized the first suffrage society long before the events of the story take place?

4. Why should Sir Rodmond's attitude toward women, the cabinet, and Indians be very similar?

Vocabulary

suffrage	florid
patronage	balked
pretentious	monologue
strenuous	ferret
W.C.T.U.	hurly-burly
jocular	

The Halifax Explosion
Hugh MacLennan

This account of a momentous event by the author of Two Solitudes *is a central scene in* Barometer Rising, *a novel focussing on Canada's coming of age.*

1   There was now only one vessel moving north towards the upper harbour, the French munition ship *Mont Blanc*. An ugly craft of little more than three thousand tons, she was indistinguishable from thousands of similar vessels which came and went during these days. She was inward bound, heading for Bedford Basin to await convoy. Moving very slowly, she had crawled through the opened submarine net and now was on her way up the Stream, past the breakwater, George's Island, and then the South End docks. She had been laded a week ago in New York with a cargo consigned to a French port, but only her crew, the Admiralty authorities, and the captain of the British cruiser in port to command the convoy, knew what her main cargo was.

2   Men on the motionless ships in the Stream watched her pass and showed no interest. The previous day they had all received orders not to move until further notification, but none had been told they were giving sea-room to a floating bomb.

3   The cruiser's captain came on deck to watch the *Mont Blanc* pass and estimate the speed she would be able to produce. He was about the only person in the vicinity of Halifax to take any overt notice of her passage up the harbour.

4   The *Mont Blanc* moved so slowly that her bow seemed to push rather than cut the water as she crept past the cruiser. The pilot was proceeding cautiously and the cruiser's captain observed this with satisfaction. What was not so satisfactory to him was the manner in which the cargo was stowed. Her fore-deck was piled with metal canisters, one on top of the other, held down with guy ropes and braced at the sides by an improvised skeleton of planks. The canisters and visible parts of the deck glistened patchily with oil. The after-deck was clear and some sailors in dungarees were lounging there out of the wind.

5   "I wonder what she's got in *those* things?" the captain muttered to his Number One. "Petrol?"

6   "More likely lubricating oil, I should think, sir."

7   "I doubt it. She's not a tanker, after all. Might be benzol from the

From Barometer Rising *by Hugh MacLennan, 1941. Reprinted by permission of the Canadian Publishers, McClelland and Stewart.*

colour of it. How much speed would you say she's got in her?"

"Ten knots at the most, I'd say." *8*

"Doubt if it's even that. I wish they'd realize that a munition ship *9* ought to be faster than the general run of ships. I can't have a cargo like that keeping station with the rest of them. She's got to cruise on the fringe and she needs about three extra knots to do it."

But the *Mont Blanc* glided on up the harbour with little sound or *10* evidence of motion except for a ripple at the bows and a thin wake. She was low in the water and slightly down by the head. A very sloppily laded ship, the cruiser's captain decided. She passed awkwardly onward, the pilot pulling her out to the exact centre of the channel as the harbour narrowed. The tricolour flapped feebly from her stern as she floated in, and as she reached the entrance to the Narrows, bells sounded in the engine-room calling for a still further reduction in speed. . . .

The *Mont Blanc* was now in the Narrows and a detail of men *11* went into her chains to unship the anchor. It would be dropped as soon as she reached her appointed station in the Basin. A hundred yards to port were the Shipyards and another hundred yards off the port bow was the blunt contour of Richmond Bluff; to starboard the shore sloped gently into a barren of spruce scrub. During the two minutes it took the *Mont Blanc* to glide through this strait, most of Bedford Basin and nearly all its flotilla of anchored freighters were hidden from her behind the rise of Richmond Bluff.

Around the projection of this hill, less than fifty fathoms off the *12* port bow of the incoming *Mont Blanc*, another vessel suddenly appeared heading for the open sea. She flew the Norwegian flag, and to the startled pilot of the munitioner the name *Imo* was plainly visible beside the hawse. She was moving at half-speed and listing gently to port as she made the sharp turn out of the Basin to strike the channel of the Narrows. And so listing, with white water surging away from her forefoot, she swept across the path of the *Mont Blanc*, exposing a gaunt flank labelled in giant letters BELGIAN RELIEF. Then she straightened and pointed her bow directly at the fore-quarter of the munitioner. Only at that moment did the men on the *Imo*'s bridge appear to realize that another vessel stood directly in their path.

Staccato orders broke from the bridge of the *Mont Blanc* as the *13* two ships moved toward a single point. Bells jangled and mega-phoned shouts came from both bridges. The ships sheered in the same direction, then sheered back again. With a violent shock, the bow of the *Imo* struck the plates of the *Mont Blanc* and went grinding a third of the way through the deck and the forward hold. A shower of sparks splashed out from the screaming metal. The canisters on the deck of the *Mont Blanc* broke loose from their bindings and some of them tumbled and burst open. Then the vessels heeled away with engines reversed and the water boiling out from their screws as the propellers braked them to a standstill. They sprawled sideways across the Narrows, the *Mont Blanc* veering in toward the Halifax shore, the *Imo* spinning about with steerage-way lost entirely. Finally she drifted toward the opposite shore.

14   For a fraction of a second there was intense silence. Then smoke appeared out of the shattered deck of the *Mont Blanc*, followed by a racing film of flame. The men on the bridge looked at each other. Scattered shouts broke from the stern and the engine-room bells jangled again. Orders were half drowned by a scream of rusty metal as some sailors amidships followed their own inclination and twisted the davits around to lower a boat. The scurry of feet grew louder as more sailors began to pour out through the hatches onto the deck. An officer ran forward with a hose, but before he could connect it his men were ready to abandon ship.

15   The film of flame raced and whitened, then it became deeper like an opaque and fulminant liquid, then swept over the canisters of benzol and increased to a roaring tide of heat. Black smoke billowed and rolled and engulfed the ship, which began to drift with the outgoing tide and swing in toward the graving dock of the Ship-yards. The fire trembled and leaped in a body at the bridge, driving the captain and pilot aft, and there they stood helplessly while the tarry smoke surrounded them in greasy folds and the metal of the deck began to glow under their feet. Both men glanced downward. Underneath that metal lay leashed an incalculable energy, and the bonds which checked it were melting with every second the thermometers mounted in the hold. A half-million pounds of trinitrotoluol and twenty-three hundred tons of picric acid lay there in the darkness under the plates, while the fire above and below the deck converted the hollow shell of the vessel into a bake-oven.

16   If the captain had wished to scuttle the ship at that moment it would have been impossible to do so, for the heat between decks would have roasted alive any man who tried to reach the sea-cocks. By this time the entire crew was in the life-boat. The officers followed, and the boat was rowed frantically toward the wooded slope opposite Halifax. There, by lying flat among the trees, the sailors hoped they would have a chance when their ship blew up. By the time they had beached the boat, the fore-deck of the *Mont Blanc* was a shaking rampart of fire, and black smoke pouring from it screened the Halifax waterfront from their eyes. The sailors broke and ran for the shelter of the woods.

17   By this time men were running out of dock sheds and ware-houses and offices along the entire waterfront to watch the burning ship. None of them knew she was a gigantic bomb. She had now come so close to the Shipyards that she menaced the graving

dock. Fire-launches cut out from a pier farther south and headed for the Narrows. Signal flags fluttered from the Dockyard and the yard-arms of ships lying in the Stream, some of which were already weighing anchor. The captain of the British cruiser piped all hands and called for volunteers to scuttle the *Mont Blanc*; a few minutes later the cruiser's launch was on its way to the Narrows with two officers and a number of ratings. By the time they reached the burning ship her plates were so hot that the sea-water lapping the Plimsoll line was simmering.

The *Mont Blanc* had become the centre of a static tableau. Her   *18*
plates began to glow red and the swollen air inside her hold heated the cargo rapidly towards the detonation point. Launches from the harbour fire department surrounded her like midges and the water from their hoses arched up with infinite delicacy as they curved into the rolling smoke. The *Imo*, futile and forgotten, was still trying to claw her way off the farther shore.

Twenty minutes after the collision there was no one along the   *19*
entire waterfront who was unaware that a ship was on fire in the harbour. The jetties and docks near the Narrows were crowded with people watching the show, and yet no warning of danger was given. At the particular moment there was no adequate centralized authority in Halifax to give a warning, and the few people who knew the nature of the *Mont Blanc*'s cargo had no means of notifying the town or spreading the alarm and no comfort beyond the thought that trinitrotoluol can stand an almost unlimited heat provided there is no fulminate or explosive gas to detonate it.

Bells in the town struck the hour of nine, and by this time nearly   *20*
all normal activity along the waterfront had been suspended. A tug had managed to grapple the *Mont Blanc* and was towing her with imperceptible movement away from the Shipyards back into the channel of the Narrows. Bluejackets from the cruiser had found the bos'n's ladder left by the fleeing crew, and with flesh shrinking from the heat, were going over the side. Fire-launches surrounded her. There was a static concentration, an intense expectancy in the faces of the firemen playing the hoses, a rhythmic reverberation in the beat of the flames, a gush from the hose nozzles and a steady hiss of scalding water. Everything else for miles around seemed motionless and silent.

Then a needle of flaming gas, thin as the mast and of a brilliance   *21*
unbelievably intense, shot through the deck of the *Mont Blanc* near the funnel and flashed more than two hundred feet toward the sky. The firemen were thrown back and their hoses jumped suddenly out of control and slashed the air with S-shaped designs. There were a few helpless shouts. Then all movement and life about the ship were encompassed in a sound beyond hearing as the *Mont Blanc* opened up.

22   Three forces were simultaneously created by the energy of the exploding ship, an earthquake, an air concussion, and a tidal wave. These forces rushed away from the Narrows with a velocity varying in accordance with the nature of the medium in which they worked. It took only a few seconds for the earthquake to spend itself and three minutes for the air expansion to slow down to a gale. The tidal wave travelled for hours before the last traces of it were swallowed in the open Atlantic.

23   When the shock struck the earth, the rigid ironstone and granite base of Halifax peninsula rocked and reverberated, pavements split and houses swayed as the earth trembled. Sixty miles away in the town of Truro windows broke and glass fell to the ground, tinkling in the stillness of the streets. But the ironstone was solid and when the shock has passed, it resumed its immobility.

24   The pressure of the exploding chemicals smashed against the town with the rigidity and force of driving steel. Solid and unbreathable, the forced wall of air struck against Fort Needham and Richmond Bluff and shaved them clean, smashed with one gigantic blow the North End of Halifax and destroyed it, telescoping houses or lifting them from their foundations, snapping trees and lamp-posts, and twisting iron rails into writhing, metal snakes; breaking buildings and sweeping the fragments of their wreckage for hundreds of yards in its course. It advanced two miles southward, shattering every flimsy house in its path, and within thirty seconds encountered the long, shield-like slope of the Citadel which rose before it.

25   Then, for the first time since it was fortified, the Citadel was able to defend at least a part of the town. The air wall smote it and was deflected in three directions. Thus some of its violence shot skyward at a twenty-degree angle and spent itself in space. The rest had to pour around the roots of the hill before closing in on the town for another rush forward. A minute after the detonation, the pressure was advancing through the South End. But now its power was diminished and its velocity was barely twice that of a tornado. Trees tossed and doors broke inward, windows split into driving arrows of glass which buried themselves deep in interior walls. Here the houses, after swaying and cracking, were still on their foundations when the pressure had passed.

26   Underneath the keel of the *Mont Blanc* the water opened and the harbour bottom was deepened twenty feet along the channel of the Narrows. And then the displaced water began to drive outward, rising against the town and lifting ships and wreckage over the sides of the docks. It boiled over the shores and climbed the hill as far as the third cross-street, carrying with it the wreckage of small boats, fragments of fish, and somewhere, lost in thousands of tons of hissing brine, the bodies of men. The wave moved in a gigantic bore down the Stream to the sea, rolling some ships under and

lifting others high on its crest, while anchor chains cracked like guns as the violent thrust snapped them. Less than ten minutes after the detonation, it boiled over the breakwater off the park and advanced on McNab's Island, where it burst with a roar greater than a winter storm. And then the central volume of the wave rolled on to sea, high and arching and white at the top, its back glossy like the plumage of a bird. Hours later it lifted under the keel of a steamer far out in the Atlantic and the captain, feeling his vessel heave, thought he had struck a floating mine.

But long before this, the explosion had become manifest in new forms over Halifax. More than two thousand tons of red hot steel, splintered fragments of the *Mont Blanc*, fell like meteors from the sky into which they had been hurled a few seconds before. The ship's anchor soared over the peninsula and descended through a roof on the other side of the Northwest Arm three miles away. For a few seconds the harbour was dotted white with a maze of splashes, and the decks of raddled ships rang with reverberations and clangs as fragments struck them.   *27*

Over the North End of Halifax, immediately after the passage of the first pressure, the tormented air was laced with tongues of flame which roared and exploded out of the atmosphere, lashing downwards like a myriad blow-torches as millions of cubic feet of gas took fire and exploded. The atmosphere went white-hot. It grew mottled, then fell to the streets like a crimson curtain. Almost before the last fragments of steel had ceased to fall, the wreckage of the wooden houses in the North End had begun to burn. And if there were any ruins which failed to ignite from falling flames, they began to burn from the fires in their own stoves, onto which they had collapsed.   *28*

Over this part of the town, rising in the shape of a typhoon from the Narrows and extending five miles into the sky, was poised a cloud formed by the exhausted gases. It hung still for many minutes, white, glossy as an ermine's back, serenely aloof. It cast its shadow over twenty miles of forest land behind Bedford Basin.   *29*

QUESTIONS

Language and Style

1. Early in the narrative one word in particular sets the suspense going. What is it? How does that word direct our attention to the details which follow?

2. Why should the account be more effective by not telling what happened to the people (the naval officer, for example) in the immediate vicinity of the *Mount Blanc*?

3. In order to produce this account the writer needed to know a bit about a number of subjects. What are some of these subjects? How is this reflected in the vocabulary?

4. How can you explain MacLennan's use of "fathoms" in paragraph 12? Notice that in paragraph 11, "yards" is the unit of measure.

5. Why do the men on the bridge of the *Mont Blanc* simply "look at each other"? Why doesn't the writer explain what they are thinking?

Organization

1. How would you describe the narrator? Where is the narrator located? Why, under the circumstances, could the narrator not have been a witness to the events in the story? Why is this an advantage?

2. Where is the climax of the narrative? What words prepare the reader for it?

3. Which small, vivid scenes help the reader picture the events in the Halifax harbour? What other features of MacLennan's account help the reader's sense of the event?

4. How does the writer organize the account of the aftermath of the explosion? How does the reader know what the organization is? In this connection, explain the organization of paragraphs 22 through 29.

5. Compare the rate at which events occur at different stages in the account. See, for example, the first ten paragraphs and paragraphs 13 and 14. How can you explain the difference?

Content

1. Consider in what particulars MacLennan's account might differ from a literal account. Which would be more realistic?

Vocabulary

laded	consigned
overt	dungarees
benzol	fathom
hawse	forefoot
steerage-way	davits
opaque	fulminant
scuttle	graving
Plimsoll line	staccato
flotilla	ironstone

The Diary of One Now Dead
George C. Hodge

The diary of Lt. Hodge has no literary ambitions. It simply recounts the day-to-day affairs of a flight crew lost on the coast of Labrador.[1]

NOVEMBER 12, 1942: We are still sitting here with 16 minutes of daylight, each day we have less than six hours of daylight between sunrise and sunset. Had about two inches of snow last night and everything was real pretty. Spent most of the day sweeping it off the plane. They said there's a chance of leaving tomorrow but this place seems so much like home that it doesn't seem like we should leave.   *1*

NOVEMBER 16: This place is full of changes. Yesterday Jansen and I walked down to the river. There was a solid sheet of ice resting on the rocks, and it was covered with two inches of snow. Last night we had rain and a warm wind, with gusts up to 60 mph. We've had all kinds of weather. One day it was six degrees.   *2*

NOVEMBER 26: I still say this is screwy weather. We were alerted at 0330 there was solid overcast. We killed time until 0600 then we got briefed. It was still overcast and seemed to be getting worse. The A-10s and B-25s started kicking off, but about then, it started to rain and the ceiling looked very low. About ten minutes later it stopped raining and an A-20 came over at 600 feet with room to spare. By 0830 the sun was shining but it was too late to take off.   *3*

NOVEMBER 30: At last we took off for Goose Bay. About 1315 we ran into a few clouds and I turned around and called for the formation to turn around also. One plane dropped out. I think I saw the two P-40s later. I lost the others while letting down below the clouds. We saw an opening to the south at about 2,000 feet and after flying in that direction we broke out. We finally had to go back up to 13,000 feet, but it was clear sailing, so we kept on. Lt. Josephson gave me a new heading to get back on course, but we know it was too much of a correction. About halfway I picked up the Goose beam, but the set went dead after a few minutes.   *4*

It was too late to turn back, so we tried to get it on the compass but couldn't. We finally hit the coast. We decided we were south of Goose Bay, so we turned to the north until we realized we must be north of Goose. We were almost out of gas, so I started looking for a place to land. I wanted to get back to where there was trees, but the engines started missing so we had to come down.   *5*

[1]Spelling and grammar as in original.

"The Diary of One Now Dead," by George C. Hodge. From The Sunday Sun, *Toronto (Oct. 7, 1984). Reprinted by permission.*

6   The crew never batted an eye, when told we were going to make a crash landing. Even if I do say so myself it was a good landing and Lt. Josephson did a good job cutting the switches. We did hit a rock that tore the bombay open and the prop tips went through the fuselage behind me. Outside of that the ship was intact. It swung around 90 degrees until stopping, but made a good wind break that way.

7   It was almost dark, so after eating a cold ration we went to bed inside the ship, and we slept very well. We had 17 blankets, a comforter and a bedroll.

8   Lt. Josephson took a star shot and decided we were 300 minutes north of Goose Bay.

9   DECEMBER 11: Lt. Josephson walked to a ford to the west and Golm to the one to the east. We spent most of the day clearing the ship and pooling the rations. I climbed the mountain [where Saglek Air Station was later located] but didn't learn too much.

10   Nolan worked on the put-put all day without any results. We cranked the dingy radio. It was pretty windy and we spent the night in the ship.

11   DECEMBER 12: Made three big improvements in our situation. Lt. Jansen and Golm discovered a lake close to the ship and they saw a fox. Waywrench and I saw about 50 seals, we knew there was food there. We made a lean-to out of tarps under the wing of the ship and slept there. It was much better.

12   DECEMBER 13: When the star shots were figured out, it showed us to be close to the town of Hebron. We worked on the put-put all day with no success, so we tried the liaison set on the batteries but they were too weak. Tonight we pooled all the blankets and slept together.

13   DECEMBER 14: Wind blowing hard with driving snow, so we stayed in all day. Our lake went dry so we went back to melting snow. We went to bed early.

14   DECEMBER 15: Had to eat a cold breakfast, after the wind blew too much on the fire. Nolan changed the voltage regulators and got 25 volts, long enough for me to get a couple of stations on the liaison receiver. The put-put stopped. We hope we know what is wrong with it. Hope to get a message out soon.

15   DECEMBER 17: The put-put went out, and we tried the batteries they were too dead.

16   DECEMBER 19: More snow last night. Nolan and Mangins worked on the put-put again, but it was too cold. We built a fire in the lean-to and thawed out.

17   DECEMBER 20: So windy we stayed in bed all day.

18   DECEMBER 21: Everything was really snowed in, so we spent the day eating, thawing out blankets and planning a trip south. Lt. Josephson, Lt. Jansen and Sgt. Nolan plan to head south on the first warm day.

19   DECEMBER 22: Had a perfect day, the first clear day in over a week. We worked on the boat and shoveled snow away from the

lean-to. We ate a pretty big meal with the three boat men eating a little extra.

DECEMBER 23: Got up at 0715, got the boat ready and started *20* carrying it. The wind was very strong and the boat was very heavy, so we had a pretty hard time of it. We didn't get to the water until noon, and then it took quite a while to find a place to put it in the water.

We intended to put them off shore, but they appeared to be *21* making slow headway to the south. That was the last time we saw them. We had a hard time coming back across the snow. We had some peanuts and caramels.

DECEMBER 24: Christmas Eve and we've been here two weeks *22* today. We got up early and got out the gas strainer so we could make a fire. It was so windy we couldn't go out so we dried out the blankets. It was pretty lonesome – just the four of us. Golm got blistered pretty bad and had swollen hands, which have to be doctored.

We stretched out our eating to cover most of the day. We had a *23* sardine sized can of herring with crackers, a spoonful of peanuts, one black cough drop each, a caramel, a cup of grape drink and lots of coffee, using the same grounds over and over. It's really a surprise how much one can get from a small caramel but we all look forward to it every day with anticipation.

DECEMBER 25: What a Christmas! Mangins' feet pained him so *24* much, we had to get up at 0330. He was in agony before that, but was better after that, although his arches pain him pretty bad. Got up again at 0900. Golm went exploring, I massaged Mangins' feet and Waywrench started to fix up the floor, which was in pretty bad condition from the fire. Later we dug out the rear entrance of the ship to repair a window. After that we had a first aid lesson. The only one who doesn't have anything wrong is me. We are about to eat our Christmas dinner and go to bed.

DECEMBER 26: Had another swell day. The weather was perfect. *25* Waywrench cleaned up the back of the ship while Golm dug out the bombay, uncovering a can of fruit cocktail and a can of chicken a la king.

I worked on Mangins' feet and did a few odd jobs. Everyone is *26* feeling better and I hope Mangins is up in a few days. We aren't starving by any means but the conversations are mostly about food. One surely can remember tasty food.

DECEMBER 27: Started today as usual by treating the casualties. *27* Mangins feet are better, but he has a big blister on each foot. Golm and Mangins spent the day drying blankets. Waywrench finished cleaning the ship, and I climbed the mountain to see if I could see anything out to sea. The enforced diet is starting to tell on us, but will eat a little more tomorrow.

DECEMBER 30: Today was overcast with snow showers. Spent *28* most of the day working on the inside. Golm lost a fingernail and may lose another, I'm just thankful his hand doesn't pain him.

Worked a little on the put-put, and may have made some progress, but it was too dark to work much. Got up a game of 500 rummy which everyone seemed to enjoy. The boys have been gone a week today. God grant they are still going.

29   JANUARY 1, 1943: Happy New Year. It snowed and blew all night and kept it up all day. So since we had no fire we stayed in bed all day.

30   JANUARY 2: More wind and snow. It slacked at noon, so we got up with the aid of a fire in a peanut can. Waywrench got the prop and diver tank out with a gallon of alcohol and glycerine. I dug out the oil drain.

31   After that we had a couple of hot fires and plenty of hot coffee, a lemon powder, and a cup of boullion. Our main dish was the last can of datenut roll with jelly and it was good. Then I worked on Mangins feet.

32   There was quite a lot of loose snow outside, but the very shape of the ship keeps it fairly clear. It actually rained today. I don't know what effect that is going to have on our situation. The boys have been gone 10 days today, which is the time we figured it would take them to make the trip. We hope they made it and can bring help soon.

33   JANUARY 3: There wasn't much wind last night, so we thought we would have a good day, but the wind picked up, and it snowed all day. The ship has a coat of ice on it and is covered with snow. Besides that the drifts are higher and closer than they have ever been before. We hooked up the hand fuel pump transfer, and I'm positive we pumped fuel to the other side but couldn't get it to drain out, so we used the alcohol to cook with. I got into a big hurry once and caused a fire, in which I got burned, but not too bad. Now we are all wearing bandages.

34   I found two boullion cubes in the radio operator's drawer. Spent a lot of time putting snow under our bed. There is quite a hole there, so we should be able to sleep better tonight. It must be raining outside now. It couldn't be melting ice on the wing.

35   We keep praying for clear weather, and hope the boys got through. Also to try out our new theory on where Hebron is.

36   JANUARY 4: Had a blue sky when we got up, but it got overcast all day. Then we got wind. Waywrench got quite a lot of gas out of the other wing. We are all praying for good weather both in hopes of a rescue plan (if the boys got through). I am cutting down – still on rations.

37   JANUARY 5: It started off like a beautiful day, but turned to a low overcast. Waywrench and I cleaned the plane of snow and Mangins finished the put-put, which was to be in pretty good shape.

38   JANUARY 6: This is the eighth day of bad weather. The entrance is blocked and doesn't do any good to dig it out. It's now 2 weeks since the boys left, but spirits are high in spite of the bad weather.

39   JANUARY 7: We've been here 4 weeks today. The entrance was

blocked up this morning. As I was going into the ship I saw a little bird. We caught him, and boiled him for a couple of hours. Then made stew by adding a boullion powder. It was really delicious. Golm started to go looking for Hebron, but the snow was too soft.

Mangins got outside today, the first time in 13 days. If we can't　*40* find a town or get the put-put going in three days we are going to have to sit and wait until the weather clears and pray that the boys got through because we are too low on food to do anything else.

God help us get out of here safely.　*41*

JANUARY 8: Today was the most strenuous day since we got　*42* here. I tried to get Hebron, and I think I know where it is, but there are two mountains in the way. I can feel myself growing weaker. We have less to eat each day.

I don't know what we would do if we didn't have that 3 lbs. of　*43* coffee. We sit around and drink coffee and talk about all kinds of food, but I think we all crave chocolate candy more than anything else. The boys have dug out the back of the ship, so if tomorrow is clear we will still have one last try with the put-put radio.

JANUARY 9: We put the put-put back in its place and it jammed　*44* again, so that leaves us with only one possibility – the boys got through to Hebron.

JANUARY 10: We have been here one month today. 31 days.　*45* Spent most of the day, which was perfect as far as the weather was concerned looking after the plane and fixing up bandages. The boys spirits were rather high today, after our little church service.

Only food today was 2 cups of coffee each.　*46*

JANUARY 11: The third day of perfect weather, also the coldest　*47* since we got here. Spent all day waiting for the plane that didn't come.

Oil gave out on this side, which presents another problem. The　*48* short rations are starting to tell on all of us, but we are still in high spirits. If we don't live to eat some of the food we talk about, we are mentally eating one of the best meals in the world.

JANUARY 12: Today was the boys' 20th day and our 33rd and was　*49* overcast, but was calm. We got the oil dug out, but we are all so weak we can hardly work. The boys' spirits are still high though, and we had a lively bull session on our favorite topic – food. Our ration today was 1 piece of pineapple and coffee.

JANUARY 13: Another calm overcast day. We dug out the oil,　*50* dried the blankets, made a new bed on snow, and ate our last food, 1 slice of ham and 1 soda cracker.

All we have left is a half pound of chocolate and 3 drink powders,　*51* but we talk like rescue should be tomorrow. It cleared this PM, so maybe there's hope tomorrow.

JANUARY 14: Clear day but with wind. We cleared off the plane　*52* and waited, but nothing happened. Late this afternoon we played cards, and oiled the gas too fast, and caused an explosion which burned both his and my face and hair and hands. Our rations were four chocolates, but we are still working out pretty well. After a devotional, we went to bed.

53   JANUARY 15: A perfect day, but the coldest since we got here. Spent most of the day trying to keep warm and listening for a plane. Also made big plans for a couple of days in New York when we get our furloughs. Rations were two chocolates and a boullion powder. We are getting weaker and colder because our bodies aren't putting out enough heat.

54   JANUARY 16: Another calm clear day, but the coldest we have yet had. The oil froze up, so we had to end up by burning nothing but gas. The only thing we have left is one boullion powder and two sticks of gum. The strain is beginning to tell, but we still have good bull sessions about food and the furlough in New York.

55   JANUARY 17: Couldn't have asked for a better day except that it is so cold that the oil is frozen and won't burn. So our gas is going pretty fast. Had our last food, boullion powder, so unless rescue comes in a few days $----$. The boys have been gone 25 days which is a long time, but they are our only hope; our families will really miss some swell dishes and menus.

56   JANUARY 18: Cold and clear. My watch stopped, so we didn't get up until noon. Must be a little warmer because we got a little oil. Today was our first complete day without food, but spirits are still high. It's surprising how much punishment the body and mind can take when necessary. We are still in pretty good condition but rather weak. Not much hope left.

57   JANUARY 20: It snowed and blew all night, but we all slept pretty well, and we were much more cheerful today. We stayed up longer than we should have though, and are pretty tired. That snow has been blowing pretty hard all day and is piling up in front of the door, so I don't know what we will do if it doesn't stop pretty soon.

58   JANUARY 21: Six weeks today and rough night with snow and rain, so everything was soaked when we got up. Only Waywrench and I got up and then only long enough to melt snow for water. Things could be worse.

59   JANUARY 22: Got up around noon, and was up until about 6. I cleared up the entrance and made the bed. We could stand some good weather.

60   JANUARY 23: Spent a miserable night. Everyone got crowded and nobody could get comfortable. Had a good day, but everybody is pretty discouraged although the conversation was pretty good. We haven't really felt famished but we are weak. It really gets me to see these boys start to do something and have to stop from the lack of power to go on. Waywrench has developed a case of piles and is really suffering.

61   JANUARY 24: Miserable night. Everybody got up at 0130, shot the bull, and went to bed at 0730.

62   JANUARY 25: Overcast but fairly calm. Each day we don't see how we can last another day, but each time we manage to go on.

We all smoked a pipe of tobacco this morning and Golm really got sick, and I felt pretty bad. But we came out pretty well.

FEBRUARY 3: Slept a solid week in bed: Today Waywrench died   *63* after being mentally sick for several days. We are all pretty weak but should be able to last several more days.

NOTE: This was the last diary entry. The men were found in late   *64* March by Eskimos. They were only about a three and one-half hour walk from Hebron.

QUESTIONS

Language and Style

1. If the reader were not aware that this account is an actual record of events, what features of the language would suggest it?

2. Can you explain why some of the effectiveness results from reading between the lines? Consider, for example, Hodge's remark for November 30 ("We did hit a rock that tore the bombay open and the prop tips went through the fuselage behind me.") and for December 23 ("That was the last time we saw them. We had a hard time coming back across the snow. We had some peanuts and caramels.").

3. What occasional remarks begin to express the difficulty of the crew's situation?

4. How, eventually, does the crew's state of mind become evident?

5. For whom is the diary written?

Organization

1. What themes help hold the account together? What matters are introduced but apparently dropped without explanation?

2. Why would it be helpful to accompany this account with a map?

Content

1. Why might the reader begin to sense frustration as the story progresses?

Vocabulary

star shot	put-put
liaison	minutes
glycerine	furlough

Mr. Toad
Kenneth Grahame

The Wind in the Willows, while intended as a children's book, has appeal for many adults. Mr. Toad is the most troublesome and, perhaps for that reason, the most interesting of the animal neighbours.

1   It was a bright morning in the early part of summer; the river had resumed its wonted banks and its accustomed pace, and a hot sun seemed to be pulling everything green and bushy and spiky up out of the earth towards him, as if by strings. The Mole and the Water Rat had been up since dawn very busy on matters connected with boats and the opening of the boating season; painting and varnishing, mending paddles, repairing cushions, hunting for missing boathooks, and so on; and were finishing breakfast in their little parlour and eagerly discussing their plans for the day, when a heavy knock sounded at the door.

2   "Bother!" said the Rat, all over egg. "See who it is, Mole, like a good chap, since you've finished."

3   The Mole went to attend the summons, and the Rat heard him utter a cry of surprise. Then he flung the parlour door open, and announced with much importance, "Mr. Badger!"

4   This was a wonderful thing, indeed, that the Badger should pay a formal call on them, or indeed on anybody. He generally had to be caught, if you wanted him badly, as he slipped quietly along a hedgerow of an early morning or a late evening, or else hunted up in his own house in the middle of the wood, which was a serious undertaking.

5   The Badger strode heavily into the room, and stood looking at the two animals with an expression full of seriousness. The Rat let his egg-spoon fall on the tablecloth, and sat open-mouthed.

6   "The hour has come!" said the Badger at last with great solemnity.

7   "What hour?" asked the Rat uneasily, glancing at the clock on the mantelpiece.

8   "*Whose* hour, you should rather say," replied the Badger. "Why, Toad's hour! The hour of Toad! I said I would take him in hand as soon as the winter was well over, and I'm going to take him in hand to-day!"

9   "Toad's hour, of course!" cried the Mole delightedly. "Hooray! I remember now! *We'll* teach him to be a sensible Toad!"

10   "This very morning," continued the Badger, taking an arm-chair, "as I learnt last night from a trustworthy source, another new and

From The Wind in the Willows *by Kenneth Grahame, 1960. Published by Charles Scribner's Sons. Reprinted by permission.*

exceptionally powerful motor-car will arrive at Toad Hall on approval or return. At this very moment, perhaps, Toad is busy arraying himself in those singularly hideous habiliments so dear to him, which transform him from a (comparatively) good-looking Toad into an Object which throws any decent-minded animal that comes across it into a violent fit. We must be up and doing, ere it is too late. You two animals will accompany me instantly to Toad Hall, and the work of rescue shall be accomplished."

"Right you are!" cried the Rat, starting up. "We'll rescue the poor   *11*
unhappy animal! We'll convert him! He'll be the most converted Toad that ever was before we've done with him!"

They set off up the road on their mission of mercy, Badger   *12*
leading the way. Animals when in company walk in a proper and sensible manner, in single file, instead of sprawling all across the road and being of no use or support to each other in case of sudden trouble or danger.

They reached the carriage-drive of Toad Hall to find, as the   *13*
Badger had anticipated, a shiny new motor-car, of great size, painted a bright red (Toad's favourite colour), standing in front of the house. As they neared the door it was flung open, and Mr. Toad, arrayed in goggles, cap, gaiters, and enormous overcoat, came swaggering down the steps, drawing on his gauntleted gloves.

"Hullo! come on, you fellows!" he cried cheerfully on catching   *14*
sight of them. "You're just in time to come with me for a jolly – to come for a jolly – for a – er jolly – "

His hearty accents faltered and fell away as he noticed the stern   *15*
unbending look on the countenances of his silent friends, and his invitation remained unfinished.

The Badger strode up the steps. "Take him inside," he said   *16*
sternly to his companions. Then, as Toad was hustled through the door, struggling and protesting, he turned to the chauffeur in charge of the new motor-car.

"I'm afraid you won't be wanted to-day," he said. "Mr. Toad has   *17*
changed his mind. He will not require the car. Please understand that this is final. You needn't wait." Then he followed the others inside and shut the door.

"Now, then!" he said to the Toad, when the four of them stood   *18*
together in the hall, "first of all, take those ridiculous things off!"

"Shan't!" replied Toad, with great spirit. "What is the meaning of   *19*
this gross outrage? I demand an instant explanation."

"Take them off him, then, you two," ordered the Badger briefly.   *20*

They had to lay Toad out on the floor, kicking and calling all   *21*
sorts of names, before they could get to work properly. Then the Rat sat on him, and the Mole got his motor-clothes off him bit by bit, and they stood him up on his legs again. A good deal of his blustering spirit seemed to have evaporated with the removal of his fine panoply. Now that he was merely Toad, and no longer the

Terror of the Highway, he giggled feebly and looked from one to the other appealingly, seeming quite to understand the situation.

22   "You knew it must come to this, sooner or later, Toad," the Badger explained severely. "You've disregarded all the warnings we've given you, you've gone on squandering the money your father left you, and you're getting us animals a bad name in the district by your furious driving and your smashes and your rows with the police. Independence is all very well, but we animals never allow our friends to make fools of themselves beyond a certain limit; and that limit you've reached. Now, you're a good fellow in many respects, and I don't want to be too hard on you. I'll make one more effort to bring you to reason. You will come with me into the smoking-room, and there you will hear some facts about yourself; and we'll see whether you come out of that room the same Toad that you went in."

23   He took Toad firmly by the arm, led him into the smoking-room, and closed the door behind them.

24   "*That's* no good!" said the Rat contemptuously. "*Talking* to Toad'll never cure him. He'll *say* anything."

25   They made themselves comfortable in arm-chairs and waited patiently. Through the closed door they could just hear the long continuous drone of the Badger's voice, rising and falling in waves of oratory; and presently they noticed that the sermon began to be punctuated at intervals by long-drawn sobs, evidently proceeding from the bosom of Toad, who was a soft-hearted and affectionate fellow, very easily converted – for the time being – to any point of view.

26   After some three quarters of an hour the door opened, and the Badger reappeared, solemnly leading by the paw a very limp and dejected Toad. His skin hung baggily about him, his legs wobbled, and his cheeks were furrowed by the tears so plentifully called forth by the Badger's moving discourse.

27   "Sit down there, Toad," said the Badger kindly, pointing to a chair. "My friends," he went on, "I am pleased to inform you that Toad has at last seen the error of his ways. He is truly sorry for his misguided conduct in the past, and he has undertaken to give up motor-cars entirely and for ever. I have his solemn promise to that effect."

28   "That is very good news," said the Mole gravely.

29   "Very good news indeed," observed the Rat dubiously, if only – *if* only – "

30   He was looking very hard at Toad as he said this, and could not help thinking he perceived something vaguely resembling a twinkle in that animal's still sorrowful eye.

31   "There's only one thing more to be done," continued the gratified Badger. "Toad, I want you solemnly to repeat, before your friends here, what you fully admitted to me in the smoking-room

just now. First, you are sorry for what you've done, and you see the folly of it all?"

There was a long, long pause. Toad looked desperately this way *32* and that, while the other animals waited in grave silence. At last he spoke.

"No!" he said a little sullenly, but stoutly; "I'm *not* sorry. And it *33* wasn't folly at all! It was simply glorious!"

"What?" cried the Badger, greatly scandalized. "You backsliding *34* animal, didn't you tell me just now, in there – "

"O, yes, yes, in *there*," said Toad impatiently. "I'd have said *35* anything in *there*. You're so eloquent, dear Badger, and so moving, and so convincing, and put all your points so frightfully well – you can do what you like with me in *there*, and you know it. But I've been searching my mind since, and going over things in it, and I find that I'm not a bit sorry or repentant really, so it's no earthly good saying I am; now, is it?"

"Then you don't promise," said the Badger, "never to touch a *36* motor-car again?"

"Certainly not!" replied Toad emphatically. "On the contrary, I *37* faithfully promise that the very first motor-car I see, poop-poop! off I go in it!"

"Told you so, didn't I?" observed the Rat to the Mole. *38*

"Very well, then," said the Badger firmly, rising to his feet. "Since *39* you won't yield to persuasion, we'll try what force can do. I feared it would come to this all along. You've often asked us three to come and stay with you, Toad, in this handsome house of yours; well, now we're going to. When we've converted you to a proper point of view we may quit, but not before. Take him upstairs, you two, and lock him up in his bedroom, while we arrange matters between ourselves."

"It's for your own good, Toady, you know," said the Rat kindly, as *40* Toad, kicking and struggling, was hauled up the stairs by his two faithful friends. "Think what fun we shall all have together, just as we used to, when you've quite got over this – this painful attack of yours!"

"We'll take great care of everything for you till you're well, Toad," *41* said the Mole; "and we'll see your money isn't wasted, as it has been."

"No more of those regrettable incidents with the police, Toad," *42* said the Rat, as they thrust him into his bedroom.

"And no more weeks in hospital, being ordered about by female *43* nurses, Toad," added the Mole, turning the key on him.

They descended the stair, Toad shouting abuse at them through *44* the keyhole; and the three friends then met in conference on the situation.

"It's going to be a tedious business," said the Badger, sighing. *45* "I've never seen Toad so determined. However, we will see it out.

He must never be left an instant unguarded. We shall have to take it in turns to be with him, till the poison has worked itself out of his system."

46　　They arranged watches accordingly. Each animal took it in turns to sleep in Toad's room at night, and they divided the day up between them. At first Toad was undoubtedly very trying to his careful guardians. When his violent paroxysms possessed him he would arrange bedroom chairs in rude resemblance of a motor-car and would crouch on the foremost of them, bent forward and staring fixedly ahead, making uncouth and ghastly noises, till the climax was reached, when, turning a complete somersault, he would lie prostrate amidst the ruins of the chairs, apparently completely satisfied for the moment. As time passed, however, these painful seizures grew gradually less frequent, and his friends strove to divert his mind into fresh channels. But his interest in other matters did not seem to revive, and he grew apparently languid and depressed.

47　　One fine morning the Rat, whose turn it was to go on duty, went upstairs to relieve Badger, whom he found fidgeting to be off and stretch his legs in a long ramble round his wood and down his earths and burrows. "Toad's still in bed," he told the Rat, outside the door. "Can't get much out of him, except, 'O, leave him alone, he wants nothing, perhaps he'll be better presently, it may pass off in time, don't be unduly anxious,' and so on. Now, you look out, Rat! When Toad's quiet and submissive, and playing at being the hero of a Sunday-school prize, then he's at his artfullest. There's sure to be something up. I know him. Well, now I must be off."

48　　"How are you to-day, old chap?" inquired the Rat cheerfully, as he approached Toad's bedside.

49　　He had to wait some minutes for an answer. At last a feeble voice replied, "Thank you so much, dear Ratty! So good of you to inquire! But first tell me how you are yourself, and the excellent Mole?"

50　　"O, *we're* all right," replied the Rat. "Mole," he added incautiously, "is going out for a run round with Badger. They'll be out till luncheon-time, so you and I will spend a pleasant morning to-gether, and I'll do my best to amuse you. Now jump up, there's a good fellow, and don't lie moping there on a fine morning like this!"

51　　"Dear, kind Rat," murmured Toad, "how little you realise my condition, and how very far I am from 'jumping up' now – if ever! But do not trouble about me. I hate being a burden to my friends, and I do not expect to be one much longer. Indeed, I almost hope not."

52　　"Well, I hope not, too," said the Rat heartily. "You've been a fine bother to us all this time, and I'm glad to hear it's going to stop. And in weather like this, and the boating season just beginning! It's too bad of you, Toad! It isn't the trouble we mind, but you're making us miss such an awful lot."

"I'm afraid it *is* the trouble you mind, though," replied the Toad *53* languidly. "I can quite understand it. It's natural enough. You're tired of bothering about me. I mustn't ask you to do anything further. I'm a nuisance, I know."

"You are, indeed," said the Rat. "But I tell you, I'd take any *54* trouble on earth for you, if only you'd be a sensible animal."

"If I thought that, Ratty," murmured Toad, more feebly than ever, *55* "then I would beg you – for the last time, probably – to step round to the village as quickly as possible – even now it may be too late – and fetch the doctor. But don't you bother. It's only a trouble, and perhaps we may as well let things take their course."

"Why, what do you want a doctor for?" inquired the Rat, coming *56* closer and examining him. He certainly lay very still and flat, and his voice was weaker and his manner much changed.

"Surely you have noticed of late – " murmured Toad. "But no – *57* why should you? Noticing things is only a trouble. To-morrow, indeed, you may be saying to yourself, 'Oh, if only I had noticed sooner! If only I had done something!' But no; it's a trouble. Never mind – forget that I asked."

"Look here, old man," said the Rat, beginning to get rather *58* alarmed, "of course I'll fetch a doctor to you, if you really think you want him. But you can hardly be bad enough for that yet. Let's talk about something else."

"I fear, dear friend," said Toad, with a sad smile, "that 'talk' can *59* do little in a case like this – or doctors either, for that matter; still one must grasp at the slightest straw. And, by the way – while you are about it – I *hate* to give you additional trouble, but I happen to remember that you will pass the door – would you mind at the same time asking the lawyer to step up? It would be a convenience to me, and there are moments – perhaps I should say there is *a* moment – when one must face disagreeable tasks, at whatever cost to exhausted nature!"

"A lawyer! O, he must be really bad!" the affrighted Rat said to *60* himself, as he hurried from the room, not forgetting, however, to lock the door carefully behind him.

Outside, he stopped to consider. The other two were far away, *61* and he had no one to consult.

"It's best to be on the safe side," he said, on reflection. "I've *62* known Toad fancy himself frightfully bad before, without the slightest reason; but I've never heard him ask for a lawyer! If there's nothing really the matter, the doctor will tell him he's an old ass, and cheer him up; and that will be something gained. I'd better humour him and go; it won't take very long." So he ran off to the village on his errand of mercy.

The Toad, who had hopped lightly out of bed as soon as he *63* heard the key turned in the lock, watched him eagerly from the window till he disappeared down the carriage-drive. Then, laughing heartily, he dressed as quickly as possible in the smartest suit he could lay hands on at the moment, filled his pockets with cash which he took from a small drawer in the dressing-table, and next, knotting the sheets from his bed together and tying one end of the improvised rope round the central mullion of the handsome Tudor window which formed such a feature of his bedroom, he scrambled out, slid lightly to the ground, and, taking the opposite direction to the Rat, marched off light-heartedly, whistling a merry tune.

64   It was a gloomy luncheon for Rat when the Badger and the Mole at length returned, and he had to face them at table with his pitiful and unconvincing story. The Badger's caustic, not to say brutal, remarks may be imagined, and therefore passed over; but it was painful to the Rat that even the Mole, though he took his friend's side as far as possible, could not help saying, "You've been a bit of a duffer this time, Ratty! Toad, too, of all animals!"

65   "He did it awfully well," said the crestfallen Rat.

66   "He did *you* awfully well!" rejoined the Badger hotly. "However, talking won't mend matters. He's got clear away for the time, that's certain; and the worst of it is, he'll be so conceited with what he'll think is his cleverness that he may commit any folly. One comfort is, we're free now, and needn't waste any more of our precious time doing sentry-go. But we'd better continue to sleep at Toad Hall for a while longer. Toad may be brought back at any moment – on a stretcher, or between two policemen."

67   So spoke the Badger, not knowing what the future held in store, or how much water, and of how turbid a character, was to run under bridges before Toad should sit at ease again in his ancestral Hall.

68   Meanwhile, Toad, gay and irresponsible, was walking briskly along the high road, some miles from home. At first he had taken bypaths, and crossed many fields, and changed his course several times, in case of pursuit; but now, feeling by this time safe from recapture, and the sun smiling brightly on him, and all Nature joining in a chorus of approval to the song of self-praise that his own heart was singing to him, he almost danced along the road in his satisfaction and conceit.

69   "Smart piece of work that!" he remarked to himself, chuckling. "Brain against brute force – and brain came out on the top – as it's bound to do. Poor old Ratty! My! won't he catch it when the Badger gets back! A worthy fellow, Ratty, with many good qualities, but very little intelligence and absolutely no education. I must take him in hand some day, and see if I can make something of him."

70   Filled full of conceited thoughts such as these he strode along, his head in the air, till he reached a little town, where the sign of "The Red Lion," swinging across the road half-way down the main street, reminded him that he had not breakfasted that day, and that he was exceedingly hungry after his long walk. He marched into

the inn, ordered the best luncheon that could be provided at so short a notice, and sat down to eat it in the coffee-room.

He was about half-way through his meal when an only too *71* familiar sound, approaching down the street, made him start and fall a-trembling all over. The poop-poop! drew nearer and nearer, the car could be heard to turn into the inn-yard and come to a stop, and Toad had to hold on to the leg of the table to conceal his overmastering emotion. Presently the party entered the coffee-room, hungry, talkative, and gay, voluble on their experiences of the morning and the merits of the chariot that had brought them along so well. Toad listened eagerly, all ears, for a time; at last he could stand it no longer. He slipped out of the room quietly, paid his bill at the bar, and as soon as he got outside sauntered round quietly to the inn-yard. "There cannot be any harm," he said to himself," in my only just *looking* at it!"

The car stood in the middle of the yard, quite unattended, the *72* stable-helps and other hangers-on being all at their dinner. Toad walked slowly around it, inspecting, criticizing, musing deeply.

"I wonder," he said to himself presently, "I wonder if this sort of *73* car *starts* easily?"

Next moment, hardly knowing how it came about, he found he *74* had hold of the handle and was turning it. As the familiar sound broke forth, the old passion seized on Toad and completely mastered him, body and soul. As if in a dream he found himself, somehow, seated in the driver's seat; as if in a dream, he pulled the lever and swung the car round the yard and out through the archway; and, as if in a dream, all sense of right and wrong, all fear of obvious consequences, seemed temporarily suspended. He increased his pace, and as the car devoured the street and leapt forth on the high road through the open country, he was only conscious that he was Toad once more, Toad at his best and highest, Toad the terror, the traffic-queller, the Lord of the lone trail, before whom all must give way or be smitten into nothingness and everlasting night. He chanted as he flew, and the car responded with sonorous drone; the miles were eaten up under him as he sped he knew not whither, fulfilling his instincts, living his hour, reckless of what might come to him.

QUESTIONS

Language and Style

1. What is the reference in the phrase, " . . . how much water, and of how turbid a character, was to run under bridges before Toad should sit at ease again in his ancestral Hall"?

2. In the café scene what is unusual about the description of Toad as "all ears"? What does the phrase "all over egg" (paragraph 2) mean?

3. How would you characterize the tone of this narrative? What is the narrator's apparent attitude toward the action and the characters?

Organization

1. Beginning, "He was about half-way through his meal . . . ," the narrative's climax begins. Compare the "rate" at which things happen earlier with the rate at which they now begin to happen.

2. Why is the reader kept out of the smoking-room when Badger attempts to persuade Toad to give up his passion for automobiles? Why is it better that way?

Content

1. Explain how it is that in some ways this is a children's story yet in other ways the story is suitable for adults. Who is the reader here?

2. Strictly speaking, Toad is a car thief. Why, though, is the reader likely to be sympathetic? What is attractive about Toad?

3. Why are the café customers not identified? Why does the writer not describe the occupants of the automobile?

4. What is human about Toad? Can you cite examples of human behaviour? What are some human characteristics of Badger? How does Badger's first speech suggest some of them?

Vocabulary

wonted	habiliments
paroxysms	uncouth
prostrate	languid
mullion	Tudor
caustic	turbid
voluble	countenances
gauntleted	panoply
sonorous	

WRITING NARRATION

A writer of a narrative tells what happened and implies or says outright what it all meant or what it all was for. The simplest narrative follows exactly that pattern. It begins at the beginning and ends at the end, and only then does the writer offer an interpretation of the events. The writer presents the events and the later reflections in the order in which they occurred. This natural, or chronological, order is the basis for all other styles of narrative presentation and suggests that the writer needs to get the order of events straight before proceeding further.

One event is not necessarily as important as every other event. Some are central to an outcome and some are merely contributory to it. Moreover, events in a narrative can often be gathered into stages, i.e., events that naturally seem to group together. Some events, taken together, evidently represent the beginnings of a story. Other events represent a development of the story in a particular, significant direction which ultimately reaches an outcome. Therefore any story has at least three stages: a beginning, a middle, and an end. This arrangement is both natural and traditional and needs to be observed by the writer of a straightforward narrative. But even these fundamental stages in a narrative can be arranged in their turn into stages as a help to the reader (and also to help the writer understand and digest what has happened).

The extent to which the narrator-writer chooses to be involved in the story will depend on whether the point of the story is to reveal something about the narrator or to show how, objectively, events transpired. How important is the narrator in the story? Does the telling reflect on the narrator? Ought the narrator to be excused from any implication the story may have and therefore from playing any part in the story? What is the reader expected to get from the story?

The story of one's first public musical performance and how it ended in a demoralizing defeat may be related for a number of different reasons (to entertain, to instruct). Depending on the reasons, the writer will choose an appropriate point of view and emphasize some features of the event at the expense of others. There is only one set of events, objectively speaking, but a number of different stories to be told.

SUGGESTIONS FOR WRITING

Before actually sitting down and writing one of the stories that follow (or one of your own), do some work to recall in detail what happened. The details of a story make a difference to a reader because things are more real that way; experiences are more easily "lived" when the writer gives a reader something to smell or touch. The actual order of events needs to be recalled and noted, too, so that the writer has sufficient control over them to present events in an orderly, clear way. (Everyone has suffered the frustration of listening to stories that wandered without apparent reason in and out of sequence.) Finally, decide why the story ought to be told. Ask, "Why am I telling the reader this?" and be prepared to answer your own question.

1. My first day at work
2. An encounter with the law
3. A parable of your own or a retelling of an old parable
4. A case of mistaken identity
5. The blizzard
6. The party that got out of hand
7. My encounter with a famous person
8. Lost in the bush
9. A strange employment interview
10. The missing child.

CHAPTER THREE
COMPARISON AND CONTRAST

INTRODUCTION

Explanations which point out likenesses and differences employ the technique of comparison.[1] At the bottom of every comparison is the practice of taking two objects, placing them, as it were, side by side, and noticing various similarities and dissimilarities. Comparison is, therefore, a special way of noticing.

Comparisons sometimes serve the single purpose of informing the reader, but at other times the writer wants to take a second step and use comparison to assist in making a decision between or among alternatives. In this case the comparison, an explanatory technique, is put into the service of argument because this approach to alternatives is meant to bring down a decision on one side or another of an issue and to help generate and explain reasons for that decision. Careful buyers of automobiles are familiar with this use of comparison.

Informative comparisons can be used to put together two or more objects in order to reveal their similarities and justify treating them as similar in important and relevant respects. Comparing a complex device to a relatively simple one helps a reader understand how the complex device works or should be treated. Understanding how a pocket calculator works, for example, can be helpful in understanding the operation of a sophisticated computer. Knowing the kind of balancing required of a bicycle rider and the road hazards the rider is likely to encounter, one can better understand the techniques of safe motorcycle riding.

Comparisons between the familiar and the unfamiliar help to lead the reader into new territory by pointing out similarities between objects in the reader's experience and others which are new. If the writer is

---

[1]Explanations which emphasize likenesses are often called *comparisons*; explanations emphasizing differences are often called *contrasts*.

reasonably sure the reader is familiar with ice hockey, indicating its similarities to the less familiar game of indoor lacrosse can help explain what that game is like. In the same way a familiarity with the workings of a camera can be used to help explain how the human eye works, or a familiarity with clamps and pliers can give readers a reasonably clear idea of how vise grips work.

Making distinctions (a special application of comparison) between superficially similar objects or ideas, recording the similarities but emphasizing the differences, helps prevent confusion and keeps our thinking straight. Here is an example of a familiar (and important) distinction:

> Inductive inferences start with observations and arrive at general conclusions. For example, if the cycle goes over a bump and the engine misfires, and then goes over another bump, and the engine misfires, and then goes over another bump and the engine misfires, and then goes over a long smooth stretch of road and there is no misfiring, and then goes over a fourth bump and the engine misfires again, one can logically conclude that the misfiring is caused by the bumps. That is induction: reasoning from particular experiences to general truths.
>
> Deductive inferences do the reverse. They start with general knowledge and predict a specific observation. For example, if the reader knows the horn of the cycle is powered by electricity from the battery, then he can logically infer that if the battery is dead the horn will not work. That is deduction.[2]

One reason distinctions like this help keep our thinking straight is that in our ordinary dealings we use both forms of thinking together, combining and mixing them without too much attention to differences. But a failure to make a distinction can plague us if we fail to treat each sort of thinking differently and are unaware that we use both in the ordinary course of life without distinction. Distinctions need not be only matters of logic and straight thinking. Noticing the likenesses and differences, say, between two people can help us understand them both better.

Comparisons seem naturally to organize themselves into two patterns: blocks and points. Pirsig's comparison of inductive and deductive reasoning is organized in blocks, i.e., all of the relevant characterisitics of the inductive process are presented and then all of the relevant features of deductive reasoning are presented. Block style arrangements seem to work better for shorter comparisons – perhaps because readers are able to hold onto one side of the comparison for only the relatively short time that the second half of the comparison is brought to their

[2]Robert M. Pirsig, *Zen and the Art of Motorcycle Maintenance* (New York: William Morrow and Company, 1974), pp. 92-93.

attention and developed. For longer and more complex comparisons, point by point arrangements seem to work better. If, for example, there are three aspects of two alternatives under consideration, a point by point comparison of Canadian and American English might look like this in outline:

Point 1: Pronunciation
    a. Canadian
    b. American
Point 2: Spelling
    a. Canadian
    b. American
Point 3: Slang
    a. Canadian
    b. American

The point by point method of organizing a comparison seems to work especially well when the objective of the comparison is to evaluate alternatives, since a sort of rating system can be developed which assigns values to each of the points of the comparison.

Analogies are special forms of comparison which put together two categorically different objects, one of which is familiar to us, and assert a significant similarity between them. A successful analogy works if there is a point by point correspondence between the two sides of the comparison. A really effective analogy is illuminating and surprising because it reveals a hitherto unsuspected similarity and leads a reader to an unanticipated discovery.

Deduction and Induction
Irving Copi

This selection, excerpted from a standard text on logic, draws an important distinction between two ways in which we think of something as "true."

Arguments are traditionally divided into two different types,   *1* *deductive* and *inductive*. Although every argument involves the claim that its premises provide some grounds for the truth of its conclusion, only a *deductive* argument involves the claim that its

From. Introduction to Logic *(4th edition) by Irving M. Copi. Copyright © 1972 by Irving M. Copi. Reprinted by permission of the Macmillan Publishing Company.*

premisses provide *conclusive* grounds. In the case of deductive arguments the technical terms "valid" and "invalid" are used in place of "correct" and "incorrect." A deductive argument is *valid* when its premisses, if true, do provide conclusive grounds for its conclusion, that is, when premisses and conclusion are so related that it is absolutely impossible for the premisses to be true unless the conclusion is true also. Every deductive argument is either valid or invalid; the task of deductive logic is to clarify the nature of the relation between premisses and conclusion in valid arguments, and thus to allow us to discriminate valid from invalid arguments.

2   An inductive argument, on the other hand, involves the claim, not that its premisses give conclusive grounds for the truth of its conclusion, but only that they provide *some* grounds for it. Inductive arguments are neither "valid" nor "invalid" in the sense in which those terms are applied to deductive arguments. Inductive arguments may, of course, be evaluated as better or worse, according to the degree of likelihood or probability which their premisses confer upon their conclusions.

3   Deductive and inductive arguments are sometimes characterized and distinguished from one another in terms of the relative generality of their premisses and conclusions. William Whewell wrote in *The Philosophy of the Inductive Sciences* that " ... in Deduction we infer particular from general truths; while in Induction we infer general from particular. ... " Thus the classical example of deductive argument

> All men are mortal.
> Socrates is a man.
> Therefore Socrates is mortal.

indeed has a *particular* conclusion inferred (validly) from premisses the first of which is a general or universal proposition. By contrast, a fairly standard form of inductive argument is illustrated by

> Socrates is a man and is mortal.
> Plato is a man and is mortal.
> Aristotle is a man and is mortal.
> Therefore probably all men are mortal.

in which a general or universal conclusion is inferred from premisses all of which are particular propositions. There is some merit to this method of distinguishing between deduction and induction, but it is not universally applicable. For valid deductive arguments may have universal propositions for conclusions as well as for premisses, as in

> All men are animals.
> All animals are mortal.
> Therefore all men are mortal.

and they may have particular propositions for their premises as well as for their conclusions, as in

> If Socrates is a man then Socrates is mortal.
> Socrates is a man.
> Therefore Socrates is mortal.

And inductive arguments may have universal propositions for premisses as well as for conclusions, as in

> All cows are mammals and have lungs.
> All horses are mammals and have lungs.
> All men are mammals and have lungs.
> Therefore probably all mammals have lungs.

and they may have particular propositions for their conclusions, as in

> Hitler was a dictator and was ruthless.
> Stalin was a dictator and was ruthless.
> Castro is a dictator.
> Therefore Castro is probably ruthless.

So it is not altogether satisfactory to characterize deductive arguments as those which derive particular conclusions from general premises, or inductive arguments as those which infer general conclusions from particular premises.

A more adequate insight into the difference between deduction and induction is suggested by the following. If a deductive argument is valid, then its conclusion follows with equal necessity from its premises no matter what else may be the case. From the two premisses *All men are mortal* and *Socrates is a man* the conclusion *Socrates is mortal* follows necessarily, no matter what else may be true. The argument remains valid no matter what additional premises may be added to the original pair. Whether we add information that Socrates is ugly, or that angels are immortal, or that cows give milk, the conclusion follows strictly from the enlarged set of premises because it follows strictly from the two original premises initially given. And if the argument is valid, nothing can make it *more* valid: if the conclusion follows validly from a given set of premises it cannot follow from an enlarged set any *more* validly or strictly or logically.

But the case is different for inductive arguments. Consider the following inductive argument:

> Most corporation lawyers are Conservatives.
> Roderick Malcolm is a corporation lawyer.
> Therefore Roderick Malcolm is probably a Conservative.

This is a pretty good inductive argument: if its premises are true, its conclusion is more likely true than false. But adding new

4

5

premisses to the original pair can serve either to weaken or to strengthen the resulting argument. If we enlarge the premisses by adding that

> Roderick Malcolm is an officer of Americans for Democratic Action.

and

> No officers of Americans for Democratic Action are Conservatives.

the conclusion no longer even seems to follow, and in fact the opposite conclusion now follows deductively, that is, validly. On the other hand, if we enlarge the original set of premisses by adding the following additional premisses:

> Roderick Malcolm campaigned vigorously for Goldwater for president.

and

> Roderick Malcolm is a member of President Nixon's cabinet.

then the original conclusion follows with much greater likelihood from the enlarged set of premisses.

6   Accordingly, we characterize a deductive argument as one whose conclusion is claimed to follow from its premisses with absolute necessity, this necessity not being a matter of degree and not depending in any way upon whatever else may be the case. And in sharp contrast we characterize an inductive argument as one whose conclusion is claimed to follow from its premisses only with probability, this probability being a matter of degree and dependent upon what else may be the case.

QUESTIONS

Language and Style

1. How does the writer treat the claim of William Whewell? What single expression suggests or signals Copi's intentions?

2. Notice the writer's vocabulary. While the expressions are mostly common ones, the passage is somewhat difficult to read. Why?

3. Can you characterize the tone of the discussion? What sorts of assumptions does the writer seem to be making about the reader?

Organization

1. Copi's discussion naturally arranges itself into three parts. What is the apparent purpose of paragraphs 1 and 2? What is the relationship between the discussion in those paragraphs and that in paragraph 6?

2. Notice the connectors the writer uses, especially at the beginning of paragraphs. Can you identify some of these? How do they help the reader know what is going on?

3. Sketch a line and box chart of Copi's main ideas.

Content

1. What is the purpose of paragraphs 4 and 5?

Vocabulary

premisses	discriminate
infer	

The Next Depression
Michael Bliss

A prominent Canadian historian and commentator here draws together some features of the Great Depression of the 1930s and the "Great Recession" of the early 1980s.

Fifty years ago Canadians were entering what proved to be the worst winter of the Great Depression. Old people remember it, but two generations of Canadians know about the Depression only as a kind of nightmare their parents or grandparents endured – hard times, "ten lost years," the Dirty Thirties. Until this year we assumed that a major depression could not recur. Now we are not so sure.

There is no universally accepted definition of a depression, nor is it common to know at the time that one has started. For many months after the stock market collapse of 1929 the debate was whether or not it would trigger a recession. Mackenzie King's Liberal government went to the voters in a general election in 1930

From Saturday Night *(November 1982). Copyright ©Michael Bliss. Reprinted by permission of the author.*

claiming that the opposition's alarm about unemployment was exaggerated. It was only after the international financial panic of 1931, when a world credit system that had been teetering for two years actually started to fall, that people began using the term "depression."

3   By the winter of 1932-33 the Canadian economy was prostrate by any standard. The country's great primary industries, particularly agriculture, were devastated by a combination of low prices and disappearing markets. Wheat was selling near the lowest prices in recorded history. Canadian farmers had earned $665.6 million in 1928; in 1933 they made $142.3 million. Pre-tax corporate profits, which had totalled $433 million in 1928, were *minus* $98 million in 1932. The automobile industry was operating at sixteen-per-cent capacity. In a population of 10 million, 826,000 Canadians, or about twenty-five per cent of the work force, were unemployed. About 2 million Canadians were receiving some form of public assistance. Federal work camps were set up for single unemployed men, feared as a menace to public order as they restlessly crossed the country looking for work. There were breadlines and soup kitchens, and special collections for destitute prairie farm families. The Dominion of Newfoundland was finding that it literally could not afford democracy: bankrupt, it surrendered its self-government back to Britain and was ruled by an appointed commission.

4   The hard times had been developing gradually since late in 1929. Recovery began modestly in 1934, and seemed well in hand when a sharp downturn in 1937-38 wiped out much of the progress. By 1939, when war began, some indicators were back to the levels of the mid-1920s, but a million Canadians were still receiving relief. Through the whole decade of the 1930s there was never a year when unemployment averaged less than ten per cent of a work force that contained proportionately many more heads of families than it does now.

5   Economic historians do not agree on what causes a depression. Monetarists tend to believe the last one could have been avoided if U.S. interest rates had not been raised to try to curb stock speculation in 1928-29 or had been brought down much earlier in the 1930s (they were in the four- to six-per-cent range throughout the period, but with prices falling as much as ten per cent annually, real interest rates sometimes ran above fifteen per cent). Structuralists concentrate on the way the Western world was plagued by a surplus of productive capacity in the 1930s, a kind of hangover from the artificial stimulus that the Great War of 1914-18 had given to production in North and South America. This had been disguised for a decade while Europe recovered, but from the late 1920s through most of the 1930s world markets were glutted with goods, particularly primary products, particularly foodstuffs. World trade declined. Then governments made things worse by surren-

dering to nationalist/protectionist forces, and creating more barriers to trade with high protective tariffs and manipulated currencies. World trade declined further.

Canada was particularly hard hit by the Great Depression because it was a trading country which produced an enormous surplus of primary products – grains, wood products, minerals. (The United States was also badly hurt, but for slightly different reasons involving a much greater crisis in business confidence. Britain, by contrast, had lagged behind North America in the 1920s but suffered much less in the 1930s.) The beginning of the crisis here was symbolized not by events on Wall Street or Bay Street, but by the collapse of wheat prices on the Winnipeg Grain Exchange. The co-operative wheat pools in western Canada were that generation's equivalent of Dome Petroleum. By 1931 they were being carried by the banks with guarantees from Ottawa, and in 1935 the federal government effectively took over their primary function. Though bankruptcy rates soared, there were no spectacular corporate disasters in Canada. Scores of small American banks failed in the early 1930s, but Canada's huge chartered banks weathered the storm without serious difficulty. . . . Nor was the Depression severe enough to cause serious fluctuations in the human condition: birth, death, marriage, crime, and suicide rates were not drastically affected. Infant mortality continued to fall sharply through the Depression, thanks to pasteurization and the advance of modern medicine. A few farmers who could not afford gas hitched horses to their cars and named them "Bennett buggies" after the prime minister. The symbol was ambiguous, since only thirty years earlier the farmer who could afford his own horse and buggy was judged properous. And he didn't have movies or the radio, gifts of technology that only the most desperately poor did not enjoy in the 1930s.

6

The fear that history might burden us with another Great Depression arose from a realization this year that the international economy was perhaps as profoundly distorted in 1981 as it had been in 1929-30. As in the 1930s, it was possible to discover ominous monetary and/or structural problems underlying the severe recession. Phenomenally high real interest rates were forcing business into a liquidity crisis that raised fears of financial collapse. World trade was stagnating, and the falling prices of many commodities suggested that they might be in substantial oversupply. Many traditional manufacturing industries, including steel, textiles, and motor vehicles, seemed to be over-expanded globally, more so even than in the 1930s because of the explosion of productive capacity in the Pacific rim and other developing countries.

7

There was also the haunting possibility that OPEC and the energy crisis of the early 1970s may have had an effect similar to

8

that of the Great War in causing an artificial, unwarranted increase in capacity in a vastly important primary sector. If OPEC continues to crumble, if new finds of oil and gas continue to be made, and if energy prices continue to fall or stagnate, the consequences for energy-producing countries like Canada, or Mexico, or Nigeria, or a dozen other nations, will be harsh. Just as our western wheat economy of the first quarter of the century had been built on high prices, especially the artificially high prices of war, so our western energy economy has boomed through the 1970s because of OPEC. It could collapse just as thoroughly, just as seriously, and for just as long as the wheat economy collapsed at the end of the 1920s. It is already a fair bet that the investment boom on our energy frontiers will not, not because the country would be poorer than the rest of the world but because Canadians would refuse to share their dwindling wealth and jobs with foreigners.

9   A few years ago a despairing stockbroker in the United States dove to his death, incorrectly believing this was a classic way to go. There will be more attempts to imitate history if we have a serious depression in the 1980s. Breadlines and soup kitchens will command prime time on TV to dramatize the plight of the unemployed. Someone will harness a horse to an automobile and call it a "Trudeau-mobile." About 1985 the unemployed will trek to Ottawa, as some of them did in 1935. History mimics itself in media events.

10   It will be the depression that we watch on television, just as the 1930s generation, according to Will Rogers, went to the poorhouse in an automobile. The appropriate symbol this time would not be a Trudeau-mobile, but something like a "Trudeau-vision," a television set turned into a radio because of the expense of replacing its picture tube.

11   Canadians wanted their governments to do something to end the Great Depression, but didn't know what to recommend or who should do it. They tossed out the callous Liberals in 1930, electing the Tories because of R. B. Bennett's promise to end unemployment or perish in the attempt. Bennett, an arrogant millionaire capitalist, was actually compassionate and fairly creative, at least in extending aid to those in need, but he did not end unemployment. He perished, destroyed in the 1935 election by the Liberals running on the slogan "It's King or Chaos."

12   Canadians were not radicalized by the Depression. While a socialist national party, the Co-operative Commonwealth Federation (which became the NDP in the early 1960s), was born in 1932-33, it was not particularly successful and became firmly established only in the levelling climate of the Second World War. When Ontario voted for the maverick Liberal Mitch Hepburn in 1934, Alberta for William Aberhart and Social Credit in 1935, and Québec for Maurice Duplessis's Union Nationale in 1936, it was hard to tell whether the provinces were moving left, right, or anywhere at all.

The only common factor seemed the desire to get the old guy out and bring in a new guy who might have some new ideas.

All governments of the 1930s were trapped by the need to spend   *13*
on welfare and public works, and the equal need to retrench because revenues were shrinking drastically. Governments are not depression-proof: a number of Canadian municipalities could not pay their debts in the 1930s; nor, by the end of the decade, could the three prairie provinces, which had to be bailed out by Ottawa. The government of Canada itself had trouble borrowing money during the crisis of 1931 (foreign investment had dried up; the dollar had collapsed; would-be lenders had problems of their own), and had to run a National Service loan campaign as though the country were at war. It is not often realized that the greatest proportionate tax increases in Canadian history came during the 1930s; governments lost all margin of choice in fiscal policy, and had to raise more money to stop their unplanned, unwanted deficits from getting completely out of control.

The new Keynesian economics was still seminar talk among the   *14*
Cambridge *avant-garde* in the early 1930s. Anticipating Keynes, and drawing on old North American "soft money" movements, quite a few Canadians were already urging governments to reflate the economy through increased spending and/or reduced interest rates. Politicians resisted, worrying about the dollar and investor confidence, but gradually caved in. The Bank of Canada was created to manage the banking system, a substantial amount of provincial legislation was passed to lighten the burden of mortgages and other debts, and by 1938-39 the King government was attempting to stimulate the economy with a planned deficit. This was perhaps the most coherent economic strategy to emerge from the 1930s.

The first strategy tried, that of protecting Canadian industries by   *15*
raising the tariff, was a dismal failure. As the economy has deteriorated in the early 1980s Canadians have seen the resurgence of protectionism in attacks on imported footwear and Japanese cars. Most people who remember the Great Depression see that kind of Canada-firstism, if followed by all other nations, as the one sure path to disaster.

The trouble with the Keynesian strategy of stimulating the econ-   *16*
omy through increased spending is that since the 1930s Ottawa has fallen into the habit of stimulating even a booming economy with deficits. Keynes's injunction to balance the deficits with surpluses in good years was forgotten, and the result is that the government is probably less well situated to fight a downturn now than it was in the early 1930s, when it had been cutting taxes and running surpluses for several years.

Another factor in the current recession not present in the 1930s   *17*
is continuing inflation. As everyone knows by this time, it shouldn't happen. Prices should *de*flate in several recessions, with the prob-

lem being how to cause *re*flation. . . . On the other hand, a continuation of what we have come to call "stagflations," a situation inconceivable in the 1930s, leaves us the mind-boggling prospect of reflating a still inflating economy.

18   Even in the 1930s no amount of Keynesian stimulation in Canada would have restored prosperity so long as the country's exporting industries couldn't sell their products at profitable prices. For Canada there is no national monetarist or Keynesian solution to a truly serious international depression. There is even an outside chance that 1930s-style Keynesianism, applied to the 1980s, could make things worse. If governments surrender to tremendous pressures to increase their spending, and if they have to resort to printing money to keep spending, they could destroy lenders' confidence entirely and perhaps trigger uncontrollable inflation in the midst of on-going depression. That's why we should worry about the current financial situation of the government of Canada, and perhaps that of the major chartered banks. Thanks to deficits, inflation, and frenzied financing, we may already have less confidence in the long-term soundness of our institutions than our parents had fifty years ago.

19   There were occasional riots of the unemployed in the 1930s, and even historians sometimes write simplistically about the social order having been on the brink of collapse. A fairly common belief today is that we'd never tolerate another Great Depression: our expectations are too high; our belief in our ability to order our affairs through government action is too strong; and, perhaps, our social fabric is so weakened by the decline of non-material values that Canadians would turn violent, even revolutionary, before they would endure such sufferings again.

20   Don't be so sure of it. Given that people who made similar predictions during the 1930s were wrong, and given the deep conservatism of Canadians, it may be that history would repeat itself in the sense that people would find the resources of family, charity, self-discipline, and dumb endurance to get them through a time of retrenchment and comparative hardship. The other side of our high expectations has been an almost equally strong sense that we've been lucky to have had thirty-five years of the good life in North America. Large numbers of Canadians, even those too young to have Depression memories, sense that it's been too good to last forever. . . .

21   Because a European war broke out in 1939, and because the Depression did not resume after the war, it's fallaciously thought that the war was necessary to bring an end to the Great Depression. While it's broadly true that the war would not have occurred without the economic chaos of the 1930s, it was not a necessary event to cure the disorder. Like many illnesses, depressions cure themselves in time. The structural problems work themselves out

as supply and demand factors gradually return to equilibrium. This was well on its way to happening before the war. It's true that full employment was restored faster than would have happened otherwise, but it was done by redirecting manpower into the most hazardous possible occupation at much less than minimum wages. Also, because of war taxes and scarcities, standards of living did not rise nearly as fast as they would have in peacetime growth. Even then, some sectors of the Canadian economy, notably prairie agriculture, required another decade and more of retrenchment after 1945 before prospering again with the Diefenbaker wheat sales of the early 1960s.

Nobody knows how to measure the long-term effects of eco-   *22* nomic depressions, which are, after all, fairly short-term phenomena. We probably tend to exaggerate the Great Depression's impact. It probably had little effect on North American culture, for example, which was at once escapist *and* socially concerned both before and after the 1930s. There is also the problem of disentangling the effects of the war from those of the Depression. It may well be that the Second World War was more responsible than the Depression for our welfare state and for our infatuation with big government.

If a depression is comparable to a hangover, its over-all effect on   *23* both businessmen and ordinary people is clear enough. You become a little more conservative, take fewer risks, prefer security to adventure, or at least keep a stock of remedies at hand. The caution lasts until you or your children forget the pain, come to believe it can't happen again, or just don't care. The recession of the 1980s, even if it does not worsen, is bound to make many businessmen and consumers, perhaps even governments, proceed more soberly.

Hangovers also have cathartic aspects. The oldsters – who were   *24* young and healthy in the 1930s, and bound to have mellow memories now – tell us that the hard times were good for them. Perhaps we half-believe they'll be good for us. "Oh sure, it's tough, but it was good to make do without a lot of things ... teaches you what's important and what isn't in life ... wouldn't hurt the kids today to have to struggle a little ... think they could take it?"

Whether or not we're heading for a hangover from the spree of   *25* the past three decades, there's little doubt that our future is more uncertain than at any time since the war. Indeed, a large part of our current trouble with high interest rates and massive floating debts has been caused by the fact that we are no longer secure enough to invest in the long-term future. Why are there no more twenty-five-year mortgages? Can anyone imagine the government of Canada ever again being able to sell us perpetual bonds (bonds that never come due, the interest being paid year after year forever) as it did in 1936? The interest rate was three per cent.

There are not many parents in the 1980s who don't worry a lot   *26* about the economic future their children face. But the final and perhaps most important lesson of the 1930s is that of the unpredictability of the future. Hardly anyone guessed what was coming in 1929. A few very far-sighted investors got out of the market before the crash. Many of them bought back in again in 1930 or 1931 – fantastic bargains – and then lost everything as the market kept on going down. Through the last five years of the Depression, newspapers were full of optimistic articles about things looking up, prosperity being just around the corner, the corner having been turned. By the late 1930s the expert had been around too many corners and were sunk in gloom. Real prosperity would never return. When the Second World War ended, informed opinion feared that the Canadian economy would return to semi-permanent depression.

27   Of course the economy boomed for the next thirty years and more. Perhaps the fears we have on this fiftieth anniversary of the worst of the Great Depression will be just as unfounded. History may repeat itself in confounding us all again. Late in the summer interest rates started to come down, and stock prices soared as investors herded to get in on the ground floor of the recovery. Mexico was broke, and International Monetary Fund bigshots speculated about world financial collapse over shrimp and champagne in Toronto. But surely the good times of the 1980s were about to begin. The return to prosperity was probably just around the corner.

QUESTIONS

Language and Style

1. What is the writer's apparent attitude toward the Great Depression and, by implication, toward a new depression?

2. Consider Bliss's tone in paragraph 27, which closes the essay. How is the reader made to feel at the conclusion?

Organization

1. In this essay Bliss draws certain parallels between the Great Depression and the current economic situation. Design a table which summarizes these parallels.

2. Paragraphs 1-6 give a brief sketch of the Great Depression. Why is it useful to begin the essay with such an account?

Content

1. What does Bliss mean by suggesting that Canadian politics and society could become radicalized and what is his attitude toward the possibility? See paragraphs 19 and 20.

Vocabulary

prostrate	monetarist
structuralist	liquid
inflation	deflation
niggardly	demeaning
demoralizing	pasteurization
Keynesian	retrenchment
fallaciously	equilibrium
infatuation	cathartic

Pronunciation
Mark Orkin

In this discussion of Canadian pronunciation, Orkin attempts to distinguish Canadian usage from its two dominant influences – American and British English.

Most lay discussions about the pronunciation of Canadian English   *1*
resolve themselves into an argument about the respective vices and virtues of an English accent as opposed to an American accent, with something called a Canadian accent roughly in the middle – an ill-defined, pallid thing drifting helplessly about between the two, not knowing where to lay its head. The aimlessness of such contention results not only from a failure to define clearly what is being talked about, but also from an attempt to formulate value judgments about matters which are to a large degree social and emotive. It is further complicated by the fact that until recently there was almost no scientific investigation of spoken Canadian, so that even serious observers have had little more to go on than prejudice and the limited ambit of their own personal observation. Thanks in large measure to the work of the Canadian Linguistic Association in focussing attention upon how Canadian English is

From Speaking Canadian English *by Mark Orkin (1970). Reprinted by permission of Stoddart Publishing Co. Ltd.*

spoken, it is becoming possible to define at least the dominant tendencies of Canadian pronunciation in relation to the recognized standards of British and American English.

2   By convention among most experts, the standard of English speech is the language of the English upper classes. . . . For many years, scholars have rated all other varieties of English well below this dialect, which has been given many names. Professor H. C. K. Wyld labelled it *Received Standard*. . . . Dr. Daniel Jones called it *Standard Pronunciation*[; and] Professor Alan S. C. Ross of Birmingham University stirred up a small hornet's nest some years ago when he resorted to the single letter *U* to designate this upper-class usage, all else being non-U. For convenience here, we shall call this dialect *Standard English*. . . .

3   No one dialect in the United States occupies the same position of prestige as Standard English. This has been ascribed to the absence of a "public school" system of education on this continent and the "vaguer social boundaries and the easier circulation between classes" which impeded the development of a class dialect of this kind.[1] Some observers would divide American speech into three parts: the English of New England, Southern English, and Western or General American. Of these the most important is General American which is spoken by perhaps two thirds of the population of the United States residing in the Atlantic states (excluding New England and the South) and the Middle and Western states. General American, G. P. Krapp has pointed out, is the product of many influences, the most important being the mingling of Scots, Irish and both northern and southern English. The resultant speech is much closer to the speech of central and northern England than it is to that of southern England. This dialect, which is so prevalent throughout the entire continent that it might almost be called North American, has had an increasing influence upon the English spoken in every other country in the world. Something very close to it is used in Canada by a large proportion of the English-speaking population, in most places by a preponderance.

4   The differences between Standard English and General American are considerable, the principal phonetic distinctions being somewhat as follows:[2]

5   (1) The sound represented by *r* has been completely lost in Standard English in final position and before other consonants, as in *car*, *first* or *card*, with the result that words like *alms*, and *arms*, *father* and *farther* are identical in pronunciation. The only exception occurs when *r* is followed by a vowel sound in the same or following word. In General American *r* is sounded in all these

[1]Henry Alexander, *The Story of Our Language* (New York, Doubleday, 1969), pp. 174-75.
[2]The tabulation which follows is largely summarized from Henry Alexander, *The Story of Our Language* (New York, Doubleday, 1969) and Thorlief Larsen and Francis C. Walker, *Pronunciation: A Practical Guide to Spoken English in Canada and the United States* (Toronto, Oxford, 1930).

positions, although many Eastern and Southern speakers prefer the English pronunciation.

(2) In Standard English, the so-called "broad *a*" prevails in *bath,* *laugh, grass,* and so on, whereas in General American the "short *a*" as in *cat* or *man* is more common, except in *father, psalm, alms* and sometimes *calm....*   6

(3) The two pronunciations differ in the sound of vowels fol-   7 lowed by *r.* In Standard English, all long vowels are modified by the insertion of a vowel sound before the *r* somewhat like the vowel sound in *the,* particularly when the *r* is suppressed as in *fear,* but also when the *r* is sounded as in *fearing.* This vowel sound is never prominent before *r* in General American, except after long *i* and *ow.* American speakers usually give the vowel sound in *four* to the first syllable of words like *forest, foreign, forehead,* which Standard English pronounces with a shorter o....

(4) The tendency in England is to pronounce with long *i* such   8 words as *direction, civilization* and *organization,* and also most words which end in *-ile,* as *agile* and *docile.* In General American, the short *i* is almost universal in these positions.

(5) American English also tends to reduce the last syllable of   9 words ending in *-ile,* such as *fertile,* to rhyme with "Myrtle." The ending *-ine* as in *genuine* is usually pronounced in Standard English to rhyme with "pin" and by some American speakers to rhyme with "pine."

(6) The vowel sound in *not, block, rod* is in Standard English   10 close to the vowel sound in *nor;* in General American, it is usually shorter than the *a* in *father.*

(7) Speakers of Standard English are careful to sound a full *u,* or   11 in effect to insert a *y-sound* before the sound of *u* following *d, n, t,* and sometimes *l,* as in *duke, duty, new, student, studio,* and follow- ing *s* or *z,* as in *assume, presume.* In American speech generally, not excepting that of New England, the *oo* sound is heard in all these words.

(8) One of the most striking differences between the two lan-   12 guages is the slurring of vowels in Standard English, where General American enunciates with "full" vowels. Thus a Standard English speaker somehow manages to reduce *extraordinary* to the two syllables "kstrordnri," while a General American speaker enunci- ates five syllables, and sometimes even six. This accounts for the criticism by Americans that an English speaker "swallows" his words, while American speech sounds monotonous to the cultured English ear. Other words of this class are *medicine,* pronounced "medsn" and *interesting,* pronounced "intrsting" by English speak- ers but carefully given their full complement of syllables by most Americans.

(9) Miscellaneous differences in vowel sounds exist. Thus the   13 first syllables of words like *Berkeley, Berkshire, Derby* are pro- nounced *ar* in Standard English and *er* in General American. *Been*

is pronounced by Standard English speakers as "bean," and by most American speakers as "bin." *Shone* is always pronounced to rhyme with "on" in England and usually with "known" in America. *Leisure* rhymes with *pleasure* in Standard English, but with *seizure* in General American. *Either* and *neither* are "eye-ther" and "nye-ther" in England, and "ee-ther" and "nee-ther" in America. *Patent* is usually "pay-tent" to an Englishman and "pat-ent" to an American. *Tomato* is "to-mah-to" in Standard English, but almost always "tomayto" to a General American speaker. And *vase* usually rhymes with the first syllable of "Boswell" in England and sometimes with "case" in America.

14   (10) In Standard English, no distinction is made between initial *w* and *wh*. Such pairs as *which* and *witch*, *when* and *wen*, *whether* and *weather*, are pronounced alike. In General American, *wh* is usually more heavily aspirated than *w* at the beginning of a word.

15   (11) Minor variations in the consonants exist, as in *schedule* (Standard English "shed" – General American usually "sked"), *herbs* (Standard English sounds the *h*, while General American frequently suppresses it), *raspberry (pronounced z* in Standard English, sometimes *s* in General American), *lieutenant* (Standard English "left-" General American "loot-").

16   (12) The General American tendency is to place the accent on the first syllable in such nouns as *address, inquiry, magazine, recess, romance, spectator*, whereas Standard English usually accents the second or a later syllable.

17   It is clear that Canada does not possess anything like a standard pronunciation. The limited samplings which have been made reveal that considerable variation exists not merely from speaker to speaker, but often in the same speaker. This divided usage is probably typical of Canada as a whole; it is certainly general in Ontario, a province which some observers consider representative of English-speaking Canada. . . .

18   It is not difficult to understand why Canadian pronunciation should share many of the characteristics of both British English and American. To begin with, there are very good historical reasons for the similarities: English-speaking Canada was largely colonized from Great Britain and the United States, and Canadian pronunciation could be expected to show the influence of this mixed parentage. There are also social and educational reasons, although these are difficult to assess. Eric Partridge has recalled that few educated and cultured persons went to North America, South Africa, Australia and New Zealand until those countries were fairly well established. . . .

19   The influence of the Canadian school system in standardizing pronunciation remains to be investigated. Certainly very few Canadian school teachers are Standard English speakers, and no Canadian public school teaches either the broad *a*, or the suppressed *r* in terminal position and before consonants, which are two of the

characteristic features of Standard English. Nevertheless, an official preference for Standard English persists, to the extent that this can be reproduced by Canadian speakers. It may be seen in the conscious choice by the Canadian Broadcasting Corporation of British rather than American pronunciation for words admitting of two variants, such as *schedule* which CBC announcers sedulously pronounce "shed-yule" in preference to the American "sked-yule," although the latter is still the dominant Ontario pronunciation. Only one third of Ontarioans tested preferred "shedyule" to "sked-yule," and many informants admitted to being fairly recent converts to the British form. . . . In Montreal, three out of four English speakers tested chose "sked-yule."

Opposed to this pro-British attitude, however, which is commonest among the upper classes, there has always been at the popular level a strongly Anglophobe sentiment which left its mark on Canadian speech. In Ontario, this goes back to the days of the Family Compact, when . . . because of their association with the old colonial regime Englishmen were suspect and their distinctive accent taboo.[3] To this day, the possessor of a marked English accent often finds himself *persona non grata*, even in the heartland of Ontario. . . . In the result, authentic or even quasi-Standard English is usually heard only on the lips of transplanted Englishmen and some CBC people. . . .   *20*

Although reliable statistics on pronunciation are hard to come by, it is probable that more Canadians say "aris´tocrat," "āzha," "carbu-raytor," "dip-theria," "onvelope," "fi´nance," "re´search," "stă-tus," "strătum" and "ver-zhion" than use the forms recommended by the CBC. Avis, who has taken one of the few Canadian samplings, reported that although a small but appreciable minority of Ontarioans tested said "prŏ-cess" rather than "prō-cess," more than half of them pronounced *genuine* to rhyme with "wine" rather than "win," and preferred American "prŏgress" (noun) to British "prōgress." With words of the class *Asia, version* and so on, Canadian usage almost always coincides with General American. . . .   *21*

It is doubtful whether many of the Canadians who use the General American rather than the Standard English pronunciation of such words do so knowingly. Several factors may influence usage: one, the tendency which they share with most Americans to adopt a spelling pronunciation, resulting in such variants as "dyne-asty," "off-ten," "plebi-site," and *leisure* pronounced to rhyme with "seizure." There may also be a striving toward what is considered a more refined diction. Thus some speakers prefer "on-velope" to "en-velope" and "va-lay´" to "va´lett." One should also remember that many Canadians have no wish to sound like Americans and, indeed, if taxed with the offence would insist with some heat that they do not. When a particular pronunciation is clearly identifiable   *22*

[3]Eric Partridge, *British and American English Since 1900* (London, Andrew Dakers, 1951).

as American, the majority of Canadians tend to shun it without hesitation.... The fact that a great many Canadians pronounce their words in the same way as General American speakers does not temper the disfavour with which American speech habits are treated....

23   The pro-British bias of much of Canadian education, however, backed by the resolute stand of the CBC is still no match for the geographical proximity of the United States, the effect of which is felt everywhere across the land. The cultural and linguistic penetration of Canada by the United States is today almost complete, and the fact that the speech of these two countries is still distinguishable can chiefly be ascribed to the natural conservatism of languages generally, reinforced by Canada's own conservatism as a nation, which has made its citizens highly resistant to linguistic change.

QUESTIONS

Language and Style

1. What does the writer seem to make of the acceptance of much American pronunciation by Canadians? How, generally, would you characterize Orkin's style in this account? Is there anything of special interest in the language the writer uses?

Organization

1. How does the organization of the comparison reinforce the writer's claim that Canadian pronunciation fits somewhere between Standard English and General American?

2. Can you summarize the similarities and differences in a three-column list?

3. Into how many parts does Orkin's discussion seem to be organized?

Content

1. Why, at the beginning of the discussion, is the writer determined to avoid value judgments about accents? What is immediately suggested about the writer's attitude and point of view? How would you characterize that point of view?

2. To what extent can you relate your own experience and practice to Orkin's observations about Canadian pronunciation?

3. Does it seem, on the face of it, reasonable to take Ontario as "representative of English-speaking Canada"?

Vocabulary

ambit	prevalent
preponderance	phonetic
Family Compact	*persona non grata*
quasi-	plebiscite
linguistic	

Erotica vs. Pornography
Gloria Steinem

This essay by an American social and political critic, from her collection Outrageous Acts and Everyday Rebellions, *focusses its attention on the different ways sexuality is thought of and depicted in the media – one healthy, the other dangerous.*

Look at or imagine images of people making love; really making   *1*
love. Those images may be very diverse, but there is likely to be a
mutual pleasure and touch and warmth, an empathy for each
other's bodies and nerve endings, a shared sensuality and a spontaneous sense of two people who are there because they *want*
to be.

Now look at or imagine images of sex in which there is force,   *2*
violence, or symbols of unequal power. They may be very blatant:
whips and chains of bondage, even torture and murder presented
as sexually titillating, the clear evidence of wounds and bruises, or
an adult's power being used sexually over a child. They may be
more subtle: the use of class, race, authority, or just body poses to
convey conqueror and victim; unequal nudity, with one person's
body exposed and vulnerable while the other is armored with
clothes; or even a woman by herself, exposed for an unseen but
powerful viewer whom she clearly is trying to please. (It's interesting that, even when only the woman is seen, we often know
whether she is there for her own pleasure or being displayed for
someone else's.) But blatant or subtle, there is no equal power or
mutuality. In fact, much of the tension and drama comes from the
clear idea that one person is dominating another.

These two sorts of images are as different as love is from rape, as   *3*
dignity is from humiliation, as partnership is from slavery, as
pleasure is from pain. Yet they are confused and lumped together
as "pornography" or "obscenity," "erotica" or "explicit sex," be-

cause sex and violence are so dangerously intertwined and confused. After all, it takes violence or the threat of it to maintain the unearned dominance of any group of human beings over another. Moreover, the threat must be the most persuasive wherever men and women come together intimately and are most in danger of recognizing each other's humanity.

4   The confusion of sex with violence is most obvious in any form of sadomasochism. The gender-based barrier to empathy has become so great that a torturer or even murderer may actually believe pain or loss of life to be the natural fate of the victim; and the victim may have been so deprived of self-respect or of empathetic human contact that she expects pain or loss of freedom as the price of any intimacy or attention at all. It's unlikely that even a masochist expects death. Nonetheless, "snuff" movies and much current pornographic literature insist that a slow death from sexual torture is the final orgasm and ultimate pleasure. It's a form of "suicide" reserved for women. Though men in fact are far more likely to kill themselves, male suicide is almost never presented as sexually pleasurable. But sex is also confused with violence and aggression in all forms of popular culture, and in respectable theories of psychology and sexual behavior as well. The idea that aggression is a "normal" part of male sexuality, and that passivity or even the need for male aggression is a "normal" part of female sexuality, are part of the male-dominant culture we live in, the books we learn from, and the air we breathe.

5   Even the words we are given to express our feelings are suffused with the same assumptions. Sexual phrases are the most common synonyms for conquering and humiliation . . . ; the sexually aggressive woman is a *slut* or a *nymphomaniac*, but the sexually aggressive man is just *normal*; and real or scientific descriptions of sex may perpetuate the same roles, for instance, a woman is always *penetrated* by a man though she might also be said to have *enveloped* him.

6   Obviously, untangling sex from aggression and violence or the threat of it is going to take a very long time. And the process is going to be greatly resisted as a challenge to the very heart of male dominance and male centrality.

7   But we do have the common sense of our bodies to guide us. Pain is a warning of damage and danger. If that sensation is not mixed with all the intimacy we know as children, we are unlikely to confuse pain with pleasure and love. As we discover our free will and strength, we are also more likely to discover our own initiative and pleasure in sex. As men no longer can dominate and have to find an identity that doesn't depend on superiority, they also discover that cooperation is more interesting than submission, that empathy with their sex partner increases their own pleasure,

and that anxieties about their own ability to "perform" tend to disappear along with stereotyped ideas about masculinity.

But women will be the main fighters of this new sexual revolu-   *8* tion. It is our freedom, our safety, our lives, and our pleasure that are mostly at stake.

We began by trying to separate sex and violence in those areas   *9* where the physical danger was and is the most immediate: challenging rape as the one crime that was considered biologically irresistible for the criminal and perhaps invited by the victim; refusing to allow male-female beatings to be classified as "domestic violence" and ignored by the law; exposing forced prostitution and sexual slavery as national and international crimes. With the exception of wife beating, those challenges were made somewhat easier by men who wanted to punish other men for taking their female property. Women still rarely have the power to protect each other.

Such instances of real antiwoman warfare led us directly to the   *10* propaganda that teaches and legitimizes them – pornography. Just as we had begun to separate rape from sex, we realized that we must find some way of separating pornographic depictions of sex as an antiwoman weapon from those images of freely chosen, mutual sexuality.

Fortunately, there is truth in the origin of words. *Pornography*   *11* comes from the Greek root *porné* (harlot, prostitute, or female captive) and *graphos* (writing about or description of). Thus, it means a description of either the purchase of sex, which implies an imbalance of power in itself, or sexual slavery.

This definition includes, and should include, all such degrada-   *12* tion, regardless of whether it is females who are the slaves and males who are the captors or vice versa. There is certainly homosexual pornography, for instance, with a man in the "feminine" role of victim. There is also role-reversal pornography, with a woman whipping or punishing a man, though it's significant that this genre is created by men for their own pleasure, not by or for women, and allows men to *pretend* to be victims – but without real danger. There could also be lesbian pornography, with a woman assuming the "masculine" role of victimizing another woman. That women rarely choose this role of victimizer is due to no biological superiority, but a culture that doesn't addict women to violence. But whatever the gender of the participants, all pornography is an imitation of the male-female, conqueror-victim paradigm, and almost all of it actually portrays or implies enslaved woman and master.

Even the 1970 Presidential Commission on Obscenity and Por-   *13* nography, whose report is often accused of suppressing or ignoring evidence of the causal link between pornography and violence against women, defined the subject of their study as pictorial or verbal descriptions of sexual behavior characterized by "the degrading and demeaning portrayal of the role and status of the human female."

14   In short, pornography is not about sex. It's about an imbalance of male-female power that allows and even requires sex to be used as a form of aggression.

15   *Erotica* may be the word that can differentiate sex from violence and rescue sexual pleasure. It comes from the Greek root *eros* (sexual desire or passionate love, named for Eros, the son of Aphrodite), and so contains the idea of love, positive choice, and the yearning for a particular person. Unlike pornography's reference to a harlot or prostitute, *erotica* leaves entirely open the question of gender. (In fact, we may owe its sense of shared power to the Greek idea that a man's love for another man was more worthy than love for a woman, but at least that bias isn't present in the word.) Though both erotica and pornography refer to verbal or pictorial representations of sexual behavior, they are as different as a room with doors open and one with doors locked. The first might be a home, but the second could only be a prison.

16   The problem is that there is so little erotica. Women have rarely been free enough to pursue erotic pleasure in our own lives, much less to create it in the worlds of film, magazines, art, books, television, and popular culture – all the areas of communication we rarely control. Very few male authors and filmmakers have been able to escape society's message of what a man should do, much less to imagine their way into the identity of a woman. Some women and men are trying to portray equal and erotic sex, but it is still not a part of popular culture.

17   And the problem is there is so much pornography. This underground stream of antiwoman propaganda that exists in all male-dominant societies has now become a flood in our streets and theaters and even our homes. Perhaps that's better in the long run. Women can no longer pretend pornography does not exist. We must either face our own humilation and torture every day on magazine covers and television screens or fight back. There is hardly a newsstand without women's bodies in chains and bondage, in full labial display for the conquering male viewer, bruised or on our knees, screaming in real or pretended pain, pretending to enjoy what we don't enjoy. The same images are in mainstream movie theaters and respectable hotel rooms via closed-circuit TV for the traveling businessman. They are brought into our own homes not only in magazines, but in the new form of video cassettes. Even video games offer such features as a smiling, rope-bound woman and a male figure with an erection, the game's

object being to rape the woman as many times as possible. (Like much of pornography, that game is fascist on racial grounds as well as sexual ones. The smiling woman is an Indian maiden, the rapist is General Custer, and the game is called "Custer's Revenge.") Though "snuff" movies in which real women were eviscerated and finally killed have been driven underground (in part because the graves of many murdered women were discovered around the shack of just one filmmaker in California), movies that simulate the torture murders of women are still going strong. (*Snuff* is the porn term for killing a woman for sexual pleasure. There is not even the seriousness of a word like *murder*.) So are the "kiddie porn" or "chicken porn" movies and magazines that show adult men undressing, fondling, and sexually using children; often with the titillating theme that "fathers" are raping "daughters." Some "chicken porn" magazines offer explicit tips on how to use a child sexually without leaving physical evidence of rape, the premise being that children's testimony is even less likely to be believed than that of adult women.

Add this pornography industry up, from magazines like *Playboy*   18 and *Hustler*, to movies like *Love Gestapo Style*, *Deep Throat*, or *Angels in Pain*, and the total sales come to a staggering eight billion dollars a year – more than all the sales of the conventional film and record industry combined. And that doesn't count the fact that many "conventional" film and music images are also pornographic, from gynocidal record jackets like the famous *I'm "Black and Blue" from the Rolling Stones – and I Love It!* (which showed a seminude black woman bound to a chair) to the hundreds of teenage sex-and-horror movies in which young women die sadistic deaths and rape is presented not as a crime but as sexual excitement. Nor do those industries include the sales of the supposedly "literary" forms of pornography, from *The Story of O* to the works of the Marquis de Sade.

If Nazi propaganda that justified the torture and killing of Jews   19 were the theme of half of our most popular movies and magazines, would we not be outraged? If Ku Klux Klan propaganda that preached and even glamorized the enslavement of blacks were the subject of much-praised "classic" novels, would we not protest? We know that such racist propaganda precedes and justifies the racist acts of pogroms and lynchings. We know that watching a violent film causes test subjects to both condone more violence afterward and to be willing to perpetuate it themselves. Why is the propaganda of sexual aggression against women of all races the one form in which the "conventional wisdom" sees no danger? Why is pornography the only media violence that is supposed to be a "safety valve" to satisfy men's "natural" aggressiveness some-where short of acting it out?

QUESTIONS

Language and Style

1. How would you characterize Steinem's choice of language? What connections might there be between the language and the sensitiveness of the subject?

2. Is it accurate to describe Steinem's tone as "argumentative"? Why should it be appropriate in the circumstances?

Organization

1. Given the title, the reader might expect as much discussion of erotica as of pornography. Is that in fact the case? Why should Steinem concentrate the discussion on one rather than on the other? Having read the essay, is the reader likely to know what erotica is?

Content

1. What is the fundamental confusion that Steinem identifies? How does Steinem suggest we find our way out of the confusion?

2. If you were to write a law which forbade "pornography," how, given the discussion here, would you identify what you wanted to forbid?

3. What is the basis for Steinem's distinction between pornography and erotica?

4. Explain why Steinem believes her distinction is an important one.

Vocabulary

empathy	sensuality
blatant	titillating
sado-masochism	suffused
paradigm	labial
gynocidal	pogroms
eviscerated	

The Death of the Moth
Virginia Woolf

Virginia Woolf's sensitive essays, which include "The Death of the Moth" and "A Room of One's Own," express her not-so-ordinary experience of ordinary life.

Moths that fly by day are not properly to be called moths; they do   *1*
not excite that pleasant sense of dark autumn nights and ivy-blossom which the commonest yellow-underwing asleep in the shadow of the curtain never fails to rouse in us. They are hybrid creatures, neither gay like butterflies nor sombre like their own species. Nevertheless the present specimen, with his narrow hay-coloured wings, fringed with a tassel of the same colour, seemed to be content with life. It was a pleasant morning, mid-September, mild, benignant, yet with a keener breath than that of the summer months. The plough was already scoring the field opposite the window, and where the share had been, the earth was pressed flat and gleamed with moisture. Such vigour came rolling in from the fields and the down beyond that it was difficult to keep the eyes strictly turned upon the book. The rooks too were keeping one of their annual festivities; soaring round the tree tops until it looked as if a vast net with thousands of black knots in it had been cast up into the air; which, after a few moments sank slowly down upon the trees until every twig seemed to have a knot at the end of it. Then, suddenly, the net would be thrown into the air again in a wider circle this time, with the utmost clamour and vociferation, as though to be thrown into the air and settle slowly down upon the tree tops were a tremendously exciting experience.

The same energy which inspired the rooks, the ploughmen, the   *2*
horses, and even, it seemed, the lean bare-backed downs, sent the moth fluttering from side to side of his square of the windowpane. One could not help watching him. One, was, indeed, conscious of a queer feeling of pity for him. The possibilities of pleasure seemed that morning so enormous and so various that to have only a moth's part in life, and a day moth's at that, appeared a hard fate, and his zest in enjoying his meagre opportunities to the full, pathetic. He flew vigorously to one corner of his compartment, and, after waiting there a second, flew across to the other. What remained for him but to fly to a third corner and then to a fourth?

That was all he could do, in spite of the size of the downs, the width of the sky, the far-off smoke of houses, and the romantic voice, now and then, of a steamer out at sea. What he could do he did. Watching him, it seemed as if a fibre, very thin but pure, of the enormous energy of the world had been thrust into his frail and diminutive body. As often as he crossed the pane, I could fancy that a thread of vital light became visible. He was little or nothing but life.

3   Yet, because he was so small, and so simple a form of the energy that was rolling in at the open window and driving its way through so many narrow and intricate corridors in my own brain and in those of other human beings, there was something marvellous as well as pathetic about him. It was as if someone had taken a tiny bead of pure life and decking it as lightly as possible with down and feathers, had set it dancing and zigzagging to show us the true nature of life. Thus displayed one could not get over the strangeness of it. One is apt to forget all about life, seeing it humped and bossed and garnished and cumbered so that it has to move with the greatest circumspection and dignity. Again, the thought of all that life might have been had he been born in any other shape caused one to view his simple activities with a kind of pity.

4   After a time, tired by his dancing apparently, he settled on the window ledge in the sun, and, the queer spectacle being at an end, I forgot about him. Then, looking up, my eye was caught by him. He was trying to resume his dancing, but seemed either so stiff or so awkward that he could only flutter to the bottom of the window-pane; and when he tried to fly across it he failed. Being intent on other matters I watched these futile attempts for a time without thinking, unconsciously waiting for him to resume his flight, as one waits for a machine, that has stopped momentarily, to start again without considering the reason of its failure. After perhaps a seventh attempt he slipped from the wooden ledge and fell, fluttering his wings, on to his back on the window sill. The helplessness of his attitude roused me. It flashed upon me that he was in difficulties; he could no longer raise himself; his legs struggled vainly. But, as I stretched out a pencil, meaning to help him to right himself, it came over me that the failure and awkwardness were the approach of death. I laid the pencil down again.

5   The legs agitated themselves once more. I looked as if for the enemy against which he struggled. I looked out of doors. What had happened there? Presumably it was midday, and work in the fields had stopped. Stillness and quiet had replaced the previous animation. The birds had taken themselves off to feed in the brooks. The horses stood still. Yet the power was there all the same, massed outside, indifferent, impersonal, not attending to anything in particular. Somehow it was opposed to the little hay-coloured moth. It

was useless to try to do anything. One could only watch the extraordinary efforts made by those tiny legs against an oncoming doom which could, had it chosen, have submerged an entire city, not merely a city, but masses of human beings; nothing, I knew had any chance against death. Nevertheless after a pause of exhaustion the legs fluttered again. It was superb this last protest, and so frantic that he succeeded at last in righting himself. One's sympathies, of course, were all on the side of life. Also, when there was nobody to care or to know, this gigantic effort on the part of an insignificant little moth, against a power of such magnitude, to retain what no one else valued or desired to keep, moved one strangely. Again, somehow, one saw life, a pure bead. I lifted the pencil again, useless though I knew it to be. But even as I did so, the unmistakable tokens of death showed themselves. The body relaxed, and instantly grew stiff. The struggle was over. The insignificant little creature now knew death. As I looked at the dead moth, this minute wayside triumph of so great a force over so mean an antagonist filled me with wonder. Just as life had been strange a few minutes before, so death was now as strange. The moth having righted himself now lay most decently and uncomplainingly composed. Oh yes, he seemed to say, death is stronger than I am.

QUESTIONS

Language and Style

1. How does the extraordinary care that is taken with the description help the reader "see" and "feel" into the writer's sense of things?

2. How would you characterize the tone of the essay? Notice the opening statement. How is the tone maintained throughout the essay? What expressions and patterns of expression contribute?

3. Why should the moth be described as "dancing" (paragraph 4)?

Organization

1. What, literally, is the writer's point of view?

2. Why should the scene outside the window at first be so carefully described? What aspects of that scene are emphasized?

3. Compare the second scene outside the window with the first. Why are things "massed," "indifferent"?

4. Explain how the miniature scene inside the window works as a little summary, an epitome, of the larger one outside.

Content

1. How is the moth connected to the new-ploughed fields, the rooks, the horses, a ship steaming at sea, the speaker?

2. In what sense is this essay less about life and death and more about a realization or a perception?

Vocabulary

yellow-underwing	benignant
share	rooks
vociferation	downs
cumbered	bossed

WRITING COMPARISONS

Writing comparisons of any sort requires some special juggling because two, three, or more subjects need attention and because, unlike in some juggling, both the writer and the reader need to follow and keep track of things. The writer's problem is therefore in part a problem of organization and control.

A successful comparison makes use of an outline to keep the writer's ideas in order and to keep the order of presentation predictable for the reader. When a writer sets out to compare, for example, the benefits of owning a small automobile to the benefits of owning a large automobile, the basis of the comparison must be clear to the reader. That will happen only if the writer first has made several decisions about the comparison. On what grounds should small and large automobiles be compared? Safety? Operating and maintenance costs? Do aesthetic considerations count? Purchase price? What is a logical order in which to present these matters? Do some naturally go together? Is there an obvious order of importance or precedence? Is some information public knowledge which only needs to be pointed out to the reader? Is there new information of which a reader may be unaware? The writer also needs to select appropriate, comparable aspects of the alternatives under discussion and to be certain that they are of central importance.

How complex the comparison is likely to be will determine whether to organize it in block or point fashion since short, relatively simple comparisons seem to work best in blocks and longer ones point by point.

The writer should advise the reader, probably at the beginning, what the purpose of the comparison is – whether it is evaluative (and will suggest that one alternative is better than another), or simply informative. If the comparison reaches an outcome and makes a recommendation, then the comparison can conclude with the recommendation. An informative comparison, if it is at all lengthy, can be completed by a summary of the main points of the discussion.

The comparison writer will need to lead the reader from one part of the comparison to another, especially if the comparison is organized point by point. Therefore, the writer will need to pay attention to the transitions between parts of the discussion to avoid simply hanging the discussion on the section headings of the outline. Otherwise the reader will be forced to make the connections without the writer's guidance.

SUGGESTIONS FOR WRITING

Some of the topics suggested here may be treated either as informative or as evaluative comparisons. Before you set out to actually write the comparison, work out an outline of your approach so that a guide is available before you start. If you write an evaluative comparison, take care to be fair, to weigh all the relevant evidence, and the chances are that the reader who is following carefully will come to your conclusion at about the same time you do.

1. Your hometown newspaper or another newspaper, and *The Globe and Mail*
2. The personalities of two friends, relatives, or teachers
3. Country neighbours and city neighbours
4. AM and FM radio programming
5. Two styles of dress or fashion
6. Two schools with which you are familiar
7. Weather, sports, or news broadcasters
8. Fly fishing and bait fishing
9. Two neighbourhoods or two towns
10. Two jobs you have held or two employers for whom you have worked.

CHAPTER FOUR
CLASSIFICATION

INTRODUCTION

One of the elementary means of sorting experiences and keeping things straight is dividing and classifying. Why sorting things out is important and how people manage to find some order in the undifferentiated scheme of things are processes exemplified by an ordinary dictionary, one of the purposes of which is simply to collect the words in the language. But if the dictionary merely collected words and did not arrange those words in some order, then even though the words were collected, it would require more luck than skill to find a particular word, determine its meaning, or check its spelling. Sorting dictionary entries alphabetically eliminates the hodge-podge and makes the collection usable. For the same reasons, libraries organize their holdings so that in a library with 40,000 volumes one can find just the right book. Without a basis for sorting all those books, the library could boast an immense pile of unsorted volumes, but the librarian could only say to someone who inquired, "There you are. Help yourself." What is true of dictionaries and libraries is true of almost any collection: telephone directories, museums, tax rolls, cattle breeds, and the contents of supermarkets. Order implies manageable access.

Sorting things out seems deep-rooted. Very young children organize the objects of their play into categorical groups. Some children with an especially well developed sense of order even insist on separating the food items on their plate and are apt to lose some of their appetite if a kernel of corn strays into the mashed potatoes.

Arranging dictionaries, grouping playthings, or organizing museum collections are all examples of an analytical approach to experience which reflects an interest in treating experience in terms of its apparent components. Probably the simplest analysis is performed by dividing an object into parts. Consider a ball-point pen. The less expensive ones have four main parts: an ink tube, a barrel, a ball-point, and a cap. The ink tube is filled with semi-liquid ink and fits over the ball-point; the ball-point consists of a fitting into which is set a small roller-bearing which, as it is made to revolve in the fitting, carries ink from the tube onto a suitable surface; the barrel is a rigid plastic cylinder which fits over the ink tube and ball-point and gives the writer something solid to grip; finally, there is a small cap which fits over the open end of the barrel to seal out dirt and debris.

What is interesting and important about this analysis is its descriptive power. It can be used to describe apparently simple objects (flower blossoms, office staplers, eyeglasses), but the same approach can serve to describe much more complex objects since major components can be separated into first-order constituent parts and eventually into basic parts. An analytic description based on separating components works just as neatly for a heavy water nuclear reactor as for a filter cigarette. (The reactor description will just be longer and require special information about isotopes, pressure vessels, cooling ponds, and so on.) Notice a second aspect of the power of this analysis. A "simple" ball-point pen is not as simple as it seems. What are the components of the ink? Of the various metal and plastic parts? What are *their* components? A single hair plucked from one's head is, potentially, so complex an object (what are the components, say, of the hair's protein?) that a description might rival an engineering manual itemizing the parts of a nuclear reactor. An analytic description has a wide range of applicability and can go very deep into the make-up of things.

Besides simply dividing the individual objects of experience, that is, separating things into their various components, we very frequently want to organize related objects by types. We classify plants and animals, newspaper advertisements (the "classifieds"), soils, geological formations, and aspects of human behaviour because of the need to bring a certain order to experience. Remember dictionaries and libraries, and consider how it is that shoppers fill their carts in supermarkets.

At the bottom of each of the natural sciences (botany, zoology, and geology) and underlying the social sciences (sociology, anthropology, and psychology) are a number of classification systems which permit management of large batches of data in a systematic, orderly fashion. The natural sciences' earliest findings, for example, were the work of enthusiastic amateur naturalists who collected specimens of every sort, combed ancient herbals for information, and accompanied imperial expeditions to gather samples of exotic flora which they carefully preserved, packed, and sent home to their scientific societies. (Charles Darwin's responsibilities aboard the ship *Beagle* included just such collecting and preserving although, of course, he eventually carried matters far beyond simple data collection.) Some early criminologists studied the physiognomies (the facial characteristics) of convicted criminals in order to collect information about people's appearance so that they could identify something they called the "criminal type."

As scientific data mounted through the efforts of enthusiasts and increasingly skilled observers, it was more and more evident that some system of organizing must be found. Pioneer scientists began to identify principles which gave order to their burgeoning findings. The usual way of classifying the world's fishes, for example, follows structure ("morphology"), while geological formations tend to be classified on the basis of their origin and place in the development of the earth's crust (volcanic, sedimentary, etc.). The library mentioned earlier puts the situation exactly, for at one time our knowledge of the natural world and the humans in it amounted to a very small, unsorted collection of information. But the work of scientists who investigated the world around them by more and more powerful and sophisticated means would only have created an enormous hodge-podge of data had systems for filing and retrieving not been developed.

There are all sorts of classification systems. These range from the very formal, which support a well-organized science (as exemplified by land-use capability classes), to the very formal, without great claims to scientific usefulness, which aim at explaining, for example, the behaviour of employees in certain kinds of organizations (as in Michael Maccoby's "Winning and Losing at Work"). All of these systems of classification are readily and simply sketched out as line and box charts. The important thing is to stick with a single, relevant principle of organization – eating habits (herbivores and carnivores), structure (backbones and no backbones), or income (dollar amounts) – and to ascertain that the system of classification is inclusive (that is that no important cases are omitted by the system).

Systems of classification have not always been put to benign use. Some of the saddest and least civilized chapters in the human record open with appeals to ethnic, racial, or other social stereotypes which angry and unhappy people have used for centuries to depersonalize those whom they perceive as enemies and to justify the inhuman treatment of those unfortunate enough to have fallen into their hands. Stereotypes are hidden in racial slurs, in ethnic jokes, in the propaganda of hate literature, and in folk beliefs about religious and ethnic practices. Stereotypes always act to obscure the individuality of people and to convey one or another falsehood about them. Those who invent derogatory labels and who deliver prejudicial judgments of groups follow a practice which is as ancient as it is dishonourable.

Distance in Man
Edward T. Hall

Hall's ideas help us understand such things as the significance of the physical space we put between ourselves and others, the nature of certain cultural differences, and the effects of crowding people into cities. His observations on "The Dynamism of Space" are applied in a later selection, "The Ladies Converse."

THE DYNAMISM OF SPACE

... Man's sense of space and distance is not static, ... [and] it has   *1*
very little to do with the single-viewpoint linear perspective developed by the Renaissance artists and still taught in most schools of art and architecture. Instead, man senses distance as other animals do. His perception of space is dynamic because it is related to action – what can be done in a given space – rather than what is seen by passive viewing.

The general failure to grasp the significance of the many ele-   *2*
ments that contribute to man's sense of space may be due to two mistaken notions: (1) that for every effect there is a single and identifiable cause; and (2) that man's boundary begins and ends with his skin. If we can rid ourselves of the need for a single explanation, and if we can think of man as surrounded by a series of expanding and contracting fields which provide information of many kinds, we shall begin to see him in an entirely different light. We can then begin to learn about human behavior, including personality types. Not only are there introverts and extroverts, authoritarian and egalitarian, Apollonian and Dionysian types and all the other shades and grades of personality, but each one of us has a number of learned *situational* personalities. The simplest form of the situational personality is that associated with responses to intimate, personal, social, and public transactions. Some individuals never develop the public phase of their personalities and, therefore, cannot fill public spaces; they make very poor speakers or moderators. As many psychiatrists know, other people have trouble with the intimate and personal zones and cannot endure closeness to others.

Concepts such as these are not always easy to grasp, because   *3*
most of the distance-sensing process occurs outside awareness. We sense other people as close or distant, but we cannot always put our finger on what it is that enables us to characterize them as

such. So many different things are happening at once it is difficult to sort out the sources of information on which we base our reactions. Is it tone of voice or stance or distance? This sorting process can be accomplished only by careful observation over a long period of time in a wide variety of situations, making a note of each small shift in information received. For example, the presence or absence of the sensation of warmth from the body of another person marks the line between intimate and non-intimate space. The smell of freshly washed hair and the blurring of another person's features seen close up combine with the sensation of warmth to create intimacy. By using one's self as a control and recording changing patterns of sensory input it is possible to identify structure points in the distance-sensing system. In effect, one identifies, one by one, the isolates making up the sets that constitute the intimate, personal, social, and public zones.

4   The following descriptions of the four distance zones have been compiled from observations and interviews with non-contact, middle-class, healthy adults, mainly natives of the northeastern seaboard of the United States. A high percentage of the subjects were men and women from business and the professions; many could be classified as intellectuals. The interviews were effectively neutral; that is, the subjects were not noticeably excited, depressed, or angry. There were no unusual environmental factors, such as extremes of temperature or noise. These descriptions represent only a first approximation. They will doubtless seem crude when more is known about proxemic observation and how people distinguish one distance from another. It should be emphasized that these generalizations are not representative of human behavior in general — or even of American behavior in general — but only of the group included in the sample. Negroes and Spanish Americans as well as persons who come from southern European cultures have very different proxemic patterns.

5   Each of the four distance zones described below has a near and a far phase, which will be discussed after short introductory remarks. It should be noted that the measured distances vary somewhat with differences in personality and environmental factors. For example, a high noise level or low illumination will ordinarily bring people closer together.

INTIMATE DISTANCE

6   At intimate distance, the presence of the other person is unmistakable and may at times be overwhelming because of the greatly stepped-up sensory inputs. Sight (often distorted), olfaction, heat from the other person's body, sound, smell, and feel of the breath all combine to signal unmistakable involvement with another body.

Intimate Distance – Close Phase

This is the distance of love-making and wrestling, comforting and   7
protecting. Physical contact or the high possibility of physical
involvement is uppermost in the awareness of both persons. The
use of their distance receptors is greatly reduced except for olfaction and sensation of radiant heat, both of which are stepped up. In
the maximum contact phase, the muscles and skin communicate.
Pelvis, thighs, and head can be brought into play; arms can encir-
cle. Except at the outer limits, sharp vision is blurred. When close
vision is possible within the intimate range – as with children –
the image is greatly enlarged and stimulates much, if not all, of the
retina. The detail that can be seen at this distance is extraordinary.
This detail plus the cross-eyed pull of the eye muscles provide a
visual experience that cannot be confused with any other distance.
Vocalization at intimate distance plays a very minor part in the
communication process, which is carried mainly by other channels. A whisper has the effect of expanding the distance. The
vocalizations that do occur are largely involuntary.

Intimate Distance – Far Phase
(Distance: six to eighteen inches)

Heads, thighs, and pelvis are not easily brought into contact, but   8
hands can reach and grasp extremities. The head is seen as enlarged in size, and its features are distorted. Ability to focus the eye
easily is an important feature of this distance for Americans. The
iris of the other person's eye seen at about six to nine inches is
enlarged to more than life-size. Small blood vessels in the sclera
are clearly perceived, pores are enlarged. Clear vision (15 degrees)
includes the upper or lower portion of the face, which is perceived
as enlarged. The nose is seen as over-large and may look distorted,
as will other features such as lips, teeth, and tongue. Peripheral
vision (30 to 180 degrees) includes the outline of head and shoulders and very often the hands.

Much of the physical discomfort that Americans experience   9
when foreigners are inappropriately inside the intimate sphere is
expressed as a distortion of the visual system. One subject said,
"These people get so close, you're cross-eyed. It really makes me
nervous. They put their face so close it feels like they're *inside
you*." At the point where sharp focus is lost, one feels the uncomfortable muscular sensation of being cross-eyed from looking at
something too close. The expressions "Get your face *out* of mine"
and "He shook his fist *in* my face" apparently express how many
Americans perceive their body boundaries.

At six to eighteen inches the voice is used but is normally held at   10
a very low level or even a whisper.... The heat and odor of the

other person's breath may be detected, even though it is directed away from subject's face. Heat loss or gain from other person's body begins to be noticed by some subjects.

11   The use of intimate distance in public is not considered proper by adult, middle-class Americans even though their young may be observed intimately involved with each other in automobiles and on beaches. Crowded subways and buses may bring strangers into what would ordinarily be classed as intimate spatial relations, but subway riders have defensive devices which take the real intimacy out of intimate space in public conveyances. The basic tactic is to be as immobile as possible and, when part of the trunk or extremities touches another person, withdraw if possible. If this is not possible, the muscles in the affected areas are kept tense. For members of the non-contact group, it is taboo to relax and enjoy bodily contact with strangers! In crowded elevators the hands are kept at the side or used to steady the body by grasping a railing. The eyes are fixed on infinity and are not brought to bear on anyone for more than a passing glance.

12   It should be noted once more that American proxemic patterns for intimate distance are by no means universal. Even the rules governing such intimacies as touching others cannot be counted on to remain constant. Americans who have had an opportunity for considerable social interaction with Russians report that many of the features characteristic of American intimate distance are present in Russian social distance.... Middle Eastern subjects in public places do not express the outraged reaction to being touched by strangers which one encounters in American subjects.

PERSONAL DISTANCE

13   "Personal distance" is the term originally used by Hediger to designate the distance consistently separating the members of non-contact species. It might be thought of as a small protective sphere or bubble that an organism maintains between itself and others.

Personal Distance — Close Phase
(Distance: one and a half to two and a half feet)

14   The kinesthetic sense of closeness derives in part from the possibilities present in regard to what each participant can do to the other with his extremities. At this distance, one can hold or grasp the other person. Visual distortion of the other's features is no longer apparent. However, there is noticeable feedback from the muscles that control the eyes. The reader can experience this himself if he will look at an object eighteen inches to three feet away, paying particular attention to the muscles around his eyeballs. He can feel the pull of these muscles as they hold the two

eyes on a single point so that the image of each eye stays in register. Pushing gently with the tip of the finger on the surface of the lower eyelid so that the eyeball is displaced will illustrate clearly the work these muscles perform in maintaining a single coherent image. A visual angle of 15 degrees takes in another person's upper or lower face, which is seen with exceptional clarity. The planes and roundness of the face are accentuated; the nose projects and the ears recede; fine hair of the face, eyelashes, and pores is clearly visible. The three-dimensional quality of objects is particularly pronounced. Objects have roundness, substance, and form unlike that perceived at any other distance. Surface textures are also very prominent and are clearly differentiated from each other. Where people stand in relation to each other signals their relationship, or how they feel toward each other, or both. A wife can stay inside the circle of her husband's close personal zone with impunity. For another woman to do so is an entirely different story.

Personal Distance — Far Phase
(Distance: two and a half to four feet)

Keeping someone at "arm's length" is one way of expressing the far   *15*
phase of personal distance. It extends from a point that is just outside easy touching distance by one person to a point where two people can touch fingers if they extend both arms. This is the limit of physical domination in the very real sense. Beyond it, a person cannot easily "get his hands on" someone else. Subjects of personal interest and involvement can be discussed at this distance. Head size is perceived as normal and details of the other person's features are clearly visible. Also easily seen are fine details of skin, gray hair, "sleep" in the eye, stains on teeth, spots, small wrinkles, or dirt on clothing. Foveal vision covers only an area the size of the tip of the nose or one eye, so that the gaze must wander around the face (*where the eye is directed* is strictly a matter of cultural conditioning). Fifteen-degree clear vision covers the upper *or* lower face, while 180-degree peripheral vision takes in the hands and the whole body of a seated person. Movement of the hands is detected, but fingers can't be counted. The voice level is moderate. No body heat is perceptible. While olfaction is not normally present for Americans, it is for a great many other people who uses colognes to create an olfactory bubble. Breath odor can sometimes be detected at this distance, but Americans are generally trained to direct the breath away from others.

SOCIAL DISTANCE

The boundary line between the far phase of personal distance and   *16*
the close phase of social distance marks, in the words of one

subject, the "limit of domination." Intimate visual detail in the face is not perceived, and nobody touches or expects to touch another person unless there is some special effort. Voice level is normal for Americans. There is little change between the far and close phases, and conversations can be overheard at a distance of up to twenty feet. I have observed that in overall loudness, the American voice at these distances is below that of the Arab, the Spaniard, the South Asian Indian, and the Russian, and somewhat above that of the English upper class, the Southeast Asian, and the Japanese.

Social Distance – Close Phase
(Distance: four to seven feet)

17   Head size is perceived as normal; as one moves away from the subject, the foveal area of the eye can take in an ever-increasing amount of the person. At four feet, a one-degree visual angle covers an area of a little more than one eye. At seven feet the area of sharp focus extends to the nose and parts of both eyes; or the whole mouth, one eye, and the nose are sharply seen. Many Americans shift their gaze back and forth from eye to eye or from eyes to mouth. Details of skin texture and hair are clearly perceived. At a 60-degree visual angle, the head, shoulders, and upper trunk are seen at a distance of four feet; while the same sweep includes the whole figure at seven feet.

18   Impersonal business occurs at this distance, and in the close phase there is more involvement than in the distant phase. People who work together tend to use close social distance. It is also a very common distance for people who are attending a casual social gathering. To stand and look down at a person at this distance has a domineering effect, as when a man talks to his secretary or receptionist.

Social Distance – Far Phase
(Distance: seven to twelve feet)

19   This is the distance to which people move when someone says, "Stand away so I can look at you." Business and social discourse conducted at the far end of social distance has a more formal character than if it occurs inside the close phase. Desks in the offices of important people are large enough to hold visitors at the far phase of social distance. Even in an office with standard-size desks, the chair opposite is eight or nine feet away from the man behind the desk. At the far phase of social distance, the finest details of the face, such as the capillaries in the eyes, are lost. Otherwise, skin texture, hair, condition of teeth, and condition of clothes are all readily visible. None of my subjects mentioned heat or odor from another person's body as detectable at this distance. The full figure – with a good deal of space around it – is

encompassed in a 60-degree glance. Also, at around twelve feet, feedback from the eye muscles used to hold the eyes inward on a single spot falls off rapidly. The eyes and the mouth of the other person are seen in the area of sharpest vision. Hence, it is not necessary to shift the eyes to take in the whole face. During conversations of any significant length it is more important to maintain visual contact at this distance than it is at closer distances.

Proxemic behavior of this sort is culturally conditioned and *20* entirely arbitrary. It is also binding on all concerned. To fail to hold the other person's eye is to shut him out and bring conversation to a halt, which is why people who are conversing at this distance can be observed craning their necks and leaning from side to side to avoid intervening obstacles. Similarly, when one person is seated and the other is standing, prolonged visual contact at less than ten or twelve feet tires the neck muscles and is generally avoided by subordinates who are sensitive to their employer's comfort. If, however, the status of the two parties is reversed so that the subordinate is seated, the other party may often come closer.

At this distant phase, the voice level is noticeably louder than for *21* the close phase, and it can usually be heard easily in an adjoining room if the door is open. Raising the voice or shouting can have the effect of reducing social distance to personal distance.

A proxemic feature of social distance (far phase) is that it can be *22* used to insulate or screen people from each other. This distance makes it possible for them to continue to work in the presence of another person without appearing to be rude. Receptionists in offices are particularly vulnerable as most employers expect double duty: answering questions, being polite to callers, as well as typing. If the receptionist is less than ten feet from another person, even a stranger, she will be sufficiently involved to be virtually compelled to converse. If she has more space, however, she can work quite freely without having to talk. Likewise, husbands returning from work often find themselves sitting and relaxing, reading the paper at ten or more feet from their wives, for at this distance a couple can engage each other briefly and disengage at will. Some men discover that their wives have arranged the furniture back-to-back – a favorite sociofugal device of the cartoonist Chick Young, creator of "Blondie." The back-to-back seating arrangement is an appropriate solution to minimum space because it is possible for two people to stay uninvolved if that is their desire.

PUBLIC DISTANCE

Several important sensory shifts occur in the transition from the *23* personal and social distances to public distance, which is well outside the circle of involvement.

Public Distance – Close Phase
(Distance: twelve to twenty-five feet)

24   At twelve feet an alert subject can take evasive or defensive action if threatened. The distance may even cue a vestigial but subliminal form of flight reaction. The voice is loud but not full-volume. Linguists have observed that a careful choice of words and phrasing of sentences as well as grammatical or syntactic shifts occur at this distance.... The angle of sharpest vision (one degree) covers the whole face. Fine details of the skin and eyes are no longer visible. At sixteen feet, the body begins to lose its roundness and to look flat. The color of the eyes begins to be imperceivable; only the white of the eye is visible. Head size is perceived as considerably under life-size. The 15-degree lozenge-shaped area of clear vision covers the faces of two people at twelve feet, while 60-degree scanning includes the whole body with a little space around it. Other persons present can be seen peripherally.

Public Distance – Far Phase
(Distance: twenty-five feet or more)

25   Thirty feet is the distance that is automatically set around important public figures....

26   The usual public distance is not restricted to public figures but can be used by anyone on public occasions. There are certain adjustments that must be made, however. Most actors know that at thirty or more feet the subtle shades of meaning conveyed by the normal voice are lost as are the details of facial expression and movement. Not only the voice but everything else must be exaggerated or amplified. Much of the nonverbal part of the communication shifts to gestures and body stance. In addition, the tempo of the voice drops, words are enunciated more clearly, and there are stylistic changes as well.... The whole man may be seen as quite small and he is perceived in a setting. Foveal vision takes in more and more of the man until he is entirely within the small circle of sharpest vision. At which point – when people look like ants – contact with them as human beings fades rapidly. The 60-degree cone of vision takes in the setting while peripheral vision has as its principal function the alerting of the individual to movement at the side.

WHY "FOUR" DISTANCES?

27   In concluding this description of distance zones common to our sample group . . . a final word about classification is in order. It may well be asked: Why are there four zones, not six or eight? Why set up any zones at all? How do we know that this classification is appropriate? How were the categories chosen?

28   As I indicated earlier . . . , the scientist has a basic need for a

classification system, one that is as consistent as possible with the phenomena under observation and one which will hold up long enough to be useful. Behind every classification system lies a theory or hypothesis about the nature of the data and their basic patterns of organization. The hypothesis behind the proxemic classification system is this: it is in the nature of animals, including man, to exhibit behavior which we call territoriality. In so doing, they use the senses to distinguish between one space or distance and another. The specific distance chosen depends on the transaction; the relationship of the interacting individuals, how they feel, and what they are doing. The four-part classification system used here is based on observations of both animals and men. Birds and apes exhibit intimate, personal, and social distances just as man does.

Western man has combined consultative and social activities   *29* and relationships into one distance set and has added the public figure and the public relationship. "Public" relations and "public" manners as the Europeans and Americans practice them are different from those in other parts of the world. There are implicit obligations to treat total strangers in certain prescribed ways. Hence, we find four principal categories of relationships (intimate, personal, social, and public) and the activities and spaces associated with them. In other parts of the world, relationships tend to fall into other patterns, such as the family/non-family pattern common in Spain and Portugal and their former colonies or the caste and outcast system of India. Both the Arabs and the Jews also make sharp distinctions between people to whom they are related and those to whom they are not. My work with Arabs leads me to believe that they employ a system for the organization of informal space which is very different from what I observed in the United States. The relationship of the Arab peasant or fellah to his sheik or to God is not a public relationship. It is close and personal without intermediaries....

The ability to recognize these various zones of involvement and   *30* the activities, relationships, and emotions associated with each has now become extremely important. The world's populations are crowding into cities, and builders and speculators are packing people into vertical filing boxes – both offices and dwellings. If one looks at human beings in the way that the early slave traders did, conceiving of their space requirements simply in terms of the limits of the body, one pays very little attention to the effects of crowding. If, however, one sees man surrounded by a series of invisible bubbles which have measurable dimensions, architecture can be seen in a new light. It is then possible to conceive that people can be cramped by the spaces in which they have to live and work. They may even find themselves forced into behavior, relationships, or emotional outlets that are overly stressful. Like gravity, the influence of two bodies on each other is inversely proportional not only to the square of the distance but possibly even the cube of the distance between them. When stress increases, sensitivity to crowding rises – people get more on edge – so that more and more space is required as less and less is available.

QUESTIONS

Language and Style

1. Compare the language of the first three paragraphs with that of some of the later paragraphs (paragraphs 6-8 for example). What differences do you notice? Explain.

2. What is the point of Hall's remark (paragraph 11): "The use of intimate distance in public is not considered proper...."?

3. How can you tell for whom this discussion is intended? Why, for example, should Hall leave out the details of the research on which the discussion is apparently based?

Organization

1. Sketch Hall's system of classification as a line and box chart.

2. What makes the discussion consistent and predictable?

3. What purpose is served by the first five paragraphs? By the last four paragraphs?

Content

1. What are the implications of Hall's remark at the end of the discussion that "more and more space is required as less and less is available"?

2. What are some implications of Hall's ideas for a society like Canada's?

Vocabulary

egalitarian	syntactic	foveal
Dionysian	caste	sociofugal
intellectuals	inversely	subliminal
olfaction	Apollonian	lozenge
kinesthetic	isolates	fellah
capillaries	proxemic	cube
vestigial	sclera	

Giving Things Names
S. I. Hayakawa

S. I. Hayakawa advances the claim, common to many students of semantics, that our language sometimes betrays us into misunderstanding and causes human strife.

Let us say animals, four large and four small, a different four with   *1*
round heads and another four with square heads, and still another
four with curly tails and another four with straight tails, . . . are
scampering about your village, but since at first they are of no
importance to you, you ignore them. You do not even give them a
name.

One day, however, you discover that the little ones eat up your   *2*
grain, while the big ones do not. A differentiation sets itself up, and
abstracting the common characteristics of A, B, C, and D, you
decide to call these *gogo*; E, F, G, and H you decide to call *gigi*. You
chase away the *gogo*, but leave the *gigi* alone. Your neighbor,
however, has had a different experience; he finds that those with
square heads bite, while those with round heads do not. Abstracting
the common characteristics of B, D, F, and H, he calls them *daba*,
and A, C, E, and G he calls *dobo*. Still another neighbor discovers,
on the other hand, that those with curly tails kill snakes, while
those with straight tails do not. He differentiates them, abstracting
still another set of common characteristics: A, B, E, and F are *busa*,
while C, D, G, and H are *busana*.

Now imagine that the three of you are together when E runs by.   *3*
You say, "There goes the *gigi*"; your first neighbor says, "There
goes the *dobo*"; your other neighbor says, "There goes the *busa*."
Here immediately a great controversy arises. What is it really, a
gigi, a *dobo*, or a *busa*? What is its *right name*? You are quarreling
violently when along comes a fourth person from another village
who calls it a *muglock*, an edible animal, as opposed to *uglock* an
inedible animal – which doesn't help matters a bit.

Of course, the question, "What is it *really*? What is its *right*   *4*
name?" is a nonsense question. By a nonsense question is meant
one that is not capable of being answered. Things can have "right
names" only if there is a necessary connection between symbols
and things symbolized, and we have seen that there is not. That is
to say, in the light of your interest in protecting your grain, it may
be necessary for you to distinguish the animal E as a *gigi*; your
neighbor, who doesn't like to be bitten, finds it practical to distin-

guish it as a *dobo*; your other neighbor, who likes to see snakes killed, distinguishes it as a *busa*. What we call things and where we draw the line between one class of things and another depend upon the interests we have and the purposes of the classification. For example, animals are classified in one way by the meat industry, in a different way by the leather industry, in another different way by the fur industry, and in a still different way by the biologist. None of these classifications is any more final than any of the others; each of them is useful for its purpose.

5   This holds, of course, for everything we perceive. A table "is" a table to us, because we can understand its relationship to our conduct and interests; we eat at it, work on it, lay things on it. But to a person living in a culture where no tables are used, it may be a very big stool, a small platform, or a meaningless structure. If our culture and upbringing were different, that is to say, our world would not even look the same to us.

6   Many of us, for example, cannot distinguish between pickerel, pike, salmon, smelts, perch, crappies, halibut, and mackerel; we say that they are "just fish, and I don't like fish." To a seafood connoisseur, however, these distinctions are real, since they mean the difference to him between one kind of good meal, a very different kind of good meal, or a poor meal. To a zoologist, even finer distinctions become of great importance, since he has other and more general ends in view. When we hear the statement, then, "This fish is a specimen of the pompano, *Trachinotus Carolinus*," we accept this as being "true," even if we don't care, not because that is its "right name," but because that is how it is classified in the most complete and most general system of classification which people most deeply interested in fish have evolved.

7   When we name something, then, we are classifying. *The individual object or event we are naming, of course, has no name and belongs to no class until we put it in one.* To illustrate again, suppose that we were to give the extensional meaning of the word "Korean." We would have to point to all "Koreans" living at a particular moment and say, "The word 'Korean' denotes at the present moment these persons: $A_1, A_2, A_3, \ldots A_n$." Now, let us say, a child, whom we shall designate as Z, is born among these "Koreans." *The extensional meaning of the word "Korean," determined prior to the existence of Z, does not include Z.* Z is a new individual belonging to no classification, since all classifications were made without taking Z into account. Why, then, is Z also a "Korean"? *Because we say so.* And, saying so – fixing the classification – we have determined to a considerable extent future attitudes toward Z. For example, Z will always have certain rights in Korea; he will always be regarded in other nations as an "alien" and will be subject to laws applicable to "aliens."

8   In matters of "race" and "nationality," the way in which classifi-

cations work is especially apparent. For example I am by birth a "Canadian," by "race" a "Japanese," and am now an "American." Although I was legally admitted to the United States on a Canadian passport as a "non-quota immigrant," I was unable to apply for American citizenship until after 1952. According to American immigration law (since 1952 as well as before), a Canadian entering the United States as a permanent resident has no trouble getting in, unless he happens to be of Oriental extraction, in which case his "nationality" becomes irrelevant and he is classified by "race." If the quota for his "race" – for example, Japanese – is filled (and it usually is), and if he cannot get himself classified as a non-quota immigrant, he is not able to get in at all. Are all these classifications "real"? Of course they are, and *the effect that each of them has upon what he may and may not do constitutes their "reality."*

I have spent my entire life, except for short visits abroad, in   9
Canada and the United States. I speak Japanese haltingly, with a child's vocabulary and an American accent; I do not read or write it. Nevertheless, because classifications seem to have a kind of hypnotic power over some people, I am occasionally credited with (or accused of) having an "Oriental mind." Since Buddha, Confucious, General Tojo, Mao Tse-tung, Pandit Nehru, Syngman Rhee, and the proprietor of the Golden Pheasant Chop Suey House all have "Oriental minds," it is difficult to know whether to feel complimented or insulted.

When is a person a "Negro"? By the definition accepted in the   10
United States any person with even a small amount of "Negro blood" – that is, whose parents or ancestors were classified as "Negroes" – is a "Negro." *It would be exactly as justifiable to say that any person with even a small amount of "White blood" is "white."* Why do they say one rather than the other? Because the former system of classification *suits the purposes of those making the classification.* Classification is not a matter of identifying "essences," as is widely believed. It is simply a reflection of social convenience and necessity – and different necessities are always producing different classifications.

There are few complexities about classifications at the level of   11
dogs and cats, knives and forks, cigarettes and candy, but when it comes to classifications at high levels of abstraction – for example, those describing conduct, social institutions, philosophical and moral problems – serious difficulties occur. When one person kills another, is it an act of murder, an act of temporary insanity, an act of homicide, an accident, or an act of heroism? As soon as the process of classification is completed, our attitudes and our conduct are to a considerable degree determined. We hang the murderer, we lock up the insane man, we free the victim of circumstances, we pin a medal on the hero.

Unfortunately, people are not always aware of the way in which   12 they arrive at their classifications. Unaware of those characteristics of the extensional Mr. Miller not covered by classifying him as "a Jew," and attributing to Mr. Miller all the characteristics suggested by the affective connotations of the term with which he has been classified, they pass final judgment on Mr. Miller by saying, "Well, a Jew's a Jew. There's no getting around it!"

13   We need not concern ourselves here with the injustices done to "Jews," "Roman Catholics," "Republicans," "red-heads," "chorus girls," "sailors," "brass-hats," "Southerners," "Yankees," "school teachers," "government regulations," "socialistic proposals," and so on by such hasty judgments or, as it is better to call them, fixed reactions. "Hasty judgments" suggests that such errors can be avoided by thinking more slowly; this, of course, is not the case, for some people think very slowly with no better results. What we are concerned with is the way in which we block the development of our own minds by such automatic reactions.

14   To continue with our example of the people who say, "A Jew's a Jew. There's no getting around that!" – they are, as we have seen, confusing the denoted, extensional Jew with the fictitious "Jew" inside their heads. Such persons, the reader will have observed, can usually be made to admit, on being reminded of certain "Jews" whom they admire – perhaps Albert Einstein, perhaps former Associate Justice Arthur Goldberg, perhaps Jascha Heifetz, perhaps Sandy Koufax – that "there are exceptions, of course." They have been compelled by experience, that is to say, to take cognizance of at least a few of the multitude of "Jews" who do not fit their preconceptions. At this point, however, they continue triumphantly, "But exceptions only prove the rule!" – which is another way of saying, "Facts don't count."

15   In Marin County, California, I once attended hearings at the county courthouse concerning a proposed ordinance to forbid racial discrimination in the rental and sale of housing. (Such discrimination in Marin is chiefly directed against Negroes.) I was impressed by the fact that a large majority of those who rose to speak were in favor of the ordinance; but I was also impressed by the number who, though maintaining that they counted Negroes among their best and most admired friends, still spoke heatedly against a law that would, by forbidding racial discrimination in the sale and rental of housing, enable Negroes to live anywhere in the county. Presumably, all the Negroes whom they loved and admired were "exceptions," and the stereotyped "Negro" remained in their heads in spite of their experience.

16   People like this may be said to be impervious to new information. They continue to vote for their party *label*, no matter what mistakes their party makes. They continue to object to "socialists," no matter what the socialists propose. They continue to regard "mothers" as sacred, no matter which mother. A woman who had been given up both by physicians and psychiatrists as hopelessly

insane was being considered by a committee whose task it was to decide whether or not she should be committed to an asylum. One member of the committee doggedly refused to vote for commitment. "Gentlemen," he said in tones of deepest reverence, "you must remember that this woman is, after all, a mother."

QUESTIONS

Language and Style

1. Why should the discussion, which begins in an abstract way, become personal? At what point does the change occur?

Organization

1. Explain how the discussion develops by placing human practices in the context of a rational explanation of "naming."

Content

1. Hayakawa's discussion centres on the legitimate purposes to which systems of classification are put. Usually these purposes reflect an interest in arranging items of our experience in convenient, manageable ways. What are some examples of this practice? What is the usefulness, for example, of arranging birds into robins, sparrows, jays, and ravens?

2. The writer claims that all naming is classifying. Is it clear that, in the example mentioned in paragraph 5, naming a piece of furniture "table" classifies it? Is there a sense in which we are merely labelling rather than classifying? What might be the difference?

3. There are some practices of which the writer disapproves. How does the tone of the language change in paragraphs 8, 9, and 10? How would you characterize it?

4. The writer seems to attribute the genuinely evil applications of classification (stereotyping) to a "social convenience and necessity" (paragraph 10). Does this explanation do justice to the sort of discrimination he mentions?

Vocabulary

differentiation	abstracting
connoisseur	zoologist
extensional meaning	denotes
cognizance	ordinance
stereotype	impervious

Sheldon's Scale of Temperament

Calvin S. Hall and Gardner Lindzey

This account of Sheldon's research, drawn from a text on personality theory, is a good example of the way a system of classification can organize a large collection of information.

1   Although Sheldon was well aware of his predecessors' attempts to type or measure physique, he began his efforts inductively. The first problem he faced was to secure a large number of physiques that could be examined and re-examined. In order to make this procedure practical and efficient he devised a photographic technique that involved taking pictures from the front, side, and rear of individuals posed in a standard position before a standard background. This procedure has come to be called the *Somatotype Performance Test* and is described in full detail in Sheldon's *Atlas of men* (1954).

2   In his first important study of the human physique, Sheldon secured roughly four thousand standard photographs of male college students. These pictures were then inspected carefully by several judges with the intent of teasing out the principal variables that account for or form the basis of physique variation. Once a given characteristic was suspected of being a primary component, it was appraised in terms of the following criteria: (1) Was it possible to rank all four thousand subjects in terms of this characteristic? (2) Could different judges reach agreement independently in ranking physiques in terms of this characteristic? (3) Was it impossible to account for this variable in terms of some combination of the other variables that had already been identified?

PRIMARY COMPONENTS OF PHYSIQUE

3   After a considerable period of carefully examining and judging these pictures Sheldon and his associates concluded that, with a list of three, they had exhausted the possibilities of discovering new components. These three dimensions became the core of the technique for assessing the physical structure of the body, and their careful delineation and measurement occupied the next phase of Sheldon's investigation.

The first component was *endomorphy*. The individual who is   *4*
high in this component and low in both of the others is characterized by softness and a spherical appearance. Consistent with the
softness and rounded quality is an underdevelopment of bone and
muscle and a relatively low surface-mass ratio. Such an individual
has a low specific gravity and floats high in the water. The fact that
the digestive viscera are highly developed in this physique and that
the functional elements of those structures develop primarily from
the endodermal embryonic layer accounts for the use of the term
endomorphy.

The second component was referred to as *mesomorphy*. A phy-   *5*
sique heavily developed in this component, and showing a decrement in both the other components, is hard and rectangular, with a
predominance of bone and muscle. The mesomorphic body is
strong, tough, resistant to injury, and generally equipped for strenuous and exacting physical demands. The athlete, adventurer, or
professional soldier might best be endowed with this type of
physique. The dominant portions of this physique have derived
primarily from the mesodermal embryonic layer, hence the term
mesomorphic.

The third component was labeled *ectomorphy*. An individual   *6*
who is at the upper extreme in this component and low in the
other components is linear and fragile, characterized by flatness of
the chest and delicacy of the body. He is usually thin and lightly
muscled. Relative to his mass the ectomorph has more surface
area than the other types of physique; he shows a preponderance
of mass over surface. He also has the largest brain and central
nervous system in proportion to his size. From this, Sheldon reasons that his physique is made up, more so than the other physiques, of tissues that have derived from the ectodermal embryonic
layer. The ectomorph, because of his large proportionate surface
area, is overexposed to external stimulation. This is a physique
poorly equipped for competitive and persistent physical action.

Intervening between a general definition of the primary compo-   *7*
nents of physique and the final delineation of the somatotype are
the details of an objective measurement technique. A suitable
measurement procedure was derived from an intricate mixture of
judges' ratings or rankings and an elaborate network of physical
measurements. Each of the four thousand subjects was ranked and
rated in terms of each of the primary components. It was possible
to take a great many anthropometric measurements, most of them
consisting of diameters of various parts of the body, and determine
how effectively these measures differentiated between individuals
who were high or low in the judges' rankings for each of the
components. Those physical measurements that differentiated accurately between subjects the judges had ranked differently on the

three primary components were retained, and all other measurements were rejected. This resulted eventually in the retention of a cluster of seventeen anthropometric measures, all of which were diameters expressed as ratios to the height of the individual. It was soon discovered that these diameters could be measured at least as accurately from photographs as from the body of the subject. Thus, the technique substituted measures derived from standard photographs for the previous practice of taking measurements directly from the subject's body.

8   At this point a total of four thousand subjects had been ranked by judges in terms of the extent to which each of the primary components was present in their physical make-up. In addition, all subjects had been assigned a score of from one to seven for each of the components. Thus, for every rating or score on each variable there existed a number of concrete illustrations in the form of individuals in the original sample who had been assigned this rating. In addition, for every individual there was a set of physical measurements that had been shown to differentiate between individuals with different ratings on the three components. It was then possible for Sheldon to develop a process whereby, given the seventeen physical measurements, the appropriate ratings on each of the three components could be objectively derived. At one point in the research a collaborator, S. S. Stevens, developed a machine, which, although it required a human operator, reduced the assignment of scores to a relatively simple, though numerous, set of manipulations. Using an operator who was unfamiliar with the somatotyping procedure, except for the instructions necessary to operate the machine, it was possible to demonstrate for one hundred cases a correlation of .94 between the ratings assigned by the machine and those arrived at by the more customary observational technique. Sheldon reports (1954) that, in general, individuals who were accustomed to somatotyping the college group customarily found correlations of .90 or above between their independent somatotype ratings.

9   The physical measurements not only lead to an over-all score for each of the components; they also provide *ratings for* these components for *five different areas of the body*: head-neck, chest-trunk, arms, stomach-trunk, and legs. A complete description of the process of somatotyping the male body is contained in Sheldon's *Atlas of men* (1954) which includes representative somatotype photographs of over one thousand men derived from a total sample of 46,000 such photographs.

QUESTIONS

Language and Style

1. In paragraphs 1 and 2 the basis of the theory is stated in somewhat abstract or at least technical language. Can you restate it in ordinary language? How useful would such a restatement be? What is gained by using such expressions as "Somatotype Performance Test"?

2. What activities are probably referred to in the statement, "These pictures were then inspected carefully by several judges with the intent of teasing out the principal variables. . . . "?

Organization

1. In what way is Sheldon's approach inductive rather than deductive? See Copi's discussion.

2. Into how many main sections is this brief discussion divided? How can the reader tell what the sections are? What connection does the pattern of organization have to the topic?

Content

1. What light does Hayakawa's discussion of naming shed on the definition of new terms in this discussion?

2. What significance might be attached to the fact that the system of types was first developed exclusively with reference to males?

Vocabulary

predecessor   delineation
decrement   anthropometric
correlations

Winning and Losing at Work
Michael Maccoby

This informal system for describing people's behaviour at work, while developed through observation of electronics engineers, has a wider application.

1   What do you want from your work? Money? Promotions? Interesting challenges? Continual learning? Membership in a high powered team at the cutting edge of technology? The opportunity to develop your own ideas?

2   Have you ever thought about how your work influences the kind of person you are becoming? How possible is it in a highly competitive corporation to develop yourself emotionally and spiritually as well as intellectually while achieving your work goals?

3   We are all individuals and so our answers will differ. To find out just how they differ, my colleagues and I have been interviewing engineers and managers for the past few years in an attempt to understand them and the nature of their work: what it means to them, how it affects them, and how it may be related to their character.

4   The psychoanalytic concept of character refers to emotional attitudes that determine what satisfies or annoys an individual – what he finds attractive, exciting, or frustrating – and how he relates to himself and to others. Essentially, what we look for in the context of character is what *energizes* a person, what turns him on, what gets him up in the morning. Among people in electronics, particularly in management, two elements stand out: the desire to win, and an interest in problem-solving, building, and gaining knowledge. Naturally, we find various mixes of these two elements among people.

5   The relationship between work and character is real as well as complex. In exploring it, we have learned that the successful individual is the one who does what needs to be done to meet his organization's particular goals, *not* because he has been told to do it but because he *wants* to do it, he *enjoys* doing it, he feels *impelled* to do it. This may seem reasonable, but it is by no means obvious, and I shall consider its implications in the course of this article.

6   Once it is established that a person does his job well when his character is adaptive to his mode of work, the well-known Peter principle can be redefined to say, quite seriously, that people do

"Winning and Losing at Work" by Michael Maccoby. © 1973 IEEE. Reprinted, with permission, from IEEE SPECTRUM, *Vol. 10, No. 7, pp. 39-48, July 1973.*

not merely rise to the level of their intellectual incompetence; they rise only to a level permitted by their character. Successively promoted until their personalities no longer fit the requirements of work, even the most brilliant engineers and scientists are likely to fail. Furthermore, a character type adaptive to a high level in one kind of organization may not fit another. For example, a fast-moving aggressive manager, ideally suited to working at high levels in a computer company, might well fail in a small instrument company; whereas a responsible and respectful craftsman might succeed at a small instrument company, but not in the semi-conductor industry.

In the course of our study . . . we have identified four major   7
character types among electronics engineers and their managers, and we have learned about the relationship between these character types and different kinds of work environments. . . .

Four character types. It should be obvious that in considering   8
types of people we must really deal with a concept social scientists call "ideal type." No individual fits an exact type – everybody is a mixture of personality traits. But just as we can speak of one person as stingy and another as generous, so can we speak of types in terms of dominant tendencies. In high-technology electronics we have identified four basic types of people. I call them the craftsman, the company man, the gamesman, and the jungle fighter.

THE CRAFTSMAN

Holding all the traditional values – thrift, belief in the work ethic,   9
and respect for people as well as for craftsmanship and quality – the craftsman is rather closed and hard to get close to, but he's a man of his word and a person who can be trusted in the crunch. He is highly independent, and doesn't generally like to compete against others. One highly respected craftsman noted, "The natural stimulation for me is my interest in the work; the competition seems to me unnatural. For others, it might be different." While the craftsman loves work, he also likes to get away from it and tinker with cars or pursue other hobbies.

The craftsman is rarely satisfied in large organizations and feels   10
more at home working in a small group or on a project with a defined and understandable structure. He wants to stay with the product from conception to completion. One craftsman remarked that for him "electrical engineering is a great hobby, but I wonder about it as a profession. I'm not strongly motivated by money; I turned down jobs $300 to $400 more per month because I didn't like the work. I wanted a job like this, with the satisfaction of putting something together and seeing it work."

When he rises in the organization it is usually not above what I   11
would call an administrative maintenance position – a laboratory

or project director, for example − unless he is one of the rare entrepreneurial craftsmen-builders who create new industries. In any case, the craftsman is absolutely essential to the creation of advanced technology.

THE COMPANY MAN

12   Unlike the craftsman, the company man is much more likely to identify with the large organization and to be satisfied within large, hierarchical projects. He tends to be a submissive bureaucrat in many ways, although he is generally courteous and more concerned with people than is the craftsman. Much of his satisfaction in life comes from belonging to a powerful, important company and, unlike the craftsman, he would not like to be off on his own. He derives a certain security from knowing where he fits in the structure and perceiving that he can rise within that structure by being responsible, and loyal, and doing his job right.

13   A very ambitious company man is also driven by fear of failure. In his dreams, he is typically chased or is in danger of falling from heights. (One manager actually told us he dreamt he was a spinning top.) The successful company man is both modest about himself and energized into compulsive activity by his fear of falling behind or just losing his momentum. Further, he often displays elements of what the psychoanalyst Erich Fromm, who first developed the theory of social character, describes as the marketing character. This is a person who relates to others by making himself an attractive package, who molds himself into what people want of him; he is a kind of centerless person who is very malleable but who also makes a good salesman. The prototypical marketing man is less adaptive to high technology than he is, say, to an advertising agency. Nevertheless, one often finds such people in certain middle management positions where they serve as mediators.

THE GAMESMAN

14   This individual is in some ways uniquely a product of the U.S. He appears at the beginning of the Republic, yet is very much a modern man. Even though the gamesman comprises only 10-15 percent of our sample, certain game attitudes seem to be increasingly characteristic of the younger high-technology managers. For this reason, and because he has not been adequately recognized, the gamesman deserves an extended description.

15   Alexis de Toqueville noted the penchant in the U.S. for treating business competition as play when he wrote in the early 19th century:

16   "The whole life of an American is passed like a game of chance, a revolutionary crisis, or a battle. As the same causes are continually

in operation throughout the country, they ultimately impart an irresistible impulse to the national character."

Later, in the middle of the 19th century, a group of scientists *17* interested in developing technology in the U.S. called themselves the "Lazzaroni," after a society of Italian workmen whose goal was to make work into play, and that goal continues to be uppermost in the minds of many scientists and engineers.

Today, however, most scientific "play" in the corporation is no *18* longer indulged in by individuals, but has been structured into a kind of game, where teams compete against time, other projects, and the market. Consequently, there is a special need for people who can integrate many specialists into a unified team working at a fast pace. Those who do the job best are the ones who experience this kind of work as a game.

The gamesman often aspires to be a kind of quarterback; profes- *19* sional football is his favorite game as it is increasingly the favorite spectator sport in the U.S., replacing the slower, less aggressive, less innovative, and more individualistic game of baseball. The gamesman often sees his work in terms of the metaphors of foot- ball and its technology – he will speak of the "game plan," of making "the big play" he'll say, "we're going to have to punt now," or "let's try an end around and see if we can corner a few more yards of the market." Indeed, this language has become part of the jargon of the high-technology business world.

Like a successful quarterback, the gamesman is innovative, flexi- *20* ble, detached, and aggressive in a controlled way. He likes to take risks and is fascinated by technique and new methods. He sees the developing project (and his career) in terms of options and possi- bilities, as in a game, and tends to be turned on, energized, by competitive pressures and crises.

Often rather bored and passive when deprived of competition, *21* once the game is on, once he can feel he's in the Super Bowl, he comes to life, remains cool, and thinks hard. While others such as the craftsman may find such high-pressure competition enervat- ing, the gamesman's goal in life is to win and to be known as a winner. (Significantly, while many of the people we interviewed tended to repress or deny their interest in personal power, some of the gamesmen admitted that what they liked most about their job was being the boss and what they liked least was having to take orders from someone else. They want to call the plays.)

The gamesman and the craftsman often feel frustrated trying to *22* communicate with one another. (You might say that if the gamesman's idea of play is football, for the craftsman it is tinkering, hiking, or sailing – that is, competing against himself and nature with the overriding goal of perfecting his technique.) The gamesman thinks the craftsman is a stick-in-the-mud, is too cautious, is not ambitious enough, and does not understand the real market. A gamesman told me that he managed a group of scientists who were like children, with neither a sense of business nor the motivation to win; he even called his lab "the sandbox." The craftsman, on the other hand, thinks that the gamesman is unsound, grandiose, superficial, pushy, and not respectful of others.

23   Increasingly, these gamesmen fill the top positions of middle management. They are the project leaders and marketing directors, and they like to integrate, direct, and motivate a team of highly talented specialists who are all working interdependently to win, to be number one – goals that for other character types are irrelevant. (After all, why should winning be more important than creating something of the highest quality, asks the craftsman, or, we would add, of making people's lives better?)

24   Significantly, the game character is less prone to suffer from the emotional problems that we found to be especially common among the craftsmen and some company men we interviewed. These problems are rooted in what Fromm calls the hoarding orientation, by which he means a tendency to retreat behind an emotional shell, thus finding it difficult to communicate with others. Practically every engineer we interviewed reports as problems the kinds of symptoms that psychiatrists describe as obsessive-compulsive – keeping his feelings to himself, avoiding other people, being overly anxious and finicky, being a perfectionist, and even having difficulty making decisions. Although these problems are sometimes encountered in the gamesman, they are generally less significant for him, and that is one reason he is better able to rise to high levels.

25   Seldom, however, do the gamesmen rise to the very top, even though an increasing number of company men have elements of the gamesman's character. Many gamesmen have mixed feelings about authority, and more than a little adolescent rebelliousness. Consequently, they are often considered too free-wheeling for top management positions. While they like to run the team, they also like to circumvent the rules. Furthermore, the gamesman cannot create his own team. He lacks patience and commitment to people, principles, and goals beyond winning. He is not an independent person and tends to lose sight of realities beyond the game he is currently playing. Indeed, he can be looked upon as creating a secondary reality for himself. If life is not interesting enough for him, he makes it a game and enters a semifantasy world.

26   *Some negative consequences.* The character of the gamesman is not easy to evaluate. Besides the importance of his role in advancing technology, he supports some positive social values; he tends to be very fair, to believe that everybody should be allowed to play who is good, and that neither race, sex, nor religion nor anything

else besides contributing to the team matters. But we can see a number of elements that inhibit both his self-development and his effect on others. He is excessively competitive and aggressive. Since he makes life a game, he expects everyone else to do the same. For him, it is enough that everyone gets a "fair" chance to play the game, and he ignores the fact that some people, due to their background or temperament, never have a fair chance to compete. He has a tendency to put people into categories of winners and losers, and to be contemptuous of the losers. Beyond this, his detachment and need to win blind him to the effects of his actions on real people, so that he never seriously considers the social values of the products he makes.

Nor is he sufficiently concerned about himself. Somebody with   *27*
such a character may remain happy so long as he's a winner and so long as he is young and vigorous, but once he loses his vigor and his thrill in winning, he becomes depressed and goalless, questioning the purpose of his life because he hasn't sufficiently developed the ability to love and understand and create. This is borne out by the successful gamesman in his forties who admitted he no longer had a goal in life and felt worried and apathetic. Another gamesman whose big project "failed" has become a depressed alcoholic. In contrast, we have met craftsmen aged 70 and older who are still energetic and interested in new ideas.

In common with the company man, the gamesman also tends to   *28*
report another symptom. He often feels that he gives in to others too easily, that he doesn't control his own destiny, that he is too malleable. Even at the highest levels, such personality types may feel a kind of unconscious self-contempt that they've given in, that they are performing for others rather than developing their own goals.

The sense of guilt and self-betrayal they feel over having to   *29*
sacrifice some of their independence is usually not conscious, but it comes out in dreams and projective tests – particularly on the Rorschach test where they report self-images of humiliation and castration. Their negative self-image tends to be related to a certain suppressed anger and hardening of the heart that occurs when one gives up a part of oneself or betrays one's convictions in order to get ahead.

In contrast to this unconscious guilt, I have observed that some   *30*
of the most creative businessmen-engineers do not repress their guilt, but act to alleviate it. These individuals are deeply concerned with the effects of their actions and recognize that their behavior has sometimes been destructive to themselves or others. But rather than hiding from their conscience, rather than hardening their hearts, their guilt spurs them to better themselves and their

organizations. One corporation president told us, "I saw myself as a slave owner, ripping off the work of other people, and I knew I had to do something to change working conditions."

THE JUNGLE FIGHTER

31   This fourth character type is less frequently encountered, but nonetheless often plays a key role in advanced technology. The jungle fighter experiences the corporation as a battleground where survival and advancement depend on crushing enemies both within and outside the company. Like the gamesman he wants to be a winner, but for him the struggle is not a game but a life-and-death contest. The Rorschach images of the jungle fighters are full of lions, tigers, and panthers; sometimes pictures of these animals are hung on their office walls.

32   Many jungle fighters have strong sadistic tendencies, although it is rare that they will admit this. Nevertheless, some do admit they enjoy crushing the opponent, and seeing his ego crack. They are likely to take pride in being feared by others, but rationalize this by claiming such fear stimulates better work.

33   Sometimes a talented and brilliant jungle fighter will be brought into a corporation in trouble and given the task of reorganizing the company and getting rid of the "dead wood." (It is notable that the other types — craftsmen, game characters, and company men — deeply dislike having to fire anyone.) Consequently, in some corporations, jungle fighters rise to high levels, though they often eventually fail because others become disgusted by their hard-hearted and self-serving conduct. Speaking of the fall of a jungle fighter, one of his associates pointed out that he had "left a trail of bodies behind him and he became a victim of revenge."

34   To get ahead in the corporate world of advanced technology, it is necessary to be competitive. But the competitive urge is very different for each of these four character types. [...] A key element is that each type is energized differently: the craftsman by his interest and pleasure in his work; the company man by his fear of failure and desire for acceptance; the gamesman by the glory of victory in the "contest"; and the jungle fighter by his need for power over others. Each character has a strong need for achievement, but achievement means something different for each character type.

QUESTIONS

Language and Style

1. With what impression is the reader left after having read the entire essay? What details are likely to stick? Why?

2. The discussion begins with a number of rhetorical questions. Which of them is addressed in the essay?

3. Why should "the craftsman" be imagined as tinkering with cars as a hobby?

4. Does Maccoby's informal language make his claims more believable? Why?

Organization

1. The classification system here is based on the question, "What energizes people?" Could a chart summarize the discussion? What would it look like?

2. Why should it be that the "gamesman" section of the discussion is longer and more complex than the other three sections?

3. Is there a sense in which the discussion "builds" from the least interesting type to the most interesting? Why should that happen?

Content

1. By what specific means might the four character types have been identified? A comparison with Sheldon's method is helpful.

2. Maccoby's article applies some aspects of personality theory to help the reader understand how people behave in (the electronics) industry. Notice that the writer makes an important qualification in paragraph 8. What is it?

3. Of which type is the writer apparently most approving? Least approving? Is it clear that the writer evaluates certain types and effectively withholds judgment of others? Why does the author do this?

Vocabulary

psychoanalytic	semi-conductor
entrepreneurial	hierarchical
compulsive	malleable
prototypical	penchant
enervating	circumvent
Rorschach	

The Flames of Youth
Wayne S. Wooden

The popular periodical Psychology Today, *which helps make the study of human behaviour accessible to a wide readership, furnished this account of the different motives of child arsonists.*

1   As a researcher with a special interest in juvenile delinquency, I became interested in arson because of a distressing statistic: Children are responsible for two out of every five cases of arson, a share that also appears to be increasing rapidly. And unlike other juvenile crimes, arson is disproportionately a white, middle-class activity. What motivates these kids to set fires? What could possibly drive them to set fire to their world?

2   Our research and that of others has shown that young arsonists are not a single group with a single motivation. Psychologist Martha Lou Berkey and I studied more than 100 children apprehended for arson in San Bernardino County, California, and we found four distinct types, each with its own patterns of firesetting and each driven by somewhat different emotional forces. The youngest group (up to age 10) consists of curious youngsters who accidentally start fires while playing with matches. Those in the second, somewhat older group (a large percentage of the total firesetting group) are problem-ridden and seem to be crying for help for various reasons. In the third (also large) group are those youngsters (whom we classify as "delinquent") who use fire as a means of adolescent acting-out against authority. In the fourth group, which cuts across age lines, are the relatively few firestarters who are severely mentally disturbed.

3   Accidental fires caused by children have become so common that they seldom make the newspaper's front page anymore. Very young children who cause fires are usually not bent on destruction when they play with fire, nor do they derive satisfaction from the fires they ignite. Rather, they are simply curious and fascinated by the spark and the igniting of a match. Sadly, however, when such young children have only minimal parental supervision – as they often do in broken homes – and little or no education about proper fire safety, the fires they accidentally set can be quite dangerous and damaging.

4   What draws these youngsters to fire? It is probably the same psychological magnetism that has always attracted people to fire:

its elemental warmth and beauty. Few young children, given the opportunity to play with matches, can resist trying. But the use of fire, in its primitive form, has become more forbidden and regulated as our society has become more urbanized. The general disappearance of fireplaces from modern homes and high price of firewood, for example, have transformed a primitive element into a luxury item. With the absence of fireplaces as an integral part of the family home, children are not as likely to be exposed to, or taught about, fire as a basic lesson in growing up. Their natural childhood curiosity about fire is not satisfied through normal daily activities. The diminished exposure to the primitive uses of fire may make it a more mystifying and attractive element, one that can be explored through playing with matches.

Ironically, the efficiency of modern firefighting may actually be   5 contributing to the arson epidemic. Before the development of sophisticated firefighting technology, the word "fire" struck fear into the hearts of rural and urban citizens alike. The great Chicago and San Francisco fires dramatized for the nation the need for fire safety, and proper fire use, paramount to survival, was taught at an early age.

To the children of the past, who were taught to fear fire and   6 instructed in its proper use, we can compare the children of today, who may view firetrucks and sirens as exciting; or worse, as just another form of entertainment – like watching action-packed programs on television – having little if any comprehension of fire's danger to life and society.

Accidental fires, while an important public concern, are easy to   7 comprehend as a consequence of normal childhood curiosity. But not all juvenile fire play is a function of natural inquisitiveness, and not all fires set by children are accidental. For many children, firesetting appears to be a symbolic act, frequently a symptom of underlying emotional or physical stress. Children who do not abandon the normal childhood experiments with fire, we believe, are crying for help, using fire as a way of expressing their feelings of stress, anxiety and anger. What turns these troubled kids into repeat firesetters, according to psychologist Kenneth R. Fineman, is positive reinforcement for their incendiary activities. With "fire success," these youngsters develop an "urge to burn" as their firesetting acts provide them with a sense of power and control otherwise lacking in their lives.

Like the accidental fires, the fires that are set as a plea for help   8 follow distinct patterns. They are usually set by youngsters who are alone in, or fairly close to, their homes. Typically, they might set fire to their own bed, their mother's clothes or their sister's hair. Thus, what is set on fire is often a symbolic target of their underlying anger. Youngsters who deliberately set their beds on fire, we believe, are symbolically expressing unhappiness with their entire lives by torching the thing that usually represents security to them.

9   Take, for instance, the case of Jerry, an 8-year-old boy. Jerry's mother had died one year before the fire incident. His father had been remarried for six months, and on the weekend before the fire, Jerry's grandfather passed away. According to his father, Jerry had at one time been outgoing and verbal and had also had many friends. In recent months, the boy had become withdrawn and rarely played with his best friend. Furthermore, Jerry had begun to fight with his one sister, had disobeyed his stepmother and had received low grades for the first time that year.

10   In our interview with him, Jerry said he daydreamed about fire and dreamed about his deceased mother at night. The fire that Jerry set, considering these disruptions, was interesting: He ignited all the wedding pictures of his father's second marriage.

11   Preteenage and teenage firesetters share the emotional disturbances of the younger troubled group. But now, as older children, they are granted greater freedom and independence, and they experience heightened peer pressure — all of which contribute to their arsonist activities. Such children often have a history of firesetting and other antisocial behavior, and may require counseling, juvenile probation or incarceration. These juveniles set fires for a variety of reasons. Some are simply the kids whose cries for help went unanswered and whose firesetting behavior became a conditioned response to deal with stress. For others, firesetting is an act of vandalism, a cover for other crimes or a way of creating excitement. These kids are likely to torch objects and structures that appear safe to burn, such as an abandoned building; in contrast to the younger troubled kids, the older arsonists don't want to get caught and they don't want anyone hurt.

12   Many older firesetters take out their hostility on school property. School-related fires account for 14 percent of the fires in our study, and according to government figures, arson is the most expensive crime inflicted on our schools. A recent Senate report estimated that public schools in the United States lose close to $600 million a year to vandalism, 40 percent of it going up in smoke. According to a California fire marshal, virtually every junior high school in the state has an arson fire at least once a year.

13   One 14-year-old in our study typifies the older firesetter. He was the second of two children and was in the ninth grade. He had a history of setting fires, including, at age 4, setting his home bathroom on fire by placing toilet paper over an electric heater and, at age 12, starting a kitchen fire by placing flammables over the stove. This time, he set his junior high school on fire because, according to his parents, he did not want to participate in school graduation exercises.

14   In a 1980 psychological profile of the recidivist firesetter, Anthony

Galit Levy

O. Rider pointed out that David Berkowitz, the confessed "Son of Sam" mass murderer, reportedly set more than 2,000 fires and made 337 false alarms in New York City from 1974 through 1977. He called in the fires to the police, identifying himself as the "Phantom of the Bronx."

Berkowitz would no doubt fit our fourth category, severely disturbed firesetters. These arsonists run the gamut in age, but they generally constitute a very small percentage of all arsonists. In general, they fit one of two major personality types. There is the "impulsive neurotic"; impatient, almost hyperactive, he is a poor sleeper, he steals and he often destroys even his own possessions. And there is the "borderline psychotic," characterized by extreme mood swings, uncontrolled anger, violence, bizarre speech and numerous phobias.   *15*

One of our young firesetters, Barry, age 6, fit the pattern of the "impulsive neurotic." Barry was in the first grade and was the older of two children. According to his mother, he had been in trouble since he was 2 and was disciplined twice a day. The boy's father had recently been in court for a drunk-driving offense that had caused a fatality and was going to serve time in prison. Thus, the boy was told that he would have to become the "man of the house." In response, Barry set three fires. The first was a trash fire in the kitchen; then he burned his baseball glove; finally, he set the living-room couch on fire − on Father's Day.   *16*

According to his parents, the boy turned to setting fires when he got mad at himself. In the interview, Barry said he was "dumb and stupid," terms his parents used to describe him as well. The parents also noticed him constantly staring at the fire in the fireplace.   *17*

More typical of our sample group were the teenage boys who were categorized by their probation workers and clinical psychologists as "borderline psychotic." Jason, a 14-year-old boy, the youngest of three children, fit this second profile. His parents were divorced when Jason was 1, and originally he lived with his mother. His father was a "speed freak" who suffered the paranoid delusion that communists were stalking him.   *18*

When the boy was 10, he was treated for borderline epilepsy. According to his mother, he could not concentrate, he could not read and he was hyperactive. He had headaches and slept day and night. He was physically immature for his age.   *19*

Jason came from a family with severe disturbances. His mother appeared hostile to society. Because she was a prostitute, the father, despite his drug habit, eventually had been given legal custody of the children. The children had nearly starved while living with him. Furthermore, until the age of 5 the boy had been raised by his mother's stepmother, who had died during an abortion while Jason was at her home. For two years prior to his fires,   *20*

Jason had been out of school. Because he used profanity to a teacher, he had been expelled. His parents never bothered to re-enroll him.

21   Jason was considered "totally incorrigible." He claimed that he had frequent fights with a family of Mexicans who lived across the street. Having found a brochure on the Ku Klux Klan, he talked to an older neighbor who was a member of a Klan in Orange County. In "retaliation" against this Mexican family, Jason built a cross, painted it and stored it in his father's garage. One evening, after having words with a group of Mexicans at a fast-food restaurant, Jason set the cross up in a vacant field behind the neighbor's house, poured gasoline on it and, after lighting it, took off running. According to Jason, "The cross was meant for all Mexicans to see it."

22   As our case studies have demonstrated, broken homes and parental neglect are the common ingredients in all four categories of firesetters. With the more severely disturbed youngsters, however, there may be other factors at work – including perhaps an inborn propensity toward antisocial behavior – that override environmental ones. While we may wonder if these children would have been any different if their fathers had been living at home, from what probation officers and psychiatrists have observed, we tend to doubt it.

23   Whatever the underlying cause, these mentally ill firesetters, though bizarre and more noticeable, are rare. More typically, as our study demonstrates, it is the "normal," though troubled, middle-class kids who are torching the country.

QUESTIONS

Language and Style

1. For whom, apparently, was this account written? Take your cue from the language the writer uses.

Organization

1. Why should the writer remind the reader that, although little or no research data is presented, it could be? Why is it not necessary to cite it here? By what means does the writer remind the reader?

2. Why is it seemingly unnecessary to present an example of one of the four types of firesetters?

3. What expectations are created in the first two paragraphs?

4. What brief departure is made at the end of the discussion? Why should the writer make such a change?

5. Are Wooden's four groups clearly identified in the second paragraph? What are the age groups of the first three?

6. Why should paragraph 7 begin with a reference to a subject which, at the end of paragraph 6, seems finished?

Content

1. What observations concerning the under-ten age group lead the reader to believe that most fires set by this group are "accidental"? How scientific does his explanation seem here?

2. Can you explain the feeling of "Aha!" a reader might experience toward the end of Wooden's discussion of Jerry?

3. Is it clear why "greater freedom and independence" and "heightened peer pressure" contribute to arsonist activities (paragraph 11)?

Vocabulary

elemental	urbanized
paramount	inquisitiveness
incendiary	conditioned response
typifies	recidivist
run the gamut	phobias
epilepsy	incorrigible

WRITING CLASSIFICATIONS

The purpose of writing classifications and describing objects by the use of analysis is to reduce the complexity of the subject for the reader without losing sight of the complexities of the related parts which comprise the whole. The writer's intention, therefore, is to render the complicated manageable without doing an injustice to the reality of things.

One way to ensure that justice is done to the subject at hand is to identify the principle on which the division or classification is to be based. No writer was clearer or more direct in meeting this responsibility than Julius Caesar, who began his report on the campaign in Europe with the words, "All Gaul is divided into three parts," and proceeded to describe the various tribal groups of the region. So seemingly influential has Caesar's approach been that many writers still choose a tripartite division of their subject, as though that is the most natural arrangement, without considering the genuine possibility of another.

Just as there is no natural reason for a three-part division of a subject, there is no one, self-evident principle on the basis of which to organize a discussion. Julius Caesar emphasized the peoples of the region because it was with them, their way of life, and their methods of combat that he, as a military leader, was naturally concerned. Someone setting out to describe Canada today would not find that principle of organization a natural one but would have to consider seriously such matters as geography and climate on the basis of which to construct an account. Indeed Canada is ordinarily separated into regions (the Maritimes, Central Canada, the Prairies, etc.) because of the importance of geography and climate to the way Canadians live.

Consider what needs to happen when a writer sets out to deal with a less ambitious subject — types of teachers. First the writer assesses the potential complications by counting the number of teachers encountered in more than a dozen years of school and recalling in some detail as many as come easily to mind. Then the writer ranges back over the impressions the teachers have left of themselves. Only now have the raw materials for the description been brought to the surface. At this point the writer needs to be clear about the purpose of the description. Is the writer interested in communicating insights about teaching styles to readers who themselves are teachers? Then styles of teaching will be the organizing principle. If the writer is concerned with the influences teachers have had on the writer personally, then the organizing principle will at first work to sort the influential teachers from the less-than-influential ones and only then to distinguish the various ways in which teachers have affected the writer.

A description which proceeds on the basis of simple analysis, too, may be organized in a number of ways from among which the writer must choose. In describing a cement mixer, for instance, the writer may decide to approach the job from the standpoint of the mixer's function and to separate it into, say, barrel, frame, and drive assembly. But a writer interested in the maintenance of cement mixers will likely choose a somewhat different principle of analysis, concentrating on parts which require different kinds of upkeep such as painting, oiling, and simple cleaning.

SUGGESTIONS FOR WRITING

Some of the topics suggested here are intended to be treated using a principle of division and others by developing a system of classes. You need to know why a particular principle suggests itself and to make the principle, and the reasons for choosing it, clear to the reader. It is sometimes helpful to illustrate your description to help the reader visualize your arrangement of things.

1. The parts of an office stapler
2. The parts of a light bulb
3. The parts of a bicycle
4. The parts of a rocking chair
5. The parts of a dictionary entry
6. Types of lending institutions
7. Types of fishing reels
8. Types of cooking or cuisine
9. Types of immigrants to Canada
10. Types of dogs.

CHAPTER FIVE
EXAMPLES

INTRODUCTION

During the late war in Vietnam the American military periodically released to the news media something called a "body count" (i.e., the number of fatal casualties suffered by the enemy), but television viewers eventually became inured to these reports, perhaps because the body counts resembled, as nothing else, football scores. However the reality of the war was eventually brought directly home to television viewers when the news networks carried, among other reports, footage showing the chief of the South Vietnamese secret police firing a pistol shot into the brain of a bound prisoner who, of course, collapsed and died in the street. The difference between the two media presentations is precisely the difference between presenting ideas and information in terms of abstractions or generalizations ("body counts") and presenting them as concrete realities, and the effect is as different. What is the difference, for example, between reading that the local unemployment rate stands at nine per cent (seasonally adjusted) and reading an account of what happens to someone who has been without work for eleven months and expects that shortly unemployment insurance payments will stop?

Examples, illustrations, anecdotes, and individual cases give abstractions and generalizations concrete shape because they are capable of portraying an abstraction or generalization in imaginable terms. The reader is then literally able to form an image and will say, "Oh, now I see what that means." An example permits the reader to observe an abstraction walking, talking, and doing things. Abstractions and generalizations are very useful for making assertions about types and groups of objects. The volume of spheres is expressed as $4/3 \pi r^3$, and we may want to make generalizations such as, "Social influences encourage women to enter a

156

restricted number of female-oriented occupations and to avoid partici-
pation in conventionally male-oriented occupations." However, very
often, to gain an appreciation of their meaning, people demand that
those abstractions or generalizations be brought down to earth so that
people can see what they mean.

For an example to do its work it must fit. It must be typical of the
individual cases which are gathered up and given expression by the
generalization. To be typical the example must capture the essential,
representative features of those individual objects organized as abstractions or generalizations. For a number of reasons Wayne Gretzky is not a
typical hockey player, and therefore an account of his career, his success, his salary, and his good works, does not serve to illustrate what
happens to people who set out to make a career in professional sport.
Generally speaking, exceptional cases do not serve as effective or relevant examples.

Sometimes a writer will construct or invent an example, as distinct
from selecting and citing an example, because of the importance of
providing a particularly relevant, typical instance. Such an example is
called a hypothetical example. The writer invites the reader to make a
common assumption, to share a hypothesis, for the sake of illustrating
an idea ("Imagine if you will. . . . "). The value of a hypothetical example
is that the writer and the reader can focus on the relevant details and
can avoid getting bogged down or distracted by the less-than-relevant
specifics of a particular real case. This is especially desirable when the
writer sets out to deal with potentially complex ideas or circumstances.

Examples are stories, or narratives, and, as is the case with stories,
there are long examples and short ones. Long, or extended, examples
are most obviously narratives (as the Herriot selection suggests). But
even examples which are introduced in passing are stories too, for when
a writer can assume the reader's familiarity with a particular instance, it
is convenient for both parties that the writer do so. The writer need not
explain the already familiar, and the reader need not read through a
rehash of old information. The writer needs only to mention an example
before proceeding to the next idea, and therefore these examples in
passing, while very short, are stories "just between us," as the writer and
the reader implicitly agree.

When a writer multiplies examples and instances of a potentially
disputatious point, the effect is to change the explanatory examples into
bits of evidence which support a point of view. In this sort of situation
the writer may not really be playing fair because what is initially presented as an explanation, somewhere along the line slips into argumen-
tation and persuasion. One good, typical example – real or hypothetical
– will usually serve to illustrate. Besides, the vividness of a strong
example has its own persuasive edge. It is only when a subject has
several aspects which the writer wants to manage that an array of
examples is necessary.

The Peter Principle
Laurence J. Peter and Raymond Hull

The Peter Principle has become almost as famous as that other principle of management, Murphy's Law. Here is its original formulation.

1   When I was a boy I was taught that the men upstairs knew what they were doing. I was told, "Peter, the more you know, the further you go." So I stayed in school until I graduated from college and then went forth into the world clutching firmly these ideas and my new teaching certificate. During the first year of teaching I was upset to find that a number of teachers, school principals, supervisors and superintendents appeared to be unaware of their professional responsibilities and incompetent in executing their duties. For example my principal's main concerns were that all window shades be at the same level, that classrooms should be quiet and that no one step on or near the rose beds. The superintendent's main concerns were that no minority group, no matter how fanatical, should ever be offended and that all official forms be submitted on time. The children's education appeared farthest from the administrator mind.

2   At first I thought this was a special weakness of the school system in which I taught so I applied for certification in another province. I filled out the special forms, enclosed the required documents and complied willingly with all the red tape. Several weeks later, back came my application and all the documents!

3   No, there was nothing wrong with my credentials; the forms were correctly filled out; an official departmental stamp showed that they had been received in good order. But an accompanying letter said, "The new regulations require that such forms cannot be accepted by the Department of Education unless they have been registered at the Post Office to ensure safe delivery. Will you please remail the forms to the Department, making sure to register them this time?"

4   I began to suspect that the local school system did not have a monopoly on incompetence.

5   As I looked further afield, I saw that every organization contained a number of persons who could not do their jobs.

A Universal Phenomenon

Occupational incompetence is everywhere. Have you noticed it?   *6*
Probably we all have noticed it.

We see indecisive politicians posing as resolute statesmen and   *7*
the "authoritative source" who blames his misinformation on
"situational imponderables." Limitless are the public servants who
are indolent and insolent; military commanders whose behavioral
timidity belies their dreadnaught rhetoric, and governors whose
innate servility prevents their actually governing. In our sophistication, we virtually shrug aside the immoral cleric, corrupt judge,
incoherent attorney, author who cannot write and English teacher
who cannot spell. At universities we see proclamations authored
by administrators whose own office communications are hopelessly
muddled; and droning lectures from inaudible or incomprehensi-
ble instructors.

Seeing incompetence at all levels of every hierarchy – political,   *8*
legal, educational and industrial – I hypothesized that the cause
was some inherent feature of the rules governing the placement of
employees. Thus began my serious study of the ways in which
employees move upward through a hierarchy, and of what happens
to them after promotion.

For my scientific data hundreds of case histories were collected.   *9*
Here are three typical examples.

Municipal Government File, Case No. 17

J. S. Minion was a maintenance foreman in the public works depart-   *10*
ment of Excelsior City. He was a favorite of the senior officials at
City Hall. They all praised his unfailing affability.

"I like Minion," said the superintendent of works. "He has good   *11*
judgment and is always pleasant and agreeable."

This behavior was appropriate for Minion's position: he was not   *12*
supposed to make policy, so he had no need to disagree with his
superiors.

The superintendent of works retired and Minion succeeded him.   *13*
Minion continued to agree with everyone. He passed to his foreman every suggestion that came from above. The resulting con-
flicts in policy, and the continual changing of plans, soon de-
moralized the department. Complaints poured in from the Mayor
and other officials, from taxpayers and from the maintenance-
workers' union.

Minion still says "Yes" to everyone, and carries messages briskly   *14* back and forth between his superiors and his subordinates. Nominally a superintendent, he actually does the work of a messenger. The maintenance department regularly exceeds its budget, yet fails to fulfill its program of work. In short, Minion, a competent foreman, became an incompetent superintendent.

Service Industries File, Case No. 3

15   E. Tinker was exceptionally zealous and intelligent as an apprentice at G. Reece Auto Repair Inc., and soon rose to journeyman mechanic. In this job he showed outstanding ability in diagnosing obscure faults, and endless patience in correcting them. He was promoted to foreman of the repair shop.

16   But here his love of things mechanical and his perfectionism become liabilities. He will undertake any job that he thinks looks interesting, no matter how busy the shop may be. "We'll work it in somehow," he says.

17   He will not let a job go until he is fully satisfied with it.

18   He meddles constantly. He is seldom to be found at his desk. He is usually up to his elbows in a dismantled motor and while the man who should be doing the work stands watching, other workmen sit around waiting to be assigned new tasks. As a result the shop is always overcrowded with work, always in a muddle, and delivery times are often missed.

19   Tinker cannot understand that the average customer cares little about perfection – he wants his car back on time! He cannot understand that most of his men are less interested in motors than in their pay checks. So Tinker cannot get on with his customers or with his subordinates. He was a competent mechanic, but is now an incompetent foreman.

Military File, Case No. 8

20   Consider the case of the late renowned General A. Goodwin. His hearty, informal manner, his racy style of speech, his scorn for petty regulations and his undoubted personal bravery made him the idol of his men. He led them to many well-deserved victories.

21   When Goodwin was promoted to field marshal he had to deal, not with ordinary soldiers, but with politicians and allied generalissimos.

22   He would not conform to the necessary protocol. He could not turn his tongue to the conventional courtesies and flatteries. He quarreled with all the dignitaries and took to lying for days at a time, drunk and sulking, in his trailer. The conduct of the war slipped out of his hands into those of his subordinates. He had been promoted to a position that he was incompetent to fill.

An Important Clue!

In time I saw that all such cases had a common feature. The *23* employee had been promoted from a position of competence to a position of incompetence. I saw that, sooner or later, this could happen to every employee in every hierarchy.

Hypothetical Case File, Case No. 1

Suppose you own a pill-rolling factory, Perfect Pill Incorporated. *24* Your foreman-pill roller dies of a perforated ulcer. You need a replacement. You naturally look among your rank-and-file pill rollers.

Miss Oval, Mrs. Cylinder, Mr. Ellipse and Mr. Cube all show *25* various degrees of incompetence. They will naturally be ineligible for promotion. You will choose – other things being equal – your most competent pill roller, Mr. Sphere, and promote him to foreman.

Now suppose Mr. Sphere proves competent as foreman. Later, *26* when your general foreman, Legree, moves up to Works Manager, Sphere will be eligible to take his place.

If, on the other hand, Sphere is an incompetent foreman, he will *27* get no more promotion. He has reached what I call his "level of incompetence." He will stay there till the end of his career.

Some employees, like Ellipse and Cube, reach a level of incompe- *28* tence in the lowest grade and are never promoted. Some, like Sphere (assuming he is not a satisfactory foreman), reach it after one promotion.

E. Tinker, the automobile repair-shop foreman, reached his level *29* of incompetence on the third stage of the hierarchy. General Goodwin reached his level of incompetence at the very top of the hierarchy.

So my analysis of hundreds of cases of occupational incompe- *30* tence led me on to formulate *The Peter Principle*:

**In a Hierarchy Every Employee Tends
to Rise to His Level of Incompetence**

A New Science!

Having formulated the Principle, I discovered that I had inadvertently *31* founded a new science, hierarchiology, the study of hierarchies.

32   The term "hierarchy" was originally used to describe the system of church government by priests graded into ranks. The contemporary meaning includes any organization whose members or employees are arranged in order of rank, grade or class.

33   Hierarchiology, although a relatively recent discipline, appears to have great applicability to the fields of public and private administration.

This Means You!

34   My Principle is the key to an understanding of all hierarchal systems, and therefore to an understanding of the whole structure of civilization. A few eccentrics try to avoid getting involved with hierarchies, but everyone in business, industry, trade-unionism, politics, government, the armed forces, religion and education is so involved. All of them are controlled by the Peter Principle.

35   Many of them, to be sure, may win a promotion or two, moving from one level of competence to a higher level of competence. But competence in that new position qualifies them for still another promotion. For each individual, for *you*, for *me*, the final promotion is from a level of competence to a level of incompetence.

36   So, given enough time — and assuming the existence of enough ranks in the hierarchy — each employee rises to, and remains at, his level of incompetence. Peter's Corollary states:

In time, every post tends to be occupied by an employee who is incompetent to carry out its duties.

Who Turns the Wheels?

37   You will rarely find, of course, a system in which *every* employee has reached his level of incompetence. In most instances, something is being done to further the ostensible purposes for which the hierarchy exists.

38   *Work is accomplished by those employees who have not yet reached their level of incompetence.*

The Peter Principle   163

QUESTIONS

Language and Style

1. How would you characterize the narrator's tone here? Why is the tone appropriate to one who makes an accidental discovery?

2. What, superficially at least, gives a sense of the scientific to the discussion?

3. By contrast, what is playful about the discussion? Can you cite instances?

4. Why should it be that the examples have a way of becoming persuasive (rather than explanatory)? In what sense is *any* clear presentation persuasive?

5. Identify some instances of word play. What contribution to the tone of the discussion is made by the word play?

6. By what means does the writer suggest that the reader has always known, but perhaps not realized, that what the writer says is true?

Organization

1. How many examples, and of what kind, does Peter use in this essay?

Content

1. What makes the examples used in this essay typical? Why should a particular hypothetical example be used in place of a "more real" one? What advantage does a hypothetical example have for the writer?

Vocabulary

indolent	insolent
dreadnaught	innate
servility	hierarchy
hypothesized	inherent
affability	generalissimo
protocol	perforated
inadvertently	corollary
ostensible	eccentrics

It Shouldn't Happen to a Vet
James Herriot

*James Herriot's recollections of Yorkshire England, where for many years he practised as a veterinarian, were produced by the BBC as a very popular television series (*All Things Bright And Beautiful*). Here is a sample of Herriot's charming memoirs.*

1   The longer I worked in Darrowby the more the charms of the Dales beguiled me. And there was one solid advantage of which I became more aware every day – the Dales farmers were all stocksmen. They really knew how to handle animals, and to a vet whose patients are constantly trying to thwart him or injure him it was a particular blessing.

2   So this morning I looked with satisfaction at the two men holding the cow. It wasn't a difficult job – just an intravenous injection of magnesium lactate – but still it was reassuring to have two such sturdy fellows to help me. Maurice Bennison, medium sized but as tough as one of his own hill beasts, had a horn in his right hand while the fingers of his left gripped the nose; I had the comfortable impression that the cow wouldn't jump very far when I pushed the needle in. His brother George whose job it was to raise the vein, held the choke rope limply in enormous hands like bunches of carrots. He grinned down at me amiably from his six feet four inches.

3   "Right, George," I said. "Tighten up that rope and lean against the cow to stop her coming round on me." I pushed my way between the cow and her neighbour, past George's unyielding bulk and bent over the jugular vein. It was standing out very nicely. I poised the needle, feeling the big man's elbow on me as he peered over my shoulder, and thrust quickly into the vein.

4   "Lovely!" I cried as the dark blood fountained out and spattered thickly on the straw bedding beneath. "Slacken your rope, George." I fumbled in my pocket for the flutter valve. "And for God's sake, get your weight off me!"

5   Because George had apparently decided to rest his full fourteen stones on me instead of the cow, and as I tried desperately to connect the tube to the needle, I felt my knees giving way. I shouted again, despairingly, but he was inert, his chin resting on my shoulder, his breathing stertorous in my ear.

6   There could only be one end to it. I fell flat on my face and lay

From It Shouldn't Happen to a Vet *by James Herriot, 1972. Published by Michael Joseph Ltd. Reprinted by permission.*

there writhing under the motionless body. My cries went unheeded; George was unconscious.

Mr. Bennison, attracted by the commotion, came in to the byre just in time to see me crawling out from beneath his eldest son. "Get him out, quick!" I gasped, "before the cows trample on him." Wordlessly, Maurice and his father took an ankle apiece and hauled away in unison. George shot out from under the cows, his head beating a brisk tattoo on the cobbles, traversed the dung channel, then resumed his sleep on the byre floor.   7

Mr. Bennison moved back to the cow and waited for me to continue with my injection but I found the presence of the sprawled body distracting. "Look, couldn't we sit him up against the wall and put his head between his legs?" I suggested apologetically. The others glanced at each other then, as though deciding to humour me grabbed George's shoulders and trundled him over the floor with the expertise of men used to throwing around bags of fertilizer and potatoes. But even propped against the rough stones, his head slumped forward and his great long arms hanging loosely, the poor fellow still didn't look so good.   8

I couldn't help feeling a bit responsible. "Don't you think we might give him a drink?"   9

But Mr. Bennison had had enough. "Nay, nay, he'll be right," he muttered testily. "Let's get on with t'job." Evidently he felt he had pampered George too much already.   10

The incident started me thinking about this question of people's reactions to the sight of blood and other disturbing realities. Even though it was only my second year of practice I had already formulated certain rules about this and one was that it was always the biggest men who went down. (I had, by this time, worked out a few other, perhaps unscientific theories, e.g. big dogs were kept by people who lived in little houses and vice versa. Clients who said "spare no expense" never paid their bills, ever. When I asked my way in the Dales and was told "you can't miss it," I knew I'd soon be hopelessly lost.)   11

I had begun to wonder if perhaps country folk, despite their closer contact with fundamental things, were perhaps more susceptible than city people. Ever since Sid Blenkhorn had staggered into Skeldale House one evening. His face was ghastly white and he had obviously passed through a shattering experience. "Have you got a drop o' whisky handy, Jim?" he quavered, and when I had guided him to a chair and Siegfried had put a glass in his hand he told us he had been at a first aid lecture given by Dr. Allinson, a few doors down the street. "He was talking about veins and arteries and things," groaned Sid, passing a hand across his forehead. "God, it was awful!" Apparently Fred Ellison the fishmonger had been carried out unconscious after only ten minutes and Sid himself had only just made it to the door. It had been a shambles.   12

13   I was interested because this sort of thing, I had found, was always just round the corner. I suppose we must have more trouble in this way than the doctors because in most cases when our medical colleagues have any cutting or carving to do they send their patients to hospital while the vets just have to get their jackets off and operate on the spot. It means that the owners and attendants of the animals are pulled in as helpers and are subjected to some unusual sights.

14   So, even in my short experience, I had become a fair authority on the various manifestations of "coming over queer." I suppose it was a bit early to start compiling statistics but I had never seen a woman or a little man pass out even though they might exhibit various shadings of the squeamish spectrum. The big chap was the best bet every time, especially the boisterous, super-confident type.

15   I have a vivid recollection of a summer evening when I had to carry out a rumenotomy on a cow. As a rule I was inclined to play for time when I suspected a foreign body — there were so many other conditions with similar symptoms that I was never in a hurry to make a hole in the animal's side. But this time diagnosis was easy; the sudden fall in milk yield, loss of cudding; grunting, and the rigid, sunken-eyed appearance of the cow. And to clinch it the farmer told me he had been repairing a hen house in the cow pasture — nailing up loose boards. I knew where one of the nails had gone.

16   The farm, right on the main street of the village, was a favourite meeting place for the local lads. As I laid out my instruments on a clean towel draped over a straw bale a row of grinning faces watched from above the half door of the box; not only watched but encouraged me with ribald shouts. When I was about ready to start it occurred to me that an extra pair of hands would be helpful and I turned to the door. "How would one of you lads like to be my assistant?" There was even more shouting for a minute or two, then the door was opened and a huge young man with a shock of red hair ambled into the box; he was a magnificent sight with his vast shoulders and the column of sunburned neck rising from the open shirt. It needed only the bright blue eyes and the ruddy, high-cheekboned face to remind me that the Norsemen had been around the Dales a thousand years ago. This was a Viking.

17   I had him roll up his sleeves and scrub his hands in a bucket of warm water and antiseptic while I infiltrated the cow's flank with local anaesthetic. When I gave him artery forceps and scissors to hold he pranced around, making stabbing motions at the cow and roaring with laughter.

18   "Maybe you'd like to do the job yourself?" I asked. The Viking squared his great shoulders. "Aye, I'll 'ave a go," and the heads above the door cheered lustily.

As I finally poised my Bard Parker scalpel with its new razor-   *19*
sharp blade over the cow, the air was thick with earthy witticisms. I
had decided that this time I really would make the bold incision
recommended in the surgery books; it was about time I advanced
beyond the stage of pecking nervously at the skin. "A veritable
blow," was how one learned author had described it. Well, that was
how it was going to be.

I touched the blade down on the clipped area of the flank and   *20*
with a quick motion of the wrist laid open a ten-inch wound. I
stood back for a few seconds admiring the clean-cut edges of the
skin with only a few capillaries spurting on to the glistening,
twitching abdominal muscles. At the same time I noticed that the
laughter and shouting from the heads had been switched off and
was replaced by an eerie silence broken only by a heavy, thudding
sound from behind me.

"Forceps please," I said, extending my hand back. But nothing   *21*
happened. I looked round; the top of the half door was bare – not a
head in sight. There was only the Viking spreadeagled in the
middle of the floor, arms and legs flung wide, chin pointing to the
roof. The attitude was so theatrical that I thought he was still
acting the fool, but a closer examination erased all doubts: the
Viking was out cold. He must have gone straight over backwards
like a stricken oak.

The farmer, a bent little man who couldn't have scaled much   *22*
more than eight stones, had been steadying the cow's head. He
looked at me with the faintest flicker of amusement in his eyes.
"Looks like you and me for it, then, guvnor." He tied the halter to a
ring on the wall, washed his hands methodically and took up his
place at my side. Throughout the operation, he passed me my
instruments, swabbed away the seeping blood and clipped the
sutures, whistling tunelessly through his teeth in a bored manner;
the only time he showed any real emotion was when I produced
the offending nail from the depths of the reticulum. He raised his
eyebrows slightly, said "'ello, 'ello," then started whistling again.

We were too busy to do anything for the Viking. Halfway through,   *23*
he sat up, shook himself a few times then got to his feet and
strolled with elaborate nonchalance out of the box. The poor
fellow seemed to be hoping that perhaps we had noticed nothing
unusual.

I don't suppose we could have done much to bring him round   *24*
anyway. There was only one time I discovered a means of immediate resuscitation and that was by accident.

It was when Henry Dickson asked me to show him how to   *25*
castrate a ruptured pig without leaving a swelling. Henry was going
in for pigs in a big way and had a burning ambition to equip himself
with veterinary skills.

When he showed me the young pig with the gross scrotal swell-   *26* ing I demurred. "I really think this is a vet's job, Henry. Castrate your normal pigs by all means but I don't think you could make a proper job of this sort of thing."

27   "How's that, then?"

28   "Well, there's the local anaesthetic, danger of infection – and you really need a knowledge of anatomy to know what you're doing."

29   All the frustrated surgeon in Henry showed in his eyes. "Gaw, I'd like to know how to do it."

30   "I'll tell you what," I said. "How about if I do this one as a demonstration and you can make up your own mind. I'll give him a general anaesthetic so you don't have to hold him."

31   "Right, that's a good idea." Henry thought for a moment. "What'll you charge me to do 'im?"

32   "Seven and six."

33   "Well I suppose you have to have your pound of flesh. Get on."

34   I injected a few cc's of Nembutal into the little pig's peritoneum and after some staggering he rolled over in the straw and lay still. Henry had rigged up a table in the yard and we laid the sleeping animal on it. I was preparing to start when Henry pulled out a ten-shilling note.

35   "Better pay you now before I forget."

36   "All right, but my hands are clean now – push it into my pocket and I'll give you the change when we finish."

37   I rather fancy myself as a teacher and soon warmed to my task. I carefully incised the skin over the inguinal canal and pulled out the testicle, intact in its tunics. "See there, Henry, the bowels have come down the canal and are lying in with the testicle." I pointed to the loops of intestine, pale pink through the translucent membranes. "Now if I do this, I can push them right back into the abdomen, and if I press here, out they pop again. You see how it works? There, they've gone; now they're out again. Once more I make them disappear and whoops, there they are back with us! Now in order to retain them permanently in the abdomen I take the spermatic cord and wind it in its coverings tightly down to the . . . "

38   But my audience was no longer with me. Henry had sunk down on an upturned oil drum and lay slumped across the table, his head cradled on his arms. My disappointment was acute, and finishing off the job and inserting the sutures was a sad anticlimax with my student slumbering at the end of the table.

39   I put the pig back in his pen and gathered up my gear: then I remembered I hadn't given Henry his change. I don't know why I did it but instead of half-a-crown, I slapped down a shilling and sixpence on the wood a few inches from his face. The noise made him open his eyes and he gazed dully at the coins for a few seconds, then with almost frightening suddenness he snapped upright, ashenfaced but alert and glaring.

40   "Hey!" he shouted. "I want another shillin'!"

QUESTIONS

Language and Style

1. It is characteristic of Herriot's narrator that he is an "innocent." Can you explain how this "innocence" is suggested to a reader? How does it work to set the tone of the narrative? How often is the narrator surprised?

2. What gives the narrator a licence to exaggerate? In what sense does exaggeration make the account "truer"?

3. Herriot pays a great deal of attention to details. What details are especially emphasized? Why are they emphasized?

4. What particulars of the narration create the impression that the writer's actual experience is the origin of this account? What makes it so vivid?

5. What words and expressions might seem unusual to North American readers? Is this a problem?

6. Why should Herriot describe one of the "local lads" as a "Viking"? What does Herriot achieve by describing the talk of his audience as "thick with earthy witticisms"?

Organization

1. At the beginning of the eleventh paragraph Herriot's account makes a transition which is similar to one in Peter's essay. Explain.

2. What is the general principle that Herriot is interested in illustrating? Why might it be easy to lose track of that main idea in the course of Herriot's discussion? Is there a sense in which the main idea is presented *in order* to tell the story?

Vocabulary

beguiled	thwart
intravenous	stones
stertorous	byre
cobbles	rumenotomy
cudding	ribald
Norsemen	forceps
witticisms	capillaries
reticulum	nonchalance
peritoneum	incised
inguinal	translucent
shilling	

A Place in the Sun
Debra Black

Much of the persuasiveness of this article from Canadian Business *comes from the details included in Black's examples.*

1   The entrepreneurs have always known it, but now the economists have discovered it, too. People who run small businesses are the real heroes of the Canadian economy. In 1979, for instance, the small-business sector racked up sales of more than $120 billion, which amounted to 30 per cent of the gross national product. With unemployment at record levels, the small-business sector created 100 per cent of all new jobs in Canada between 1975 and 1982. That's right: all of them.

2   Impressive as those numbers are, we don't for one minute believe that the 150,000 people who go into business for themselves every year in Canada are motivated mainly by public-spiritedness. And it probably doesn't have much to do with greed, either. Most people do it because they want to run things. They are, at heart, lousy employees. No one says it's easy. In fact, about 60 per cent of all new businesses fail in their first year of operation. The reasons are easy to figure out: too much inventory; too little capital; poor markets or failure to know your markets, to name just a few. The good news? Of those 150,000 start-ups, 60,000 or so do survive their first birthdays. Some of them even grow up to become big businesses.

3   If you dream of self-employment, there are several steps you can take to make sure you wind up among the winners. . . . Who knows? You might even get rich. And even if you don't, you can consider yourself a capitalist hero. . . .

4   The neighborhood dress shop loaded with chic Parisian haute couture and the local New York-style restaurant dripping with brass both look like the hottest of hot prospects. Look again. Only a thorough investigation would reveal that the haute couture is really yesterday's fashion and that the polished brass hides a kitchen that's on the Public Health Department's hit list.

5   Before you put down your hard-earned, often borrowed dollars, you should remember one important rule: no one's going to tell you that his business is a dud. Seems obvious, doesn't it? Well, you'd be surprised at the number of people who will slap down the cash without finding out what, exactly, they're buying.

6   Let's use the case of one Toronto businessman who did it right

From Canadian Business *(May 1984). Reprinted by permission of the author.*

as our guiding light. Before he acquired a small plastics manufacturing company with no debt and sales of $10 million, he ran a
thorough investigation. He checked the company's financial statements, accounts receivable and inventory. He assessed the company's hard assets. He talked to customers, suppliers and former
employees. He got a full picture before he put his money on the
table.

What our 53-year-old former executive established was that the   7
owner, who was close to 70, wanted to retire, but didn't want to sell
the company to any of his competitors. No scary skeletons in the
closet there. Then he went on to establish the financial health of
the firm. He hired an accountant for a fee of $7,000. He and the
accountant went over the financial statements of the company,
checking for discrepancies. They examined the firm's accounts
receivable, its income projections and assets. They found that the
company was making a marginal profit of only $60,000 per year
because the manufacturing plant was working at only 25 per cent
capacity. The two of them also established the value of the company's "hard assets" – the machinery, building, inventory and so
on – at $2 million.

The next step for our prospective purchaser was to talk to   8
suppliers, customers and ex-employees of the firm. During this
investigation, he found that one of the problems of the company
had been a lack of sales and marketing expertise – not an insur-
mountable difficulty.

Next he turned to the business evaluation department of his   9
accountant's firm to help him come up with a viable offer. This
department suggested that, based on the profits and the value of
the company's hard assets, the offer should be made at $1.8 mil-
lion. This would still leave him some negotiating room. By the time
the deal closed, the final sale price was $2 million. Last month he
was offered $9 million by a U.S. competitor.

Sadly, there are hundreds of examples of small-business people   10
who didn't do the necessary legwork, only to be horrified months
after the deal closed. Donald Hunter, a partner in the small-business
division of Price Waterhouse, chartered accountants, points to the
example of one Toronto businessman. After a few months in business, this man found that about 30 per cent of his inventory, listed
as part of the assets of the company, was missing. Says Hunter:
"This really drives home the point that you must get professional
advice and make sure you have a handle on what you're buying."

Then there was the budding entrepreneur who wanted a fast   11
entry into the energy conservation game. He just as quickly lost
$20,000. What he ended up with was an electronic device that
conserved energy, all right. It's just that nobody wanted to buy it.
"He didn't really do a proper marketing survey," explains Hunter.

Whether buying a business or starting your own, Hunter says the   12 same rule applies: know your markets. Watch for the owner who tells you that his antifreeze product has worldwide appeal. If you don't know what your markets are, you can find yourself facing financial ruin.

13   There are other general principles to follow. Check the legal title of a company and find out if there are any liens on the business or back taxes owing. A call to local municipal offices might prove useful to find out whether the company is in violation of any local regulations. You should also check whether you're buying the shares of a company or the assets. The former can mean inheriting a company's liabilities and outstanding accounts payable, possibly putting the health of the business in jeopardy.

14   A smart small-business person will also call the local branch of the Better Business Bureau to help shake out those skeletons. But above all, you must get an idea of how the company is run and why it's successful. Then, says Michael Lauber, a partner at Thorne Riddell, chartered accountants, "You can determine whether you can carry it on in that way or if it's something unique to the personal style of the individual."

15   Investigating the industry is tough work, but worth it. One southern Ontario businessman who was looking at buying a toboggan manufacturing company found after investigating the industry that the company had no future. The influx of plastic toboggans on the market was bound to make the company's old-style wooden version obsolete. What looked like a fabulous business turned out to be a losing proposition. The businessman abandoned his takeover. A year later, the company went bankrupt.

16   Before making your final decision, you can also turn to the Federal Business Development Bank, which offers a variety of services to help the entrepreneur evaluate a business. Counselors at the FBDB will look at a company, evaluate its sales, profits and markets and put together a realistic forecast of revenues and expenditures. Then a counselor will offer you an opinion on whether it's a good or a bad buy.

17   Before you put your money down, establish how much you want to invest in the company and what kind of return you're counting on. "I wouldn't invest in anything that yielded me less than Canada Savings Bonds would," advises Hunter. "If the business yields a return of less than 10 per cent, you're better to put your money into CSBs." Once you have established your investment and return criteria — Hunter recommends a minimum of 15-20 per cent, depending on the business — you should stick to them and not buy anything that doesn't meet those criteria. It's simply not worth the aggravation.

18   A final caveat: *take your time*. Be prepared to look at scores — even hundreds — of deals. "The person who buys impulsively and doesn't study the situation," says Lauber, "will start getting surprises he hasn't budgeted for."

There's no guarantee that the company you settle on will be a   *19*
gem. In fact, no matter how much research you do, there's bound
to be a wart or two. But if you follow the right steps in buying your
business – and develop a business plan once you've acquired it –
your investment can pay off handsomely.

The newspaper advertisement reads: "Failing Retail Business for   *20*
Sale. Cheap. Great Potential. Reason for Sale: Overleveraging." Your
interest is piqued. The business looks like a turkey, but you're
convinced that under your guidance, it could be transformed into a
golden eagle. You could be right. Every year thousands of failing
businesses are turned around, reaping substantial profits for the
turnaround artist.

Scooping up one of the 10,260 businesses that failed in 1983 at a   *21*
bargain basement price is an attractive proposition. You could,
however, end up in the basement faster than the previous owner.
Take some advice and isolate the reasons for the company's sale.
Find out if the company's tumble into the cellar was prompted by
undercapitalization, high interest rates, poor management or a
lack of markets. One Manitoba businessman who was looking at
buying a nursery discovered after a little checking that the markets
for the company had all but disappeared. No amount of financial
wizardry could make this company a profitable venture.

But some failing companies can be made profitable. Another   *22*
businessman who acquired a foundering retail store realized that
the problem with the business had been a lack of merchandising
expertise. It seemed the previous owner had stocked the store to
suit his own taste, rather than market demand. "The new owner
carried products that had a better chance of selling," explains
Murray Axmith, president of Murray Axmith & Associates, a Toronto-
based management consulting firm. "He turned that business around
and added other outlets."

The reasons for business failures are not always crystal clear.   *23*
One problem should alert you to the possibility of multiple disasters. Says Donald Hunter, a partner in the small-business division
of Price Waterhouse, chartered accountants: "Often one indicative
problem, such as 'I overextended myself,' means that there may be
a lack of managerial capabilities, and that may mean other problems." Make sure you get to the bottom of the can of worms and
not just as far as the first Red Wigglers.

It's also crucial that before you sign your name to any final sales   *24*
agreement, you draw up a business plan that outlines specifically a
step-by-step recovery plan. You should determine whether you
have the expertise to change the fortunes of the company. If you
don't, and you still want to buy, make sure you bring in somebody
who can fill the gaps.

When two Toronto businessmen recently bought a small com-   *25*
pany in the service industry, they knew that bad management was
causing the company's woes. Since they already had another busi-

ness that was doing well, they believed they had the managerial skills to make the new company work. "Once they bought the firm and took over its management," says Michael Lauber, a partner at Thorne Riddell, chartered accountants, "they revitalized the company."

26   Expertise isn't enough. There's still that niggling problem of having enough capital to finance the turnaround. It's particularly important when buying a failing business that you have a substantial cushion of financing. Being able to finance a company for 48 weeks doesn't do much good if it's going to take 49 weeks to set it back on the right track.

27   Once you've isolated the reasons for a company's demise and established whether you can help change the picture, you must then continue to check out the small business as you would any other acquisition. Examine its assets and liabilities. Check the legal title, the company's financial performance and its market in the same way you would when buying a successful business.

28   Ultimately, if you can isolate the reasons for the firm's failure and can implement a solid recovery plan, odds are you can turn a company around. It won't be easy. Often only the more sophisticated business person can pull it off, say the experts. Says Michael Lauber: "It's much easier to duplicate a formula for success than bring in a new plan and turn a business around."

29   But turning a business around sure is satisfying. Profits always smell great; profits from failure smell even sweeter.

QUESTIONS

Language and Style

1. Can you identify some examples of what seems to be an intentional use of clichés and pat phrases? What purpose do they serve?

2. Where does the writer locate the reader? Why should the writer occasionally address the reader directly ("you")?

3. What are some other examples of language and tone which seem designed to appeal directly to the reader? One example occurs at the end of the first paragraph.

Organization

1. In what way does a set of rules help organize the discussion? What are the rules?

2. At what point in the discussion does the writer seem to abandon the

familiarity of an informal chat and, as it were, get down to business? Why is this change appropriate? When does the writer return to the original tone?

3. How do the cases and hypothetical examples help focus Black's more general points? How serious are these examples? How do you know?

Vocabulary

entrepreneur	chic
haute couture	discrepancies
caveat	piqued
niggling	demise

The Painful Realities of the New Technology
Rod McQueen

This comprehensive article from Saturday Night *magazine surveys the problems that the introduction of new technologies presents for Canadian industry and the people who find a livelihood there.*

The young operators sit transfixed, eyes on glowing twenty-inch   *1*
screens, oblivious of the world around. Their fingers guide fibre-optic pens and caress keyboards with the easy familiarity of high-school typing students. Yet they are developing and describing the contours of an aircraft – until recently a technique so difficult that few could master it without long training. At de Havilland Aircraft, near Toronto, twenty-year-old community college design graduates can become good junior draughtsmen in four years; such an apprenticeship once took twelve. The computer-aided design system they use, like others becoming common in Canada, has changed the work force and forever altered the way of work.

"It allows an untidy process of trial and error," says Mike Davy,   *2*
de Havilland's vice president of engineering, "using the computer at a time when a person's mind is able to grow quickly." Because the design work on de Havilland's Dash 8 commuter aircraft can be

From Saturday Night, *Annual Report on the Economy (July 1984). Reprinted by permission of the author.*

transmitted directly from the computer terminal to permanent mylar sheets and on to the manufacturing process, wasted effort is minimized and the designs achieve maximum efficiency. "The currency we have to work with is pounds weight," says Davy. "The safest plane in the world is too heavy to fly. So you design molecule by molecule because anything that is surplus must be cut off."

3   Mistakes can be found early. Inside the computer the plane makes its first test flights, under programmed simulations of stress, before it is built. As Davy says, "All our embarrassments are on paper. We can now ask: 'What's it look like?' We have had no signs of breaks yet. But I don't want to give the idea that *planes* break. Planes break privately; they break here before people pay fares to get on." In addition to giving early warnings of structural problems, the process also saves time.

4   De Havilland uses CADAM, a patented form of CAD/CAM (computer-aided design/computer-aided manufacture). Other advances in method are achieving similar change in factories across Canada. Seven years ago, robotics and CAD/CAM were all but unknown. Today they are well-known workers on the factory floor. Such advances are, depending on the spokesman, either Canada's strength – or already too late. "The issue in Canada is not simply one of catching up with the Joneses, it is surpassing them," says Roy Phillips, president of the Canadian Manufacturers' Association. "Technology is the key."

5   Between 1981 and 1983, according to the European Management Forum, Canada dropped from sixth place to eleventh among industrial nations in terms of competitiveness. And Canada ranks only fifteenth of twenty-two countries in terms of the technology-related criteria the Forum calls "innovative forward orientation." While there may be agreement that technology will lead the way in the future, there is much debate about where Canada is today. Stuart Smith, chairman of the Science Council of Canada, insists that "Canada is way behind in adapting new technology to our existing industries. In manufacturing, we are a backward nation."

6   Just how backward becomes apparent when Canada's research and development expenditures are compared with those of other industrialized countries. As a percentage of gross domestic product, according to Statistics Canada, Canadian R&D expenditure is 1.12 per cent, putting Canada well behind France (1.82), Japan (2.01), Germany (2.27), the United States (2.41), and Switzerland (2.45). Growth in R&D spending is also at the bottom of the chart. In the 1970s, annual growth averaged less than one per cent a year; Japan's was almost seven per cent. . . .

7   For more than a century, technical change meant simply that workers were replaced by machines. In this long process, working conditions generally improved, real wages rose, and employment

increased. But today there are fears that change will cost jobs; it will certainly not solve unemployment. In his book *Knights of the New Technology*, David Thomas quotes Bell-Northern Research engineer John Elliott: "There are not going to be large numbers of high-tech manufacturing jobs. I just wish the politicians would understand that. We're going through another revolution like the one in which we threw the vast majority of the population off the farm and into the city. This time we're going to move a very large segment of the population from making things to other forms of employment. I don't think we've come to grips in Canada with the fact that fewer people are going to be working for less time."

If the Canadian economy operated in a vacuum, new technology would almost automatically create wealth and thus jobs. The purchase and installation of new equipment in the first place is a creator of jobs. The second effect arises from improvement in efficiency. If, for instance, robotics is introduced in a sawmill that produces timber for new houses, the mill may be able to lower the price of timber appreciably. If this lowers the cost of new houses, it both increases the demand for houses and represents a saving to the house buyer; that saving is then spent on other goods, such as carpeting and appliances. In all of these sectors, employment is increased.   8

Changes of this kind, creating new jobs while destroying old ones, are likely to produce disruptions and considerable inconvenience, but in the long term they shouldn't − within a national economy − create structural unemployment. But international trade changes this process. If new technology is developed outside the borders of the country, and if equipment embodying the new technology (industrial robots, say) is imported, the country misses the beneficial effects of the first round though the benefits of the second round still appear. If, however, the technology is embodied in finished, imported consumer goods, the national economy misses out on both the first and a good part of the second round benefits. Then the country's only gain is the indirect effect associated with lower product prices.   9

New technology, when applied in international trade, produces a comparative advantage for the country that applies it first. In the technologically backward country, income and employment will decline. The culprit is not changing technology itself but the failure to keep up with it and use it effectively.   10

The problem is compounded by the fact that Canadian manufacturers have traditionally been slow to modernize or exploit technological advances. According to Stuart Smith, one major reason is foreign ownership of Canadian industry. "Canadian manufacturers," he says, "never were much interested in the development of new products. They just tried to make adaptations of the technology their home office was using. Many of our branch plants are not   11 modernizing." Those that do want to modernize, whether foreign-owned or Canadian-owned, don't have the cash now because it has all gone to pay off debt. Time is running out, Smith warns. He looks to business. "The lead must be with the private sector." But he adds, "The public sector must be willing to help."

12   There have been some government-spawned successes which have been turned over to the private sector. The National Research Council, for example, created the crash position indicator, a device for spotting downed aircraft. The communications research centre in the department of communications invented Telidon, the videotext system now battling British and French systems on world markets.

13   A more recent development has come from the federal department of public works. Ten years ago, worried that industry would fail to exploit the new technology in building design, the department set out to create a computer system capable of such design, including even the intricacies of heating and air conditioning duct-work. The criteria were specific: the system had to be able to reflect such factors as past weather patterns, there had to be graphics, and the price of each portable work station should not exceed $40,000. Graeme Scott of Ottawa's Bell-Northern Research invented the computer language, called "Grapple," the system would eventually use. Various firms considered it and failed to follow through, but in 1982 Cymbol Cybernetics, a consulting firm, moved into the CAD field and took the system on. It was unveiled at a Las Vegas computer show last year, and took the industry by storm.

14   While that success demonstrates government-business coopera-tion, it also sheds light on the poor opinion Canadians have of themselves in this field. "It's selling in the United States," says Douglas Hartt, director-general at Public Works. "It's the old story – we can now go to people and say the Americans bought it." Even in his own department, Hartt finds that people say "Who's bought it?" He replies, "The Americans bought it." Suddenly there's more interest. "Oh, the Americans bought it," goes the reply, "well it must be as good as IBM." Sighs Hartt, "It'll drive you nuts."

15   One customer for the system could be Douglas Cardinal, the architect who is designing the new National Museum of Man in Ottawa. Cardinal's first major project was St. Mary's Church in Red Deer, Alberta. Its sweeping brick lines have been compared both to the protective cloak of the Virgin Mary and to the skins of a prairie teepee rippling in the breeze. The design was done by computer. The roof alone required 81,000 simultaneous calculations. "It would have taken seven men working a hundred years to calculate it," Cardinal points out. "The computer did it in hours."

16   Not every government move has been so productive as the one that led to Cymbol Cybernetics. There is, for example, the sad tale

of UTEC, a full-scale prototype of a computer developed at the University of Toronto. Some still believe that it could have put Canada in the forefront of big computers had the university and its sponsor, the federal government, paid for further development. Instead, in 1952, they bought a made-in-England Ferranti computer and scrapped the Canadian project.

Stuart Smith believes that a history of importing foreign technol-   *17*
ogy has left Canada with too few risk-takers. "There's far too much foreign ownership in our economy," he says, "but we can't afford to buy them out and I don't think we can afford to kick them out. Therefore, we've got to live with them. We've got to get into new industries that are high risk, but the big capital is staying away. Only the government is left to fill the vacuum – and governments do it badly. We end up with Canadairs."

Ken Jones is president of the Ontario Centre for Advanced Manu-   *18*
facturing. His background includes six years as chairman and president of Standard Modern Tool. He oversees the robotics and two of the six CAD/CAM technology centres established by the Ontario government in 1983 to advise industry and provide assistance in technology application. His opinion of Canada's technical situation is blunt. "We're heavy net importers. We're using somebody else's equipment. On average, we're behind in the extent of application by three or four years."

The reason, says Jones, is the inherent conservatism of Canadi-   *19*
ans. "We don't bat an eye about major resource investments, but in manufacturing we tend to be a little more conservative than the Japanese or the Americans. We have a penchant for running to the government for help. It's part of our national psyche." For him, technological change is essential unless governments erect protectionist trade barriers and let the standard of living fall. "We compete, or else we live by selling our resources."

Conservative tendencies notwithstanding, a few technological   *20*
giants, such as Northern Telecom, do operate in Canada. With twenty-seven plants and annual revenues of more than $3 billion, Northern Telecom is the country's largest manufacturer of telecommunications equipment. In 1982, it launched its most ambitious product development programme ever, OPEN World. The firm will spend $1.2 billion on new products, enhancements, and services in the first five years. During that time, new revenue is expected to reach $13 billion.

In addition, many smaller firms are entering the arena. While   *21*
most are based in Ontario, Saskatoon and Burnaby are emerging as growth centres. In Saskatoon, Develcon Electronics, founded in 1974, produces the Dataswitch, a device that can make up to 2,000 computer connections to a central computer. Each Dataswitch is worth $30,000 to $100,000, and most of the market is outside

Canada — two thirds of sales are in the U.S. Similar success has come to Imapro, in Charlottetown. There, company founder and president Fred Andreone came up with some unique technology capable of converting computer-generated information from digital form into full-colour images of excellent photographic quality.

22   The largest concentration of high-tech innovators is in the so-called Silicon Valley North area near Ottawa. Forty advanced-technology companies are located in suburban Kanata, and 350 more are clustered within the region. Ninety per cent are Canadian-owned. They have located there partly because of federal government influence, but mostly because Ottawa's Bell-Northern Research laboratories have, for the last twenty years, spun off a multitude of products, engineers, and entrepreneurs. A partial list of Canada's high-tech hot-shots would include:

· Bytec-Comterm, of Montreal, producers of the Hyperion portable computer;

· Gandalf Technologies, of Nepean, Ontario, inventors of the Gandalf box, which is used to transmit computer data over local telephone lines;

· Linear Technology, of Burlington, Ontario; half of the world's 2.6 million hearing aids are based on LTI's technology;

· Lumonics, of Kanata, manufacturers of industrial, scientific, and medical lasers, now the world's third-largest laser maker;

· Mitel, of Kanata, maker of telecommunications equipment and large-scale integrated circuits;

· Nabu, of Ottawa, which produces systems linking home computers to cable television networks;

· Orcatech, of Ottawa, which makes graphic computer systems;

· Spar Aerospace, of Toronto, whose products include the celebrated Canadarm;

· Sydney Development, of Vancouver, which makes micro software programs.

23   In many cases, such companies have depended upon a single entrepreneur and one new product for initial success. For the country as a whole, however, and the manufacturing sector in particular, broader responses are required. The two most promising are robotics and CAD/CAM. In simplest terms, CAD/CAM is to the design engineer or draughtsman what the word processor is to the typist — both a productivity tool and a creative force. It's the system that's letting twenty-year-olds learn airplane design at de Havilland. According to the U.S. National Science Foundation, "CAD/CAM has more potential to improve productivity than any technological development since electricity."

24   CAD/CAM allows a design engineer to use a special computer input device, rather than a lead pencil, to "draw" on a monitor screen and get geometry into the computer. Both configuration and dimensions can be changed instantly as the designer, in effect,

creates a model on the screen that precisely represents the product – either as a wire-frame rendering or as a solid three-dimensional model. Once the model is in the computer, the operator performs functions that would be impossible on paper. The model can, for example, be rotated to permit viewing from any angle; parts of the image can be magnified up to 1,000 times in order to view detail; stress can be calculated; data can be transferred to plotters or printers so that drawings can be produced. The CAM half comes into play later, when the data base created by the design engineer is fed by the computer to a production machine or manufacturing system, which in turn makes the finished product.

The Japanese are leading in the application of CAD/CAM technology. Of all the CAD/CAM systems installed in the world in 1982, Japan installed more than half. Ironically, ninety per cent of the $100 million worth of CAD/CAM equipment installed in Japan in 1982 was made in North America. In Canada, according to a 1983 survey by Evans Research, the CAD/CAM market grew from $7 million in 1977 to $57 million in 1982. Future growth would occur at a rate of forty per cent a year, the firm predicted, to $300 million by 1987.   *25*

Large engineering firms, such as H. A. Simons (International) of Vancouver, are among the early converts to CAD/CAM. At Simons, a computer program has been developed that can display the Vancouver skyline on a video terminal as it would be seen from any vantage point – the top of nearby Grouse Mountain, say, or the downtown intersection of Georgia and Howe streets. It answers a concern that development at B.C. Place might block the view of the surrounding mountains. Models of the 220-acre site – to be developed over thirty years – were of little help. Now Simons can feed in information about any proposed building and see immediately how the skyline and the view will be affected. According to Kent Fletcher of H. A. Simons, "Large-scale three-D modelling is just beginning. We hope we're a step or two ahead of everyone else on the learning curve. For a stodgy old engineering company, it's been quite an undertaking."   *26*

CAD/CAM has uses for small companies as well. A. G. Anderson, of London, Ontario, was the first pattern shop and foundry in North America to install a CAD/CAM system. "We're pioneers and always have been," says executive vice president Geoff Anderson. What began as a one-man shop in 1948 now employs sixty, melting a wide range of metals. Employees can be more quickly trained than in the past. "Although traditional pattern-making skills will always be highly valued," Anderson remarks, "the fact is that there is a continuing decline in the availability of these skills. This void will be breached to some extent by the CAD/CAM technologists now being trained at our community colleges."   *27*

28   Meanwhile, however, demand for good designers is so high that most firms must train their own. At Microtel Pacific Research, in Burnaby, 320 employees (of whom 150 are engineers) produce telecommunications equipment including satellites. Outside hiring is almost impossible for some positions. Microtel has been advertising for a year for an integrated circuit designer. Even with the promise of a $60,000 salary, it has had no success. "We can't hire them, so we've had to create a system to train them ourselves," says Paul Thiel, Microtel's manager of component and technology development. Because so much of the basic design information can be captured in the CAD system, however, a standard electronics designer can now become an integrated circuit designer in one month — a metamorphosis that used to take four to five years.

29   Thiel sees a creativity explosion as well. Designs that once took ten man-years now take one man-year. "An integrated circuit designer used to have to draw every line himself," says Thiel. "We've captured his thoughts in a software program. All the computer-aided design tools we're developing are an extension of the mind, versus the traditional design stations that were an extension of the hands." According to industry-wide statistics, in a typical application, one hour on a CAD terminal is worth about three hours on a traditional drawing board. On detailed designs, the advantage becomes five to one, on revisions ten to one.

30   The number of jobs, however, does not grow in the same way. At Simons, for example, the new technology means fewer people. The recession cut staff from 1,500 to 600. Now that the economy is perking up, staff has been bolstered to 800. But 1,000 employees would have been required were it not for the CAD/CAM installations.

31   While estimates vary, each robot does the work of anywhere from 1.7 to 6 employees. . . . In Canada, most robots have been installed by auto manufacturers. Donald Hackworth, former president and general manager of GM Canada, points to the 117 robots at the company's Oshawa, Ontario, plant. As he said last year when they were being installed, "We don't anticipate that our head count will be less. There will be, however, a big difference in what those people do. For 117 people there won't be any more personal 'totin' that barge, liftin' that bale.' Instead, they will let the robots do the dirty work. Their job will be to baby-sit the robots."

32   Robotics began with hydraulic controls. With the advent of microelectronics and the microcomputer, it became possible to program multijointed manipulators to carry out complex, repetitive tasks with consistency and precision. The first robots were in place in the late 1960s. Today, there are about 2,000 types of robot, but the technology is still in its infancy. At the present level of development, only about three per cent of all manufacturing tasks can profitably be done with robotics. Current applications include welding, spray painting, grinding, assembly, and materials handling. Again, the Japanese are the leaders. No accurate count of the number of industrial robots at work in Japan seems to exist; estimates range up to 54,000, depending on how robots are defined. But according to the Robot Institute of America, there are 18,000 robots in Japan, 8,000 in the U.S. – and 600 in Canada.

As costs fall, more will be installed. At General Electric, which   *33*
manufactures robots, "one of our assembly robots goes for about the price of a Corvette," says executive vice president James Baker. "On a two-shift basis over a five-year period it can perform at an average of $4 an hour, about a third the cost of a very bored human." Computerized vision is being added to robots. "It's being used to inspect pizzas to see if they have enough pepperoni slices. It will shortly be inspecting disposable diapers moving at thirty miles per hour down the assembly line."

For all of the auto makers, the race is to catch the Japanese.   *34*
Japanese cars have been entering North American markets with a $1,500 manufacturing labour cost advantage over North American cars, largely because Japan can make a car in about fifty-seven man-hours, compared with an average of 100 man-hours in North America. To date, most robots are used for what are known as the three-D tasks – dirty, dull, or dangerous – or the three-H ones – hot, heavy, and hazardous. In the auto industry there are plenty of both. In some cases, while an employee costs about twenty-four dollars an hour, an industrial robot can perform the same job for six dollars. At U.S. General Motors, for example, where employee wages increased 200 per cent during the 1970s, robot costs increased only forty per cent, causing GM chairman Roger Smith to observe dryly, "Every time the cost of labour goes up a dollar an hour, 1,000 more robots become economical." That's why GM will invest an estimated $1 billion to install 14,000 robots throughout its operations by 1990.

The effect of those first 117 robots in Oshawa was to increase the   *35*
production rate from forty-five vehicles an hour to fifty-two. By this year's end, GM will have 300 robots in Canada; by 1990, 1,200. Already, lasers are used to check body openings on the assembly line. Optical scanners are mounted on the rotating arms of the robots to shoot two laser beams at each vehicle body. Twelve key areas are checked – including the windshield, deck lid, tail lamp, and door and window openings – while the assembly line is moving at rates of over fifty vehicles an hour.

At the $400 million Chrysler assembly plant in Windsor, robots   *36*
are essential in the production of the firm's new mini-vans. When the plant produced New Yorkers and Fifth Avenues, there was only one robot. After conversion to van production last year, the plant

has 125 robots of eight types. Uses include spot and arc welding, sealing, interior painting, material handling, urethane application to glass, and hot-melt glue applications. According to plant manager George Hohendorf, the Windsor assembly plant is "the most technologically advanced vehicle assembly system within the new Chrysler corporation. The role of the robot, integrated with sophisticated automation, reflects all of our factories of the future."

37   How many workers will be needed in those factories of the future? Beyond predicting that work patterns, working hours, and the nature of the work itself are all bound to change, no one is prepared to guess. Is the robot being perceived as a job threat? According to Ken Jones of the Ontario Centre for Advanced Manufacturing, workers are accepting their robot partners. "In most plants in which robots have been installed, there has been general acceptance by the work force." He has some suggestions for future dealings, however. "The new technology is making obsolete the traditional division between labour and management. For society to derive the maximum benefit from the technology, new relationships will need to be established."

38   However the debate is resolved, robotics is here to stay. And not just at the auto factories. Harber Manufacturing, in Fort Erie, Ontario, is assembling and marketing a British-designed robot system for North American distribution. Harber, a manufacturer of wood-burning stoves and aluminium boats, had purchased a robot for its own needs and was impressed with the unit's ability to do fast and accurate seam welding of sheet metal. Blair Harber, the president, says, "With robots for welding, everybody wins. Management gets better productivity, workers better working conditions, and the consumer a better product."

39   Modernization of Canadian manufacturing can include processes other than robotics and CAD/CAM. At Haley Industries, of Haley, Ontario, new casting technology has enhanced the Ottawa Valley firm's position as one of the top three aerospace foundries in North America. It produces gearbox and transmission housings for a range of aircraft from executive jets through the F-18 fighter to the Boeing 767. The company, formerly Light Alloys, was federally owned until 1967 when it was bought for one dollar by Bartaco Industries, of Orillia, Ontario. The company has since spent $2.7 million on R&D. Microprocessors and fluoroscopic inspection govern everything in production from sand distribution to heat treatment to quality control. Today, annual sales have reached $23 million; according to chief executive officer Robert Turnbull, the success formula is "modernization and keeping pace with the latest developments in technology. About ninety per cent of our

castings are exported, so we have to compete in the toughest markets."

Fisher Gauge, of Peterborough, Ontario, has had equal success in   40
foreign markets. The company developed Fixturblok, a machining process for turbine blade production now in use among the world's leading engine builders – General Electric, Pratt & Whitney, and Rolls-Royce. "The application of technology and improvements in productivity are something that you've got to be working on continuously," says Fisher Gauge president Bill Fisher. Exports are essential to the firm's livelihood, because the Canadian market is small. With annual sales in excess of $20 million, he urges other Canadian manufacturers to sell the new technology. "You can carve out a niche for yourself in the world markets," he insists.

While there are specific success stories, the broader implica-   41
tions are not yet clear. There are, after all, far too many Canadian firms that have not modernized. To change that, the Science Council's Stuart Smith calls for a cooperative national strategy that would include governments at all levels as well as business and labour. "Reality is hitting home," he says. "The labour unions are being more reasonable, management is more enlightened. In the best-case scenario, we will make a concerted effort to get into new industries that we're not in now. By the end of the 1980s, we'll be holding our own in the knowledge-intensive areas." But, he notes, the clock is close to midnight for Canada's manufacturers. "The new world is one of world markets and modern technology. They've got to adapt to both of those very, very quickly."

There, are, however, few signs yet of national leadership. Even   42
for those in the vanguard of technological change, the future is unpredictable. "We have a lead today," says Microtel Pacific's Thiel, "but whether we can hold that or not...." His voice trails away as he considers the competition. "There's $200 million going into this software annually in the U.S." For the successful, the recipe seems so simple. Says Fisher Gauge's Bill Fisher: "We're taking Canadian zinc and converting it into small precision components and exporting it at very substantially enhanced value. This is something Canadian industry should be striving to do."

Perhaps the dialogue about jobs can never be anything more   43
than an academic exercise. The real question is not how many jobs technology will or will not create but how far behind Canada can be allowed to fall, and whether human concerns can remain central to our thinking. As Stuart Smith argues, "We have to make sure that those who are displaced by modernization are not just put on the rubbish heap." But from all sides – government, business, and labour – there is agreement that technical change is essential. As Ken Jones puts it: "In the next ten years, twenty years, if we are not

using technology appropriate to that period, we won't be in business. The new technology is the difference between life and death."

QUESTIONS

Language and Style

1. What aspects of the discussion might lead the reader to feel that the whole subject is very complicated and that crucial decisions need to be taken by people perhaps better informed than the reader? To what extent could this be due to the "level" and "speed" of the discussion?

2. Given the apparent assumptions about what will cause the reader concern (a comparatively low level of spending on research and development), who is the reader?

3. Why should the writer use the expression "took the industry by storm" (paragraph 13)?

4. When does it become clear what the example in the first few paragraphs is an example of? Why should the reader be made to wait?

Organization

1. Into what obvious parts is this discussion organized? How does the reader know to anticipate this pattern?

2. In paragraph 8 the writer sets out to explain the theoretical results of the introduction of new technology. Why is an example appropriate here? How does it work? Is it clear where the example stops?

3. Explain the sense in which the discussion touches down, here and there, to give the reader a glimpse of the realities of the new technology.

4. In paragraph 8, the writer takes time to explain certain technicalities. Why would it have been helpful to some readers to have the technicalities in paragraph 6 explained as well? Are there other instances where similar explanations would have been helpful?

Content

1. What observations might lead the reader to conclude that "it could go either way"? What are the dangers? What sorts of things give hope?

Vocabulary

oblivious	transfixed
mylar	comparative advantage

ductwork	penchant
enhancements	stodgy
metamorphosis	laser
urethane	fluoroscope
niche	man-year

Motorcycle Maintenance
Robert M. Pirsig

Pirsig's ability to connect practical and everyday matters with complex theoretical questions of human understanding is illustrated in this excerpt from his best-selling book Zen and the Art of Motorcycle Maintenance.

On this machine I've done the tuning so many times it's become a   1
ritual. I don't have to think much about how to do it anymore. Just mainly look for anything unusual. The engine has picked up a noise that sounds like a loose tappet but could be something worse, so I'm going to tune it now and see if it goes away. Tappet adjustment has to be done with the engine cold, which means wherever you park it for the night is where you work on it the next morning, which is why I'm on a shady curbstone back of a hotel in Miles City, Montana. Right now the air is cool in the shade and will be for an hour or so until the sun gets around the tree branches, which is good for working on cycles. It's important not to tune these machines in the direct sun or late in the day when your brain gets muddy because even if you've been through it a hundred times you should be alert and looking for things.

Not everyone understands what a completely rational process   2
this is, this maintenance of a motorcycle. They think it's some kind of a "knack" or some kind of "affinity for machines" in operation. They are right, but the knack is almost purely a process of reason, and most of the troubles are caused by what old time radio men called a "short between the earphones," failures to use the head properly. A motorcycle functions entirely in accordance with the laws of reason, and a study of the art of motorcycle maintenance is really a miniature study of the art of rationality itself. I said yesterday that the ghost of rationality was what Phaedrus pursued and what led to his insanity, but to get into that it's vital to stay with down-to-earth examples of rationality, so as not to get lost in generalities no one else can understand. Talk about rationality can

get very confusing unless the things with which rationality deals are also included.

3   We are at the classic-romantic barrier now, where on one side we see a cycle as it appears immediately – and this is an important way of seeing it – and where on the other side we can begin to see it as a mechanic does in terms of underlying form – and this is an important way of seeing things too. These tools for example – this wrench – has a certain romantic beauty to it, but its purpose is always purely classical. It's designed to change the underlying form of the machine.

4   The porcelain inside this first plug is very dark. That is classically as well as romantically ugly because it means the cylinder is getting too much gas and not enough air. The carbon molecules in the gasoline aren't finding enough oxygen to combine with and they're just sitting here loading up the plug. Coming into town yesterday the idle was loping a little, which is a symptom of the same thing.

5   Just to see if it's just the one cylinder that's rich I check the other one. They're both the same. I get out a pocket knife, grab a stick lying in the gutter and whittle down the end to clean out the plugs, wondering what could be the cause of the richness. That wouldn't have anything to do with rods or valves. And carbs rarely go out of adjustment. The main jets are oversized, which causes richness at high speeds but the plugs were a lot cleaner than this before with the *same* jets. Mystery. You're always surrounded by them. But if you tried to solve them all, you'd never get the machine fixed. There's no immediate answer so I just leave it as a hanging question.

6   The first tappet is right on, no adjustment required, so I move on to the next. Still plenty of time before the sun gets past those trees . . . I always feel like I'm in church when I do this . . . The gage is some kind of religious icon and I'm performing a holy rite with it. It is a member of a set called "precision measuring instruments" which in a classic sense has a profound meaning.

7   In a motorcycle this precision isn't maintained for any romantic or perfectionist reasons. It's simply that the enormous forces of heat and explosive pressure inside this engine can only be controlled through the kind of precision these instruments give. When each explosion takes place it drives a connecting rod onto the crankshaft with a surface pressure of many tons per square inch. If the fit of the rod to the crankshaft is precise the explosion force will be transferred smoothly and the metal will be able to stand it. But if the fit is loose by a distance of only a few thousandths of an inch the force will be delivered suddenly, like a hammer blow, and the rod, bearing and crankshaft surface will soon be pounded flat, creating a noise which at first sounds a lot like loose tappets. That's the reason I'm checking it now. If it *is* a loose rod and I try to make it to the mountains without an overhaul, it will soon get

louder and louder until the rod tears itself free, slams into the spinning crankshaft and destroys the engine. Sometimes broken rods will pile right down through the crankcase and dump all the oil onto the road. All you can do then is start walking.

But all this can be prevented by a few thousandths of an inch fit   *8* which precision measuring instruments give, and this is their classical beauty – not what you see, but what they mean – what they are capable of in terms of control of underlying form.

The second tappet's fine. I swing over to the street side of the   *9* machine and start on the other cylinder.

Precision instruments are designed to achieve an *idea*, dimen-   *10* sional precision, whose perfection is impossible. There is no per- fectly shaped part of the motorcycle and never will be, but when you come as close as these instruments take you, remarkable things happen, and you go flying across the countryside under a power that would be called magic if it were not so completely rational in every way. It's the understanding of this rational intel- lectual *idea* that's fundamental. John looks at the motorcycle and he sees steel in various shapes and has negative feelings about these steel shapes and turns off the whole thing. I look at the shapes of the steel now and I see *ideas*. He thinks I'm working on *parts*. I'm working on *concepts*.

I was talking about these concepts yesterday when I said that a   *11* motorcycle can be divided according to its components and ac- cording to its functions. When I said that suddenly I created a set of boxes with the following arrangement:

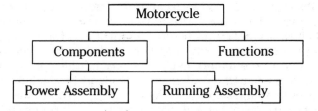

And when I said the components may be subdivided into a   *12* power assembly and a running assembly, suddenly appear some more little boxes:

And you see that every time I made a further division, up came   *13* more boxes based on these divisions until I had a huge pyramid of boxes. Finally you see that while I was splitting the cycle up into finer and finer pieces, I was also building a structure.

14   This structure of concepts is formally called a hierarchy and since ancient times has been a basic structure for all Western knowledge. Kingdoms, empires, churches, armies have all been structured into hierarchies. Modern businesses are so structured. Tables of contents of reference material are so structured, mechanical assemblies, computer software, all scientific and technical knowledge is so structured — so much so that in some fields such as biology, the hierarchy of phylum-order-class-genus-species is almost an icon.

15   The box "motorcycle" *contains* the boxes "components" and "functions." The box "components" *contains* the boxes "power assembly" and "running assembly," and so on. There are many other kinds of structures produced by other operators such as "causes" which produce long chain structures of the form, "A causes B which causes C which causes D," and so on. A functional description of the motorcycle uses this structure. The operators "exists," "equals," and "implies" produce still other structures. These structures are normally interrelated in patterns and paths so complex and so enormous no one person can understand more than a small part of them in his lifetime. The overall name of these interrelated structures, the genus of which the hierarchy of containment and structure of causation are just species, is *system*. The motorcycle is a system. A *real* system.

16   To speak of certain government and establishment institutions as "the system" is to speak correctly, since these organizations are founded upon the same structural conceptual relationships as a motorcycle. They are sustained by structural relationships even when they have lost all other meaning and purpose. People arrive at a factory and perform a totally meaningless task from eight to five without question because the structure demands that it be that way. There's no villain, no "mean guy" who wants them to live meaningless lives, it's just that the structure, the system demands it and no one is willing to take on the formidable task of changing the structure just because it is meaningless.

17   But to tear down a factory or to revolt against a government or to avoid repair of a motorcycle because it is a system is to attack effects rather than causes; and as long as the attack is upon effects only, no change is possible. The true system, the real system, is our present construction of systematic thought itself, rationality itself, and if a factory is torn down but the rationality which produced it is left standing, then that rationality will simply produce another factory. If a revolution destroys a systematic government, but the systematic patterns of thought that produced that government are left intact, then those patterns will repeat themselves in the succeeding government. There's so much talk about the system. And so little understanding.

That's all the motorcycle is, a system of concepts worked out in   *18*
steel. There's no part in it, no shape in it, that is not out of someone's mind . . . number three tappet is right on too. One more to go. This had better be it. . . . I've noticed that people who have never worked with steel have trouble seeing this – that the motorcycle is primarily a mental phenomenon. They associate metal with given shapes – pipes, rods, girders, tools, parts – all of them fixed and inviolable, and think of it as primarily physical. But a person who does machining or foundry work or forge work or welding sees "steel" as having no shape at all. Steel can be any shape you want if you are skilled enough, and any shape *but* the one you want if you are not. Shapes, like this tappet, are what you *arrive* at, what you give to the steel. Steel has no more shape than this old pile of dirt on the engine here. These shapes are all out of someone's mind. That's important to see. The *steel*? Hell, even the steel is out of someone's mind. There's no steel in nature. Anyone from the Bronze Age could have told you that. All nature has is a *potential* for steel. There's nothing else there. But what's "potential"? That's also in someone's mind! . . . Ghosts.

That's really what Phaedrus was talking about when he said it's   *19*
all in the mind. It sounds insane when you just jump up and say it without reference to anything specific like an engine. But when you tie it down to something specific and concrete, the insane sound tends to disappear and you see he could have been saying something of importance.

The fourth tappet *is* too loose, which is what I had hoped. I adjust   *20*
it. I check the timing and see that it is still right on and the points are not pitted, so I leave them alone, screw on the valve covers, replace the plugs and start it up.

The tappet noise is gone, but that doesn't mean much yet while   *21*
the oil is still cold. I let it idle while I pack the tools away, then climb on and head for a cycle shop a cyclist on the street told us about last night where they may have a chain adjuster link and a new foot-peg rubber. Chris must have nervous feet. His foot pegs keep wearing out.

I go a couple blocks and still no tappet noise. It's beginning to   *22*
sound good, I think it's gone. I won't come to any conclusions until we've gone about thirty miles though. But until then, and right now, the sun is bright, the air is cool, my head is clear, there's a whole day ahead of us, we're almost to the mountains, it's a good day to be alive. It's this thinner air that does it. You always feel like this when you start getting into higher altitudes.

The altitude! That's why the engine's running rich. Sure, that's   *23* got to be the reason. We're at twenty-five hundred feet now. I'd better switch to standard jets. They take only a few minutes to put in. And lean out the idle adjustment a little. We'll be getting up a lot higher than this.

QUESTIONS

Language and Style

1. Why should the final paragraph give the reader a sense of satisfaction?

2. In what sense is the writer talking to himself? Where does the writer locate the reader?

3. How is the writer's tone appropriate to his apparent relationship with the reader?

4. How does Pirsig's choice of language, his vocabulary, reflect his determination to "stay with down-to-earth examples"?

Organization

1. What is Pirsig's discussion about? In what ways is it about tuning a motorcycle? In what ways about the meaning of rationality? What is the relationship between the two? How does Pirsig help make the connections?

2. Is it clear that this excerpt is part of a wider, more ambitious, continuing discussion? How do you know? Is this a problem?

Content

1. Considering the writer's apparent double subject, what do you make of the closing statement?

Vocabulary

tappet	porcelain
loping	icon
crankshaft	phylum
genus	inviolable
molecules	gage

Canada's Forgotten Poor

Leonard Shifrin

The living, concrete reality of poverty in Canada is portrayed largely by the force of the examples in Shifrin's article from Maclean's.

The old woman hesitated, then she put the can of tuna fish back on   *1*
the supermarket shelf. Maybe next week, when her pension cheque arrives, she will be able to afford it; until then she will make do with toast and tea. In a schoolroom a child tries to concentrate on his lesson, but his mind wanders. He cannot play in the after-school hockey league because there is not enough money in a welfare cheque for things like hockey equipment. His mother explained it all to him, and he knows there is nothing she can do. Still, it seems unfair.

Those scenarios of genuine poverty are played out in Canada   *2*
every day. In 1981, according to Statistics Canada, 3.5 million Canadians were living within its definition of poverty. In 1982 the number jumped to 4.1 million. The 1983 figure, which will not be available until fall, will probably be roughly 4.4 million. After a dozen years of decline, poverty has returned in earnest, largely because of unemployment. And now a jobless economic recovery threatens to make poverty a lasting legacy of the great recession.

Echoing the 1930s, churches and social agencies are again   *3*
attracting long lines at their soup kitchens and depots offering free groceries to the needy. "A few years ago," said Brother Justin Howson of the Little Brothers of the Good Shepherd order, who runs the organization's centre in Hamilton, Ont., "it would be an unusual day if we served 80 dinners. Now we often have 240 people in line for the meal." As well, there has been a big change in the kind of people coming for the free meal. It used to be mainly transients, "hobo types," he declared. Now there are people of all ages, including teenagers and even five-year-olds. "These are not starving children," he added, "just children who are hungry because there is not enough food in the house anymore."

Indeed, Canada's poverty is not the abject sort found in the Third   *4*
World. The common measure is what Statistics Canada delicately calls its "low income cutoffs," the levels at which families must spend more than 58.5 per cent of their incomes on the three chief necessities of life: food, shelter and clothing. Because those costs are highest in big cities, StatsCan calculates five sets of cutoffs for

"Canada's Forgotten Poor," by Leonard Shifrin and Maclean's correspondents. From Maclean's *(January 30, 1984). Reprinted by permission.*

each size of family, with the lowest set being for rural areas and the highest applying to metropolitan areas with populations of more than 500,000. For a family of four in 1983 the poverty lines ranged from $14,110 in rural areas to $19,180 in the largest cities. "Those numbers may seem fairly high," said National Council of Welfare Director Kenneth Battle, "but the Statistics Canada figures are actually the lowest poverty thresholds anyone has formulated in Canada." Both the Senate committee on poverty and the Canadian Council on Social Development have suggested ways of measuring the phenomena that produce higher poverty lines. "In any event," added Battle, "most poor Canadians have incomes thousands of dollars below even the lowest of those standards."

5   Between 1969 and 1981 the proportion of Canadians living in poverty was almost cut in half, to less than 15 per cent from more than 25 per cent. In part, that reflected a variety of government initiatives, instituted mainly in the early 1970s, as Ottawa expanded the unemployment insurance program, tripled family allowances, increased pensions for low income senior citizens and added a spouse's allowance for 60- to 64-year-olds married to low income pensioners. At the same time, six provinces established additional supplements for the poorest older people. But that was only part of the explanation for the decline in poverty rates. There was also a major influx of married women into the labor force, increasing the number of two-paycheque families at the same time that lower birthrates were reducing the number of people to be cared for in those families. Then the crush of unemployment descended, and hundreds of thousands of households suddenly found that the paycheques they counted on had disappeared.

6   The measure of a society's social safety net is not how effective it is in good times but how efficient it is in the bad. The 1982 poverty data published recently by Statistics Canada showed where the nation's safety net held up and where it let people down badly. Single workers were no more successful at holding their jobs than were those with families, but the big increase in poverty levels was in the family categories. That is because Canada's unemployment insurance plan is primarily a system designed for singles, providing benefits high enough to keep one person above the poverty line, but not a family. The most striking demonstration of that was the 1982 experience in the 25 to 34 age bracket. Among singles, the poverty rate actually went down by half a per cent. Among families, it went up by four per cent.

7   But hardest-hit of all were female-headed, single-parent families, whose already sky-high poverty rate jumped a further eight per cent, driving fully half of those families below the poverty line. That turn from bad to worse is all the more chilling because the number of mother-led families is growing at such a rapid rate that

one in six of all families with children is now headed by a single
female parent.

The poverty figures for 1982, when unemployment averaged 11   *8*
per cent, startled many experts. But the numbers will be even
worse for 1983, when the jobless rate increased further to a post-
Depression record average of 11.9 per cent. What is more, by the
end of last year the unemployment insurance safety net was becoming less effective. In the spring of 1982 the number of people
receiving benefits was 95 per cent of the number unemployed. By
the fall of 1983 it was down to 75 per cent, despite the efforts of
federal and provincial governments to recycle the unemployed
back onto the unemployment insurance rolls through job creation
projects offering just enough weeks of work to qualify participants
for another round of benefits.

A missing link in Canada's income security system, as the pov-   *9*
erty figures demonstrate, is any provision for the children in the
families of the unemployed. That was not always the case. From
the time of the 1972 expansion of the unemployment insurance
program until 1975, when the provision was repealed, unemployment insurance used to provide benefits of as much as 75 per cent
of former earnings to those with dependents. Now there is a 60-
per-cent maximum for everyone and, as a result, the poverty rates
for both one- and two-parent families have jumped substantially.

When the federal government repealed the dependency rate   *10*
provision, it said the measure would no longer be needed because
a federal-provincial social security review was to produce a comprehensive income supplement program for all low income families. Instead, the federal-provincial process collapsed a few months
later, producing nothing. Saskatchewan launched its own family
allowance supplement for low income households, a program that
now provides up to $91 per month per child. Manitoba later
followed with a more modest version, offering $30 a month per
child.

In 1982, with its low income families on unemployment insur-   *11*
ance able to collect the supplement, Saskatchewan was the only
province in which the poverty rate did not increase. In fact, it
actually went down slightly. And in Manitoba, with its smaller
supplement, the rate went up by only half the national average.
Ottawa had offered to pay two thirds of the cost of the supplement
programs before the federal-provincial negotiations fell apart more
than eight years ago. But it has since declined to make the amend-
ments necessary for such programs to qualify even for the
50-per-cent cost sharing that it provides to traditional welfare
programs under the Canada Assistance Plan. Its only move to help
low income families was the creation in 1978 of the refundable

child tax credit, which now provides mothers with a maximum annual payment of $343 per child.

12   For the most part, the federal government's recent antipoverty efforts have been directed toward pensioners. It increased the guaranteed income supplement for low income senior citizens in 1979 and 1980 and promised another increase in last month's throne speech. Two years ago Ottawa created the Labor Adjustment Benefits program, which helps some people in the pre-pensioner category. Laid-off workers over the age of 55, if they have spent most of their working lives in an industry designated by the government as undergoing severe economic dislocation, can receive the equivalent of continued unemployment insurance benefits until they turn 65. Qualifying industries can be designated on either a national or a regional basis but, because very few have actually been designated, fewer than 3,000 people are currently receiving benefits under the program.

13   The most hard-pressed of pre-pensioners are widows, and only a tiny proportion of them qualify for federal benefits. When a person aged 60 to 64 and married to a low income pensioner begins receiving a federal spouse's allowance, she (or in rare cases he) continues to get it until age 65, even if the pensioner-spouse dies before then. But only 6,000 widows and 200 widowers are currently in that situation. Last year Alberta became the first province to try filling the gap by providing the equivalent of a full pension to all low income widows and widowers over the age of 55.

14   There are many measures available to combat poverty. It would take just a few programs aimed at the various groups among the poor to reduce Canada's poverty rate to almost zero. "The problem," said Patrick Johnston, executive director of the National Anti-Poverty Organization, "is that poverty does not have a high enough visibility so that governments are pushed to adopt the measures." Every month Statistics Canada provides updates on how many people are unemployed and what is happening to inflation. But poverty figures are only reported annually and not until almost the end of the following year. "If Canada had a monthly poverty index and we had been getting new instalments of the bad news every 30 days for the past two years," added Johnston, "there would have been such a groundswell of demand for government action that maybe by now the poverty news would not be bad anymore."

15   Divorced, 37, and a father of four, Arthur Gouchie of Amherst, N.S., has two formidable adversaries in his struggle against poverty. One is the fragile economy, which the former crane operator and carpenter blames for his inability to find steady work since he was laid off three years ago when a local steel company closed down.

The other is the Nova Scotia government, which refuses to pay Gouchie family benefits, even though he supports the children. Under provincial law, family benefits — which would amount to substantially more than Gouchie's $121 a week from unemployment insurance — are paid to single parents only if they are women. In the fall of 1981 Gouchie set out to challenge the law but was finally defeated in the Supreme Court of Nova Scotia last June.

Gouchie's total income last year from unemployment insurance   *16*
and intermittent work was $6,800. Besides unemployment insurance payments, Gouchie also receives about $120 monthly in federal family allowance for his children, aged 11 to 15. He spends about $80 a week for food and once he pays the bills (Gouchie owns his small bungalow, but he must pay his ex-wife $30 a month to purchase her share of the house), there is little money left. To save money, he quit smoking last year and instead of toys he gave his children clothes and boots for Christmas. As well, he asked his sister to give him several rolls of wallpaper for Christmas to upgrade the house. His one treat to himself during the festive season was a case of beer.

Still, while Gouchie tries to remain cheerful, he is finding it   *17*
difficult to deal with the constant idleness and isolation. "One of the worst parts of it is being home all the time with no money to get out — to go somewhere," he said. "I have not been to a dance since I don't know when. I feel like an old maid, stuck in the house all the time."

Although he realizes that the recession has a lot to do with his   *18*
situation, Gouchie also blames himself because he left school after Grade 10. "I could kick myself for not staying in school longer," he said. "I would tell people, if you have a good job, hang onto it. Do not abuse it."

At 61, Bert Vokey says that his life has come full circle — from   *19*
destitution to destitution. When Vokey was a child in Newfoundland during the Depression, his family often experienced severe poverty, especially when his fisherman father had a bad season. But Vokey, himself a father of five and a onetime janitor who has been out of work since the mid-1970s, said that he is facing even greater hardship now than in the 1930s. "I have had it worse in the past 12 months than I ever did since the day I was born," he said.

Vokey, his wife, Remona, 50, and their children, aged 15 to 25,   *20*
have been struggling for more than a decade to avoid poverty. But they say that they began to lose the battle a year ago, when a chimney fire destroyed their subsidized house in Harbour Grace, on the west side of Conception Bay. Provincial authorities moved them to a public housing development on the outskirts of St. John's, but they have found it difficult to adapt to their new home. The Vokeys were on welfare even before they left Harbour Grace,

but Bert Vokey says that his family could manage then because elder sons William, 25, and Lorne, 20, brought in extra income from casual labor or jobs in local fish plants. But in St. John's none of the Vokeys' four children who are not still in school have been able to find work, mainly because they can scarcely read or write. At the same time, Bert and Remona say they are not healthy enough to work themselves.

21   The family receives $650 a month from social assistance, in addition to almost $60 in monthly family allowance payments for the two youngest children. They do not pay rent, but they have to lay out an average of roughly $140 a month for heating. The lack of money and jobs is taking a severe toll. Said Bert Vokey: "My wife and I are not getting along; none of us are. My 18-year-old daughter twice tried to kill herself since we came here, and my wife was in the hospital for the same thing [taking an overdose of medication] in September." The family has become dependent on the Salvation Army and other charities. Added Remona Vokey: "We are beggars, and me and my husband and children are not used to that. If changes are not made soon here, this family is going to be broken up."

22   Marlene Fidler, 26 and twice divorced, lives with two of her children, Anson, 9, and Joulene, 7, in an old downtown Vancouver hotel, The Hazelwood, on the fringes of the city's skid road. "I don't mind it here, but I don't like it for the kids," she said. "It is hard to judge people around here. You just do not trust the people." But it is hard to find better accommodation when a social worker advised her not to spend more on rent than $410 out of the $760 that she receives in welfare payments.

23   Fidler has been on welfare since she was laid off as a waitress two years ago. She has lived in the hotel ever since she moved to Vancouver from Saskatchewan three years ago, after leaving her husband. There is a padlock on her door to discourage thieves, but there is little of value inside — a bed and dresser in one room, and a bed, one chair, a desk, a small fridge, a sink and a two-burner hotplate in the other. There is no telephone and she shares a hallway bathroom with other residents. The one luxury is a small color TV. Said a stoic Fidler: "I would feel better if I had a different place, with a bathroom and a kitchen. Other than that, I think I'm doing okay. I keep things to myself." Then, she added, "I don't say I'm on welfare, more or less because I'm ashamed."

24   Job hunting is frustrating because she has few skills; her father made her leave school early to look after her brothers and sisters. Now her main challenge is stretching the welfare cheque each month. "I borrow from friends and pay them back when I get my cheque. Then, before the third week is up, I've got to borrow again. It goes like that from month to month," she said.

Fidler needed a crisis grant from welfare to buy clothing for her *25* children this month. She gets her own second-hand clothing from a nearby church. Concluded Fidler: "I was better off when I was working. I was bringing home the bread. This way you are dependent on someone else."

For Sandra Sundquist, a poverty-level income means constantly *26* having to say "no" to her five children, aged 7 to 16. The 37-year-old Surrey, B.C., divorcee, who has relied on public assistance since her marriage ended nine years ago, had to rule out Cub Scouts for her son Robert, 9, because she could not afford the $25 registration fee. Nor could she allow 10-year-old Cathy to join Girl Guides, because Sundquist does not have a car to drive her daughter to the meeting hall. Recently, some of the children wanted to go to the Ice Capades, but that, too, was unaffordable – as are movies. "Sometimes the kids will run to their bedrooms crying and say, 'You don't like me,'" said Sundquist. "But I know when they are older they will understand."

Sunquist faces formidable obstacles as she tries to support her *27* family with the $582.50 a month she receives from welfare and family allowance. She last worked full-time, stocking shelves at Woolco, 11 years ago. Since then the responsibilities of motherhood have limited her to occasional part-time work. The $600-a-month rent on her five-bedroom house is provided by the province, but Sundquist still has to pay $180 a month for heating oil. She makes her own jams, jellies, bread and baked goods, and every fall she buys a few hundred pounds of vegetables to store in the garage. "But lots of times, we do not have money for meat for weeks," said Sundquist, "or we go for weeks without milk – and that bothers me." Sundquist is somewhat better with clothing because she is a skilled seamstress and has a knitting machine. Besides making a lot of her children's clothes, she sews clothes and crafts for other people in order to barter for food and other necessities.

At times, the problems become overwhelming for Sundquist. *28* "When my kids go to bed at night and I am all alone, I think, 'Is it always going to be like this?'" she admitted. But, for the most part, Sundquist retains her optimism. "I have a house that looks reasonably nice," she said. "I have a lot of friends. 'Poor' is the people in other countries you see on television who do not have any food and who live in shacks. I feel very fortunate."

Frederick Robertson, 44, has been separated from his wife and *29* two sons for 1½ years because of unemployment. He has not even had enough money to visit them in Blairmore, Alta. – a $14.90 bus trip from Calgary where he is looking for work – since October. Robertson said that he is "surviving, not living" on $87 a week from unemployment insurance benefits. He cannot afford to telephone his 12- and 14-year-old sons because neither he nor his wife, who is on welfare, can afford a telephone.

30   Only four years ago Robertson was living relatively comfortably in Victoria and working as a hotel desk clerk. But as interest rates increased he found it difficult to meet his mortgage payments. As a result, he decided to leave Victoria three years ago, and that is when his descent into poverty began. Robertson moved with his family to their native Blairmore. But there was no work there, and he went on alone to Calgary to look for a job. He eventually found a $4.50-an-hour position as a dishwasher and later as a short-order cook for a Calgary restaurant. But four months ago, after one year in that job, the restaurant closed. Now he has given up on any chance of going back to the hotel business. "Things happen to poor people," he said. "I'm sitting here with no upper denture plate; my hair is down to my neck; I do not have a decent suit. I could not present myself to the front desk of a hotel like this."

31   Robertson can scarcely afford to buy food for himself on $87 a week. He said that he has difficulty cashing his weekly unemployment insurance cheque at most banks because he has no bank account of his own. As a result, he takes them to a broker, who subtracts a $5 service charge. That leaves him with $82, and $55 of that is used to pay rent.

32   When he is not looking for a job, Robertson works as a volunteer at Calgary's Unemployed Action Centre, where he counsels other impoverished people and hands out food hampers. "I talk to guys in here who were making $25,000 a year a couple of years ago, and all they can say now is, 'I never thought I would have to do this,' " Robertson said. "It drives you crazy and makes you bitter."

33   It is difficult for Patricia Watson of Nanaimo, B.C., to ask her two teenage daughters to drink only one glass of milk or orange juice a day. And it hurt to tell 16-year-old Jennifer recently that she would have to wear a beat-up, three-year-old coat again this winter because there was no money for a new one. "It is just all the little things like that that add up," said Watson, a 36-year-old former bookkeeper who lost her job a year and a half ago when business slowed down. Since then, she has exhausted her unemployment insurance and resorted to welfare. Jennifer, Patricia and her common-law husband, Wayne Bouchard, 39, live on $840 a month in welfare, as well as $29.95 monthly in federal family allowance. (Daughter Carol, 14, has been in a foster home since October because of learning and behavioral problems.)

34   Like Watson, Bouchard has exhausted his unemployment benefits. "I cannot give my family what I think a man should be able to

give his family," he said. He has held several jobs in the past as a sales manager, but the only work he has been able to find during the past year and a half was a job shovelling gravel on a construction site – and that lasted only a few weeks. The transition to unemployment and idleness has been tough. "I was more or less a workaholic," said Bouchard, "and stopping dead after 22 years was a real blow to the system." It is still a struggle to keep his spirits up. "It is a waiting game, and you just have to bear with it. You just have to keep yourself in the right frame of mind," he said.

Both Watson and Bouchard say that the fight against depression   *35* is a difficult one when they are left with only $345 a month after paying bills, including $400 rent for their three-bedroom house. It means that they cannot buy fruit because it is too expensive, they can seldom use their car because of the cost of gas. Meanwhile, Watson says that she has almost given up all hope of finding a job. "I have called every bank, every department store, every place that has financial jobs," she said. "The banks just laughed. They said, 'You can come down and put in your application, but every three months we just throw them away.'" Bouchard tries to be philosophical about his plight: "We all got spoiled in the good old days, back when we worked," he said.

Claude Beaudry, like many other Canadians in 1984, has been   *36* out of work so long that he no longer qualifies for unemployment insurance. For him, poverty does not just involve pinching pennies and frantically searching for another job. It is also a form of psychological oppression. "It makes me feel like nothing, if you want to know the real truth," said Beaudry, a 31-year-old Sudbury father of three sons, aged 1 to 8, who was laid off for a second time by Inco Ltd. at the end of 1982. "It is not something to be proud of. Every man wants to be able to provide for his own family on his own." Added his wife, Deborah-Ann, 29: "You have to worry that there is enough food to eat, that the kids are not going to starve."

After losing his $9.35-an-hour laborer's job, Beaudry collected   *37* unemployment insurance until the eligibility period expired last July. His family now depends on $645 a month from welfare (up from $614 last year) and $89.85 in federal family allowance payments. The Beaudrys said that as they began to adjust to not having any money, their car and television both broke down, aggravating the boredom and sense of claustrophobia. Meanwhile, their financial situation has become desperate. Last October Beaudry took a job as a door-to-door vacuum cleaner salesman and borrowed $350 from a finance company. But Beaudry had little success selling a relatively expensive item in a community where many people are unemployed and he gave up after a month. Now

Beaudry is three months behind on his $70 monthly payments for the loan, and he is concerned that his furniture or his broken-down car will be confiscated. The family has had to turn to the Salvation Army, the Roman Catholic Church and the United Steelworkers — Beaudry's former union — for help at times when even their welfare money ran out.

38   For now, the Beaudrys are looking forward to moving into a $151-a-month, four-bedroom apartment in a public housing development after a 1½-year wait — a welcome change from their $235, two-bedroom flat. Still, the Beaudrys expect that life will remain a grim struggle unless Claude finds another job. He is often depressed and irritable, and he is now convinced that only a "miracle" will create more work. "I don't know what I'm going to do," he said. "I have to find a way to pay that finance company."

QUESTIONS

Language and Style

1. Why are the first fourteen paragraphs expressed in such general terms? What is the eventual effect on the reader?

2. Compare the effect of the opening paragraphs with that of the seven "cases" which make up the balance of the discussion. What are some differences in the language?

3. Where, for instance, would you expect to find phrases like "low income cutoffs," "major influx of married women," and "lowest poverty thresholds?"

Organization

1. Is there a sense in which the examples, arranged as they are, represent a sort of parade of misery? To what extent does this manner of presentation encourage the reader's sympathy and understanding? Could it discourage such reactions? Explain.

2. Why should it be difficult to connect the examples to relevant elements in the opening discussion? What different arrangement of the material might help?

Content

1. What facts do the examples tend to emphasize? Is there a consistent pattern throughout? How would you describe it?

2. What comparisons with "The Painful Realities of the New Technology" suggest themselves?

Vocabulary

abject	influx
groundswell	intermittent
workaholic	claustrophobia

WRITING EXAMPLES

The simplest pattern of development in which examples are used is a statement of a generalization followed by a single extended example which illustrates the generalization:

> Sometimes American tourists arrive in Canada with peculiar impressions of the country.

This generalization can be illustrated by one of many (probably apocryphal) tales of American tourists who arrive in summer looking for snow and the ski slopes. But notice that a claim as broad as this one is not completely illustrated by the snow-seeking Americans example. One sort of mistaken impression, about our climate, *is* illustrated, but the writer's main point demands the additional support of several examples which illustrate other sorts of false impressions of the country tourists are likely to have.

Sometimes a writer can manage a short-cut in this situation and not discuss real tourists at all. The writer can invent a hypothetical touring family and capture many of the common misapprehensions about the country. The writer might invent "a typical American family" whose members are, for the sake of an effective example, appallingly misinformed. They might expect that Canadians speak with clipped British accents or that Canadian police officers wear scarlet tunics and ride horses. They might worry about wolves. The example, a composite, may be fictional, but so long as the facts are representative and the writer makes clear that the example *is* fictional, constructed for convenience, no one is misled.

Another approach to illustrating a broad generalization such as the one about tourists is to break the generalization into parts, each of which is then illustrated with a suitable example:

> Sometimes American tourists arrive in Canada with peculiar impressions of the country's weather, geography, or culture.

Here the writer has broken open the generalization to make it more accessible to illustration and is, by implication, committed to at least three examples (a weather example, a geography example, and a culture example). This way of managing examples is effective because the writer can target examples more accurately and because the connection between the illustrations and the generalization is easier to make out.

The writer should remember that examples are a particular application of narration, or story-telling, and therefore many considerations which apply to creating narratives apply to the use of examples as well. It might be helpful to think of examples as shortened stories which select details for their relevance to the generalization at hand.

SUGGESTIONS FOR WRITING

Before setting out to illustrate any of the topics suggested here, consider modifying the generalizations in order to make them more manageable. Try opening the generalization somewhat so that the contents of the generalizations are more obvious and are more easily exemplified.

1. Sometimes it is better to tell a white lie.
2. It is easy to become entangled in a bureaucratic mess.
3. We can give people offence without knowing it.
4. An easy, relaxed manner may conceal someone's real feelings.
5. Most of the time I am level-headed, but sometimes. . . .
6. If something *can* go wrong, it *will* go wrong.
7. There is more than one way to skin a cat.
8. Your appearance can determine how people react to you.
9. It is not *what* you know, but *who* you know that matters.
10. It is more painful to be poor in the city than in the country.

CHAPTER SIX
CAUSE AND EFFECT

INTRODUCTION

The twinned concepts of cause and effect are used to make connections between events and to develop whole chains of connections. If it were not possible to connect events and to identify chains of connections, sometimes called "causal chains," events could only be understood as accidents. Things would just "happen," and the world as people ordinarily know it would be governed by fate or luck only. So, to explain a disaster, these forces would be called forward, perhaps in the shape of a personified but disinterested power (we still retain the expression "Lady Luck") whose whim dictated that, say, a plague of grasshoppers be made to descend on the ripening grain crops and winter bread be made scarce.

People who live without much hope of changing their circumstances are reminders of what life would be like without the concepts of cause and effect: they have a sense of fatedness about them, a sense of powerlessness before the unpredictable vagaries of things. They shrug and assert that an epidemic of bad luck or poor harvests just has to be endured and lived with. It is out of their hands.

But the ability to establish reliable connections and chains of connections gives people power over their environment, over their circumstances, and over their fate. If people can say why an event occurs, then they can predict that, given similar circumstances, the event is likely to occur again. Predictability is the source of human power over events because sometimes it is possible to alter circumstance and therefore to change the eventual outcome of things. Power over events is demonstrated in the development of a successful vaccine for poliomyelitis by Dr. Jonas Salk, a discovery which freed literally millions of people from the fear of this often fatal, paralytic disease. The basis of modern science, the scientific method, itself amounts to a general procedure for connecting causes and effects by using a system of tests for connectedness. These connections are followed, or "read," forward from cause to effect and back from effect to cause. In the former case the question which gets answered is whether an event is likely to occur, and in the latter, following events back to causes, the question is why an event has occurred.

When a reader sets out to understand a chain of events, how that explanation works will depend on whether the writer has set out to explain why an event has occurred or has set out to determine whether it will occur. In either case the writer is plainly engaged in a special application of narrative because what is explained is how one event leads to another.

One difficulty a reader encounters is the reliability of the connections since it may be that several different outcomes are possible, each with a different degree of probability. Further, it may be that a number of different candidates for causes suggest themselves. The reader must then work to sort out and evaluate them since there is always more than a single obvious hypothesis which can be advanced to explain why a set of circumstances occurred. The connections are therefore not always obvious and require sorting and evaluating, as the following makes clear:

> No single explanation can really explain human behavior; it can at most illuminate human behavior and allow us to see something we had not seen. . . . An accident may be considered a paradigm. Why did it happen? The road was icy at that point. And the driver of the small car was in a great hurry because he was late for a crucial appointment, because the person who had promised to pick him up had not come. And his reflexes were slower than usual because he had had hardly any sleep that night because his mother had died the day before. And just before the accident his attention was distracted for one crucial second by a very pretty girl on the side of the road, who reminded him of a girl he had once known. Yet he might have regained control of his car if only a truck had not come toward him just as he skidded into the left lane. The truck driver might have managed not to hit him, but. . . . If we add that the truck driver had just gone through a red light and was, moreover, going much faster than the legal speed limit, the policeman who witnessed the accident, as well as the court later on, might discount as irrelevant everything said before the three dots and be quite content to explain the accident simply in terms of the truck driver's two violations. He caused the accident. But that does not rule out

the possibility that the other driver had a strong death wish because his mother had died, or that he punished himself for looking at an attractive girl the way he did so soon after his mother's death, or that the person who had let him down was partly to blame.[1]

The causal chain is often tangled. Readers need to be aware that some causes are partial and contributory, that a particular outcome may not be the result of a single cause or a string of concatenated events, that, indeed, sometimes we just cannot determine why some things occur. Some events occur due to a number of independently occurring causes which, taken all together, yield a result. Some causes are more important than others since some circumstances are absolutely necessary to an outcome while others may only speed the outcome or heighten the result.

[1]Walter Kaufmann, *Discovering the Mind*, Vol. III: *Freud vs. Adler and Jung* (N.Y.: McGraw-Hill, 1980). Reproduced with permission.

Being a Man
Paul Theroux

In this essay Paul Theroux, author of The Mosquito Coast, *examines some of the less attractive aspects of his subject.*

There is a pathetic sentence in the chapter "Fetishism" in Dr. Norman Cameron's book *Personality Development and Psychopathology*. It goes, "Fetishists are nearly always men; and their commonest fetish is a woman's shoe." I cannot read that sentence without thinking that it is just one more awful thing about being a man — and perhaps it is an important thing to know about us.   1

I have always disliked being a man. The whole idea of manhood in America is pitiful, in my opinion. This version of masculinity is a little like having to wear an ill-fitting coat for one's entire life (by contrast, I imagine femininity to be an oppressive sense of nakedness). Even the expression "Be a man!" strikes me as insulting and abusive. It means: Be stupid, be unfeeling, obedient, soldierly and   2 stop thinking. Man means "manly" — how can one think about men without considering the terrible ambition of manliness? And yet it is part of every man's life. It is a hideous and crippling lie; it not only insists on difference and connives at superiority, it is also by its very nature destructive — emotionally damaging and socially harmful.

3   The youth who is subverted, as most are, into believing in the masculine ideal is effectively separated from women and he spends the rest of his life finding women a riddle and a nuisance. Of course, there is a female version of this male affliction. It begins with mothers encouraging little girls to say (to other adults) "Do you like my new dress?" In a sense, little girls are traditionally urged to please adults with a kind of coquettishness, while boys are enjoined to behave like monkeys towards each other. The nine-year-old coquette proceeds to become womanish in a subtle power game in which she learns to be sexually indispensable, socially decorative and always alert to a man's sense of inadequacy.

4   Femininity — being lady-like — implies needing a man as witness and seducer; but masculinity celebrates the exclusive company of men. That is why it is so grotesque; and that is also why there is no manliness without inadequacy — because it denies men the natural friendship of women.

5   It is very hard to imagine any concept of manliness that does not belittle women, and it begins very early. At an age when I wanted to meet girls — let's say the treacherous years of thirteen to sixteen — I was told to take up a sport, get more fresh air, join the Boy Scouts, and I was urged not to read so much. It was the 1950s and if you asked too many questions about sex you were sent to camp — boys' camp, of course: the nightmare. Nothing is more unnatural or prison-like than a boy's camp, but if it were not for them we would have no Elks' Lodges, no pool rooms, no boxing matches, no Marines.

6   And perhaps no sports as we know them. Everyone is aware of how few in number are the athletes who behave like gentlemen. Just as high school basketball teaches you how to be a poor loser, the manly attitude towards sports seems to be little more than a recipe for creating bad marriages, social misfits, moral degenerates, sadists, latent rapists and just plain louts. I regard high school sports as a drug far worse than marijuana, and it is the reason that the average tennis champion, say, is a pathetic oaf.

7   Any objective study would find the quest for manliness essentially right-wing, puritanical, cowardly, neurotic and fueled largely by a fear of women. It is also certainly philistine. There is no book-hater like a Little League coach. But indeed all the creative arts are obnoxious to the manly ideal, because at their best the arts are pursued by uncompetitive and essentially solitary people. It makes it very hard for a creative youngster, for any boy who

expresses the desire to be alone seems to be saying that there is something wrong with him.

It ought to be clear by now that I have something of an objection   *8* to the way we turn boys into men. It does not surprise me that when the President of the United States has his customary week-end off he dresses like a cowboy — it is both a measure of his insecurity and his willingness to please. In many ways, American culture does little more for a man than prepare him for modeling clothes in the L. L. Bean catalogue. I take this as a personal insult because for many years I found it impossible to admit to myself that I wanted to be a writer. It was my guilty secret, because being a writer was incompatible with being a man.

There are people who might deny this, but that is because the   *9* American writer, typically, has been so at pains to prove his manliness that we have come to see literariness and manliness as mingled qualities. But first there was a fear that writing was not a manly profession — indeed, not a profession at all. (The paradox in American letters is that it has always been easier for a woman to write and for a man to be published.) Growing up, I had thought of sports as wasteful and humiliating, and the idea of manliness was a bore. My wanting to become a writer was not a flight from that oppressive role-playing, but I quickly saw that it was at odds with it. Everything in stereotyped manliness goes against the life of the mind. The Hemingway personality is too tedious to go into here, and in any case his exertions are well-known, but certainly it was not until this aberrant behavior was examined by feminists in the 1960s that any male writer dared question the pugnacity in Hemingway's fiction. All the bullfighting and arm wrestling and elephant shooting diminished Hemingway as a writer, but it is consistent with a prevailing attitude in American writing: one cannot be a male writer without first proving that one is a man.

It is normal in America for a man to be dismissive or even   *10* somewhat apologetic about being a writer. Various factors make it easier. There is a heartiness about journalism that makes it accept-able — journalism is the manliest form of American writing and, therefore, the profession the most independent-minded women seek (yes, it is an illusion, but that is my point). Fiction-writing is equated with a kind of dispirited failure and is only manly when it produces wealth — money is masculinity. So is drinking. Being a drunkard is another assertion, if misplaced, of manliness. The American male writer is traditionally proud of his heavy drinking. But we are also a very literal-minded people. A man proves his manhood in America in old-fashioned ways. He kills lions, like Hemingway; or he hunts ducks, like Nathanael West; or he makes pronouncements like, "A man should carry enough knife to defend himself with," as James Jones once said to a *Life* interviewer. Or he says he can drink you under the table. But even tiny drunken

William Faulkner loved to mount a horse and go fox hunting, and Jack Kerouac roistered up and down Manhattan in a lumberjack shirt (and spent every night of *The Subterraneans* with his mother in Queens). And we are familiar with the lengths to which Norman Mailer is prepared, in his endearing way, to prove that he is just as much a monster as the next man.

11   When the novelist John Irving was revealed as a wrestler, people took him to be a very serious writer; and even a bubble reputation like Erich (*Love Story*) Segal's was enhanced by the news that he ran the marathon in a respectable time. How surprised we would be if Joyce Carol Oates were revealed as a sumo wrestler or Joan Didion active in pumping iron. "Lives in New York City with her three children" is the typical woman writer's biographical note, for just as the male writer must prove he has achieved a sort of muscular manhood, the woman writer – or rather her publicists – must prove her motherhood.

12   There would be no point in saying any of this if it were not generally accepted that to be a man is somehow – even now in feminist-influenced America – a privilege. It is on the contrary an unmerciful and punishing burden. Being a man is bad enough; being manly is appalling (in this sense, women's lib has done much more for men than for women). It is the sinister silliness of men's fashions, and a clubby attitude in the arts. It is the subversion of good students. It is the so-called "Dress Code" of the Ritz-Carlton Hotel in Boston, and it is the institutionalized cheating in college sports. It is the most primitive insecurity.

13   And this is also why men often object to feminism but are afraid to explain why: of course women have a justified grievance, but most men believe – and with reason – that their lives are just as bad.

QUESTIONS

Language and Style

1. How would you describe the tone of paragraphs 5, 6, and 7? How does the tone change in paragraph 8? What words suggest this change? Why should the writer change his tone?

2. How important are the references to writers toward the end of the essay? Who are these people?

3. What aspects of the language in the essay are especially suited to expressing the anger in the essay?

4. What does the writer assume about what the reader feels? For whom might this account prove unconvincing?

Content

1. From what cultural assumptions come the different sorts of unhappiness mentioned in the essay?

2. What characteristics of manliness does Theroux identify? Is it clear what values and behaviours could replace it?

3. What connections can you make with "Pornography vs. Erotica" by Gloria Steinem?

Vocabulary

pathetic	philistine	oaf
coquettishness	pugnacity	neurotic
latent	fetishist	aberrant
puritanical	grotesque	literariness

Guilty Verdict
Kirk Makin

This newspaper story demonstrates the difficulty of explaining why people do what they do – and the occasionally speculative nature of such explanations.

He was a classic example of a cop who went wrong.   *1*

From interviews with people who knew ex-Mountie Patrick   *2* Michael Kelly, convicted last night of murdering his wife, there emerges a picture of a man with many enemies whose shameless braggadocio left a sour taste in the mouths of acquaintances.

"I don't think there are too many people out there rooting for   *3* Kelly," Paul Copeland, a lawyer uninvolved in the case, said in an interview, mirroring the sentiments of several of those interviewed.

Several friends of Jeanette Kelly attended most of the trial out of   *4* a mixture, as Judy Seres put it, of fascination and moral obligation to see it through to the end.

In keeping with the general lack of sympathy for the accused   *5*

From The Globe and Mail *(Toronto), June 1, 1984. Reprinted by permission.*

man, the group had a party planned if the jury returned with a conviction.

6   People didn't always feel this way toward Mr. Kelly. In the early 1970s, he was the fair-haired boy, considered a bright police prospect. His guts, enthusiasm, resourcefulness and relatively slight build made him ideal for undercover drug work.

7   And he was tough — a karate blackbelt, he could lift his wife by the neck with one hand and demolish a tennis ball with his serve.

8   Mr. Copeland, an experienced Toronto lawyer who represents many alleged drug dealers, tells of how Mr. Kelly turned some heads in police college during a class assignment.

9   Each student was given $20 to purchase a small amount of soft drugs. "Everyone came back with little bags of marijuana," Mr. Copeland said, chuckling. "Kelly brought in an ounce of heroin."

10   Filled with ambition, he learned to speak fluent French and Spanish, the latter through a course in South America.

11   But not long after starting his work as an underworld drug buyer for the Royal Canadian Mounted Police, something began to go wrong. His testimony sent drug dealers to jail, but there were ugly rumors.

12   "There are certainly rumors of a 'not guilty' club down Kingston (Ont.) way," where several prisons are located, Mr. Copeland said. "They are people who maintain they may have sold drugs, but they didn't sell to him. . . . The cop is nearly always believed."

13   His sentence will truly be "hard time" because of his former job and his reputation, another lawyer said. "But ask the people who are doing time because of his evidence if their time is harder than his."

14   Eventually, Mr. Kelly's behavior at trials became antagonistic and most unhelpful to Crown attorneys and defence lawyers alike, said one criminal lawyer who often faced him. This made him "a real black sheep" on a force made up mainly of dependable, professional officers, said the lawyer, who asked to remain anonymous.

15   "He felt it was far beneath him to be acting as an assistant to the Crown. He was upbraided by Crowns several times. . . . Kelly always had a chip on his shoulder. You always got the impression he was looking to aggrandize himself."

16   Perhaps the best theory of Mr. Kelly's fall from grace is that he lived his underground cover so effortlessly that it became his civilian life as well.

17   Certainly, people began to wonder out loud when he and his wife acquired their Porsches, travelled extensively and joyfully embarked on life in the fast lane.

18   "It's a weird experience being undercover," Crown counsel Wade Nesmith says. "His cover was being a high-roller. I guess it was easy — his wife had all those passes for airlines, for example, so they

could travel. (Mrs. Kelly worked as an airline reservations clerk.) But it's a far cry from leading the fast life undercover to throwing your wife off a balcony."

Another lawyer said the lifestyle of the undercover drug officer *19* can be "very seductive. They get used to a certain lifestyle whether it is artificial or not. They want to maintain it." But you can't maintain a $150,000-a-year lifestyle on a police constable's salary.

In 1978, the suspicions about his drug activities dovetailed with *20* criminal charges of arson in connection with a disastrous fire at his home. Mr. Kelly was suspended while a full internal investigation was launched.

Several drug cases were dropped or made considerably more *21* difficult for the Crown because it chose not to use Mr. Kelly's evidence.

Mr. Copeland handled one case in which his client stoutly maintained he was a hashish dealer and didn't touch cocaine, the drug *22* he was accused of trafficking. The $3,000-worth of cocaine entered as an exhibit was only 0.3 per cent pure and would probably never have been bought or sold by anyone, the lawyer said.

On appeal, the Crown said the only evidence against the man *23* was Mr. Kelly's and that they were not satisfied with his credibility. On the suggestion of the Crown, the appeal was allowed.

Mr. Kelly had resigned under a cloud shortly before Jeanette *24* Kelly fell from their 17th floor balcony.

Within days of the murder, he was in Hawaii with Jan Bradley, his *25* lover. Then it was Victoria, for a few months, where he lavished his attentions on at least three women. One of these was Hanna Kirkham.

"I didn't like him," she said in an interview this week. "I just *26* didn't have a good feeling about him.

"I'm a widow and when you have been through something like *27* that, you know there is a natural course of events you go through. I didn't smell any kind of regret, sorrow or grief about him. He was just having a good time. Maybe he didn't feel he had to act."

Although she was portrayed as his lover during the trial, Ms. *28* Kirkham said she was anything but that. She said she was turned off by his boastfulness about his police life and the overkill he indulged in when courting, such as constantly sending flowers and even dropping roses at her feet on a tennis court.

"He just seemed phony, a real phony. Afterward, I made a crack *29* to a girlfriend of mine that I bet he threw his wife off that balcony."

In British Columbia and later at a villa in the south of France *30* with his new wife, Ms. Bradley, Mr. Kelly spent money lavishly.

According to a Toronto lawyer very familiar with the case and *31* with Mr. Kelly, the 34-year-old man was doing all he could to back up the lies he had told Ms. Bradley about his lifestyle and resources.

"I think he was a pathological liar. He would meet girls and tell *32* them the most unbelievable (lies)." A girl friend he was once at the beach with remarked on the beauty of two yachts passing by, the lawyer said. "Kelly said, 'I'm glad you think so. They're mine.' " He refused to let her go and see them at the dock because they were "leased out," the lawyer recounted.

33   At other times, Mr. Kelly boasted to people of having two Rolls-Royce dealerships, several expensive sports cars and several homes. He told a friend he had once beat off seven or eight assailants in three-and-a-half seconds, but he required plastic surgery to reconstruct his face.

34   Within a year and a half of Mrs. Kelly's death, Mr. Kelly had exhausted the $270,000 insurance money from his wife's death and could no longer even pay the phone bill at the French villa, said the lawyer, who asked to remain anonymous.

35   Ms. Seres, a good friend of the dead woman, said she had always found Mr. Kelly show-offish and artificial. She said she wished in retrospect she had watched the signs of marital discord more closely.

36   In August, 1980, Ms. Seres recalled, Mrs. Kelly came to work at CP Air with three odd injuries. She explained away a sprained finger as having been accidentally caught in a car door by Mr. Kelly. A leg fracture occurred when she tripped during an argument with her husband.

37   The third injury was a dislocated jaw. "She said she had bent down to kiss the dog when she got home and it decked her. I wish at times I had asked more questions."

38   To Mrs. Kelly's friends, she was a fun-loving, ostentatious and somewhat spoiled woman. At 33, she still bore the hallmarks of a finishing school education and well-to-do upbringing.

39   Mrs. Kelly, who grew up in Scotland, was also something of a world traveller, having worked in New Zealand, Colombia, and Tunisia.

40   She wore beautiful clothes, had a lot of class and wanted people to know it, Ms. Seres said. She was also outrageous enough, for example, to go up to a table of people at a full restaurant and ask them pointedly how long they intended to stay.

41   The day before her death, Mrs. Kelly was very distraught about a fight she had the night before with her husband, Ms. Seres said. "I broke a personal rule and asked her something I had never asked anyone before — 'Why don't you leave him?' She said she was not going to give up her lifestyle."

42   Ms. Seres theorized that when the Kellys met in Mexico, each though the other had lots of money. This mutual misconception appeared to be at the root of the tragedy that was to come, she said.

43   "They spent money in the most frivolous manner. For no reason

at all, they would fly from France to the Bahamas for the weekend. He was the kind of person who would go out and order 15 suits of different colors."

Evidence from a formerly close lawyer-friend of Mr. Kelly's at the trial indicated Mr. Kelly had made off with large sums of money which belonged to the friend or, in one case, a client of his.   *44*

"He was doing the old shell game," said the Toronto lawyer who knows the case intimately. "He burned every one of the friends he had. It was just unbelievable."   *45*

Mr. Kelly was finally brought down with a large body of circumstantial evidence and the sudden willingness of an eyewitness to testify.   *46*

Metro Toronto Police Sergeant Ed Stewart charged Mr. Kelly with the first-degree murder of his wife. Sgt. Stewart, who had relentlessly gathered evidence for two years, won a police award for his efforts.   *47*

But why did Dawn Bragg, the eyewitness, agree to testify that she had seen the murder? Why would he kill his wife in front of a woman who was no longer his lover?   *48*

It couldn't have been revenge on her estranged lover, Mr. Kelly, said the Toronto lawyer. "I believe her absolutely. Kelly is a megalomaniac – he thought he could control her."   *49*

QUESTIONS

Language and Style

1. Some ready-made phrases appear in this newspaper article ("life in the fast lane," "stoutly maintained"). What are some others that appear here? How does this practice affect the reader's interest?

Organization

1. Explain how this discussion is organized on a "before and after" pattern. What is characteristic of the "before" Kelly? The "after" Kelly?

2. In what way is the explanation fragmentary and "jumpy"? What makes it seemed patched together? Does the reader feel an urge to reconstruct events?

Content

1. How are the first changes in Kelly's behaviour explained? What light

does the account of Kelly's private life shed on the question?

2. Does the description of Kelly's style of living lend support to the theory of the "underground cover"? Is there reason to believe that Kelly may *not* have changed?

3. What other theories or explanations are offered? Why should it be so difficult to decide which explanation is the best?

4. Does the reader come away from the article with a sense that the matter is decided? Why? Why not?

Vocabulary

braggadocio
aggrandize
pathological
megalomaniac

upbraided
dovetailed
ostentatious

Why Are Movies So Bad?
Pauline Kael

In this article, the New Yorker *movie critic Pauline Kael explains how the economics of the movie business influence the productions that make it to the screen.*

1   The movies have been so rank the last couple of years that when I see people lining up to buy tickets I sometimes think that the movies aren't drawing an audience – they're inheriting an audience. People just want to go to a movie. They're stung repeatedly, yet their desire for a good movie – for *any* movie – is so strong that all over the country they keep lining up. "There's one God for all creation, but there must be a separate God for the movies," a producer said. "How else can you explain their survival?" An atmosphere of hope develops before a big picture's release, and even after your friends tell you how bad it is, you can't quite believe it until you see for yourself. The lines (and the grosses) tell us only that people are going to the movies – not that they're having a good time. Financially, the industry is healthy, so among the people at the top there seems to be little recognition of what miserable shape movies are in. They think the grosses are proof that people are happy with what they're getting, just as TV executives think that the programs with the highest ratings are what TV viewers want, rather than what they settle for. (A number of the new movie executives come from TV.) These new executives don't necessarily see many movies themselves, and they rarely go to a theatre. If for the last couple of years Hollywood couldn't seem to do anything right, it isn't that it was just a stretch of bad luck – it's the result of recent developments within the industry. And in all probability it will get worse, not better. There have been few recent American movies worth lining up for – last year there was chiefly *The Black Stallion*, and this year there is *The Empire Strikes Back*. The first was made under the aegis of Francis Ford Coppola; the second was financed by George Lucas, using his profits from Star Wars as a guarantee to obtain bank loans. One can say with fair confidence that neither *The Black Stallion* nor *The Empire Strikes Back* could have been made with such care for visual richness and imagination if it had been done under studio control. Even small films on traditional subjects are difficult to get financed at a studio if there are no parts for stars in them; Peter Yates, the director of *Breaking Away* – a graceful, unpredictable comedy that pleases and satisfies audiences – took the project to one studio after another for almost six years before he could get the backing for it.

There are direct results when conglomerates take over movie companies. At first, the heads of the conglomerates may be drawn into the movie business for the status implications – the opportunity to associate with world-famous celebrities. Some other conglomerate heads may be drawn in for the girls, but for them, too, a new social life beckons, and as they become socially involved, people with great names approach them as equals, and it gets them crazy. Famous stars and producers and writers and directors tell them about offers they've had from other studios and about ideas they have for pictures, and the conglomerate heads become indignant that the studios they control aren't in on these wonderful projects. The next day, they're on the phone raising hell with their studio bosses. Very soon, they're likely to be summoning directors and suggesting material to them, talking to actors, and telling the company executives what projects should be developed. How bad are the taste and judgment of the conglomerate heads? Very bad. They haven't grown up in a show-business milieu – they don't have the background, the instincts, the information of those who have lived and sweated movies for many years. (Neither do most of the current studio bosses.) The conglomerate heads may be business geniuses, but as far as movies are concerned they have virgin instincts; ideas that are new to them and take them by storm may have failed grotesquely dozens of times. But they feel that they are creative people – how else could they have made so much money and be in a position to advise artists what to do? Who is to tell them no? Within a very short time, they are in fact, though not in title, running the studio. They turn up compliant executives who will settle for the title and not fight for the authority or for their own tastes – if, in fact, they have any. The conglomerate heads find these compliant executives among lawyers and agents, among lawyer-agents, among television executives, and in the lower echelons of the companies they've taken over. Generally, these executives reserve all their enthusiasm for movies that have made money; those are the only movies they like. When a director or a writer talks to them and tries to suggest the kind of picture he has in mind by using a comparison, they may stare at him blankly. They are usually law-school or business-school graduates; they have no frame of reference. Worse, they have no shame about not knowing anything about movies. From their point of view, such knowledge is not essential to their work. Their talent is being able to anticipate their superiors' opinions; in meetings, they show a sixth sense for guessing what the most powerful person in the room wants to hear. And if they ever guess wrong, they know how to shift gears without a tremor. So the movie companies wind up with top production executives whose interest in movies rarely extends beyond the immediate selling possibilities; they could be selling neckties just as well as movies, except that they are drawn to glamour and power.

3   This does not prevent these executives from being universally treated as creative giants. If a studio considers eighty projects, and eventually twenty of them (the least risky) go into production, and two of them become runaway hits (or even one of them), the studio's top executive will be a hero to his company and the media, and will soon be quoted in the *Los Angeles Times* and *The New York Times* talking about his secret for picking winners – his intuitive understanding, developed from his childhood experiences, that people want a strong, upbeat narrative, that they want to cheer the hero and hiss the villain. When *Alien* opened "big," Alan Ladd, Jr., president of the pictures division of Twentieth Century-Fox, was regarded as a demigod; it's the same way that Fred Silverman was a demigod. It was nothing to do with quality, only with the numbers. (Ladd and his team weren't admired for the small pictures they took chances on and the artists they stuck by.) The media now echo the kind of thinking that goes on in Hollywood, and spread it wide. Movie critics on TV discuss the relative grosses of the new releases; the grosses at this point relative to previous hits; which pictures will pass the others in a few weeks. It's like the Olympics – which will be the winners?

4   There are a lot of reasons that movies have been so bad during the last couple of years and probably won't be any better for the next couple of years. One big reason is that rotten pictures are

making money – not necessarily wild amounts (though a few are), but sizable amounts. So if studio heads want nothing more than to make money and grab power, there is no reason for them to make better ones. Turning out better pictures might actually jeopardize their position. Originally, the studios were controlled by theatre chains – the chains opened the studios in order to have a source of supply. But the studios and the theatre chains were separated by a Supreme Court order in 1948 and subsequent lower-court rulings; after that, the studios, operating without the protection of theatres committed in advance to play their product, resorted to "blind bidding" and other maneuvers in order to reduce the risk on their films. It's only in the last few years that the studios have found a new kind of protection. They have discovered that they can get much more from the sale of movies to television than they had been getting, and that they can negotiate presale agreements with the networks for guaranteed amounts before they commit themselves to a production. Licensing fees to the networks now run between $3,000,000 and $4,000,000 for an average picture, and the studios negotiate in advance not only for network showings and later TV syndication (about $1,500,000 for an average picture), and for pay television (between $1,000,000 and $1,500,000), but for cable TV, the airlines, cassettes, and overseas television. And, of course, they still sell to foreign distributors and to exhibitors here, and much of that money is also committed in advance – sometimes even paid in advance. So if a film is budgeted at $8,500,000, the studio may have $14,000,000 guaranteed and – theoretically, at least – show a profit before shooting starts, even if $4,000,000 is allowed for marketing and advertising. And the studio still has the possibility of a big box-office hit and *really* big money. If a picture is a large-scale adventure story or has superstars, the licensing fee to the networks alone may be between $15,000,000 and $25,000,000, and the total advance guarantees may come to almost double the budget. Financially, the only danger in an arrangement like this is that if the film goes seriously over budget the studio can still lose money. That's why directors who have the reputation of always coming in on schedule are in steady demand even if they've had a long line of box-office failures and their work is consistently mediocre, and why directors who are perfectionists are shunned as if they were lepers – unless, like Hal Ashby, they've had some recent hits.

The studios no longer make movies primarily to attract and   5
please moviegoers; they make movies in such a way as to get as much as possible from the prearranged and anticipated deals. Every picture (allowing for a few exceptions) is cast and planned in terms of those deals. Though the studio is very happy when it has a box-office hit, it isn't terribly concerned about the people

who buy tickets and come out grumbling. They don't grumble very loudly anyway, because even the lumpiest pictures are generally an improvement over television; at least, they're always bigger. TV accustoms people to not expecting much, and because of the new prearranged deals they're not getting very much. There is a quid pro quo for a big advance sale to television and theatres: the project must be from a fat, dumb best-seller about an international jewel heist or a skyjacking that involves a planeload of the rich and famous, or be a thinly disguised show-business biography of someone who came to an appallingly wretched end, or have an easily paraphrasable theme – preferably something that can be done justice to in a sentence and brings to mind the hits of the past. How else could you entice buyers? Certainly not with something unfamiliar, original. They feel safe with big-star packages, with chase thrillers, with known ingredients. For a big overseas sale, you must have "international" stars – performers who are known all over, such as Sophia Loren, Richard Burton, Candice Bergen, Roger Moore, Clint Eastwood, Burt Reynolds, Alain Delon, Charles Bronson, Steve McQueen. And you should probably avoid complexities: much of the new overseas audience is subliterate. For a big advance sale to worldwide television, a movie should also be innocuous: it shouldn't raise any hackles, either by strong language or by a controversial theme. And there must be stars, though not necessarily movie stars. It has recently been discovered that even many Americans are actually more interested in TV personalities than in movie ones, and may be roused from their TV-viewing to go see a film with John Denver or John Ritter. In countries where American TV series have become popular, our TV stars may be better known than our movie stars (especially the ones who appear infrequently). A 1979 Canadian film, *Running*, starring Michael Douglas, who has appeared in a TV series and was featured in *The China Syndrome*, cost $4,200,000; by the time it was completed, the various rights to it had been sold for over $6,000,000. The lawyer-financier who set up the production of *Foolin' Around*, which stars Gary Busey, said he would not have made the picture without the television insurance of a supporting cast that included Tony Randall, Cloris Leachman, and Eddie Albert. Nobody needs to have heard of these independently packaged pictures for them to be profitable, and, in some cases, if it were not contractually necessary to open the film in theatres in order to give it legitimacy as a movie, it would be cheaper not to, because the marketing and advertising costs may outstrip the box-office revenue (unless that, too, was guaranteed). On productions like these, the backers don't suffer the gamblers' anxieties that were part of film business in the fifties and sixties, and even in the early seventies. Of course, these backers don't experience the gamblers' highs, either. Movie executives now study the television Q ratings, which measure the public's familiarity with performers, and a performer with a high rating (which he attains if he's been in a long-running series or on a daytime quiz show) is offered plum movie roles – even if this means that the script will have to be completely rewritten for his narrow range or bland personality.

There is an even grimmer side to all this: because the studios   6
have discovered how to take the risk out of moviemaking, they don't want to make any movies that they can't protect themselves on. Production and advertising costs have gone so high that there is genuine nervous panic about risky projects. If an executive finances what looks like a perfectly safe, stale piece of material and packs it with stars, and the production costs skyrocket way beyond the guarantees, and the picture loses many millions, *he* won't be blamed for it – he was playing the game by the same rules as everybody else. If, however, he takes a gamble on a small project that can't be sold in advance – something that a gifted director really wants to do, with a subtle, not easily summarized theme and no big names in the cast – and it loses just a little money, his neck is on the block. So to the executives a good script is a script that attracts a star, and they will make their deals and set the full machinery of a big production in motion and schedule the picture's release dates, even though the script problems have never been worked out and everyone (even the director) secretly knows that the film will be a confused mess, an embarrassment.

Another new factor makes a risky project still riskier; if a movie   7
doesn't have an easily paraphrasable theme or big stars, it's hard to sell via a thirty-second TV commercial. (The networks pay a lot for movies, but they get much of it back directly from the movie industry, which increasingly relies on TV commercials to sell a film.) It's even hard for the studio advertising departments to figure out a campaign for newspapers and magazines. And so, faced with something unusual or original, the studio head generally says, "I don't know how to market it, and if I don't know how to market it, it will lose money." The new breed of studio head is not likely to say, "It's something I feel we should take a chance on. Let's see if there's somebody who might be able to figure out how to market it." Just about the only picture the studios made last year that the executives took a financial risk on was *Breaking Away*. And despite the fact that it cost what is now a pittance ($2,400,000) and received an Academy Award Best Picture nomination, Twentieth Century-Fox didn't give it a big theatrical re-release (the standard procedure for a nominated film) but sold it to NBC for immediate showing, for $5,000,000. So a couple of weeks after the Awards ceremony, just when many people had finally heard of *Breaking*

Away and might have gone to a theatre to see it, it appeared, trashed in the usual manner, on television. The studio couldn't be sure how much more money might come in from box offices, and grabbed a sure thing. In order to accept the NBC offer, the studio even bypassed pay TV, where the picture could have been seen uncut. It was almost as if *Breaking Away* were being punished for not having stars and not having got a big advance TV sale. And the price was almost insulting: last year, Fox licensed *The Sound of Music* to NBC for $21,500,000, and licensed Alien to ABC for $12,000,000, with escalator clauses that could take the figure up to $15,000,000; Columbia licensed *Kramer vs. Kramer* to ABC for nearly $20,000,000, and United Artists got $20,000,000 for *Rocky II* from CBS. But then how do you summarize in a sentence the appeal of a calm, evenhanded film about fathers and sons, town boys and college boys, and growing up – a modest classic that never states its themes, that stirs the emotions by indirection, by the smallest of actions and the smallest exchanges of dialogue?

8   When the numbers game takes over a country, artists who work in a popular medium, such as the movies, lose their bearings fast. There's a pecking order in filmmaking, and the director is at the top – he's the authority figure. A man who was never particularly attractive to women now finds that he's the padrone: everyone is waiting on his word, and women are his for the nod. The constant, unlimited opportunities for sex can be insidious; so is the limitless flattery of college students who turn directors into gurus. Directors are easily seduced. They mainline admiration. Recently, a screenwriter now directing his first picture was talking about his inability to find a producer who would take some of the burden off him; he said he needed a clone – someone who would know what was in his mind and be able to handle a million details for him. But anyone observing this writer-director would know that he needs a real producer, and for a much more important reason: to provide the sense of judgment he has already lost. Nobody really controls a production now; the director is on his own, even if he's insecure, careless, or nuts. There has always been a megalomaniac potential in moviemaking, and in this period of stupor, when values have been so thoroughly undermined that even the finest directors and the ones with the most freedom aren't sure what they want to do, they often become obsessive and grandiloquent – like mad royalty. Perpetually dissatisfied with the footage they're compulsively piling up, they keep shooting – adding rooms to the palace. Megalomania and art become the same thing to them. But the disorder isn't just in their heads, and a lot of people around them are deeply impressed by megalomania. What our directors need most of all, probably, is a sense of purpose and a subject that they

can think their way through. Filmmakers want big themes, and where are the kinds of themes that they would fight the studios to express? It's no accident that the two best recent American movies are both fantasy fairy tales – childish in the fullest, deepest sense. Working inside a magical structure, Carroll Ballard in *The Black Stallion* and Irvin Kershner in *The Empire Strikes Back* didn't have to deal with the modern world; they were free to use the medium luxuriantly, without guilt. You can feel the love of moviemaking – almost a revelry in moviemaking – in their films, as you can also in Walter Hill's *The Long Riders*, despite its narrative weaknesses and a slight remoteness. But we don't go to the movies just for great fairy tales and myths of the old West; we also hope for something that connects directly with where we are. Part of the widespread anticipation of *Apocalypse Now* was, I think, our readiness for a visionary, climactic, summing-up movie. We felt that the terrible rehash of pop culture couldn't go on, mustn't go on – that something new was needed. Coppola must have felt that too, but he couldn't supply it. His film was posited on great thoughts arriving at the end – a confrontation and a revelation. And when they weren't there, people slunk out of the theatres, or tried to comfort themselves with chatter about the psychedelic imagery. Trying to say something big, Coppola got tied up in a big knot of American self-hatred and guilt, and what the picture boiled down to was: White man – he devil. Since then, I think, people have expected less of movies and have been willing to settle for less. Some have even been willing to settle for *Kramer vs. Kramer* and other pictures that seem to be made for an audience of over-age flower children. These pictures express the belief that if a man cares about anything besides being at home with the kids, he's corrupt. Parenting ennobles Dustin Hoffman and makes him a better person in every way, while in *The Seduction of Joe Tynan* we can see that Alan Alda is a weak, corruptible fellow because he wants to be President of the United States more than he wants to stay at home communing with his daughter about her adolescent miseries. Pictures like these should all end with the fathers and the children sitting at home watching TV together.

The major studios have found the temporary final solution for movies: in technique and in destiny, their films *are* television. And there's no possibility of a big breakthrough in movies – a new release of energy, like the French New Wave, which moved from country to country and resulted in an international cross-fertilization – when movies are financed only if they fall into stale categories of past successes. But once the groups that are now subsidizing studio-made films begin to weary of getting TV shows when they thought they were buying movies, there should be a chance for some real moviemaking. And when the writers and directors have

9

confidence in what they want to express, if they can't find backing from the studios they ought to be able to find backers outside the industry who will gamble on the money to be made from a good picture, once it is completed. It's easier to make money on movies now: there are more markets, and we know now that the films themselves have a much longer commercial life than early moviemakers could have guessed. The studios may find that they need great moviemakers more than the moviemakers need them. Billy Wilder may be right that you can't make pictures with 'em, but of course he's wrong that you can't make pictures without 'em. There are problems both ways, but there may be fewer problems without them, and less rage.

10   It would be very convincing to say that there's no hope for movies – that audiences have been so corrupted by television and have become so jaded that all they want are noisy thrills and dumb jokes and images that move along in an undemanding way, so they can sit and react at the simplest motor level. And there's plenty of evidence, such as the success of *Alien*. This was a haunted-house-with-gorilla picture set in outer space. It reached out, grabbed you, and squeezed your stomach; it was more gripping than entertaining, but a lot of people didn't mind. They thought it was terrific, because at least they'd felt something; they'd been brutalized. It was like an entertainment contrived in Aldous Huxley's *Brave New World* by the Professor of Feelies in the College of Emotional Engineering. Yet there was also a backlash against *Alien* – many people were angry at how mechanically they'd been worked over. And when I saw *Black Stallion* on a Saturday afternoon, there was proof that even children who have grown up with television and may never have been exposed to a good movie can respond to the real thing when they see it. It was a hushed, attentive audience, with no running up and down the aisles and no traffic to the popcorn counter, and even when the closing credits came on, the children sat quietly looking at the images behind the names. There may be a separate God for the movies, at that.

QUESTIONS

Language and Style

1. How would you characterize the writer's tone in this essay? See, for example, the comments on *Kramer vs. Kramer* and *The Seduction of Joe Tynan*, and the comments on television ("TV accustoms people to not expecting much. . . . ").

2. Is there a sense in which Kael's language varies from "high" ("an

appallingly wretched end") to "low" ("fat, dumb best-seller")? Can you locate other examples?

3. How does the high and low range of the writer's language match her treatment of good and bad movies? How does this use of language affect the tone of the essay?

Organization

1. What, in summary, are the main causes for the state of the movie industry? Why do they not arrange themselves in a neat chain?

2. How can you explain the organization of Kael's essay? Notice the length of the paragraphs and the fact that some of them (paragraphs 2 and 4 are examples) begin with a "topic sentence."

3. How much effort does Kael commit to supporting the claim that movies are bad and likely to get worse? What is assumed about the reader?

Content

1. Many of the movies Kael mentions have not been shown in the theatres for some time. What responsibility does the reader have in the circumstances?

Vocabulary

grosses	aegis
conglomerates	milieu
compliant	echelons
demigod	syndication
quid pro quo	subliterate
hackles	innocuous
plum	paraphrasable
pittance	padrone
guru	stupor
grandiloquent	posited
jaded	trashed

Ice and Light
Barry Lopez

This excerpt from Lopez's Arctic Dreams, *an extraordinary account of the North, manages to combine scientific explanations and personal experience in a particularly effective way.*

1   At first it seems that, except for a brief few weeks in autumn, the Arctic is without color. Its land colors are the colors of deserts, the ochers and siennas of stratified soils, the gray-greens of sparse plant life on bare soil. On closer inspection, however, the mono-tonic rock of the polar desert is seen to harbor the myriad greens, reds, yellows, and oranges of lichens. The whites of tundra swans and of sunlit ice in black water are pure and elegant. Occasionally there is brilliant coloring – as with wildflowers in the summer, or a hillside of willow and bearberry in the fall; or a slick of vegetable oils shining with the iridescent colors of petroleum on a tundra puddle; or the bright face of a king eider. But the bright colors are more often only points in a season, not brush-strokes; and they are absorbed in the paler casts of the landscape.

2   Arresting color in the Arctic is found more often in the sky, with its vivid twilights and the aurora borealis. (The predominant col-ors of the aurora are a pale green and a soft rose. I turned over a weathered caribou antler once on the tundra and found these same two colors staining its white surface. Such correspondence, like that between a surfacing guillemot and an Eskimo man rolling upright in his kayak, hold a landscape together.)

3   Arctic skies retain the colors of dawn and dusk for hours in winter. On days when the southern sky is barely lit for a while around noon, layers of deep violet, of bruised purples and dense blues, may stretch across 80° of the horizon, above a familiar lavender and the thinnest line of yellow gold. The first sunrise/ sunset of spring may glow "carmine and lake [red], fading off into crimsons, yellows, and saffrons," as a British naval surgeon wrote in his winter journal. In the spring and fall, when sunrises and sunsets are more widely separated, vivid reds, oranges, and yel-lows shine through washes of rose and salmon, of pale cyan, apricot and indigo, as they do in other latitudes. In summer, the skies have a nacreous quality, like the inside of an abalone shell. The colors of summer skies are pastel; the temperature of the light, however, varies enough so that around midnight yellows in the landscape fade noticeably and blues deepen.

The striking phenomena in the arctic sky for a newcomer are the   *4*
unsuspected variety of solar and lunar rings, halos, and coronas;
the aurora borealis itself; and the mirages that occur at sea, including fata morganas. These events are especially apparent in the Far
North for several reasons. The kinds of ice crystals that cause solar
and lunar refraction are often present in the arctic atmosphere.
The air itself is clear. Slight inversions in the lower atmosphere and
sharp temperature differentials at the surface of the ocean in
summer, which cause mirages, are common. And the arctic region
lies directly underneath the part of the earth's atmosphere that
makes the auroral display, or northern lights, visible.

When he was in winter quarters on the coast of Melville Island in   *5*
1819-20, William Parry drew a picture of the sun's halos, arcs, and
parahelia, or sun dogs, that is now famous. He captured in that
single drawing many of the effects that are regularly seen in the
Arctic either alone or in some combination. The sun, at the time,
was about 22° above the southeastern horizon. It was surrounded
by a halo that measured 44° across the horizon and by a second
halo 92° across the horizon, part of which was cut off below by the
line of the earth. (These are called, after their degree of radius, the
22° and 46° solar halos.) Both these halos were subtended by
other arcs, while yet another arc cut across the sun and swept
away east and west, parallel to the horizon (the parahelic arc).
Where the parahelic arc crossed the 22° halo, two brilliant sun
dogs appeared. And below the sun, just at the horizon, gleamed a
third sun dog (actually a subsun).

This picture can be readily explained by physicists in terms of   *6*
ray mechanics, a precise bending of sunlight through certain types
of ice crystals aligned in a specific way. In fact, a physicist named
Robert Greenler reproduced the elements of Parry's drawing almost perfectly in a computer illustration generated by the formu-
lae involved – a tribute to the accuracy and completeness of
Parry's work.

Francis M'Clintock, another British explorer, was presiding at a   *7*
burial through the sea ice in Baffin Bay in 1857 when he took notice
of a stark December moon. A "complete halo encircl[ed] the moon,"
wrote M'Clintock, "through which passed a horizontal band of pale
light that encompassed the heavens; above the moon appeared the
segments of two other halos, and there were also mock moons or
paraselenae to the number of six. The misty atmosphere lent a
very ghastly hue to this singular display, which lasted rather more
than an hour."

The physics involved in the refraction and reflection of sunlight   *8*
by ice crystals and water droplets, and its diffraction by airborne
particles, is dauntingly complex. The arcs and halos produced are
sometimes very faint; they also occur in unexpected combinations.
Seeing them, however, is largely a matter of training yourself to

look. On a single spring day over Lancaster Sound I saw a soft, opaque white pillar or feather (the shape was like a passerine bird's tail feather) standing between the sun and the southeastern horizon (a sun pillar); and that evening, a few minutes after midnight, two long, rainbow-hued shields standing on the horizon on opposite sides of the sun, an unusual pair of sun dogs.

9   The aurora borealis, pale gossamer curtains of light that seem to undulate across arctic skies, are transfixing in part because of their diffidence. "It is impossible to witness such a beautiful phenomenon without a sense of awe," wrote Robert Scott, the British Antarctic explorer, "and yet this sentiment is not inspired by its brilliancy but rather by its delicacy in light and colour, its transparency, and above all by its tremulous evanescence of form. There is no glittering splendour to dazzle the eye, as has been too often described; rather the appeal is to the imagination by the suggestion of something wholly spiritual...."

10   It is unusual in the literature of exploration to find a strictly consistent reaction, but virtually everyone who wrote down his thoughts about the aurora described, first, the inadequacy of his language and, second, a pervasive and stilling spiritual presence. Among Eskimos the descriptions are often of events that precede or follow life on earth, of the play of unborn children, or of torches held by the dead to help the living hunt in winter. In more southerly latitudes of the Northern Hemisphere, where the aurora is occasionally visible, its connotations are much different, largely because its predominant color when it becomes visible that far south is a deep red. The apparition suggested conflagration and holocaust to Europeans in the Middle Ages. Vikings thought it a reflection in the sky of Vulcan's forge. Miners in Alaska at the turn of the century, of a more scientific and prosaic bent, thought the aurora was a gaseous form of lightning or the glow from radium mines.

11   The first time I recognized the northern lights was on a flight from Seattle to Anchorage, when I saw them above the Wrangell Mountains. It was a clear night, and at first I thought it was only a long, moonlit orographic cloud, the kind one often sees isolated over a mountain. Then I saw it move. Completely absorbed, I watched the long banner of pale light, unfurling in lateral movements over the snow-white mountains until the plane turned away. The motions were like a t'ai chi exercise: graceful, inward-turning, and protracted.

12   The bottom of an auroral display rarely comes as close as 100 miles above the earth. To the human eye, however, the thin wall of light sometimes appears actually to touch the earth because of a problem of depth perception with objects of unknown size in space. Accurate descriptions are further complicated by its

overwhelming size, and its movement. The light wall is often hundreds of miles long and 150 miles or more high; as the intensity of auroral activity increases, the "curtain" of light begins to undulate in a horizontal direction, folding back on itself in huge S-curves and then unfurling again.

There are additional problems with perspective and scale. To   *13* someone underneath the display (the top of the wall is tipped toward the south), the aurora may appear like a convergence of rays toward an apex above. Seen edge-on (from directly beneath the bottom edge), the display may seem like luminous smoke rising from the earth. From a distance it may look like a weightless curtain of silk, hanging straight down and rippling in the night air.

The aurora occurs in a thin corridor called the auroral oval   *14* centered on the North Magnetic Pole. The display is created by an electric discharge in the earth's ionosphere and is apparent to us because some of the energy released is visible light. The most common tinting, of pale, whitish green and pinkish rose, is light emitted from oxygen atoms. During intense periods of auroral activity, nitrogen molecules release a crimson light, usually apparent only at the bottom edge of the auroral curtain.

Imagine that your view is from the sun and that you are facing   *15* the earth. To your far left on the earth's surface are the penumbral shadows of dawn. Before you is the bright light of noon. To your far right the border between evening and night. Streaming outward from the sun is a gas of ionized, or charged, particles, mostly helium and hydrogen nuclei, called the solar wind. These particles pass around the earth as though it were a rock in a stream of water. In doing so they flatten the planet's magnetic field (the magnetosphere) on the near side (day) and elongate it on the far side (night). As it flows past the earth, the solar wind generates an electric current from left to right. The path of least resistance for the solar particles that carry this current is along force lines in the earth's magnetic field that curve down to the earth's surface in the polar regions (like the embrasure of an apple, where the stem is). Particles pouring into the polar regions from a positive terminal on the left create the aurora. As they flow up and out to a negative terminal on the right, they constitute a separate invisible phenomenon, the polar wind.

As the stream of particles flows earthward down the funnel-   *16* shaped surface of the magnetosphere at the Pole, it excites electrons in oxygen atoms and nitrogen molecules which, as they settle back into a stable state, emit energy – X-rays, infrared and ultraviolet light, radio waves, and visible light.

The still wall of light we perceive curved along an east-west arc   *17* is the calmest sort of auroral display. The more energetic the sun's streaming particles, the deeper they penetrate into the earth's ionosphere and the taller the wall of light becomes. Varying intensities in the electric field produced by the solar wind, and in the solar wind's own magnetic field, cause the wall to develop a series of fine corrugations and folds perpendicular to its east-west extension, to surge in several directions, and to break up into patches. The changes in the electric and magnetic fields that produce, respectively, the changes in color and motion are caused by magnetic storms on the sun. Major magnetic storms occur in an eleven-year cycle, in association with solar flares in the vicinity of sunspots and in solar features called coronal holes. Magnetic substorms, far more common, create the sequence of auroral events that arctic viewers think of as "typical" for an arctic winter evening. First, a sudden brightening resolves itself into a transparent auroral curtain. Its fine corruscations (rays) become more prominent. There are surges of movement east and west across the curtain, which starts to develop deep folds. The entire display may then move steadily north. Toward dawn it breaks up into isolated luminous patches, like clouds.

18   The power produced in this generator is astonishing – 1 trillion watts with a current of 1 million amperes. The most violent solar storms affect magnetic compasses, wreak havoc with radio communications and certain navigational systems, and create induced electric currents in long conductors like the trans-Alaska pipeline.

19   Many people claim the aurora makes a sound, a muffled swish or "a whistling and crackling noise, like the waving of a large flag in a fresh gale of wind," as the explorer Samuel Hearne wrote. And some Eskimos say "the lights" will respond to a gentle whistling and come nearer. They easily evoke feelings of awe and tenderness; the most remarkable effect they seem to have, however, is to draw a viewer emotionally up and out of himself, because they throw the sky into a third dimension, on such a vast scale, in such a beautiful way, that they make the emotion of self-pity impossible.

20   I remember flying from Prudhoe Bay to Fairbanks one winter night. The sky was clear and the aurora borealis was very strong. With moonlight from the south the snow-covered landscape below was bright, its relief evident in ground shadows. Even the faint line separating the snow-covered tundra from the snow-covered ice was apparent. The auroral curtain stretched out to the west from my view, toward the Village of Wainright and the Chukchi Sea. It was in its early, quiescent form of diaphanous rays, a long, pale ghost fire. I could see the edge of the Brooks Range and the plain of the North Slope below. I recalled days of camping in the mountains, of traveling on the tundra, and the times I'd camped on the arctic coast west of Prudhoe. I could see these places clearly, but it was the aurora, towering over the earth, that resolved what could have been only a map into a real landscape, making the memories seem immediate and tangible.

No one knows whether the first Europeans found their way to   *21*
Iceland, and thence to Greenland and North America, by accident
or by design. A reasonable thought is that Iceland occasionally
appeared to people in the Faroe Islands as a great looming mirage,
like the one of Somerset Island I saw that day. Such mirages often
occur whenever a mass of warm air lies over a body of cold water.
Light rays that under other conditions might travel straight off into
space are bent, or refracted, back earthward in a series of small
steps as they pass through layers of air at different temperatures.

Mirages are usually divided into two categories: in superior   *22*
mirages, like the one of Somerset, the image the eye sees of an
object is a false image above the actual object; in an inferior
mirage, the false image occurs below the object. Superior mirages
are commonly seen at sea in the Arctic in summer, especially late
in the afternoon of a clear day. Distant islands, ships, coastlines,
and icebergs lying beyond the real horizon all appear to be closer
than they are, the sea itself appears slightly concave, and the
horizon seems unusually far off.

Superior images are created when light waves pass from denser   *23*
(or cooler) air in the lower atmosphere into air that is less dense
(or warmer). Evenly spaced layers of successively warmer air (i.e.,
layers of air arranged in a perfect temperature gradient) work like
a series of eyeglass lenses, each of which is successively less
corrective. A ray of light passing through them all is bent back
earthward in a smooth arc. The viewer sees a single clear image of
the real object.

If the lenses are arranged, however, so that a more corrective   *24*
lens comes between two less corrective lenses, the ray of light is
turned back on itself. If it is turned back sufficiently (e.g., because
of a strong temperature inversion in the lower atmosphere), a
viewer will see not only the primary image but a second, inverted
image on top of it. Another series of corrective lenses "out of
sequence" (i.e., a second temperature inversion in the lower atmosphere) will create a third image, this one right-side-up on top of
the second image. With other changes in the order of the lenses,
the primary image itself will disappear entirely, leaving an empty
space between the horizon and the second, inverted image.

The degree of "stooping" (the vertical compression common   *25*
with superior mirages), as well as the number of images that
appear, and any apparent magnification of the image, depend on
the rate of change of air temperature vertically and the presence of
reversals in that rate of change. Mirages, of course, are always
imprecise. The distortions come about because of shimmering
(due to slight turbulence in the air) and because the entire atmospheric lens itself is astigmatic – it curves more strongly in one
direction (vertically) than the other (horizontally). All mirages,

therefore, are vertically fuzzy. It is this astigmatic quality of the atmosphere, in combination with complex atmospheric inversions above uniformly bright objects like the sea ice, that gives rise to the most impressive of arctic mirages, the fata morgana. These extensive "mountain ranges" or "urban skylines" seem utterly real to the soberest viewer because of the combined effect of several optical phenomena.

26   Under mirage conditions, sunlight reflecting off the sea ice, through layers of successively warmer air, in which there is a sequence of slight temperature inversions, creates the appearance of a high grayish rampart in the distance. The wall appears in outline and detail exactly like a distant palisade seen through the earth's blue haze because the astigmatic atmospheric lens has broken the white ice up into areas of light and shadow, and vertical blurring has eliminated any recognizable features. If the layers of air are then slightly tipped by a breeze and return to the horizontal in a regular rhythmic pattern (which occurs because of gravity), the alternation will produce permanent peaks and spires on an already steady image and the illusion is complete. The upper edge of the mirage appears serrated, like the arête of a mountain range; the gray walls suggest snow-covered slopes, even down to dark ridge lines where wind has apparently blown the snow away; and the clefts of steep montane valleys are apparent.

27   Mirages were a source of delight and amusement to many arctic travelers. They brought lighthearted feelings and a sense of mock astonishment to the serious, sometimes tedious business of making coastal surveys and plotting a course. Fata morganas stand somewhat outside this tradition of innocent whimsy. Seasoned explorers, vehemently insisting on what they had seen, set down mountains and islands on their charts where there was nothing but empty sky. So convincing were these apparitions that the skepticism of other explorers (or even a member of the same expedition) was met with contempt. Expeditions sent out later to verify these new lands sometimes saw the same fata morgana, further confusing the issue. Only by prolonging their arduous journeys, thereby observing a constant receding of the image, did they prove that the land was not there at all.

28   So it was for the Macmillan Expedition (1913), sent to confirm the existence of a "Crocker Land," reported by Robert Peary northwest of Cape Thomas Hubbard, northern Axel Heiberg Island. The "Barnard Mountains," reported by John Ross in 1818 to extend from Devon Island to Ellesmere Island across Jones Sound, were found not to exist by Edward Inglefield in 1852. American explorer Charles Francis Hall's "President's Land" proved an ephemera. The "King Oscar Land" and "Petermann Land" described by an Austrian army officer from Cape Fligeli, Franz Josef Land, in 1884 were never

seen again. Vilhjalmur Stefansson set off twice in search of "Keenan Land" in the Beaufort Sea.

Some arctic experts conjecture, especially in Stefansson's case,   *29*
that these fata morganas were actually tabular bergs or ice islands. It may, indeed, have been a tabular berg hundreds of square miles in extent that a Cossack explorer named Alexei Markoff found far north of the Yana River delta in 1715. The "prodigious mountains" of ice that blocked his path were never reported again.

The monotonic surfaces of the Arctic create frequent problems   *30*
with scale and depth perception, especially on overcast days. Arctic hare and willow ptarmigan sometimes disappear against the snow when they are only two or three yards away. Even when a contrasting animal like a caribou or a brown bear is visible on snow or ice, it is sometimes hard to determine whether it is a large animal at a distance or a small animal at close range. In *My Life with the Eskimo* Stefansson recalls spending an hour stalking a tundra grizzly that turned out to be a marmot. A Swedish explorer had all but completed a written description in his notebook of a craggy headland with two unusually symmetrical valley glaciers, the whole of it a part of a large island, when he discovered what he was looking at was a walrus. Johann Miertsching, travelling with M'Clure aboard the *Investigator*, wrote of a polar bear that "rose in the air and flew off" as the hunting party approached. A snowy owl. "These comical deceptions," wrote Miertsching, "are a frequent occurrence."

The white-out is another familiar deceptive phenomenon. It   *31*
commonly occurs under an overcast sky or in a fog bank, where light traveling in one direction at a certain angle has the same flux, or strength, as light traveling at any angle in any other direction. There are no shadows. Space has no depth. There is no horizon. On foot you stumble about in missed-stair-step fashion. On a fast-moving snow machine your heart nearly stops when the bottom of the world disappears.

William Scoresby, in his *Account of the Arctic Regions* (1820),   *32*
offered an original explanation for mistakes in depth perception that are frequently made along certain arctic coasts. The coasts he had in mind are characterized by an extreme degree of contrast between their barren rock walls and expanses of snow and ice. With no middle tones to work with, the eye has trouble resolving these two-dimensional vistas into three dimensions. The human eye also commonly uses the relative density of blue light scattered in the air to judge distance (this is the light that softens the edge of a far mountain); but the clear arctic atmosphere scatters very little light. Faced with these high-contrast, black-and-white coasts, having no knowledge of their real height, and staring at them through

an exceedingly clear atmosphere, early mariners had no idea whether they were 5 or 25 miles offshore. Mogens Heinson, sent out to search for lost colonies in Greenland by Frederick II of Denmark in the sixteenth century, battled ice and snow squalls across the North Atlantic for weeks before he raised Greenland's southeast coast. With a fresh gale blowing favorably and clear skies, he laid a course for those towering cliffs. After several hours he appeared to be no closer to the coast than when he began. The effect was so convincing that he succumbed to the belief that his ship was being held motionless over an undersea lodestone. Frightened, he put about until the coast of Greenland was far behind, and then set course for Denmark.

QUESTIONS

Language and Style

1. In what way is Lopez's discussion a mixture of things? How does this fact affect the language here?

2. How does the writer help the reader understand some of the technical matters here? See paragraph 15.

3. What is Lopez referring to when he mentions "the temperature of the light" (paragraph 3)?

Organization

1. Can you find examples of personal observations, historical reference, scientific explanation, and humour in this account?

2. Can some of the phenomena be thought of as accidental causes? As mechanical causes? Are the effects of the phenomena always predictable? Why?

3. Into approximately how many parts is the discussion divided? Where do the introductory matters end? How is the section which deals with the *aurora borealis* organized?

Content

1. Explain the "correspondence" Lopez remarks in paragraph 2. How could it "hold a landscape together"?

Vocabulary

ochers	lodestone	embrasure
stratified	diaphanous	serrated
iridescent	passerine	montane
tundra	evanescence	marmot
cyan	sienna	sun dogs
orographic	monotonic	clefts
palisade	eider	diffidence
arête	guillemot	
ephemera	opaque	

The Ladies Converse
Robert Sommer

Sommer's interesting and humorous account of the results of a plan to rearrange a hospital ward lends insight into the ways of institutions and how people adapt to them.

My interest in environmental engineering dates from the time an   1
internist for an elderly ladies' ward at a state hospital asked for help in discovering what was wrong with the place. Several thousand dollars had been spent to improve the ward – curtains framed the windows, the reflection of fluorescent lights danced on the new tile floor, tubular steel chairs with brightly colored plastic seats gave a Mondrian touch to the walls, and several air conditioners guarded the windows. The renovation is instructive since it reveals what can happen when people discover money. The old folks' ward was located in Western Canada where extensive federal, provincial, and local welfare programs were in force. In the 1950s a bright civil servant deduced that inmates of institutions were indeed citizens and eligible for federal old age pensions. Seventy-five dollars a month may seem small in absolute terms, but it was a great windfall to all players in the institutional game – custodians, patients, and relatives – since the pensions had accumulated over the years. Some patients had comfortable nest eggs when they were discharged, but if a patient died at the institution, his estate, including the accumulated pension funds, went to his relatives. At

From Personal Space *by Robert Sommer* © *1969. Reprinted by permission of the publisher, Prentice-Hall, Inc., Englewood Cliffs, N.J.*

this particular hospital the administration decided to spend some pension funds on amenities for the elderly.

2   New furniture, air conditioners, and a television set were purchased for the ward. There is no record of what the ladies said about the change since no one solicited their opinions before or after. This is the customary state of affairs in custodial institutions where, in return for the beneficence of free room and board, the grateful inmates are expected to accept their environment as it is. The patients have privileges rather than rights, visitors instead of families. This became painfully evident when I interviewed patients about their wards. The patients were taken by surprise, and the nurses were suspicious. Of course, no one had solicited their opinions about the renovations either. The changes were planned and initiated from above, and completed by people who spent no time on the ward. The floor tiles, for example, were all the same pattern and ran the same way, which made the large lounge look even larger and more institutional than it had before. This singular style was not due to deliberate planning or economy but stemmed from inertia and the inability to realize that floor designs (or the color scheme or chair arrangement) made any difference. Most items were purchased and positioned for ease of maintenance rather than comfort or therapy. Occasionally the outcome bordered on the bizarre from the standpoint of human relationships. Most of the chairs on this ward stood in straight lines along the walls, but there were several rows back-to-back in the center; around several columns there were four chairs, each chair facing a different direction! The tragedy was not that these arrangements existed but that they were accepted as normal and reasonable throughout the institution. To compound the irony, pictures of this ward before and after the renovation formed a major portion of the hospital's application for an improvement award. The pictures revealed such a dramatic improvement in the physical conditions of the ward that the hospital won its award easily.

3   Despite the good publicity, the ward physician was dissatisfied with the outcome, although he could not specify his reasons. The ward looked better, but the ladies' mental state was unchanged. We visited the ward together, and I took to sitting there alone on long afternoons. Initially I shared his enthusiasm for the new furnishings. There was no denying that it was the best furnished ward in the hospital; as such it was regarded as somewhat of a model to be seen by visitors on tour. It took several weeks of sitting and watching before I could sort figure from ground and see what was not happening as well as what was. With as many as 50 ladies in the large room, there were rarely more than one or two brief conversations. The ladies sat side by side against the newly painted walls in their new chrome chairs and exercised their options of gazing down at the newly tiled floor or looking up at the new

fluorescent lights. They were like strangers in a train station waiting for a train that never came. This shoulder-to-shoulder arrangement was unsuitable for sustained conversation even for me. To talk to neighbors, I had to turn in my chair and pivot my head 90 degrees. For an older lady, particularly one with difficulties in hearing and comprehension, finding a suitable orientation for conversation was extremely taxing. I hardly need add that there was no conversation whatever between occupants of the center chairs that faced different directions.

In retrospect, the reasons for the straight-row arrangement are   4
not difficult to understand. First, there is the lack of explicit principles relating furniture arrangement to social intercourse. Sensitive individuals intuitively know that there is a connection, and people who want to converse will, consciously or unconsciously, occupy chairs with a suitable orientation and distance, but this is on a prescientific and nonverbal basis, something that is unlikely to play much part in the bureaucratic intricacies of institutional architecture. Magazines in medical specialties and allied fields devote considerable space to hospital construction and ward design, but the published plans and blueprints reveal only bare walls and rooms. The arrangement of furniture is left to the ward staff who do not realize the therapeutic potential of furniture arrangements. Ward geography is taken for granted, and a chair becomes something to sweep around rather than a necessary tool for social interaction. . . .

The inadequacy of the ward arrangement was also apparent   5
when we contrasted it, not only with the conversational groupings in private homes, but also with the arrangement in the corridor outside the ward. Because of the absence of special visiting rooms (space was short and patients' families had a low priority in the competition for available space), this corridor was used by families and friends during visiting hours. Before the building opened to the public at 8:00 a.m., the custodian arranged the chairs in straight rows shoulder to shoulder against the walls. Several hours later relatives had moved the chairs into small groups so that they could face one another and converse comfortably. This was the typical situation in the corridor, but it *never* occurred on the ward. It was clear that families and friends arranged their environment to suit their needs, but the patients were being arranged by it.

Certain arrangements of furniture are very efficient from the   6
standpoint of ward chores. It is a sad commentary that more is known about this aspect of furniture arrangement than about its therapeutic use. Nurses often complain about a ward that looks "junky" or cluttered. A quasi-military arrangement of chairs in neat rows along the wall appears neater, besides making it easier to sweep and survey the ward at a glance. It takes only a second to look down a continuous row of chairs against the wall, compared

with the several seconds required to survey a cluttered room with an irregular seating pattern. Placing chairs along the walls left wide pathways for foodcarts and cleaning wagons to pass freely. Food service personnel and maintenance employees often came through this ward because of ease in transit. The large highway converted the ladies' living space into corridor space that could not be occupied without the risk of injury from the express traffic passing through.

7   Another factor responsible for the straight-row arrangement was the "institutional sanctity" that prevails whenever people spend long periods of time in any environment. After a time, no matter how unusual or unpleasant it seemed at first, the customary becomes fixed and natural. This can apply to the deafening noises of an auto assembly plant as well as the straight-row classrooms in schools. Hospitals, too, have a way of seeming right and efficient to their inhabitants, no matter how they appear to outsiders. In the old folks' ward, the staff no longer noticed the odors and clanking of keys that bothered visitors. The same was true of hospital routines, including the fact that patients were awakened every morning at 5:30. The old-line attendants who were the moral arbiters of the hospital had decreed that the night shift had a "soft touch" and so should bear the additional responsibility of getting the ladies dressed and ready for breakfast before the day shift arrived. Since there were 83 ladies on the ward who averaged 74 years of age and only two nurses on the graveyard shift, this meant starting early in order to get everyone up. The first ladies up and dressed waited two hours until the day shift arrived and served breakfast. Knowing this, it is not difficult to understand why the ladies were tired and ready for bed at 7:00 p.m. This time schedule produced awkward results when several ladies left the ward to live outside. It was the goal of social service to place as many of the ladies as possible in private homes in the belief that from the patient's standpoint as well as the cost to the state, this was preferable to living in an institution. Several ladies had to return to the hospital because people objected to their rising at 5:30 a.m. only to sit in the living room waiting for breakfast. Going to bed at 7:00 p.m. did not endear them to households where courtesy dictated a minimum of noise and disturbance while someone sleeps.

8   The effects of institutional sanctity are most pernicious for individuals who are infirm, helpless, or passive. For schizophrenic people, whose withdrawal and passivity can be compounded by disturbances of perception and thinking, objects may appear fixed and immutable or charismatic and magical. The pattern of a chair may have a symbolic meaning and a patient will not sit down until he has performed a special ritual. There may be gross perceptual distortions of size and distance that affect his view of the environ-

ment in addition to secondary disturbances of hospitalism, institutionalitis, and disculturation resulting from living in a large impersonal institution. It is common to find inmates whose original symptoms have abated, but who have become maladapted to life outside. Inmates and keepers alike come to accept routine as sacred and stability as an absolute value. When we tried to rearrange ward furniture, we encountered patients (and nurses, too) who considered it their duty to correct any deviation from "the way things belonged." After cleaning time, it was surprising to see how quickly furniture returned to its original location. . . .

Individual patients mark out territories on the ward, and any 9 territorial violation produces disturbance. That the nursing staff come to accept the territorial boundaries set by patients in one of the chief impediments to close staff-patient contact. Typically one finds the nurses driven back to a small area around their station. This is nonverbal and inexplicit, but an impressionist painting of a mental ward would show patches of white around the nurses' station surrounded by a sea of blue and gray representing the patients in their drab clothing. When I sat in the dayroom making observations, not only did patients and staff feel uncomfortable to see me there, but I felt personally unwanted. Robert Pace, an anthropologist, spent considerable time charting the location of patients and staff in a veterans' hospital. He found that the attendants were seen near the entrance of the dayroom three times as often as they were in the middle or rear of the room. When questioned, the attendants explained that if they lingered in the rear, "it upset the boys back there," but "you can talk to these men here." Pace described how the patients' nonverbal cues as to space ownership forced him back into the "staff area." On one occasion he was hit by a patient when he unwittingly occupied the patient's chair. . . .

The existence of "favorite chairs" is a typical feature of 10 institutional life. In interviews with staff and residents in 17 English old folks' homes, Lipman found the "habitual occupation of particular chairs" in each institution. Over 90 per cent of those patients who regularly sat in the sitting rooms occupied the same chairs in the same positions each day. Attendants and domestics located the residents in relation to their favorite chairs. Furthermore, when anyone assisted a patient to and from the sitting room, he was invariably told by the person himself or by neighbors where "X's chair" was in the room. It was clear that both nurses and other residents by their behavior reinforced the system of chair ownership. This situation was a source of great confusion to newly admitted patients who had difficulty locating an unowned chair. Sometimes a new resident would be driven from seat to seat until he found one that did not belong to anyone. Interestingly, in their administrative rules and official statements, the nursing staff attempted to discourage space ownership. Senior welfare officials and the matrons of the homes claimed that this policy was intended to avoid feelings of favoritism and possessiveness among the residents and to encourage them to "mix with the others." However, as we have mentioned, the behavior of the nurses in reinforcing the ownership system as well as the inmates' desires for places of their own undermined the official policy, which was ignored in practice.

11   The hospital administrator who does not arrange his wards to facilitate interaction will find the wards arranging the patients to minimize it.

12   Before undertaking our experiment, we spent some time observing seating patterns in a variety of places – homes, bus depots, railway stations, theaters, and hotel lobbies. We became aware of how incorrect our assumptions about public places had been. We had naively believed that hotel lobbies and railway stations were full of people sitting and talking. In actuality, most people sat alone reading or looking at new arrivals. People who were talking invariably had arrived together. People who came alone sat alone and did not interact at all. This provided very little precedent for developing institutional architecture that would bring the residents of this old folks' home into greater contact with one another. The resort hotel might have provided a suitable model, but the clientele usually is young, active, and eager for new friends and social activities in contrast to our own population of elderly men and women incarcerated, often against their will. Organized games or musical activities might have brought younger people together, but our ladies were, if not infirm, at least sedentary. After reviewing the various possibilities, we decided that the ladies would be more likely to converse if they sat facing one another rather than shoulder to shoulder. Our initial view (which was modified later) was that the people should be pointed towards one another like projectiles in order to maximize conversation. We also felt that the large open areas should be broken into smaller spaces, so that each person could select one or two others with whom to interact. Partitions might have served our purpose, but we decided to start with small tables placed around the ward. This upset the highway patrol no end, since they now had to navigate food carts and cleaning wagons around the tables instead of the long open stretch that they had before. Several of the nurses remarked that the tables made the ward look "junky." It seemed reasonable that we should give the ladies these islands of security around which they might group their chairs. We felt that the ladies would feel uncomfortable if their chairs were out in the oceanic spaces. Square tables have the advantage of letting a person know the boundaries of his territory. This seemed an important consideration for an older

person whose sole personal area might be the table space in front of her. With round tables a person never knows where his territory ends and another's begins.

The dayroom was a large open area that, prior to the study, contained 43 chairs, four couches, and four small tables. The tables were placed out in the center of the room, too far from the chairs to be useful, and were employed only for formal activities and for patients whose special diets required them to eat separately. For two weeks prior to the beginning of the study, we recorded all interaction that took place in the dayroom. At various times of the day an observer visited the ward and recorded everything that happened during five-minute periods. So little interaction took place on the ward that longer sessions added little new information. Anything that occurred was recorded on mimeographed floor plans. *13*

After two weeks we removed three of the old couches and introduced five additional square tables (30 inches per side), making a total of nine tables. The chairs were moved away from the walls and placed around the tables in various parts of the room. The first two weeks following the change was a stabilization period and no interaction counts were taken. During this time the nurses encouraged the ladies to sit at the tables. On the morning when the ladies first discovered the change there were spontaneous comments such as, "Where is our chesterfield? We miss our chesterfield." "This is a nice table, but I don't want to eat all day." and "Is this my chair now?" The last comment reflects the fact that individual chairs were moved to new locations. The maintenance and food service employees complained loudly that the tables and chairs cluttered their route through the ward. An occupational therapist inquired whether we were getting ready to hold a party. *14*

It soon became apparent that if we wanted the ladies to remain at the tables, we would have to make the new locations more attractive. Put another way, we had to give the ladies some reasons for remaining at the tables. We hoped that this would become less necessary as the advantages of the tables for social intercourse became evident. We had imagined that the ladies would initially resist a new furniture arrangement and endeavored to counteract this by associating the tables with pleasant experiences and objects. Artificial flowers and vases were placed on the tables (later, real flowers were used) and magazines were laid out every day. Even so, it was difficult to persuade the ladies to remain at the tables. The ladies moved their chairs back against the walls at every opportunity. Indeed the movement of chairs back to the walls continued for some years afterwards and seems to have important psychological significance. Later studies of seating patterns of groups of people, both healthy individuals and patients of *15* various sorts, also showed that people like to sit with their backs to walls and other tangible barriers. Part of this is simply because of comfort and the possibility of leaning one's chair back against a solid surface, but there also seems to be a need for security.

16   A wall location facing out enables one to see what is going on. In a barren institutional environment, this is exceedingly important, since the most exciting events are people coming and going. A good vantage point can provide advance information on meals, medication trays, and craft periods. When we mapped room density, we found that the highest concentrations of persons occurred in the small corridor at the entrance to the dayroom. Further observation and interviewing disclosed three major factors responsible for the high density: the certainty of seeing visitors to the ward from this location, its proximity to the dining hall, and the fact that the corridor contained the only windows low enough to permit an outside view.

17   Our primary concern was to see whether the new arrangement would increase interaction between the ladies. The record sheets distinguished between transient verbal interaction (asking a question, shouting at another patient, extending a greeting) and sustained verbal interaction (reciprocated conversations maintained over two seconds). Because of the difficulty of deciding what constituted nonverbal interaction (touching hands or giving food), recording was limited to verbal interaction between patients. . . .

18   . . . Both transitory and sustained interactions increased during the second period. There was also a remarkable increase in the amount of reading at this time. Before the study was begun, very few magazines were seen in the dayroom despite the fact that large quantities were purchased for the patients or donated each month. One reason for this was that there was no place to store magazines when they were not in use. If a magazine were to be placed on the floor, a nurse was likely to consider this untidy and remove it. The tables now provided places where printed materials could be left without fear of their immediate disappearance. Patients had formerly hoarded magazines, carrying them around in bundles or keeping them under mattresses where they would not be taken away. The same hoarding, which had been a sensible reaction considering the circumstances, appeared when we first laid out magazines on the tables. The first week we supplied 20 magazines a day but they disappeared as rapidly as we put them out. Later, when the ladies found that the magazines were brought to the ward regularly and could be left on the table safely, hoarding decreased.

19   At the same time the ward physician was so impressed with the transformation of the ward, that he sent an occupational therapist to the ward to develop a crafts program. He felt that craftwork could be done at the tables. None of our interaction recording was

done during the crafts sessions, but there was an increase in craft activities throughout the day. Like magazine reading, this was a serendipitous outcome of the new ward arrangement, and has the further implication that it is difficult to keep change isolated and circumscribed. A hospital ward, like a commercial office or an army barracks, is a social system, and a change in any single element will change other parts too. When one introduces tables into a room, it is likely that the occupants will try to make the tables attractive and functional. Except under highly artificial and restricted laboratory situations, it is unlikely that environmental changes can involve only a single factor. If we study the effects of decreased noise in a commercial office, we might find that it produced lower absenteeism and fewer outside trips. One would thereby be recording interaction among more inhabitants than were present in the office before the change. Initial change produces secondary changes, which then affect the initial change, and it is difficult to determine whether an observable effect resulted from the initial change, one of the secondary changes, or a combination of all.

I found this study in the old folks' ward to be instructive, not only   *20* from the standpoint of improved institutional architecture, but also for the possibilities it presented of undertaking environmental research. It is standard procedure in psychological research to taken environment for granted, or to consider it as a background against which interaction takes place. This study convinced me of the potentialities of behavioral research in which the total environment could be altered systematically according to an experimental plan. The pitfalls of undertaking this research using a single variable laboratory model were also apparent. Yet experimentation is only one of the methods used in the behavioral fields, and it is generally supplemented by interviews, natural observation, and questionnaire methods.

QUESTIONS

Language and Style

1. Can you identify those places where the writer's personal reactions come to the surface? What is his apparent attitude toward institutional values and arrangements?

2. How, in particular, would you characterize the writer's tone in paragraph 1? What particular expressions or choices of words contribute to the tone? Is this same attitude evident in the paragraphs which follow? Where does the tone change?

3. Can you explain the writer's apparent surprise at the end of the discussion?

Organization

1. In what ways is this essay organized as a typical scientific report? Where does the report of the experimental work begin? What procedures did Sommer employ?

2. Although Sommer does not describe the ward in detail, an impression does emerge. Can you identify those passing remarks which contribute to the reader's sense of the place?

Vocabulary

internist	schizophrenia	inertia
Mondrian	charismatic	retrospect
amenities	serendipitous	pernicious
beneficence	fluorescent	immutable
figure and ground	windfall	impediments
moral arbiters	custodial	

WRITING ABOUT CAUSES AND EFFECTS

When the writer wants to explain why something happened, the writer is committed to exploring causes and therefore aims at connecting one or another prior event with the result in question. When a writer wants to determine whether an event will transpire, the writer is committed to exploring the future effects of existing or anticipated circumstances and therefore aims at linking events to give the explanation predictive force. In both cases the writer constructs a special sort of narrative.

One of the problems a writer needs to solve in putting together such narratives arises because the connections between events are not self-evident and because an event, understood as a cause, has a number of effects, some of which are more important or obvious than others. Scientists have an advantage here, for in limiting their explanations to observable and testable data they can apply a dependable test of connectedness and predictability. So the non-scientific writer needs a sense of limits, a degree of modesty, and a willingness to explore various possibilities.

A writer who, for example, sets out to explain why, given prison populations, males commit more violent crimes than females needs to realize that such a complex question probably has no definitive answer. Several available explanations suggest themselves, and the most a writer can hope for in the end is a helpful exploration of possibilities in which various causes are considered and weighed. Some may be discounted along the way, while some may still stand for further investigation. In the end a writer may only produce a short-list of potential explanations, but at least the list has been shortened.

A writer who wants to explain the possible effects of high levels of fossil fuel combustion (the burning of larger and larger quantities of oil and coal for industrial and domestic purposes), will quickly encounter something called the Greenhouse Effect. This hypothesizes that large amounts of carbon dioxide released by fossil fuels will cause a marked heating of the earth's atmosphere with attendant flooding and other catastrophies. However, almost as soon as the Greenhouse Effect presents itself as an apparent outcome, the writer will encounter the perhaps equally likely possibility that the earth's oceans will act to absorb the abundant carbon dioxide, thus eliminating the problem and forestalling the catastrophic consequences. The fact is that no one knows which will happen, but the writer has enlightened a reader along the way.

SUGGESTIONS FOR WRITING

Many of the topics which are suggested here are intended for exploration. The writer should not expect to produce a final or definitive explanation, nor should the writer expect to predict the future accurately. Possibilities, though, need to be weighed and considered. Other topics admit to surer treatment because most of the facts are known and their relationships are predictable, so a careful explanation is called for.

1. Why do some leaves change colour in the fall?
2. Why are some people shy?
3. Why do airplanes stay up?
4. In what ways are Canadians influenced by their proximity to the United States?
5. What will happen if you fail to check the oil level in your car's engine?
6. Why do men commit more violent crimes than women?
7. Why does it snow?
8. Why are people who are victims of child abuse likely to abuse *their* children?
9. What effects are likely to follow from the adoption of computers in business and everyday life?
10. Why is it so difficult to quit smoking?

CHAPTER
SEVEN
PROCESSES

INTRODUCTION

Process is a notion which grows out of the ideas of cause and effect, and it is central to the understanding and management of things. A process consists of a linked series of actions or events which, given a particular "input" or beginning, yields a predictable result. The linkage in a process is a cause-and-effect linkage, and it is this causal relationship which gives the predictability of the result. Describing a process, therefore, requires a special sort of narration.

A sample of the great number and variety of processes with which people are involved suggests how important processes are: bureaucratic (getting a driver's licence), biological (digestion), industrial (steel-making), chemical (oxidation), social (mating), botanical (photosynthesis), intellectual (concept formation), political (elections), commercial (lending and borrowing), legal (civil litigation), manufacturing (making pantyhose).

Processes are presented in two different ways: as directions and as information. The purpose of presenting directions is to complete a job of work, to explain to a reader how to put a process in action and see it through. The purpose of an informative presentation of a process is to give the reader a general idea of how a process works. It is the difference between a set of instructions explaining how to change a flat tire, which is successful to the extent that it produces the desirable result with the least effort, and a description of how tires are made, which is intended to give the reader an idea of how tires are produced by the industry.

Very simple processes consist of events arranged as a simple series of actions which occur one after another, but more complex processes show a branching, feedback, or loop pattern. So-called "streaming" procedures followed in some schools show a branching of the education process in which, at a certain time in their school career, students are directed to one of several presumably suitable specialized programs of instruction. In the manufacture of paper it sometimes happens that shredded-wood material is not sufficiently fine to be accommodated by the machinery at the next step in the process, and it is therefore fed back, recirculated, to be chipped or ground a second time before reentering the pulping process proper. A loop in a process occurs when, for example, in a wood products plant waste materials such as sawdust are redirected to a secondary process which produces heat energy for the plant.

The more complex a process is, the more likely it is that it will comprise a number of subsidiary processes, as well as branchings, feedbacks, and loops. Anyone who has toured a modern steel mill or negotiated a mortgage will understand the relationship, for, while securing a mortgage is on the face of it a matter of completing certain application forms for consideration by the lenders, it may very well include along the way the self-contained processes of real estate appraisal, title clearance, etc.

Whether a process is simple or complex, instructive or informative, it shows a common pattern of arrangement consisting of steps or phases. A recipe is typical and is arranged this way:

Casseroled Octopus[1]
To prepare octopus and squid, remove the beaklike mouth, anal portion and the eyes — being careful not to pierce the ink sack which lies close by. If the ink fish are small, this may be done with scissors; if large and tough, you will need a knife to penetrate far enough to slip them inside out and remove and discard the yellowish pouch and the attached membranes. On octopus the very ends of the tentacles are also discarded. Wash well in running water to remove gelatinous portions. Octopus, which has eight arms, comes in enormous sizes, but is apt to be very tough if over 2 to 2½ pounds in weight. Both these and the eight to twelve inch squid, which have six arms and two tentacles, need tenderizing. This can be done in two ways: by merciless beating — native fishermen pound them on the rocks — or by adding tenderizer to a marinade.

The arms and tentacles are cut cross-wise in 1 to 1¼ inch rounds and the white portions of the body meat are often cut in diamond shapes of about the same size to equalize the cooking time. . . .

Clean, pound, and cut up as described previously and place in a casserole:

6 small octopus
½ cup olive oil
⅓ cup vinegar or ½ cup dry wine
2 cups julienned mushrooms
1 cup chopped onions
1 pressed clove garlic
1 tablespoon each fresh chopped parsley, chervil and
     basil
⅓ bay leaf

Cover and bring to a boil. Reduce the heat at once and simmer, very tightly covered, 2½ to 3 hours. You may add the ink to the pan drippings just before serving. Do not boil. Serve with creamed spinach.

Recipes, like all descriptions of processes, begin with raw materials (here octopus or squid, but bureaucratic processes use information) and describe how those raw materials need to be treated or prepared so that they will work in the process (the octopus is cleaned, trimmed, pounded, cut up). Once the raw materials are prepared, they are combined with supplementary ingredients at various points in the process (olive oil, chopped onions). The actual process of cooking an octopus is fairly simple compared to the procedures (more processes) for preparing the materials and consists of four or five steps (cover, bring to a boil, reduce heat, simmer, add ink).

Many accounts of processes conclude with a description of the final product and an indication of how to treat or use it. The octopus recipe suggests a suitable accompaniment for casseroled octopus but does not describe the end result ... which may be just as well.

The Oxford English Dictionary

Paul Roberts

*Roberts's account of how the great dictionary was assembled features
details that help the reader imagine what actually happened.*

The greatest lexicographical effort in England in the nineteenth *1*
century – perhaps the greatest of any century anywhere – was the
Oxford English Dictionary. This has gone under various names in
its long career. It is sometimes called the *Oxford Dictionary*, the
Historical English Dictionary, and the *New English Dictionary*, and
it is variously abbreviated the OED, the OD, the HED, and the NED.
It is usually bound in ten or twelve or twenty volumes, and it costs
in the neighborhood of 250 dollars.

The idea for the *Oxford English Dictionary* was born and nurtured *2*
in the Philological Society in England. In the year 1857 one of its
members read a paper criticizing existing dictionaries. He pointed
out that the best of them were hit-and-miss affairs, unscientifically
produced, impressionistic. He suggested that the Society undertake a new dictionary to be planned along quite different lines. The
Society agreed enthusiastically, not knowing that none of them
would live long enough to see the project completed.

The idea was that the dictionary would draw its data from *3*
English writing and would not only give word meanings but would
systematically cite contextual evidence to verify the meanings
given. The dictionary would include all words in use between the
year 1100 and the date of publication. It was intended to cite the
first occurrence of each word in English writing and the last
occurrence if the word had dropped out of use, together with other
citations across the centuries to show developments in meaning. It
was decided that all extant English writing dating from before 1500
should be read and as much of the later writing as possible. In the
end, practically all of English literature was covered, together with
great quantities of cookbooks, religious tracts, trade manuals, newspapers, and the like.

The reading was done by thousands of volunteers. If you *4*
volunteered to read for the dictionary, you would be assigned, say,
the works of Jane Austen. You would be told to read the novels

carefully, looking for any unusual word, any word unusually used, any word that struck you as new or old or in any way remarkable. When you came on such a word, you wrote it on a slip together with the sentence in which it occurred, noting the page or chapter number and the edition. You were also instructed to excerpt as many ordinary words and their contexts as time permitted. In the end some five million quotations were gathered, of which about a million and a half appeared in the dictionary.

5   As the slips came in, they were sorted and filed in storehouses and eventually studied by the editors and their assistants. When an editor came to write the entry for the word *buxom*, for example, he began by assembling all the slips on *buxom*. He then deduced its meaning and its changes of meaning from those slips. It didn't matter what he thought it meant or ought to mean or what other dictionaries said about it. He was bound by the slips. They gave him all the variant spellings and different usages and displayed the whole history of the word. Everything he had to say about *buxom* came out of those slips, and in the finished article, he included quotations to demonstrate the meanings given.

6   In the first quarter of a century, progress on the dictionary was spasmodic. The Philological Society found the undertaking vaster than it had imagined; financial troubles arose; editors died; interest flagged. But in the 1880s a man named James Murray was hired as editor, and the work picked up again. Murray got out the first volume, A to Ant, in 1884. About this time Henry Bradley, a young philologist, was hired as coeditor, and the pace was doubled. After the turn of the century, two more editors, William Craigie and Charles Talbot Onions, were added to the staff. These last were the only ones who saw the work completed in 1928. Murray and Craigie were knighted for their work on the dictionary.

7   Anyone with any curiosity at all about words should make the acquaintance of the *Oxford English Dictionary*. It is to be found in the reference room of any college library, along with its abridgement, the two-volume *Shorter Oxford*. You may find it rather a maze at first. The entry on the word *set*, the longest entry in the dictionary, runs to some twenty-three small-type, triple-columned pages; there is a good deal to say about *set* if you say everything. But brief acquaintance will quickly make the plan and possibilities clear. You will find there everything known about most English words and, through the words, the key to much in the development of English culture. The *Oxford* has contributed to thousands of scholarly studies that would have been altogether impossible without it. The *Oxford* is itself one of scholarship's greatest triumphs and a monument to the thousands of men and women who contributed their leisure hours for years and decades, for neither money nor fame but only for the satisfaction of extending human knowledge.

QUESTIONS

Language and Style

1. How does the writer include the reader in the process of dictionary making? Why should he do this?

2. Given the subject's size, how do the examples selected by the writer help communicate a sense of the way the project was organized? What are the examples?

3. Why should the writer make a point of mentioning that, after thirty years' work, the first volume finally appeared, covering *A* to *Ant*?

Organization

1. How does the focus change between paragraphs 4 and 5? Why?

Content

1. How does Roberts manage to convey a sense of the magnitude of the dictionary project?

Vocabulary

lexicographical	philological
contextual	extant
spasmodic	tracts

How to Weave a Basket
Susan Sargent

Sargent's article furnishes a clear account of how popular traditional baskets are made, for those who might consider making one themselves.

1   Ask Bliss McIntosh, a basket maker . . . , what she uses her black-ash baskets for, and she will be hard pressed to give a brief answer. Hanging on the wall of her cabin are baskets filled with socks, sweaters, yarn, laundry, and tools. Smaller baskets sit on the kitchen counters, holding everything from eggs, onions, herbs, and pencils

From Country Journal *(October 1983). Reprinted by permission.*

to stray Christmas-tree ornaments and seed packets. Piles of pack baskets, market baskets, melon baskets, cheese baskets, and others lie about in various stages of completion, waiting to be finished and sold. Bliss's daughter, Annika, age four, has her own basket, which once was her cradle and now holds her toys. Baskets on top of the piano hold knitting needles, sheets of music, clothes to be mended, and books.

2   As Bliss's home demonstrates, splint baskets remain as functional and decorative today as they were in early American times. Bliss has been making baskets professionally – and teaching others the craft – for about six years, and she produces beautiful examples of basket weaving. But you don't have to be an expert to make your own baskets. Some designs are simple enough to be made by anyone with a little time and patience.

3   Most of the baskets used by American Indians and early white settlers were made of splint: long, flexible strips of wood peeled from a tree, generally ash, oak, or hickory. Bliss's baskets are made of black ash, with white-ash handles and rims. She makes her own splint from black-ash logs. First she fells a black-ash tree with a minimum number of knots and bends. She cuts it into 8- to 10-foot logs (black ash doesn't grow to more than a foot in diameter), which she stores underwater in a stream to loosen the wood's fibers. Then she peels 2- to 3-inch-wide strips off a log after softening it by repeated pounding with a heavy wooden mallet. Once the splint is off the log, it can be hung to dry and stored indefinitely. Bliss encourages her students to be cautious in taking trees. Good black ashes are not common, and one tree will yield about fifty baskets. Don't cut one until you know you'll be able to use that much splint; or divide one tree among several friends.

4   Most beginning basket weavers will probably prefer not to start with a standing tree. Fortunately, prepared splint – generally white ash and oak – can be purchased by mail from commercial suppliers.... Commercial splint is fine for the market basket Bliss demonstrates....

5   The basic technique for plaiting a basket is the same as for any kind of splint construction. The *spokes* are the vertical strips in the weave and are also known as "ribs" or "uprights." The *weavers* are the horizontal strips, which are woven in an over-under pattern, working from the bottom up. In "spiral" baskets, the weavers are cut as long as possible, and as each new length is woven in, it overlaps the previous piece. In "circular" baskets, the weavers are cut just long enough to go around the basket once and overlap themselves. The directions provided here are for what Bliss calls a market basket – a spiral-weave, round-bottomed basket with a hump inside. The hump prevents the basket's bottom from sagging, since it keeps the weight of the contents from settling in the center and forcing the bottom outward.

MATERIALS

For this basket you will need: 6

· 12 *spokes*, 23 inches by ½ to ¼ inch. These should be cut 7
narrower in the middle than at the ends so that the woven strips of
splint can be pushed tightly together to make a solid bottom. Do
this by marking the center of each spoke with a dot, then trimming
down the spoke to a ¼-inch width for 3½ inches on either side of
the dot.

· 4 to 8 *weavers*, cut as long as 8 to 10 feet if possible. The first few 8
weavers are cut narrow at one end and gradually widen out, with
the narrowest strips going into the basket bottom. For example, cut
the first weaver so that it increases in width from a point to, say, ½
inch; then cut the second so that it increases from ½ inch to the
full width of the splint you're working with – an inch or so. The last
weaver you use in the basket should taper back down to a point.

· A ½-inch-wide *rim piece*, which will be cut to length after you 9
finish weaving. Its length will be equal to the circumference of the
top edge of the basket plus 2 inches. Note that the rim piece is
distinct from the rims themselves (below). The rim piece is the
final weaver of the basket, and should be made of slightly heavier
splint than any of the other weavers.

· *Binders*, ¼ inch wide and as long as possible. These should be of 10
the finest splint, carefully cut along the grain, because they bind
the rims to the basket and hold the entire assembly together.

· Two *rims*, made of white ash or heavy splint, ¾ to 1 inch wide and 11
as long as the circumference of the basket's top edge plus 3 to 5
inches.

· A *handle* is optional and may be made from white ash or, for a 12
lightweight basket, from heavy splint.

· *Tools*. If you decide to make your own splint and handles, you'll 13
need more tools than if you construct a basket simply with commercial splint. Making splint, for example, will require a wooden
mallet, putty knife, and heavy scissors or tin snips. For shaping the
rims and handles you'll need a froe or hatchet to split the ash; a
pocketknife; a shave horse or other surface; a fine-toothed saw and
a chisel; and two clamps to hold the handle in place while you cut
the notches. If you don't make your own materials, you will need
only a small screwdriver, three metal clamps, and one pair of vise
grips with the gripping surface wrapped with tape.

WEAVING

The first step in making a basket is to soak the splint until it is 14
flexible enough to be woven; that usually takes thirty minutes to an
hour. The splint is then cut to the proper length and width for the
basket you plan to make. (Use heavy scissors or tin snips, taking

care to cut along the spoke, leaving a 2-inch tail to tuck in later.) Weave over the Number 9 spoke, under Number 5, and so on, working around clockwise. When you arrive back at the Number 1 spoke, take up the slack and force the weaver to lie as tight and close to the center of the spokes as possible. Shape it into a neat circle and adjust the spokes so they are evenly spaced. Start around a second time by laying the weaver over or under *two* spokes, then resume the same over-and-under pattern. When you begin weaving the third round, instead of going under two spokes, make the required odd number of spokes by cutting one of them – whichever one is widest – in half along its length down to the weaver. From now on, treat those two halves as separate.... Long, awkward pieces can be loosely coiled and secured with a wooden clothespin until needed.

15   To start the basket, lay out the twelve spokes like the spokes of a wheel, all intersecting at the center. The order is important: the first spoke is laid horizontally and marked at one end with Number 1. The second is laid on top, perpendicular to the first. Starting at Number 1, fill in the spaces, working clockwise around and bisecting angles between spokes with each new piece.

16   The thin, pointed end of the first weaver is laid under the Number 1 spokes. The second and third rounds should be woven with the basket bottom on your knee ... to form the hump.

17   Continue to shape the basket bottom on your knee until the woven part is several inches in diameter. Then lay the basket on a table and start to flatten out the bottom. To do that, you have to weave more loosely. Continue around until the diameter of the woven part is about 7 inches. The nose of each new weaver should overlap the tail of the previous one, and the ends should be tucked out of sight behind the nearest spoke....

18   After you've woven a 7-inch bottom, start to turn the sides up. Fold and bend the spokes to make them stand upright ... and pull the weaver tight to hold the spokes in position. The shape of the basket depends on how tight you pull the weavers and how abruptly the sides turn up. Continue the weaving, pushing the rows together ... until 2 to 3 inches of the spokes are left for finishing.... Plan ahead and finish with a weaver that tapers down to a point.

19   After the last weaver is in place, weave the rim piece through the spokes.... The rim piece will eventually be hidden between the inner and outer rims. It should overlap itself by about 2 inches.

20   The basket can now be put aside to dry for a day or two. It will shrink a little, and the weavers should be tightened down using your fingertips, a small screwdriver, or a knitting needle.

21   Now it's time to turn down the spokes. Cut the spokes on the inside of the rim piece flush with the upper edge. Then trim all the outside spokes into points, cutting on a diagonal across the

top. . . . Leave the spokes long enough to bend over and tuck down inside the basket to a depth of three to five weavers. . . . Before bending them over, set the basket upside down in water just deep enough to soak the tops of the spokes and the rim piece.

MAKING THE RIMS

The two rims give strength and rigidity to the basket. Experienced basket makers like Bliss McIntosh generally use hand-carved hoops of white ash. The rims are made by dividing an ash log into sections of approximately the correct size (¾ to 1 inch wide) using a mallet, froe, and hatchet. Then, using a drawknife, shave the rims to the proper thickness on a shaving horse (the thickness will vary somewhat from one basket to the next, but ¼ inch should be thick enough in most cases). Then whittle them into shape with a pocketknife. You can do the job more simply using heavy pieces of splint. Even light splint can be doubled up and used, if that is all you have available. If you are using carved ash rims or heavy splint, thin the overlap with a knife so it doesn't create too much of a bulge. Beveling the edges of the rims slightly is also a nice touch. *22*

To bend the rims to shape, soak them and lay one over the rounded part of a shaving horse or over a log. Starting at one end, press the rim gently against the curve with the palms of both hands, working along inch by inch. Repeat until the rim is curved enough to fit as the inner or outer hoop on the basket edge. Using the basket to measure, determine the shape of the rims and clamp them for drying. . . . *23*

THE HANDLE

Handles are more difficult to make, and you may not want to attempt one on a first basket. Bliss prepares hers just as she does the white-ash rims, first shaping the wood with a drawknife. The handle should be long enough to allow the ends to be inserted into the basket to a depth of three to five weavers, and it should be thick enough at the points where it intersects the rim to allow you to cut notches in it. When the handle is in place and the basket bound together, the inside rim will be locked into the notches on the handle. The ends of the handle, beyond the notches, should taper in both width and thickness so that they will slip easily between the weavers. *24*

To shape a notched handle, set the inside rim in place in the basket, and mark with a sharp knife or pencil the two points where the handle will sit. Mark the rim, the edge of the basket, and also the handle (to show the depth of the notch). Clamp the handle to a table edge with two clamps or a small vise. Mark the handle with *25* the width of the inside rim and cut the notch with a fine-toothed saw. . . . Use a small, sharp chisel to remove the chip of wood. Soak the handle for an hour, bend it into shape, and tie the ends with a piece of cord so it will hold its shape until dry. . . .

26   A simple handle for a lightweight basket can be fashioned from plain splint. Take the heaviest piece you have and tuck the ends down into the basket between weavers; then bend them up and tuck them in again.

BINDING

27   When the rims and handle are completed, the basket is ready to be put together. This process, called binding, or crossed lashing, is the final step. First, set the rims and handle in place and hold them with clamps (or clothespins for a more fragile basket). . . . The overlapping sections of the inner and outer rims should lie close together, but not in exactly the same spot, to avoid a bulge. The overlap should not line up with the handle, either. The binding piece should be narrow enough to fit between the spokes, but should be strong so it will not break halfway through the binding.

28   To start binding, pick a point just past the overlapping sections of the rims. Start from the inside of the basket and poke the end of the binder up between the outside rim and the rim piece. Bend over ½ inch of the binder and tuck it back down between the rim piece and the inside rim. . . .

29   Now, begin lashing with the loose end of the binder, working counterclockwise around the basket. Loop the binder between each pair of spokes, over the top of the rims, and down between the next pair of spokes. You can use a small screwdriver to push the spokes apart to get the binder through. Leave 3 inches of slack in your first loop; you'll use that later to tighten the binding after you've gone all the way around the basket. . . .

30   To tighten the binding, you will need a pair of vise grips with the nose covered in tape so as not to mark the basket. The vise grips hold the two rims together far more tightly than you can by hand. Clamp the vise grips onto the rims just past the point where the binding begins, then pull the binder taut with the 3-inch slack you left for a handhold at the beginning. Shift the vise grips along inch by inch, pulling the binder-slack up as you go. . . .

31   After you've tightened the binding all the way around, reverse direction and bind the rims again. The second round of binding will crisscross the first round. You won't be using the vise grips to tighten this round, so take up all the slack as you go. If the binder is not long enough to make it all the way around the basket, lap in another strip.

32   After you've completed the second round of binding, finish by tucking the binder down inside the basket through three weavers

and trim it close. Splint baskets traditionally are not treated with preservatives such as oil or varnish, though some people do paint them.

Your basket is done..., and it will quickly fill up with stray *33* objects or even a picnic. Now that you have the knack of weaving splint, you'll probably want to make another basket, and then another. You'll find, as Bliss McIntosh did, that basket making can become a habit that's tough to break.

QUESTIONS

Language and Style

1. Why might the reader be led to believe that the first step in the process is the selection of a black-ash tree? The writer suggests that, because an average black ash will yield about fifty baskets, it might be a good idea to "divide one tree among several friends." How is the suggestion likely to strike a reader?

2. How would you characterize Sargent's remark that "most beginning basket weavers will probably prefer not to start with a standing tree"?

3. What aspects of the description of the procedure tend to give a beginner confidence? What difference does personalizing the process make?

4. How does the writer's choice of language help the reader who actually wants to use these directions?

5. Notice that occasionally the writer shifts from the second person ("you") to the third person ("it") and back. Why is this shift appropriate?

Organization

1. At what point does the discussion shift from a general process description to an actual set of directions? How can the reader tell?

Vocabulary

plaiting   froe

Secrets of the Squash King
J. L. Welch

Although Dill no longer holds the record for growing "huge enormous-size punkins," this account from Harrowsmith *magazine describes what are, no doubt, approved methods for giant pumpkin culture.*

1   The letter from New York was addressed to "Mr. Pumpkin, Ontario, Nova Scotia." That it made its way to Howard Dill's mailbox in Windsor, Nova Scotia, says less about life on the rural routes, where postmen still know who lives where, than it does about Dill's fame and field of expertise. Windsor had been dubbed by the *Wall Street Journal* "pumpkin capital of the world."

2   All because of a modest man with what he calls "competitive spirit." If Howard Dill is disappointed that his 1981 champion fell short of the 500 pounds he'd hoped for, he manages to conceal it. "I'm pleased," says the farmer. "It's still a world record and my third straight win. No one else has ever won in international competition three years in a row."

3   The object that garnered Dill his 1981 triumph is, or rather was, a 493-pound specimen of the squash family. Reaching the 500-pound mark, the four-minute mile of pumpkin growing, is Dill's greatest dream. Though he has a good chance of claiming the glory – and a prize of $1,000 offered by octogenarian pumpkin-fancier Raymond Cornell of Pennsylvania – the gap between his weighty cucurbits and those of his competitors is narrowing. Every year the race becomes more intense.

4   What drives otherwise sane and modest people to squander precious hours of each day, immense portions of garden space, rich loads of manure, costly bags of fertilizer and hundreds of gallons of water on the cultivation of bloated, not particularly tasty monsters of the vegetable kingdom? Dill, one of the most unpretentious, soft-spoken fellows you'll ever meet, cites his competitive spirit. Others speak of fun. The truth dawns only when one finally encounters one of the giants, reposing like an obese and pacific Buddha amidst its riotous leaves and vines, and contemplates the fact that, in peak growing season, the seemingly inert spheroid gains the weight of a full-size "normal" pumpkin – 10 or 15 pounds – every day. What attracts, fascinates, compels is the very mystery of growth itself.

5   To raise what Dill calls "a huge enormous-size punkin" you need,

From Harrowsmith *(February/March 1982). Reprinted by permission of the author.*

first of all, space. *Territory*. Plants should be placed at least 20 feet apart each way for best results. Some of Dill's dozen or so plants occupy close to 2,000 square feet *each*. They clamber up fences and engulf whole apple trees. Dill once counted all the leaves on one plant: there were more than 100, each one almost two feet wide. He figures he gets four pounds of pumpkin per leaf.

Dill raises his pumpkins in several spots on his farm, but the favoured location is what was for many years ("til oil came in") the family woodpile. The soil there is deep, loose and rich in potash. Into this already rich soil he works generous quantities of manure from his own cows, leaves (which he gets from the highways department), rotted hay and other organic matter. The manure is applied during winter and tilled 16 to 20 inches deep in spring. For additional grow-power, Dill twice uses commercial 6-12-12, first before setting out the plants and later as a side-dressing along principal vines. He does *not* feed his pumpkins milk. "I don't know how many times I've heard that," chuckles Dill. "Some people will never believe I don't milk-feed 'em." The truth is, Dill did try milk once just in case there might be some truth to the old story. As far as he is concerned, there isn't.

Dill starts his seeds indoors in Nova-Mix at the beginning of May. As soon as the seedlings are strong enough he begins feeding them with liquid fertilizer, and during the first week of June sets the young leviathans outdoors. He covers them in chilly weather. Each plant is sheltered within a high, irregular pen constructed of plywood and whatever else comes to hand to protect them from wind, which can lift the young vines and prevent them from rooting at every joint. More roots provide more nourishment, according to Dill. As they grow, he stakes down runners to encourage the growth of roots. By late August, the place looks like a pig farm with pumpkins for porkers.

Choosing the right time to allow fruit to begin setting is a matter of experience. The plants must first be mature, says Dill; otherwise it is "like getting a cow bred too soon." When the time for fruit setting arrives, on a morning "unfavourable for the bees to do their work," Dill begins the careful job of artificially pollinating the flowers.

Here, too, breeding is of utmost importance. Dill's monsters are the result of years of selection for size, shape, rapid weight gain and long maturation. Both the strains he began working with, *Hungarian* and *Mammoth Chile*, were a diminutive 75 to 100 pounds when first grown in Hungary and Chile respectively. Many obese strains of both have since been developed, including Dill's *Show King* from the former and his *Atlantic Giant* from the latter. Both, in fact, are in one botanical slot, *Cucurbita maxima*, but *Show King*,

6

7

8

9

the heftier, produces a long, high fruit with white seeds while *Atlantic Giant* is "not quite as upright but better looking," says Dill. Neither one is a "true" pumpkin, which will not grow over 40 or 50 pounds, but only a stickler would call them squash. Certainly they are known as pumpkins at the increasingly popular festivals held every year in Philadelphia, Circleville, Ohio, and Half Moon Bay, California, where pumpkin judging now attracts thousands of spectators.

10   Growing seed from his own best efforts, Dill allows two or three fruits to begin developing on most vines, later removing all but the one with the most potential. How to spot these? Dill chooses by shape as well as size. "I'll take length over circumference," he says. The ideal pumpkin should be extra long as well as high.

11   While he believes that "the difference between being good and being great is just a little extra effort," Dill attributes some of his success to Nova Scotia's relatively long summer days and cool nights. Giant pumpkins, unlike giant watermelons, are not inordinately fond of a steamy climate. Dill thinks hot, humid weather causes them to ripen before they get up to championship weight. "Texans just can't understand why they can't grow 'em as big as we can up here," he says. "It's the heat."

12   After the first "perfect specimen" has set well, Dill picks off all other fruit and blossoms. Thereafter he nips off new blossoms twice a week. He never prunes the vines, believing that "the only thing that will increase the fruit size comes out of the vine."

13   Dill's pumpkins expand steadily until August when, if they've got the stuff champions are made of, they embark on an orgy of spectacular growth. In a small, dog-eared notebook Dill inscribes each day the length, height and distance from side to side over the middle of each fruit. This chore he calls "taking my daily girth." His records show that on August 1 his 1981 champion was 12½ inches from stem to blossom end. By August 31, it measured 51¼ inches in length. During this period of explosive growth the pumpkins are at risk of coming loose from their vines or breaking off at their stems, which grow thicker but not longer as the fruit balloons. From experience Dill can sometimes spot which young pumpkins may have stem trouble. These he turns or elevates on pedestals of packed earth.

14   Pumpkins are thirsty plants, and giant pumpkins particularly so. They are monstrous sponges. Last August Dill supplied each of his hopefuls with something like 100 pounds of water a day. Pounds? That's how he recorded it, and understandably so. He carried it all in five-gallon (50-pound) containers, one in each hand. Throughout the season he monitored the moisture content of his soil. Like fertilizer, water is applied in critical amounts just short of the harmful dose.

Dill has had few serious problems with insects or fungus over   *15*
the years. Occasionally he uses a commercial fungicide; against
striped cucumber beetles, he employs rotenone. Last spring he
had trouble with salt-spotting on several plants, which he blamed
at first on the leaves from the highways department. Ultimately,
however, the salt was traced to some contaminated commercial
fertilizer.

Dill has yet to devise a means of weighing his pumpkins *in situ*   *16*
and his consequent uncertainty causes some anxiety as the day of
reckoning approaches. Appearances can deceive – some strap-
ping specimens have proved to be disappointingly hollow. "He's
looking real good," said Dill, fervently, of his 1981 contender a few
weeks before it was to be cut from the vine. At that point there was
nothing left to do but hope.

On October 8 Dill carved through the monster's stem, by now as   *17*
burly as a stevedore's forearm. The stump was wet and sticky: "he"
was still "taking in." Dill and several strong helpers rolled the
massive vegetable onto a tarp and strained to hoist it to the bed of
his pickup truck. Its peak weight, 493 pounds, was recorded that
day by an agriculture department official in Windsor. Dill then sped
away with his "big one" to the Cornell Pumpkin Show in Philadelphia. Placed on the scales there two days later, the big squash had
slimmed to 469½ pounds, a decrease due to loss of moisture, one
of the hazards of the game. (A few years back one well-heeled
competitor took the extravagant precaution of airfreighting a giant
pumpkin, fresh from the vine, to an Ohio contest. He lost to Dill
anyway.) In spite of moisture loss, Dill's entry still had 80 pounds
on its nearest rival.

On October 12, back in Windsor for the Atlantic Winter Fair,   *18*
Dill's pumpkin, now weighing 466 pounds, was declared World
Champion in a weighoff conducted via telephone with competitors
at Half Moon Bay, California. Admired, gaped at for a few days by
incredulous spectators ("he must've grew that indoors"), the mammoth then went "on tour" courtesy of Sobey's department stores
which, in national bidding, purchased it from Dill.

One may question the rectitude of growing massive vegetables   *19*
merely for display. But Dill, who saves or sells all his seeds (about
700 per squash), uses the flesh for cattle fodder. His local competitor, Knowles, declares he wouldn't grow anything he couldn't eat
but admits his wife is getting tired of putting up and freezing
pumpkin. And what was the champion's ultimate destiny? Sobey's
pies. Its seeds, by the contractual agreement, went to Dill. Half of
those ended up at the Cornell pumpkin show and thence in the
hands of rival growers. Dill expects some day to be beaten by his
own seeds. (Owen Woodman, another local enthusiast, took the
1981 Hants County ribbon from him with an entry developed from

Dill's seeds and fertilized with Dill's manure.) Meanwhile, he hopes 1982 will be his best year yet. Growing that 500-pounder is his current ambition. "Getting to the top takes a long time," he says, "but I do believe the biggest joy is staying there."

QUESTIONS

Language and Style

1. What do you make of the claim that Windsor, Nova Scotia, "has been dubbed by the Wall Street *Journal* 'pumpkin capital of the world' "?

2. Describe the difference between the writer's language and Dill's. What is the effect of this play of language on subject?

3. Is the writer's choice of language consistent throughout? Discuss.

4. How would you characterize the attitude of the narrator in this account?

5. Explain the special effectiveness of the observation, "By late August, the place looks like a pig farm with pumpkins for porkers."

Content

1. If the purpose of this account is not especially to instruct growers of giant pumpkins, what is its purpose? Which is more interesting here – the pumpkin or the pumpkin-grower? Why?

Vocabulary

octogenarian
unpretentious
inert
clamber
leviathans
obese
fungicide
in situ
rectitude

cucurbits
Buddha
spheroid
potash
pollinating
inordinately
rotenone
incredulous
fodder

The Basque Connection

Harry Thurston

Thurston's account captures the extraordinary archaeological work that went into the discovery near Red Bay, Labrador, of the remains of a Basque whaling station and an all-but-perfectly preserved sixteenth-century whaling vessel.

Midnight, Christmas Eve, 1584. Joanes de Echaniz, in his early 20s, a Spanish Basque whaler from the town of Orio, lies dying in the high forecastle of a galleon. The air around the vessel is soured by the smell of blubber rendering in copper cauldrons, and as whale-oil-filled oaken barrels thunder across the rough planks of a nearby wharf, en route to join hundreds of others in the galley's hold, Echaniz dictates his last will and testament. The young man's first wish – vain as he knows it to be – is to be buried at home, in his family tomb. To his wife and daughter, Echaniz assigns all of his worldly goods, save a pound of wax, which is to be given to Our Lady of Aizarnazabal.   *1*

Not a particularly remarkable will for its time, but with these words, the dying whaler unwittingly composed what would become one of the most intriguing documents in Canada's history. Echaniz's bequest casts a clear shaft of light into five decades of European settlement and exploitation of this country that, until recently, lay cloaked in obscurity, unfamiliar to even the most well-versed historical scholars. For although Echaniz's will was no different in content from any other commoner's of that era, it was composed in a quiet cove along the Labrador shore of the Strait of Belle Isle a full two decades before a Frenchman named Samuel de Champlain sailed into the Gulf of St. Lawrence to found what was once assumed to be the first European colony in Canada.   *2*

Ironically, it was just one year before Echaniz's premature demise that Sir Humphrey Gilbert had sailed into what is now St. John's Harbour and claimed Newfoundland for Queen Elizabeth I of England, thus launching the British Empire. Gilbert's presumptuousness must have provided more than a few hearth-side belly laughs (or curses) among the whalers living a mere 300 miles northwest of where he proudly planted the ensign. Spanish Basques had been coming to North America for two generations. At least nine whaling stations had been established, one of which boasted a summertime population of 900.   *3*

From Equinox *(November/December 1983). Reprinted by permission of the author.*

4 This Basque whaling enterprise was Canada's first full-blown industry, and documents such as Echaniz's will are the nation's first recorded history. It is curious that this chapter had, until recently, fallen into the hiatus which spans the 70 years between Jacques Cartier's voyage in 1534 and Champlain's colonization. Able-bodied seaman Joanes de Echaniz, doomed to die an ocean away from his birthplace, had to wait nearly 400 years to be accorded the dignity of a historical footnote. His will provided one small clue toward unravelling a mystery that would eventually lead a team of 20th-century archaeologists to the site where he and his fellow whalers toiled six months of the year.

5 In the process of probing into the lives of the forgotten Basque North Americans, the archaeologists have also uncovered two of the continent's most important archaeological sites. On a small island near Red Bay, Labrador, their trowels scraped soil and peat away from the remains of the oldest known whaling station, providing a first glimpse at a now disreputable endeavour that was a crucially important industry in its age. And several yards offshore, archaeologists using scuba tanks have found the world's most intact remains of a 16th-century galleon, one of those small, functional and little-understood vessels whose decks and holds cradled the settlement of this continent.

6 Even more so than many archaeological success stories, the rediscovery of Labrador's Basque communities resembles something plucked from the eccentric pages of Sir Arthur Conan Doyle or Agatha Christie than dry fodder for ponderous Ph.D. theses. In the real-life mystery that once shrouded this chapter of Canadian history, the chief sleuth is a self-styled expert on Basque history named Selma Barkham. Her work would entitle her to a place beside the most eminent fictional detective heroines, but it has also earned her the very real honours of The Order of Canada and the Gold Medal of The Royal Geographical Society. A librarian by training and a historical geographer by obsession, Barkham spent five years in Basque country, pawing through mouldering notarial documents in provincial Spanish centres for references to Grand Baya and Tierra Nova.

7 Perhaps it took a person of Barkham's tenacity and background to tackle single-handedly the Basque/Canada connection. Until she began poking through Spanish archives, few Canadian academics appeared willing to risk grant monies and reputation by plotting the New World history of an ethnic group that neither French nor English acknowledge as nation builders. Not only was Barkham free from the shackles of academic peer pressure, but she came from a family with a long history of intellectual audacity. Her father, Michael Huxley, founded the British *Geographical Magazine*, and she numbers Thomas Henry Huxley, a cohort of Charles

Darwin, and Aldous Huxley, author of *Brave New World*, among her relatives.

Barkham immigrated to Canada in 1950 and married a McGill   *8* University architecture student, whose thesis was on Basque rural construction and design. Brian Barkham's singular interest led to a trip to Spain soon after their marriage, where Selma clearly remembers Basque acquaintances complaining that no one was interested in their documents relating to 16th-century Canada. After her husband died in 1965, Barkham was determined to return to Spain and search out these early Canadians, even though doing so would involve a long uphill struggle against the skepticism and polite tolerance of her academic superiors and barely polite cold shoulders from all sources of research funds.

Undaunted, she went to Mexico for three years to learn Spanish,   *9* supporting herself and her four children by teaching English. Then, in 1972, shortly after being refused financial assistance from the Canada Council, she set off to the Basque port of Bilbao. An anonymous gift of $1,000 got her and her children through the first winter, barely. "We very nearly starved," she says.

Sacrifice soon paid off. During that lean winter, in a cupboard in   *10* the Consulado archives of Burgos, she found the first references to Canadian ports used by Spanish Basques for whaling. They were among leather-bound volumes of marine insurance policies, penned on parchment with excruciating embellished calligraphy.

These first discoveries earned Barkham seasonal support from   *11* the Public Archives of Canada, and over the next five years, she pored through 50,000 dusty documents. They led her from one provincial Basque archive to another, to Paris and the British Museum and, finally, to the Canadian source of this Holmesian peregrination: Tierra Nova, or Labrador.

In order to pinpoint the best locations for searching out archae-   *12* ological remains of the Basque presence in Canada, Barkham painstakingly decoded Spanish rutters, sailing directions that gave detailed descriptions of the Labrador coastline. The rutters proved surprisingly accurate. These 16th-century navigators provided Barkham with exact soundings, compass bearings, directions for entering harbours and distances between capes. Barkham correlated this information with modern maps to identify nine likely whaling-station sites along the Strait of Belle Isle.

In the summer of 1977, accompanied by Arctic archaeologist   *13* Graham Rowley and his geographer wife, Diana, and by Dr. Walter Kenyon of the Royal Ontario Museum and Dr. James Tuck of Memorial University in St. John's, Newfoundland, Barkham tramped the glacial terraces of Labrador's southern coast. For a historical geographer, there could have been no better vindication of a decade's dogged, almost bloody-minded determination. Evidence of the Basque occupation was almost embarrassingly visible. Her son Michael, then 18, discovered an artifact that would have pleased a seasoned field veteran by merely bending over and pointing out a 400-year-old harpoon head half exposed in an eroded marine terrace near Schooner Cove. The story was the same in every suspected Basque port that the Barkham expedition investigated. At Chateau Bay and at St. Modeste and at Red Bay, they found red tiles, evidence of "ovens" or tryworks, and a few scraps of earthenware ceramics.

14   As significant as they were, these discoveries held nothing new to local outport children who, for generations, had used centuries-old whaling artifacts as handy playthings and had crushed the red clay of Basque roof tiles to concoct Indian paint. Turfed-over hummocks that local lore held to be French forts proved to be Basque whale-oil works. Throughout the region, there was other, more grim evidence of the once-booming enterprise. Along the shore, whalebones were visible, and at the tryworks sites, charred blubber mixed with clay still clung to the rocks like black lichen.

15   The most valuable Basque artifact on the Labrador coast, however, was not so easily found. Legal documents contained in the archives of the Spanish town of Oñate alerted Barkham to the possibility that the Belle Isle shore might hold the wrecks of several Basque galleons. In one case, according to the documents, two harpooners had invoked power of attorney to collect their share of whale oil that had been salvaged from a ship by a man named Joanes de Portu. Their testimony revealed that the ship had been blown ashore when the cables broke and that it was carrying a full load of cargo. By piecing together a complicated series of cross-references, Barkham was able to identify the ship as the *San Juan*, and more important, she found that in 1565, it went to the bottom of the harbour at Buytres (Les Buttes), a Basque whaling establishment on the present-day site of Red Bay. Barkham wrote to the head of Parks Canada's Marine Excavation Unit, Robert Grenier, suggesting that he reconnoitre the depths of Red Bay harbour.

16   On Labour Day weekend 1978, to the good-natured jibes and skeptical glances of local residents, Grenier and a three-person crew dove into the frigid but gin-clear water of Red Bay near a swaybacked landform called Saddle Island. On their first dive, they surfaced with an oak plank – oak was preferred by 16th-century Basque shipwrights and is not found within hundreds of miles of the barren Labrador coast. A few feet under the silt near where the plant rested, largely intact and remarkably well-preserved, lay the *San Juan*.

17   It was a red-letter day for marine archaeology. Not only was the *San Juan* the earliest shipwreck ever found in Canada, it was the most complete 16th-century working galleon anywhere. Other ship-

wrecks of the same period had been found in the Caribbean, but warm-water parasites had reduced the wood to fragments that barely resembled ships' parts, let alone suggested the look of the vessel itself. Of equal importance to the archaeologists was the fact that the *San Juan* lay a mere 90 feet from shore and in only 40 feet of water − a comfortable diving depth. Its location near Saddle Island's land-based whale-oil tryworks meant that research teams could examine the ship in its working context, and to the archaeologist, context is crucial. As Grenier says, "It was not just a preserved box thrown somewhere."

All of these discoveries, both land-based and undersea, sparked   *18* a human migration the likes of which the area had not seen since the days of the annual spring arrival of the Basque whaling fleets. A crew of 50 archaeologists and support staff floated trailers to the village of Red Bay, which lies at the end of a redoubtable road along the shore of Labrador's Strait of Belle Isle. Two fishing stages and a merchant's loft were converted into bustling field laboratories complete with computer terminals for cataloguing the tens of thousands of artifacts that have been preserved and stored with the aid of the Canadian Conservation Institute. It was decided that Memorial University's archaeology unit would concentrate on the land dig on Saddle Island and that Parks Canada, through an agreement with the Newfoundland government, would undertake excavation of the *San Juan*.

Today, Red Bay boasts 350 residents. But 400 years ago, it was   *19* the largest of the Basque whaling ports, with as many as 900 seasonal residents. Enclosed by two red granite cliffs that gave the town its modern name, Red Bay has always had the best harbour on the Belle Isle coast. During the town's heyday, as many as 10 galleons lay like floating warehouses in the protected lee of Saddle Island.

Because subsequent house construction and garden digging   *20* have altered many of the potential land-based dig sites, Tuck and his Memorial University crew decided to centre their efforts on undisturbed Saddle Island. For Tuck, like Barkham, the initial success at Red Bay represented the vindication of considerable academic risk-taking. Tuck came to Memorial in 1968, after being educated at Syracuse University in New York State. His instinct told him that Newfoundland and Labrador were the last frontiers of North American archaeology. "There are not many places in North America where things are virtually unknown, which is the way it was in Newfoundland 15 years ago," says Tuck.

The same fortitude that allowed Tuck to turn his back on the   *21* surer bets of more established archaeological areas is a necessary quality of leadership on the Saddle Island project. There, either fog and cold wind wrap and whip researchers or, if the sun shines, a miasma of blood-starved blackfies rises from nearby peat bogs to form clouds about the bent heads of Tuck's field crews. These dogged crews pass their summers scraping the soil and peat away, layer by layer, with trowels, toothbrushes, wooden picks and whisk brooms. What has emerged is a picture of the New World's proto-type whaling station.

22   Men wielding long knives minced the strips of whale blubber for rendering in copper cauldrons set atop fieldstone fireboxes. A man stood on a platform erected at the back of this primitive processing plant. Occasionally, he skewered a limp piece of whale fatback and unceremoniously forked it into the fire, to a crackling explosion of burning fat: literally the sound of the leviathan stewing in its own juices. Behind the tryworks, a labourer ladled the finished oil into half barrels of water, where it was purified. The dross sank to the bottom, and the whale oil that lit 16th-century cities rose to the top.

23   Basques, in fact, developed the industry of whaling. It is known that they were hunting the great mammals from small boats in the Bay of Biscay as early as 1000 A.D. Even so, it was the search for cod, not whales, that probably brought the first Basque ships into the Strait of Belle Isle. Logistically, crossing the Atlantic Ocean was no great feat for the Basques. They regularly provisioned ships to make the three-month journey to the fishing grounds off the coast of Ireland, and from there, it would have been a fairly straight-forward run to Tierra Nova.

24   Shrewd in money matters, Basque cod fishermen would have quickly realized the commercial potential of the numerous whales off Newfoundland and probably would have had difficulty tending their cod lines when the spouts of leviathans plumed in a tight, narrow strait that seemed made for shore-based whaling. Eventu-ally, tales reached Spanish shores, and monied burghers began devising ways to turn Labrador's whales into profits. Barkham has uncovered a document which reveals that as early as 1547, whale oil was being exported directly from Tierra Nova to Bristol, Southampton, London and Flanders. Tuck compares the whale-oil industry of 400 years ago with the imminent oil boom in today's Newfoundland. "They were over here for the main chance, like people who go on the offshore today," he says. "It was an oil boom. Maybe the world's first oil boom."

25   Tuck's excavations indicate that the Labrador Basques had tapped a veritable gusher of whale oil. As the ancient ovens took shape stone by stone from under the turf canopy, the archaeologists were surprised at their size. The Red Bay tryworks contain a half-dozen fireboxes aligned in a row instead of a single firebox as was typical of later shore-based whaling stations, such as the ones at Spitz-bergen. Tuck suggests that the multiple ovens might be a measure of the density of the migratory whales as they passed through the strait.

26   After being killed, the whales were towed ashore for flensing, in

the age-old pattern established by the Basques in the Bay of Biscay. Bones found just off Saddle Island indicate that the flippers and tail flukes were removed first to streamline the transport-truck-sized carcasses, which had to be rotated during flensing. The remains of a substantial wharf at Saddle Island also led archaeologists to speculate that some whales may have been brought alongside the wharf, rather than beached. This would have saved a great deal of time and effort. According to Barkham, some whales may also have been lashed to the side of the galleons for flensing, in the style of later generations of British and New England pelagic whalers. In every case, after the whales were stripped of their insulating layer of blubber, they were towed across the harbour to what Red Bay residents have always called the Bony Beach. Even today, the beach is littered with the pocked and mouldering remains of 40 whale skulls. Dr. Stephen Cumbaa, head of the Zooarchaeological Identification Centre at National Museums of Canada, says that the carcasses were taken to the beach simply to get them out of nose range of the Saddle Island settlement.

Although the Basque whalers were obviously tapping a rich *27* resource, Tuck's work shows that they lived spartan lives. Charred layers of peat surrounded by collapsed chimney stones have been found in context with other domestic artifacts, such as cooking and storage pots and majolica, a tin-glazed pottery that has a characteristic pastel blue or green hue. Otherwise, though, the dwellings can charitably be described as utilitarian, probably very similar to outbuildings still found in Basque country – nothing more than lean-tos that often incorporate local topography into their design. At one Saddle Island living site, a steep bank formed one side and the sloping shed-style roof was supported on the other side by a low fieldstone retaining wall. The two ends and roofs were framed by locally available timber.

Other homesites have led Tuck to surmise that important *28* craftsmen like the coopers rated substantial tile-covered roofs, while lower-class crewmen had only sailcloth between themselves and the often hostile elements. This theory of class distinction is reinforced by the quality of personal possessions associated with the tile-roofed cooperages. Among the assemblage of coopers' tools that have been unearthed were a fine Venetian wine-glass stem and a decanter bearing a raised wishbone design. These are objects of discriminating taste, compared to the pedestrian earthenware typically found in what Tuck calls "lower-class dwellings."

By midsummer of 1982, Tuck had good reason to believe that he *29* had gone about as far as he could with his fieldwork. The tryworks were exposed, and the settlement pattern on Saddle Island was taking shape under his team's trowels. However, a routine test hole sunk into the island's rocky eastern point plunged Tuck into an entirely new sphere of speculation. Wherever he dug, there were human bones. It seemed that he had stumbled onto Red Bay's

Basque graveyard. That there should be one was predictable, considering the inherent hazards of whaling and that Red Bay was occupied for six months of the year for more than half a century. What surprised Tuck was that not all the burials conformed to the tidy practice of God-fearing Europeans. At the most extreme point on the island, Tuck exposed a mass burial. Only a layer of sod covered the poorly preserved skeletons that, in some cases, were barely distinguishable from the tea-coloured background. It initially appeared that the bodies had never been buried, merely dumped on the beach.

30   This was grist for the rich imagination of the archaeologist. A whalebone found near one of the skulls inspired speculation on a barbaric theme: Perhaps the skull had been impaled on the whale rib as a grizzly warning to passing ships. But closer examination of the interrelationship of the bones plus the lack of any other evidence of warlike contact between the Basques and local natives led to the abandonment of that theory.

31   Further excavation this past summer revealed that the dead men were lying on domestic debris — charcoal, food bone, ceramics, nails — associated elsewhere with living quarters. Tuck now says that someone probably placed them there with a little care. They may have been laid out on a platform with a tent to protect them from scavengers such as foxes and polar bears.

32   The 1983 field season also revealed more mass burials, although these bodies (in groups of four, six and eight) were properly laid out, albeit in shallow graves and, except in two cases, without coffins. Some of the multiple burials may have been the result of whaling accidents. "It's possible to imagine a whale boat stove in or capsized," says Tuck. But he is reserving judgment until the bones have been subjected to closer scrutiny by his Memorial colleague Sonja Jerkic, a physical anthropologist. Analyses of the bones may indicate disease or inadequacies in diet as the cause of death.

33   The unburied bodies are less amenable to simple explanations. They haunt Tuck. "You know," he says, "there's more questions than answers. Why didn't they clean them up when they came back? And I guess the answer to that has to be that it might have been one of the last episodes in the whole business of 60 or 70 years of whaling."

34   While the artifacts found on land and underwater sometimes provoke conflicting views of Basque adaptations to conditions in the New World, in other ways, the two sites complement each other perfectly. The cold Belle Isle waters have preserved the wooden artifacts to such a degree that the honey hue of the oak still shines through four centuries of wear. But the same salt water has so badly corroded all submerged iron artifacts that only two, a small swivel gun and an anchor, survive. The opposite situation

exists on the land, where the iron samples are intact, and the wood has been mulched in the acidic peat soil. Thousands of nails and spikes and the occasional valuable artifact, like a harpoon or 16th-century coin, have been recovered from Saddle Island.

Despite a lack of metal artifacts, the *San Juan* stands as a virtual   *35* time capsule of the golden age of Basque commerce, and it represents the apex of their shipbuilding skills. Unfortunately, however, even the best craftsmanship could not have protected the *San Juan* from the vagaries of the weather and the sea on that December night 418 years ago. The 300-ton vessel was moored in the centre of Red Bay harbour, with its profitable whale-oil ballast packed so snugly that there was hardly a chink of light between the 1,000 barrels in its capacious hold.

The prospects of a homecoming and of sharing the season's   *36* bounty were perhaps fateful distractions. In any event, someone neglected to check the mooring lines, and when the wind came suddenly and ferociously out of the north, it was too late to do so. The gale drove with full force over the barrens, catching the *San Juan*'s lofty forecastle like a sail. The ship swung around on its broad beam; the mooring snapped. In a matter of minutes, the boat's oak hull crushed sickeningly against Saddle Island's rocky shore. Crew members scrambled to land through the icy, white-capped water as the *San Juan* settled onto its keel. The stern and masts were left exposed above the surface, but over time, the actions of wind, waves and ice pried open the hull like two halves of an oyster, and the ship found its watery grave, buried under conserving layers of silt that gently laved her like a shroud.

It is one of those propitious quirks of history that Grenier was   *37* the one to disinter the *San Juan*. Although he hails from Trois Rivières, Quebec, Grenier might easily have walked among the whalers of Red Bay without anyone questioning his status as a fellow countryman. Physically, he is poured in the Basque mould, short and sturdy like the men buried on Saddle Island. And Grenier shares the Basques' consuming passion for the sea. It was this that prompted him to abandon his sedate post as a classics professor at Collège des Jesuits in Quebec City in 1969 to don scuba gear as part of Parks Canada's then neophyte Marine Excavation Unit. "For me, it was the adventure," he says. "It was an occasion to be on the sea. And when I switched from land to underwater archaeology, it was not very rational. It was more because of my love of boats, the sea and fishermen."

Grenier canoes to work each morning. His headquarters, on an   *38* orange and yellow barge moored off Saddle Island, is the staging area for one of the most technically advanced underwater projects in the world. The barge reverberates with the lulling din of oil-fired generators and boilers that run the support system for the dive crew working in the crystalline but fatally cold Belle Isle water.

"When we go to the United States or Europe," Grenier says, with an irritable undertone stemming from what he considers Canadians' false modesty, "people are amazed at what we're doing. I think it's quite an achievement to be able to produce the quality of research and the amount of work that we're producing in this sort of environment, where the water is zero degrees Celsius."

39   The hot-water system that makes Red Bay submarine work practical, despite conditions every bit as harsh as those in the high Arctic, seems simple at first glance. Two home oil furnaces heat raw seawater to 107 degrees Fahrenheit (42 degrees Celsius). The warm liquid is then pumped to as many as eight divers through a series of umbilicals. Each diver has a valve on his suit to control the incoming flow. The suit itself is loose-fitting and floppy and is supplied with a series of perforated "arteries" that channel warmth across the diver's body.

40   Keeping warm is imperative not only to the diver's safety but also to his efficiency. Exposure to the cold water, even with the protection of a diving suit, can rapidly dull a diver's senses to the point where he is unable to carry out the painstaking work of mapping the ship's timbers on the harbour floor. This mapping procedure indicates where each timber was found in relation to the rest of the wreck and is vital to the goal of reconstructing the *San Juan*'s architecture.

41   Still, the lot of the archaeological divers in Red Bay is difficult. Most of the wreck lies in water shallow enough to permit day-long diving. But even when working on deeper sections of the *San Juan*, Grenier's researchers go down for 200 minutes in the morning and then, after one and a half hours for lunch, return for an additional 100 minutes — the maximum daily amount of time allowable without risking decompression sickness, more commonly known as the bends. The underwater season begins in May as soon as the ice is out — or most of it. Occasionally, members of Grenier's team have looked up from their work to see the greenish white underbelly of an approaching iceberg. Diving continues until the end of October, when shortening days force the archaeologists to spend all of the sunlit hours underwater. Colds and flu are common; home life is difficult to maintain. The work is so strenuous that researchers often return to Red Bay in the evening and immediately fall into their beds.

42   Nonetheless, the team is slowly managing to piece together the *San Juan*. After mapping, each timber is brought to the surface to be precisely measured and drawn to scale. Finally, Grenier scrutinizes each piece, a hands-on analysis that he insists is indispensable to the reconstruction of the ship's integrity and function. "It's one thing to look at drawings and say, 'Well, this piece fits here,'"

he says. "But at some points, it doesn't make sense. You have to play with the three-dimensional object. Then you realize where it goes. With drawings, you couldn't do that. There are too many elements involved. People have even tried to use computers. But these boats were not designed that way. The *San Juan* is a poem."

Grenier has difficulty talking about the *San Juan* without waxing   43 poetic. It is not that the ship was, to extend his own metaphor, an intricately fashioned sonnet. It was utilitarian, as vessels go, its grace of a more homely sort, like a ballad. "The builder had some general shape in mind when he began, but the material itself dictated the final outcome," he says. For this reason, Grenier feels that the ship exhibits more than its share of eccentricities. Even the hull is somewhat asymmetrical, each side having assumed its own idiosyncratic lines.

Far from diminishing the *San Juan*'s archaeological value, these   44 irregularities make it all the more interesting. One reason the vessel is no paragon of naval architecture is that it could have been knocked out hurriedly to meet a buoyant market. The ship, like a good fishing boat, was built with just enough care to meet its purpose. Grenier and his team are, in effect, examining an early example of planned obsolescence.

In terms of design intricacy, the *San Juan* pales when set beside   45 military vessels such as the recently raised *Mary Rose* or *Nelson's Victory*. But such comparisons merely whet Grenier's enthusiasm for this little wreck. "You take the *Mary Rose*," he says. "That's very fascinating. But it was the Rolls-Royce of ships for that era. At the time, there might have been a few dozen *Mary Roses* in the world. But there were thousands of *San Juans*. The *San Juan* was the Volkswagen of the period which made things go. Boats like it built the trade in Europe and assisted in the exploration, then exploitation, of the New World. It's the type of vessel that helped to build our country."

The *San Juan* and its ilk were country makers not only for   46 Canada but for the whole continent – all of the Americas. Historical records show that galleons like the *San Juan* were built specifically for the Labrador fishery. After two or three years, by which time they had more than paid for themselves, they were often resold in Seville for service in the Caribbean. Fragmentary remains of similar ships have been found in warm southern waters but always in a very sorry state of decay. Students of 16th-century Spanish naval architecture have had to rely on rudimentary line drawings that survive in English and Venetian documents to recreate the lines of these "workhorses of Europe," to use Grenier's coinage. The *San Juan* represents the first opportunity not only to reconstitute the exact look of a 16th-century galleon but also to understand the techniques that accounted for its design. Grenier even claims that he can tell whether the shipwright was having an off day.

47   The *San Juan* was a beamy craft. Its beam, or width, was 26 feet, and it had a relatively short keel length of 50 feet. A considerable overhang and rake of the forecastle and stern, however, gave it the appearance of a much longer ship. From stem to stern, it might have measured 90 feet. The *San Juan* was also squared off at either end. This boxiness was a case of design suiting function. The Basques' prime concern was capacity; therefore, they were willing to sacrifice a degree of seaworthiness and speed. The *San Juan* probably ploughed through the water at a top speed of a few miles per hour.

48   Although galleons would hardly qualify for the America's Cup, Grenier feels that Basque shipwrights had little to apologize for. The *San Juan*'s pragmatic design may not have provided comfortable passage, but the boat was eminently seaworthy.

49   Because the *San Juan* is so complete, many non-archaeologists wonder why it will not be raised and reconstructed, like the much-touted *Mary Rose*. Instead, Parks Canada intends to use information from the wreck to construct a 10-to-1 scale model. After analysis, each timber of the ship is returned to Red Bay and reburied under a protective layer of silt and sandbags. "Reburying for some is a horror," admits Grenier, "but I think that what we're doing is more important – getting the knowledge out of it. And in 10 years, if the technology and money are available [it would cost millions], the wood will still be there."

50   There are practical reasons beyond economics for not making the *San Juan* a showcase. Because the ship's stern and three or four of its masts remained above water, they have been smashed and scattered by winter ice. As a result, the *San Juan*, although complete for marine archaeologists, has retained less of its original integrity than the *Mary Rose*, which sank quickly to the bottom. And even if Grenier had been able to raise the ship intact, he would have learned less about it than he has learned piece by piece. Intact, it would have been too precious to examine. "We are trying to ensure that when we finish the project, we will know how each piece was put in the ship and in what sequence," says Grenier. "And then we will understand how the Basques built boats."

51   Analyses of the material collected to date will take Grenier another decade and will constitute a major chapter in the annals of nautical archaeology. For many, it would be crowning professional achievement. Grenier, his rubber boots propped on his desk and surrounded by blueprints of ancient ships and lithographs depicting Basque whaling activities, is not content. "What I would like to find," he muses, "is at least one musical instrument. There must

have been incredible evenings here when the dangerous work was done, like with fishermen today. Chasing whales must have been more than work."

Finding a musical instrument? Such an ambition seems facetious coming from a man who has honestly earned his reputation as one of Canada's most eminent archaeologists. But Grenier's sentiments are a curious key to the personal motivation that has made Red Bay a world-class dig and given Canadians a once lost chapter of this nation's history. Hoping to find a musical instrument is no more farfetched than Barkham's early unfinanced sojourns to obscure Spanish archives, no more flighty than Tuck's speculation about the fate of the Basques in that unmarked grave site.   *52*

Ultimately, the value of the Red Bay dig will not be simply to reconstruct the material culture of the New World Basques – no matter how much implicit value there is locked up in the form and function of the 16th-century galleon or prototype whale-oil station. Archaeologists seek to understand what made their subjects tick, how and why they worked, played and, finally, died. They attempt to expose the mentality of an era. This concern is vitally interesting at Red Bay because the Basques set the stage for resource exploitation of the New World by later waves of Europeans. On the whole, it is a sad legacy that has seen the extinction or serious depletion of scores of species.   *53*

Perhaps the single most perplexing question for Red Bay archaeologists is posed by the mass burials on Saddle Island: Why, after four generations, did the ships fail to return one spring? No one has the answer to that question – yet. One possibility is that the Basques simply hunted themselves out of business. The whalebone record lends credence to this theory, for most of the massive remains belong to two species, the Arctic bowhead and right whales. Both species were prized by whalers because they carried a thick layer of oil-bearing blubber, possessed long plates of baleen and were lethargic swimmers, thus providing easy targets for harpooners. Today, both species are conspicuously absent from Labrador waters.   *54*

The slaughter that must have occurred defies imagination. In 1705, a French sealing captain, Sieur de Courtemanche, commented on the unearthly sight of thousands of whale skulls littering the beach near Red Bay. Barkham estimates that 2,000 whalers worked the Strait of Belle Isle every summer. Over five decades, they probably killed 20,000 rights and bowheads, more than enough to deplete a local population.   *55*

But even if they did not hunt their quarry to extinction, there is evidence that the Basque fishery was itself a victim of changes in the social climate. Many of the ships lost in the ill-fated Spanish Armada of 1588 were the same Basque commercial vessels used on   *56* the Labrador run, pressed into military service much against the wills of their independent-minded owners. The debacle of the Armada not only resulted in the loss of many ships but dealt a crippling blow to the Spanish economy. In the end, capital may simply not have been available to rebuild the Labrador fishery.

QUESTIONS

Language and Style

1. Can you explain the apparent similarity between the land-based researchers and the Basque whalers? What aspects of language and detail contribute to the effectiveness of the account here?

2. How is the writer's choice of language influenced by the immediate subject? Compare, for example, paragraph 22 with the paragraphs which precede it.

3. Can you explain the apparent shift of subject between paragraph 21 and paragraph 22?

Organization

1. How many different processes are discussed in Thurston's account? What are they?

2. Where is the interest focussed in Thurston's account?

3. To what extent are the actual findings at Red Bay discussed and evaluated? Can you summarize those findings as they are explained here?

4. Towards the conclusion of his account what are some of the means Thurston uses to tie together the different subjects?

Content

1. What is ironic about the use by outport children of whaling artifacts and tiles?

2. Some of this account may be especially interesting. Are there reasons, for example, why the account of Barkham's work should be particularly interesting?

Vocabulary

outport	dross	forecastle	strait
Basque	burghers	galleon	flensing
ensign	flukes	hiatus	pelagic
notarial	spartan	mouldering	utilitarian
cohort	topography	calligraphy	surmise
peregrination	cooperages	rutter	decanter
bloody-minded	grist	artifact	albeit
tryworks	ballast	hummocks	capacious
lichen	laved	reconnoitre	neophyte
jibes	paragon	redoubtable	ilk
miasma	baleen	prototype	credence
heyday	lethargic	lee	Spanish Armada

A Day's Fishing
Tiny Bennett

Bennett's "over the shoulder" advice to the beginning angler imagines a very successful first day's fishing. Notice the conversational nature of the explanation and the roles the narrator and the new angler play.

It is time to gather together our beautiful new tackle, and head out for a day's fishing. We need to learn how to put the gear together with the proper knots, and to learn a few different angling techniques.   1

I have chosen a favorite fishing hole that has a good head of fish and conditions that are easy for the beginning angler. It is less than pastoral, being close to a busy highway, and most anglers sweep by it without a second look. But it is a good place to fish and has characteristics that may be found all over North America.   2

Picking a warm day in early summer, let's take all the gear, including the lures you have so carefully selected, for you never know what fish might happen along in this type of fishing hole. We will start with dew worms and live minnows for bait and these we will pick up at the site. While we do that, we can take a good look at the water and start learning how to recognize a good fishing spot.   3

Our fishing hole was once just a marsh, with a deep-water channel running through to connect a big lake with a smaller,   4

From The Art of Angling *by Tiny Bennett, 1970. Reprinted by permission.*

weedy inland bay. It was an interesting place when wild, but a highway bridge built at a narrow point changed it into a hotspot.

5   When the traffic got too heavy for the old single-lane bridge, the makers of highways threw a massive broken-rock causeway across the marsh, covered this with fill, and put a four-lane highway on top. Across the deep, fast channel went a bridge with solid concrete piers set fast in the current flowing back and forth in the gut, thus creating a water race. The closing in of the channel speeded the flow, and this cut deep holes and created massive eddies on each side of the bridge.

6   The deepened water attracted channel catfish, the eddies became the feeding places of walleye and other species, and the various obstructions and covering spots brought along minnow shoals and a trailing tail of resident and visiting predators. In fact, we now have a typical rich fish-population because of works that provided suitable habitation for all indigenous species.

7   We'll use bottom gear and a worm for our first attempt here, in one of the big eddies below the downstream side of the bridge. The water in these massive swirls is around 20 feet deep, and when the current swings to flow through the other way, we will still be able to fish in comfort, and hold bottom.

8   An early start lengthens the angling day, so here we are at 5 a.m., having coffee with the owner of the boat and bait livery, and chatting about conditions and learning which fish have shown recently. Advice from someone who lives right on the water is valuable indeed; and he tells us that the white bass are in, and that pike seem to have followed them and are being taken in the shallows on each side of the new bridge.

9   So, in addition to our worms we buy a couple of dozen small minnows. One dozen of these are less than 2 inches long, the right size for white bass, and the other dozen, for pike, are good-sized chub about 5 inches long. These go into our double-bait bucket and on reaching the point that we will fish from on the bank, the bucket liner is pulled out, sunk in the water and tied to a rock. It is going to get warm and this precaution will keep all the minnows lively.

10   At 20 feet the eddy is too deep for comfortable bobber fishing, even with a slider float, so we will use a sliding leger and, since the bottom is fairly clean, a dipsey sinker of 1 ounce.

11   The ferrule of the rod joint is rubbed between nose and cheek to add a little lubricating skin oil. The rod is pushed together, the reel screwed home and the line is threaded through the guides with about 10 feet pulled out of the tip ring so that we can build our terminal tackle. To make our sliding leger we need a dipsey sinker, two split shot and a size No. 6 standard hook. The sinker is slid up the line two feet and clamped in place. Now comes the important

part – knotting the hook on the end of our nylon monofilament line.

Nylon can slip with a poor knot, and worse still be reduced in test strength. Some of the knots used with silk line hold well with nylon, but can drop the test strength by as much as 50 per cent. Since we are going to use 8-pound monofilament, it would be foolish to use a knot reducing its effective value to 4-pound test, so we will settle for the *clinch knot* which, under scientific testing, has been shown to retain as much as 87 per cent of the line strength.   *12*

The clinch is *the* knot to use in fastening the end of a length of nylon to a rigid eye, including those on the hook, the swivel, or the end of a leader. Since it is a knot that we will be using regularly in all branches of angling, it is just as well to learn how to tie it properly.   *13*

This can be awkward to tie at first, giving most beginners the idea that a third hand is needed. But a little practice quickly brings proficiency in tying and in as few as six practice ties, it becomes second nature.   *14*

The end of the line is brought to the hook eye and 6 inches are pulled through and doubled back on the main line. This short end is twisted five times around the main part, by holding onto both ends and twisting the hook. The end is now brought forward and passed through the eye formed above the hook eye in the nylon. This end, together with the main line, is carefully pulled taut against an even strain on the hook. The spare end is now burned off with a cigarette or snipped, leaving a small tag.   *15*

With light lines, many anglers, including myself, prefer to use the slightly more complex, but superior *improved* clinch knot. In fact, once mastered, this can be used all the time.   *16*

In the improved version, the line is passed twice through the eye of the hook, twisted five times as before, poked through both loops in the nylon above the hook eye and then through the next twist up the line. It is pulled taut on all three ends: the hook, the main line and the short end. Both of these knots form a neat wrap that allows the line and hook to be positioned at the best level for setting and holding a fish.   *17*

For clipping the end of the nylon, and for a score of other jobs, I always carry an over-sized pair of nail clippers in my tackle box. These are good for cutting anything from spare ends of nylon to the lighter-weight leader wires, and are available at drug stores. I keep mine tied with a length of strong line to a strut of my box, so that they are always ready.   *18*

Now that the hook is tied to the end of the line it is time to put the bait on, but since this is a first angling trip, it will be wise for a few practice casts to be made to make sure that we can plop the bait into the edge of the eddy. It is a pretty big target, less than 40   *19* feet offshore, so it shouldn't take us long to pick up the necessary skills. But we had better take time out now for a few words on casting.

20   The best way to pick up casting skill is by practicing with a rubber sinker tied to the end of the line. Some level piece of ground, lawn or a local park is a good place, but most folks are more at ease and feel less conspicuous practicing over water.

21   Casting with spinning and spincast gear is a matter of *feel* and *timing*. It is more easily taught by a practical method than by a written description, so if you know someone willing to give a short lesson, that will be best. It is hard to explain in writing how much power to apply, or when to release the line, but I will take a stab at it, using the clock-face system to describe positions. So let's see what we can do.

22   When facing the water squarely, your head is at 12 o'clock, your feet at 6 o'clock. When you point your right arm forward, level with your shoulder, you mark 9 o'clock; with your arm behind, you mark 3 o'clock. All the other positions are relative to these.

23   Facing the water, reel the sinker to 18 inches below the rod tip and put the rod back over your shoulder until the tip is at 2 o'clock.

24   By moving your wrists slightly up and down you can get the feel of the weight of the tackle as the sinker draws the rod tip down. When you have done this, release the line and hold it either with your finger tip or with the spincaster button, so that it is set to flow when the pressure is released.

25   Next, dip the rod tip slightly, lift it to feel the sinker weight, and as it comes up taut, use wrist action to power it forward in a straight line over your shoulder towards the target. When the point hits 10 o'clock release the line and allow the rod to follow through until it is possible to sight the target over the tip.

26   If the direction is right and the correct amount of thrust is applied, the sinker will plop right in at the desired spot. Too much power and it flies over the mark, but can be reeled back into the proper spot. Too little power and it falls short, and will need to be thrown again.

27   If the line is released too soon, the sinker will fly almost straight up in the air, or at whatever angle the tip was at when the line was released. If freed too late, the sinker will crash into the water just in front, or wheel around in a full arc to smack painfully into your shins.

28   This is the overhead cast – quite simple really, and the one to be used 99 per cent of the time. It provides for the safety of others on the bank, and is mandatory for use in a boat holding other anglers.

29   After several practice casts and a couple of fair fumbles, you appear to have the range and the timing, so we will bait with a big dew worm and start fishing.

30   Since it is important to have a lively bait wriggling on the bottom to attract fish, it is a mistake to thread it up the hook, as this will

confine it. The pointed end of the worm is the head, the flat end the tail. The hook is pushed through the thick collar ring, one-third down from the head. Bring it right out, hook eye as well, and stick it in again halfway down the worm. Don't push it through this time, but just far enough to allow the point and barb to show. This will sit the worm in the bend.

When using a worm on travelling-float gear I would only hook it *31* once through the collar ring, as this allows the worm full move- ment and lets it swim like a small eel or live leech. But in our swim we can expect small fish, and the big double hook-hold saves bait when the eager biters are around. A big fish will suck it straight in.

Now you make your cast and it is successful, landing the hook *32* bait into the eddy, so sit down and make yourself comfortable. Put the end of your rod up on that forked stick left by another angler, allow the bait to settle on the bottom and when the line sinks slack, reel in until it is taut to the rod tip and then slack off a bit. This will allow bites to register, without a sudden pull warning off a fish. Sit tight on the rod, concentrate on the line and tip, and be ready to pick it up and offer slack when you see a bite.

Shut and lock the tackle box, so the gear won't be upset if it gets *33* knocked over in the excitement of a fighter with a lunker.

Yes, I saw that. It wasn't a fish, just a small piece of floating weed, *34* or maybe a sunken stick washed against the line by the slow- moving current. The line tightened slowly to the rod and put a slight bend in the tip before it came loose and let the tackle go slack gain. A number of small things like that happen in a day's fishing. When a true bite occurs it will show itself as a definite *jag-jag-jag* or, in the case of a big fish, as a solid pull that will jerk hard at the rod. With experience, you can read what is going on below by the behaviour of the rod and line.

This is the moment of truth for the angler: waiting for something *35* to happen. It is important to have quite a bit of confidence in what you are doing, to be able to say to yourself. "I'll give them time . . . I know there are fish here . . . my bait is still on . . . and I'll stick it out to give the fish a chance to find the bait."

The biggest problem is always the waiting. Not waiting all day *36* without a bite: that's being dumb, not patient. But we must wait for a reasonable amount of time. Anglers too often give a bait just a few minutes, then pull it out to see if it is still on, or to move it a few feet in either direction. The truth is that it takes a little time for a fish to find the bait. Sometimes the starting technique is wrong, and we need to run through a few different plans to get into contact with the fish. But it never hurts to give the fish enough time to come around.

Your bait is settled where there *are* fish and it would show poor *37* judgement to keep hauling it out. So leave it there. No, look! Quick! You've got a bite. Now pick up the rod gently without tightening the line and when you get a long pull or a heavy feeling, raise the rod to bring the line taut, and when you can actually feel the fish, jerk the rod up with a firm wrist movement to set the hook. Good. You have him. Now keep that rod point well up to act as a spring. Keep the line tight and reel slowly. Always take it easy at first. I once had a little bite here, set the hook, reeled easily for about 20 feet and suddenly a great boil erupted and a 27-pound channel catfish took off for the other side of the channel. I thought at first I'd set the hook into a small fish that had been taken by a big one, but in fact I'd hooked the cat right away and he had come along in docile fashion for the first stage. You must always be prepared for that type of reaction from a lunker.

38   Well, you've landed the fish and it's a rock bass. Now these fellows have a sharp dorsal fin (that's the one on top of the back) so fold down his fin, by bringing your half-closed hand over his head and down. Then grip him firmly behind the gills. You must have timed the strike perfectly, for the hook is right in the lip. Just take a firm hold of the shank, push the hook straight back and twist out. Fine. Now put him back to grow bigger – he's too small to keep.

39   Small fish such as the rock bass and sunfish are eager biters and often gulp the hook so that it finishes by sticking firmly in the throat. For this I carry a long pair of surgical forceps, the narrow kind with a long nose and a clip system in the handle that can lock the ends onto the shank of the hook for disgorging without damage. These are particularly good for use on a throat-hooked pike, as they keep fingers clear of the sharp teeth.

40   It is now 7 a.m. and you have taken eight fish: three small rock bass and two sunfish which you put back to grow, plus a nice-sized crappie and two brown bullheads of 1 pound which we have on the stringer in the water so that they will stay alive and fresh until we are ready to go home. I think it is about time to change to a large minnow for a while, to see if there are any decent walleye hanging around the swim. So, take off the small hook by cutting it close to the knot, and leave it to dry before putting it back into the box. Now, using the clinch knot, tie on a size 4 medium hook, and I'll get a minnow out of the bucket liner in the water.

41   You hear a lot of arguments over the best way to put a live fish on the hook as bait. Some people suggest a hook hold on the back, just in front of the dorsal fin, others stick it carefully through the side just in front of the tail.

42   Both these hook positions are useful and can be used for different circumstances, but for our purposes we'll use the one I believe best for leger fishing a live minnow. So hold the fish firmly, but not hard enough to hurt it, and gently push the point and barb through both lips, into the bottom and out of the top. I prefer this hook style because we are using 5-inch minnows which are fairly large for the job at hand, and since predators swallow prey head first, we give

the biting fish time to turn the bait, so that when we strike, the hook should be well in its mouth.

A gentle overhead cast now, and check the line with your finger *43* tip, just before the bait reaches the spot. This slows the bait and allows it to drop into the water softly, with less chance of being stunned. A *lively* bait tugging away at the tackle, will bring in predators from a considerable distance, and for this reason, let it sit there so that they have time to find it. Your cast was fine, so put the rod down on the rest. But this time allow more slack, for you may need to let the fish move off several feet before you set the hook. Any bite now will likely be a decent fighter, as the bait is really too big for small rock bass. You may need to wait longer for a take, but you have caught a few fish and it is worthwhile spending an hour or so on the chance of a better size.

While we are waiting let us again run through what to do on a *44* bite, as it will be too late to do so when a fish takes.

When your line and rod tip show action, pick up the rod, set the *45* reel to give free line and let the fish move off. When he stops and then swims away again, flip in the line retrieve on the reel, put the rod point out towards the fish, and when the line comes tight, or a heavy pull is felt, reel to get the line taut, flip up the rod to set the hook and bring the rod up to take the strain on the limber tip. Got it? Now make yourself comfortable on that rock, sit over the rod and be ready for action. While you wait, I'll get out my rod and see if I can pick up something on float tackle. I'll fish right here where my bait can run down the edge where the fast stream and the slack water meet. It is 8 feet deep and I can handle that with a fixed-position float on my long steelhead spinning rod. There's no argument that a 9-foot light rod comes in mighty handy at times.

With the rod put together, and a spinning reel loaded with 8- *46* pound nylon clamped on the butt, I thread the line through the guides and the rubber ring on top of the float and then through the metal eye on the bottom. Since I'm going to try with the small minnows first, I'll put on a size 10 standard shank hook, with three swan shot clamped 2 feet up from the hook to weigh down the minnow and balance the bobber so that it sits well, with just a couple of inches of the tip showing. My guess is that the water is 7 feet deep so the float is pushed up 8 feet, dropped into the water and allowed to swim down in the medium-speed current. Whoops! It's gone under – a slow shuddering sink. It's touched bottom. So out it comes and the float is pushed down 6 inches.

Drop it in again, and this time it runs the full length of the swim *47* without catching. I will allow it to go down this straight length, then check it at the bottom, and by turning the rod over, will make it turn in and hang still in that tiny eddy 25 feet below where we are fishing. This will make the minnow swim along the bottom and into that little bit of slack water where fish often lie in wait for an item of food washed down by the current. Now the gear is running properly, so I put a small minnow hooked through both lips and, my line of swim assured, out it goes.

48   Since I have a long rod in full control of the tackle, the overhead cast is not applicable. My swim starts 10 feet out from the bank, and with the bobber gear hanging below the rod point, I flip over the flier and swing the terminal gear out gently. When the minnow reaches the chosen mark, I release the line as smoothly as possible and the bottom gear slides out and lands where I aimed. With the rod held high and a finger set on the lip of the spool, I allow the tug of the float to slowly pull line off the spool. The idea is to make the tackle swim down without a pause until it reaches the desired point, where it will be checked. With my finger on the spool, I can quickly clamp down on the line if I need to strike. Now it is in the little eddy, so the line flier is thrown in and the live bait allowed to wander around in that hotspot.

49   Hey! There it goes! Down in one smash. It's up again, but look now! It's going *bob-bob-bob*. That means the fish has it and is turning it. Since it's a small minnow, just give it a second . . . down again, right under this time, so it's up with the rod. I've got him – a nice white bass. There must be a school of them huddled in that swim, so I string the fish and start again. We're going to have a fish supper tonight.

50   By the time I string the fifth white bass I can see that you are looking uneasily at your still tackle and I know that you want to join in the fun. Then, as you open the tackle box to sort out a float, there is a clatter and your rod is pulled hard. Forgetting the advice about the time needed for a fish to take a big minnow, you rear back and to our mutual surprise and delight, meet the strong pull of a fair-sized fish. Come on, get your rod up. Don't panic. Sure, let him take line. If you try to stop him something's going to give. I wrap up my tackle and lean it against the bridge support. It looks as if we have a two-man fish on the line now.

51   Stand up straight, face the direction of the run of the fish, and keep that rod up to cushion his pull. Don't worry about the line peeling off, we set the drag to the rod and if you do everything right, the fish can't get a dead-weight pull on your 8-pound line. There are no snags at all, and lots of room for him to run and fight. Now look out! He's swimming back this way and your tackle is going slack.

52   There must never be slack line to a fish, so reel in to put that bend back into the rod and keep reeling as long as the fish keeps coming. But keep that rod up because your fish will turn away and bolt, and when that happens there's going to be a sudden strain on the tackle . . . you have to be ready with the rod point up where the slash of the fish will be cushioned by the steely bend of the rod.

There he goes. He's turned and is running, so stop reeling at once. If you continue reeling while the fish is taking line, it will become strained, and worse, develop masses of twists. Wait till the fish stops. Pull very steadily and smoothly with the rod straight back, then reel the tip down the line gained. Keep repeating this procedure. It is known as pumping and is the only way to use tackle to fight a fish. Don't jerk – keep a steady strain and reel down smoothly without giving slack.

I am certain that you have tied into a fair-sized channel cat, for *53* he's slugging away down deep and hasn't shown yet. If it was pike or bass it would have come up and tried to throw the hook by jumping, or by shaking its head out of the water. A walleye, unless it was a monster, would have started to weaken by now. I doubt that a carp would take a minnow as big as the one you used. By the process of elimination we can be almost certain that it is a channel catfish. So watch it; once you get him up near the surface where he meets the light, he's going to make one hell of a fast run. Be prepared for this to happen just when you start to believe that you have the fish licked.

Meanwhile I'll get the landing gear ready, for it is obvious that *54* you have a fish that will give us trouble at the bankside. You won't be able to swing it ashore, as you did earlier with the smaller fish. So, as we have not yet studied landing techniques, I'll run through the basics, while you struggle on with your first big fish.

QUESTIONS

Language and Style

1. How would you characterize the tone of the writing? What sorts of things does Bennett do to create such an effect? Is there a good reason for adopting the tone – from the reader's point of view?

2. Where, so to speak, is the narrator "standing"? Who is the narrator?

3. Compare Bennett's description of the clinch knot (and the improved clinch knot) with some of the other directions. How might some of the differences be accounted for?

4. What do you make of the expression "lunker"? Can you explain the apparent contradiction in the suggestion, "So hold the bait fish firmly, but not hard enough to hurt it, and gently push the point and barb through both lips, into the bottom and out the top"?

5. What aspects of Bennett's directions contribute to a reader's sense that they just might work?

Organization

1. Why should the writer do so much explaining for the reader? Would the processes be more effectively presented as a simple list of steps?

2. How does the fact that the writer needs to deal with several related processes affect the progress of the narrative as a whole?

Vocabulary

head	pastoral
habitation	indigenous
eddies	livery
leger	ferrule
monofilament	swim
steelhead	drag
dead-weight	shoals
gut	causeway
chub	

WRITING ABOUT PROCESSES

Anyone who has tried without success to follow a set of instructions will sense intuitively what can go wrong. Here is a set of "instructions" for writers of directions which assures failure (compare it to the octopus recipe, which works):

1. Always assume that the meanings of special terms are known to the reader. (Everyone knows what "simmer" means.)

2. Do not dwell too long on the initial preparation of materials. (It's more trouble than it's worth to pound octopus.)

3. The order of operations is not preordained, so if it's not terribly clear, no harm is done. (What difference does it make whether an octopus is tenderized before or after it is cut up?)

4. Always assume the reader knows as much about the subject as you do. (Why bother to explain that large octopuses are apt to be impossibly tough and unsuitable as food? Everyone knows that.)

5. Provide no warnings along the way. (If someone wants to boil octopus into mucilage, it's not the writer's concern, and they'll know better next time.)

6. Once all the steps have been completed, the results are obvious, and you needn't bother describing them or explaining what to do with them. (Everyone knows that creamed spinach goes with octopus *en casserole*.)

7. Above all you should assume an attitude of complete superiority. (It gives readers confidence.)

These "directions," in their wrong-headedness, point to the importance of keeping the reader posted along the way, making certain that the manner in which an operation is carried out is clearly explained, furnishing the reader with necessary background information, and making allowances for variations in procedure.

The best test of a set of directions is whether it works or not. The writer of the assembly instructions accompanying boxes of Lego blocks knew the probable age of the blocks' owners-to-be and produced a set of directions which consists of a series of diagrams without a word of explanation (these instructions work very well). Test your own directions that way. Ask yourself, "If I knew what I tell the reader and what I assume the reader knows, could I follow these directions?"

The main principle of direction writing, that the discussion must be adapted to the reader, is also the main principle of writing informative process accounts. What are the reader's needs, and what does the reader know about the subject? The writer must know before proceeding further.

An account of a process is a special form of story-telling and, like all stories, has a beginning, a middle, and an end. In the beginning the writer needs to answer such questions as: What is this process? Who performs it? Why is it important? What are its main parts or steps? Why is it being described? For whom? In the middle of the story the writer needs to give an account of the phases or steps in the process in the order in which they ordinarily occur (that is, chronologically), needs to describe the manner in which they are done, and needs to identify necessary tools, equipment, or materials. The end of the story fixes the chief steps in the reader's mind, points out how the process is related to other connected or similar processes, and reminds the reader of any special matters which bear emphasis.

SUGGESTIONS FOR WRITING

Some of these suggestions will result in a set of directions; others require an informative treatment of a process. In certain cases a sketch or some other illustration may prove helpful.
1. Explain how to make a box kite or a paper airplane.
2. Explain how to unclog a stopped-up sink.
3. Explain how to clean and fillet a fish.
4. Explain how to make a spaghetti sauce from scratch.
5. Explain how to raise rabbits for meat.
6. How do the gears on a ten-speed bicycle work?
7. How does a vacuum cleaner work?
8. How is paper made?
9. How does a Wankel engine work?
10. How is instant coffee manufactured?

CHAPTER EIGHT
DEFINITION

INTRODUCTION

It would be fair to say that there are two general kinds of definitions: definitions which are meant to give information about how an expression is used and definitions which are meant to give persuasive force to a writer's ideas.

Persuasive definitions ought to be suspect because they represent something of a masquerade. It is as though a writer has a concealed purpose and is interested in convincing the reader of an idea's validity under the guise of constructing a helpful explanation of an expression's meaning. This is particularly true of certain "loaded" expressions associated with partisan matters. How, for example, would the expression "socialism" likely be defined by a proponent of capitalism or "capitalism" by a supporter of Marxist theories? Consider how "life" is managed by competing sides in the ongoing debate over legalized abortion. In these cases there is sometimes a trap built into the persuasive definition because a reader may be asked to accept the legitimacy of a definition housing a number of questionable assumptions which, once allowed, lead to overwhelming conclusions. If, for example, "life" were taken by definition to begin at conception, then abortion would probably be considered an act of homicide and abhorrent to right-thinking people.

Informative definitions, by contrast, work to lay all the writer's cards on the table in order to avoid confusion and to clarify ideas. Different sorts of informative definitions can be distinguished by the procedure the writer adopts for the purpose: dictionary definitions, formal definitions, and extended definitions.

Dictionary definitions are, of course, familiar to everyone. If there is a question about what a word means, careful people naturally look to a dictionary for an authoritative answer and find an explanation given mostly in terms of synonymous expressions. An unusual word like "lachrymose" is defined in one dictionary as:

> 1. given to or characterized by shedding tears; tearful. 2. suggestive of or tending to cause tears; mournful.[1]

And this works very well provided that the terms of the definition are sufficiently familiar to the searcher. However, when the synonymous terms are nearly as obscure as the one the dictionary sets out to define, a frustrating circularity arises:

> ligule . . . 1. a thin membranous outgrowth from the blade of most grasses. 2. a strap-shaped corolla, as in the ray flowers of the head of certain plants.[2]

There is a point at which dictionary definitions run out, throw up their hands, and say, "Well, look. We must start *somewhere*."

There are two other limitations to which dictionary definitions are subject: the dictionary as arbiter and the dictionary's completeness.

Everyone has heard the claim that because "ain't" is or is not in the dictionary, it either is or is not an acceptable expression. Beneath this kind of claim is the assumption that dictionaries are a social register of the language, telling people what expressions are "in" and what expressions are "out," that they are arbiters of linguistic good taste and appropriate usage – the dictionary as rulebook. It can be argued, however, with equally good reasons, that a dictionary is more like a catalogue which serves as a record of language use and therefore should collect expressions as they are ordinarily employed by native speakers. Commonly, dictionaries will come down in the middle of this argument and, while including an expression like "ain't," will indicate in some way that it is non-standard or colloquial.

A dictionary's completeness or comprehensiveness is sometimes also questionable, for most dictionary making has been undertaken by British and American lexicographers and reflects the assumption that Canadian expressions and spellings are somewhere in between the British and the American practices. Usually dictionaries which are not expressly Canadian in origin, and a large majority are not, will indicate that "color" is the preferred American spelling and "colour" the preferred British spelling, leaving Canadians to choose between the two as they like. There are, moreover, many Canadianisms which do not appear in Anglo-American dictionaries. "Shad fly" comes to mind, and "Inuit," although the latter expression may not appear in dictionaries as a preferred replacement for "Eskimo" because it has only lately come into common use at the behest of native peoples, and dictionaries, which

---

[1] From *The Random House Dictionary of the English Language:* College Edition, rev. ed., ed. in chief, Jess Stein (Random House, Inc., © 1975). Reprinted by permission of Random House, Inc.
[2] *Ibid.*

take a long time to compile, have yet to catch up with some modern expressions.

Dictionary definitions not only have cultural and technical limitations. They do not readily serve as the beginning for orderly, rational inquiry since they record common usage and are not intended to explore meanings so much as to give them. Formal definitions are required, definitions which function in connection with systems of classification (classes and subclasses) to narrow the meaning of the term in question by identifying those qualities which distinguish all members of a subclass from members of all other subclasses of the same order. Aristotle (384-322 B.C.) intended this sort of formal definition when he claimed that what distinguished humans from all other animals was their rationality. He claimed that humans were the only rational animal.

Two other more recent definitions which are constructed like Aristotle's try on the face of it to accomplish the same formal classification:

Humans are the only animals which blush, or need to,
— Mark Twain

and

Humans are the only animals that hoard their dead.
— Ambrose Bierce

Dictionary definitions record use, and formal definitions can sometimes be used to construct systematically a theory in science or morality, but to explore meanings of important ideas extended definitions are needed, and they are controlled by no lexicographical or theoretical procedures. Virtually any explanatory device may be put into service for an extended definition. The definition of "cliché" and "arrest" which appear in this section illustrate this fact. Examples, accounts of personal experience, the origins of words, are all used to develop and explore the meanings of these and other expressions in the readings which follow.

Only some expressions seem suitable for extended definitions: those expressions which have a special importance or significance and which interest the writer not so much as words, but as concepts whose implications, or "contents," need to be brought to light.

The Meaning of Cliché
Bergen Evans and Cornelia Evans

Here is an authoritative definition of the term from the Evanses' book on contemporary usage.

Cliché is a French word meaning a stereotype block and is used in   *1*
English to describe those phrases (there are thousands of them),
originally idioms, metaphors, proverbs, or brief quotations, which
overuse and, sometimes, changing circumstances have rendered
meaningless. Many of them just fill out the vacancies of thought
and speech. A man goes to say *far* and he says *far and wide*. Speech
is a difficult thing. We spend more time learning to talk than
anything else we do. It is an effort, an unceasing effort. There is
strong resistance in us to it and the inertia which this resistance
sets up is probably the chief cause of our use of clichés.

Many clichés are alliterative, that is, their words begin with the   *2*
same sound. We do not say we are *cool*, but *cool as a cucumber*.
Unless one is *slow but sure*, things go to *rack and ruin* and he may
be thrown out *bag and baggage*.

Historical changes have made many clichés utterly meaningless.   *3*
What does *fell* mean in *one fell swoop*? Or *halcyon* in *halcyon
days*? Or *moot* in *moot point*? Yet these and hundreds of other
phrases, totally devoid of meaning to those who speak them, are
heard every day.

Many clichés were once original and clever, but repetition by   *4*
millions, possibly billions, of people for hundreds and even thousands of years in some instances has worn all originality and
cleverness away. They were fresh-minted once, but are now battered
beyond acceptability. And their use is doubly bad because it char-
acterizes the user as one who thinks he is witty, or would like to be
thought witty, and yet is a mere parroter of musty echoes of
long-dead wit. His very attempt to sound clever shows him to be
dull.

Our speech is probably more crammed with clichés today than   *5*
ever before. The torrent of printed and recorded matter that is
dumped on us every day in newspapers and from radio and television is bound to be repetitious and stereotyped. The brightest day
in the world's history never produced one-millionth, in fresh, original, and honest expression, of the bulk of what cascades over us
every day. All this stuff is prepared in furious haste. There is
neither time nor energy for care or thought and the inevitable

result is a fabric woven of stereotyped phrases. Ninety per cent of what the public reads and hears is expressed in fossilized fragments and, naturally, ninety per cent of its own expression, apart from the necessities of life, is also expressed in them.

6   This makes the task of the man who wants to speak and write clearly and honestly a difficult one. He must be on his guard all the time, especially against anything that seems particularly apt. That doesn't mean that he is never to use a current phrase or even a hackneyed one. It may be, for example, that after consideration he really does want to say that the pen is mightier than the sword. And if he does, he'd better say it in the cliché form that in some labored circumlocution. But he mustn't expect to be thought clever for saying it. And, of course, he may deliberately choose to speak in clichés in order that his speech may be common and familiar.

7   Wits often use clichés as the basis of their wit, relying on the seeming familiarity of the phrase and the expectation of its inevitable conclusion to set the trap for the innocent reader – such as Oscar Wilde's "Punctuality is the thief of time" or Samuel Butler's "It's better to have loved and lost than never to have lost at all" – but that is a wholly different thing.

QUESTIONS

Language and Style

1. How does the reader know what "alliterative" means?

Organization

1. What is the apparent purpose of the last paragraph? What is it doing there?

2. Why are examples of special importance in this brief essay? Can you supply some of your own?

3. Why, according to the authors, do people use clichés? In what two places is this question addressed?

4. In what ways does this definition bear a resemblance to a dictionary definition?

Vocabulary

idioms	circumlocution	parroter
proverbs	halcyon	hackneyed
fossilized	metaphors	moot

Profits

John Kyle

Oil company economist John Kyle here explores, in informal language, a key economic concept and its implications.

During the past few years I've found that almost every time I go to a   1
dinner party and the other guests discover that I'm an economist
working for an oil company, the questioning becomes as predictable – and sometimes as aggressive – as that of a prosecutor in a
courtroom. Of course, with all the attention given to the oil industry ever since the first big OPEC price increases in 1973, it would
be surprising if I were not drawn into discussions of oil company
profits and the like. But, while the interest is understandable, I am
always puzzled (and somewhat distressed) by both the misinformation that abounds about the oil industry and the confusion that
exists about the concept of profit in general and the role it has in
our economic system. And this in a country that is historically
committed to the concept of private enterprise, free markets, and
consumer choice.

Given that background I welcomed the invitation . . . to write   2
something explaining "the size, source, and use of oil-company
profits." I will certainly force me to organize my thoughts, and then
at least *I'll* be ready at the next party.

Besides, as an economist I am seriously worried that widespread   3
failure to understand what profits are all about will lead to well-
intentioned but misguided legislation that will create serious problems for us all. So, the opportunity to try to clarify how the system
works is too good to pass up. First, a few basics.

What are profits?   4

It's surprising (to me), but many people I know who are upset   5
about oil-company profits don't really seem to understand what
profits are in our type of mixed economy. (Mixed economy, by the
way, is one of those favorite buzz-word terms that simply means we
have neither a pure Adam Smith type of capitalist system nor a
centrally controlled socialist system. Rather, we have an economy
where most goods and services are supplied by privately owned
enterprises responding to market incentives, with governments
also providing some goods and services. Governments, in addition,
watch over the economy to ensure that such things as health
standards, environmental protection regulations, and the like are
observed.)

"Profits" by John Kyle, in The Review *(Nov. 2, 1980). Reprinted by permission.*

6   Profits, in our type of economy, are defined as the difference between revenues and costs in a business activity. These costs include all wages and salaries, payments for raw materials and other items used in the production process, and – ever more important these days – the obligations to governments incurred by the firm, such as royalties and taxes. However, in this definition (which is basically the one used by the tax authorities) costs do *not* include any payments to the owners of the machinery and equipment used in the firm nor is there any adjustment for the distortions caused by inflation.

7   While this definition is adequate for some purposes, it does not really do much to help us understand how profits contribute to the efficient working of our economic system. For that, we must broaden our viewpoint to look at the role of profits as a reward to the owner or owners of a business and a key signal to the marketplace. Both of these roles are necessary if the market system is to work, and both must be understood before any judgment can be made on the "reasonableness" of any particular firm's or industry's level of profits.

8   By producing a product or service desired by the public, the owners of a business are hoping that the capital they have supplied to make that happen will grow. But their eventual reward, if any, will depend on another critical factor: how efficiently the business operates. Profits are the incentive our economic system provides to the businessman to strive to keep the costs of production as low as possible, thereby making the gap between revenues and costs as wide as possible. Of course, as all businessmen try to do this, the competition that takes place for the consumer's dollar results in much of this efficiency being passed on to purchasers in the form of lower prices. (Lest you think that prices are never lower, look at the effect of high profits and competition on electronic calculators and the computer industry. A decade ago both prices and profits were very high and only a few firms were in the business. Now dozens of firms compete, and prices have fallen steadily for several years.)

9   Without the promise of profits as a reward for supplying capital to a successful business, it would be unreasonable for anyone to give up the ability to make some other use of his money. For, when an individual invests in a business, he gives up the chance to buy something else with the money – a new car, perhaps, or a vacation or some other goods or service. Thus profits are, in effect, a payment to the owner of the capital for waiting. As a reward for giving up current consumption in order to increase the productive capacity of the economy, the supplier of capital receives a profit from the sale of an additional output made possible by his investment.

10   In addition to providing rewards to suppliers of capital for doing things society indicates it wants done (and the very fact that we

buy the goods and services offered indicates that we want the efficient production of these goods or services to take place), profits also serve as a signaling device. That is, they indicate which industries are producing those goods and services most desired by the public and which, therefore, ought to expand the fastest. In industries where profits are "high" — relative to the risk involved — new capital will tend to be invested, more labor will be hired, more raw materials purchased and, as a result, output will be expanded. Conversely, in those industries where profits are "low," production will tend to contract and labor and capital will tend to migrate to other industries.

To take only one example of this process, in the early years of   *11* this century, coal was a major source of energy in Canada. Many homes were heated by it and most industries and the railroads ran on it. But as oil and natural gas were discovered and began to be delivered to markets, their lower prices and greater convenience caused profits in the coal industry to decline. As a result coal dealers gradually went out of business (or became fuel-oil dealers). Oil and gas expanded and coal contracted until today virtually no homes are heated this way, the railroads now run on diesel, and industrial activity is largely fueled by oil and gas.

So, how should we measure profits? What is the correct way to   *12* tell whether they adequately perform their tasks of rewarding investors and signaling markets?

Earlier, I gave you the tax-collector's definition of profits as the   *13* difference between revenue and costs. This definition leads, obviously, to the measure of profits headlined in the newspapers, annual reports, and the like: the absolute dollar amount earned in a particular quarter or year. A roundup in *The Financial Post* of the returns to 125 of Canada's larger shareholder-owned companies showed, for instance, that in the second quarter of 1979 net profits were, in total, 47 per cent higher than a year earlier and, during a 12-month period, 40 percent ahead of the previous 12 months. The gains varied widely from industry to industry, especially when year-to-year comparisons were examined — metals and minerals up 312 percent, uranium and coal up four percent, integrated oil and gas companies up 45 percent, forest products up 77 percent, autos and parts up 112 percent.

While these figures provide the media with eye-catching head-   *14* lines, the story changes when profits are reported in the context of overall sales. For example, the profit margin (that is, net income as a percentage of sales) was 20.8 percent in the metals and minerals group that had the huge 312-percent year-to-year increase in net profits. The profit margin for oil and gas companies was 7.2 percent, for all the 45-percent jump in income. And it was a smallish three percent in autos and parts, where net profits had risen 112 percent.

Moreover, even comparisons of profit margins are really only   *15* useful when you want to see how a company is doing from one period to another — a measure of profitability over time. Also, while they are useful in comparing the progress of similar companies within a single industry, they are not very valuable (and can be misleading) when comparing one industry with another. For example, in retailing — where sales volumes are high — a one-percent or two-percent profit margin can be considered good; but in high-risk operations, such as mining, nine to 10 percent may not be enough to attract the investors or lenders to finance expansion.

16   In fact, the *only* reasonable measure of profits insofar as their role in the economy is concerned is as a rate of return. Or, to put it more simply, you have to look at the profit as a share or percentage of the total capital invested in the business in order to get a realistic idea of their size. The reason for this, quite simply, is because investing funds in a business (that is, supplying capital) is, except for the risk factor, basically the same thing as putting money in a savings account or purchasing a Canada Savings Bond. Just as $1,000 per year would be considered a "high" return on a CSB for which you had paid $5,000 (a 20-percent per year rate of interest, in fact), it would be a "low" return on CSBs for which $20,000 had been paid (only a five-percent a year rate of interest). So, too, profits can only be measured relative to the amount of capital invested and the risk involved. Regardless of the absolute dollar amount of profits, if the rate of return adjusted for risk is lower than that available elsewhere, then capital will tend to flow out of the business and be invested where it can earn the higher return.

17   Incidentally, before you rush to grab your copy of Imperial Oil's annual report to shareholders to calculate the rate of return ... you should be aware of another complicating factor. The basic profit numbers reported there are misleading. Not in a legal or accounting sense, of course. The statement of earnings provides exactly the information required by law, and it is as accurate as modern accounting techniques can make it. But it is still misleading in an economic sense because of the high rates of inflation we have been experiencing in recent years. And, what's more, the statements and annual reports of every company in Canada are misleading in exactly the same way.

18   The problem, in brief, is in the calculation of costs. Recall I said that the technical definition of profits was revenue less costs. Included in costs is something called depreciation, which is basically a recognition of the fact that capital equipment wears out as it is used in production. In order for any firm to remain in business, obsolete or worn equipment must be replaced. The depreciation allowance is used to create a fund, in essence, that will permit this replacement. It is established by letting the company set aside a

certain percentage – say, five percent or 10 percent – of the original cost of the equipment each year so that when equipment finally needs replacing, after say 10 or 20 years, replacements can be purchased.

Unfortunately, in a period of high inflation, the cost of a new   *19* piece of equipment will generally be much higher than the cost of the original. (If you want an idea of how much, take a look at the price of a new car and compare it with prices nine or 10 years ago. Prices of capital equipment have been doing much the same thing.) Thus, the true cost to the company for "using up" the machine is much higher than the amount that the government allows as a deduction for depreciation. Total costs, in other words, are much greater than those reported in the official statements.

Another way of looking at it is to consider your own income.   *20* According to official government statistics, the average worker in Canada earned more than twice as much in 1978 as he or she did in 1970. But in real terms, if you're that average worker, you know you can't buy twice as many goods and services as you did in 1970. That's because prices have soared. In fact, prices were 80 percent higher in 1978 than they were in 1970, so that you could only buy 16 percent more goods and services in 1978 than you did in 1970, despite the fact that your nominal income was up by a much larger amount.

Partially in recognition of this problem of inflation, the federal   *21* government has indexed the personal income-tax system since 1974 so that personal exemptions and marginal tax brackets are adjusted to compensate for inflation. The basic idea is that you should not move into a higher tax bracket just because of inflation. Instead, the government agrees that you should only pay taxes based on your "real," or inflation adjusted income.

No such adjustment is permitted for corporations. However,   *22* many economists and other experts have urged the government to permit adjustments to corporate taxes similar to those allowed individuals. In 1978, in response to a suggestion from the accounting profession, Imperial – along with several other companies – tried to estimate the real value of its profits by adjusting its depreciation and other items to reflect today's costs. This figure is reported at the back of the 1978 annual report (it has to go there because there are rules on how and where the basic figures are to be reported). For 1978 this adjustment for inflation reduced profits from the "official" $314 million derived from the basic revenue-less-costs rule to $122 million on an inflation adjusted basis. In other words, some $192 million of the company's reported "profit" in 1978, or about 60 percent of reported earnings, were only an inflationary illusion. They were, in fact, really revenues that will have to be used to replace capital that has worn out as a result of the company's current operations, unless Imperial is prepared to go out of business, which it's not.

23   To some extent, of course, all companies face the same problem, so a comparison of rates of return across industries, while they are biased upward because of inflation, can provide some indication of their relative profitability. However, before you make that comparison, there is another factor to take into account, namely risk.

24   There are varying degrees of uncertainty, of course, to various investments — and I've qualified statements several times with a phrase such as "aside from the risk factor." At one extreme are such investments as Canada Savings Bonds. Here, the Canadian government guarantees both the return you will receive on any invested funds (in terms of the interest rate) and what is called the "liquidity" of the investment. All that means is that you can convert your CSB into cash at any time and the government guarantees to pay you the face value of the bond plus any accrued interest. Now before you say that is only reasonable, remember that very few investments are that safe. If you buy a share of corporate stock, for example, neither the dividend you will receive nor the price at which you will be able to sell the share in the future is guaranteed by anyone. And, in order to get people to invest in the more risky stock, investors have to expect that they will earn a greater total return (dividends plus capital gains) than they would receive if they had left their money in CSBs, at least on average. Moreover, within that average, some people will be outright losers, while others will earn handsome returns, indeed.

25   As everyone who reads the daily stock-exchange quotations knows, companies and industries also differ in their riskiness. And, in order to attract investors, the riskier industries must promise higher potential returns than the more secure businesses. Yet the after-tax rate of return on capital employed has not been substantially different between total manufacturing and the petroleum industry during the past decade.

26   In 1968, for example, the after-tax profit on capital employed — that is, the rate of return — in the petroleum and coal industries averaged 6.8 percent, while for total manufacturing the comparable figure was 6.7 percent. For the nine years from 1968 through 1976, profits as a percentage of capital employed averaged 8.5 percent in the petroleum and coal industries and 7.8 percent in all manufacturing. Of course, the rate of return in individual years can vary somewhat more, largely as a result of fluctuations in economic activity in the country as a whole. Manufacturing tends, on average, to be hit harder by recession, for example. As a reflection of this, in 1971 the rate of return on capital employed was 7.6 percent in petroleum and coal and 6.4 percent in manufacturing. However, the basic point — that returns in the mineral-fuels industries are

hardly out of line with those in total manufacturing when risk factors are recognized – should be fairly clear.

Incidentally, I would like to draw to your attention the fact that *27* these profit levels are a far cry from the 50 percent, 100 percent, 150 percent, and larger profit-percentage increases you see reported in the media. And, as I indicated earlier, it is rates of return that are the most relevant measures of a company's performance.

Let's turn now to two more important terms that should be *28* understood if profit levels, including those of the oil industry and Imperial, are to be evaluated fairly. They are before-tax and after-tax profits.

Critics of the oil industry, and sometimes of private enterprise in *29* general, often object to looking at after-tax rates of return rather than before-tax. They argue that the returns to individuals from, say, CSBs are before-tax returns, so the appropriate comparison with a corporation ought to be before-tax corporate rates of return as well. Regardless of the superficial appeal of this "logic," however, the argument is invalid because corporations are not real people, and since they are not they do not earn anything for themselves directly. Instead, they exist to earn a return for the people who have invested in the business. And that return, quite simply, is the return earned by the corporation after its corporate-income taxes have been paid. Just as a bank depositor is not concerned with the money earned by the bank, but rather with the interest paid on savings deposits, the intelligent investor in a corporation is not interested in the earnings of a corporation before taxes. Instead, his concern is what available after taxes, either to be paid out in dividends to shareholders or reinvested in the business in the hope of providing a capital gain.

So, when you see a businessman pointing to his after-tax rate of *30* return or suggesting that after-tax returns are insufficient to justify a particular project, he is not really trying to trick you, nor is he demanding "exorbitant" profits. He is only drawing attention to what is a more relevant figure for anyone interested in investing in the business.

Even after-tax profit figures, however, are widely misused or *31* misinterpreted in reports on corporate activities – and nowhere is this as apparent as when people talk about oil companies. One of the problems, I have to admit, is the often obscure way economists "explain" complex issues. So, I'll keep professional jargon to a minimum.

Although after-tax profits are the amount of earnings available to *32* a corporation, either to pay out in dividends or reinvest in the business, most companies, in fact, reinvest the major portion of these funds. That is not the impression the casual observer gets from newspaper reports and TV newscasts. In the case of foreign-owned companies, there are often misleading stories about a drain of profits, equal to after-tax profits, out of the country.

33   The truth is quite different. At Imperial, for example, after-tax profits in 1979 (without any of the adjustments for inflation I argued earlier ought to be made) totaled $493 million. Of that, only $150 million, or about 30 percent of after-tax profits, was actually paid to shareholders in dividends. The remaining funds are, in fact, reinvested in the business. While every company is different, Imperial's behavior is still fairly typical of most corporations.

34   Still, many Canadians wonder if the oil companies are spending a reasonable portion of their share of extra revenues from higher energy prices to develop new energy sources. How much, in other words, is enough?

35   To look at that question fairly, another concept — net cash flow — has to be introduced. That means the total amount of cash available to a company. How is that calculated? First, there are after-tax profits. Add to that depreciation, the allowance I've already mentioned that business can charge against its taxable revenues to cover part of the cost of wear and tear on equipment. There are also the tax dollars governments forego in the form of tax and some other minor incentives to encourage development of new Canadian supplies, if certain types of investment expenditures are made. (Of course, governments hope that those incentives will eventually produce new royalty and tax revenues.) However, even after using up all of those funds, Imperial borrowed about $300 million in 1979 to help pay for its investment.

36   The federal government has been monitoring the performance of 31 of the largest petroleum companies in Canada for several years to see what in fact happens to the money they bring in. For the period 1973 to 1978, the total cash generated by these companies (before borrowing), including the depreciation I mentioned, amounted to some $18.5 billion. Investment spending in Canada during the same period amounted to $14.3 billion or 77 percent of total cash generated, while dividends paid to shareholders came to $2.4 billion or 13 percent of total cash. Profits, on the other hand, totaled $9.4 billion or only 65 percent of investment spending. And that is the average for a number of years, including a period of sluggish investment in 1975.

37   More recently, as the search for new reserves of oil and gas has speeded up, even higher percentages have been reinvested. As a result, industry has had to borrow capital from others to supplement internally generated funds. And, as the industry is forced to turn to more exotic, higher technology sources of energy, such as the Athabasca oil sands and heavy-oil deposits, deep-basin gas, offshore Atlantic, and the like, costs will escalate even more.

38   To put some of these costs in perspective, a few more numbers

may help. The first of the new generation of oil-sands plants – Syncrude Canada Ltd. – of which Imperial owns 25 percent, began production in mid-1978. Its planned capacity is 129,000 barrels a day of synthetic crude oil, and the cost of the plant was about $2.2 billion. Another heavy-oil plant, at Cold Lake, which Imperial hopes to be permitted to build in the early 1980s, will have a planned capacity of 140,000 barrels per day and will cost an estimated $7 billion by the time it is completed. Much of the increased cost over Syncrude, by the way, aside from the extra 11,000 barrels per day of capacity, reflects the impact of inflation on construction bills.

To raise the funds necessary to pay for these investments, Impe- *39* rial expects to have to augment the cash it will generate internally from its operations with substantial external financing. Even at that, partners will likely be required to help assume some of the financing load and to share the risk. The promise of profits from this venture is what will, of course, be the attraction.

I hope, at this point, that I have said enough to convince you of *40* two things. First, rather than being a rip-off of the Canadian public, profits are an integral and important part of our economic system. They are what motivate individuals to place their savings at the disposal of a business. And they lead to the investment that, in the final analysis, provides our economy with growth and jobs. In fact, they are the major reason why, if the system is allowed to function as it can without excessive governmental interference, consumers in market-oriented economies enjoy the highest standard of living in the world. Second, insofar as the oil industry is concerned, the profits earned are helping, in fact, to achieve Canada's goal of energy independence. That is because they help directly to finance new investments and provide the incentives necessary to entice potential investors to supply the industry with the extra capital it will require for the huge projects necessary in the years ahead.

As I said, I hope I have convinced you of these two points. *41* Because if I have not, and if enough Canadians do not also come to the same understanding, there is a very serious danger that in the name of taxing "excess profits," we will emasculate private industry to the point where it will be unable to do the job we so badly need done.

QUESTIONS

Language and Style

1. Can you identify a change in tone as the discussion moves ahead? How would you characterize the change?

Organization

1. Where does the introduction to the discussion end? How do you know?

2. Why should the formal definition of "profits" require amendment or expansion?

3. Notice how the definition tends to reveal the subject's complications (see paragraph 18 and following, for example). What are some of the complications?

4. What comparison is implied in paragraphs 20 to 22? In paragraphs 24 and following?

5. How is "risk" defined? What is the connection to the notion of profit?

6. How many examples are used in this definition? Why are there so many?

Content

1. Having read as far as paragraph 8, what elements do you see as comprising a definition of profits? Can you write an informal definition of the word?

Vocabulary

OPEC
Adam Smith
depreciation
exorbitant

buzz-word
conversely
indexed

The Female System
Anne Wilson Schaef

A noted therapist and social commentator, Schaef explores features of the Female System, which, she claims, has been submerged in the dominant White Male System, touched on by Paul Theroux's essay earlier.

My observations about the Female System and the White Male System come from women who have begun to trust their own perceptions and feel safe in expressing them. I have found that an amazing number of women with very different backgrounds and experiences tend to agree on many of these issues; this points to the existence of a clarity and commonality that are rarely observed or credited.   *1*

Far too frequently, women say only what is expected of them or acceptable in this culture. Their input generally falls into one of two categories: "women's talk" and "peacekeeping talk." Women's talk is stereotyped as useless. It is "all anyone can expect from a woman." It is allowed to exist because it does not threaten the White Male System. Peacekeeping talk does not threaten the White Male System either. In fact, it supports its concepts and ideas. It is women's way of demonstrating their understanding of the System and their reluctance to challenge its myths.   *2*

Women who have never stepped outside the . . . White Male System almost always communicate in one of these two modes. Even women who have begun to trust their own perceptions often fall back into one of these ways of speaking when they do not feel safe. *3*

There is another kind of "women's talk," however. It is the kind that emerges during individual therapy, groups, and private conversations – situations in which women feel safe to explore their own evolving System. I have often been privileged to hear this meaningful and moving "women's talk." The ideas presented here were developed with the help of women who were free to voice their own perceptions. They provide us with a solid beginning as we seek to define the White Male System and our own Female System and explore other realities.   *4*

Whenever I am comparing the White Male System with the Female System, I like to begin with a discussion of time.   *5*

In the White Male System, time is perceived as the numbers on the clock. In other words, men believe that the numbers on the clock are real and that time itself is nothing more than what those   *6* numbers measure. Five minutes equal five minutes; one hour equals one hour; one week equals one week; and so on. Time is what the clock or calendar measures. One who accepts this believes that it is possible to be early, late, or on time, and that these concepts have real meaning.

7   In the Female System . . . time is perceived as a process, a series of passages, or a series of interlocking cycles which may or may not have anything to do with the numbers on the clock. Frequently, the clock is irrelevant and may even be seen as interfering with the process of time. Early, late, and on time are concepts that have no real meaning.

8   There is an interesting correlation here between how much one buys into the White Male System and how he or she views and uses time. White women have bought into the System the most, and they are usually within fifteen minutes or so of being "on time" for an appointment. Blacks have bought in second most, and they are usually within a half hour or so of being "on time." Chicanos and Asian Americans tend to arrive within the hour. Native Americans – who have bought into the System the least – may be days or even weeks "late". . . .

9   Let me illustrate this . . . with some examples from my own experience. When my son was little, I used to try to have dinner on the table by six o'clock. That meant that I usually started preparing it around five o'clock, when I got home from work. Unfortunately, this was just about the time when my son's internal time mechanism started running down. He would begin fussing and pulling at me. When I continued to go by "clock time" and focused my attention on preparing a meal, I frequently discovered that I had developed a "growth" on my leg. My son had wrapped himself around it, hanging on for dear life while I dragged him around the kitchen with me! One day I decided to treat time as a process. When I stopped what I was doing and responded to him, which only took a few minutes, he toddled off happily and kept himself amused until dinner was ready.

10   Neither approach to time was "right." It just happened that the process approach worked better for all concerned in this situation.

11   Several years ago I was an administrator in a mental health facility, where one of my assigned tasks was to run the weekly staff meetings. I soon discovered that the people who got to the meetings "on time" were not really there at all. Their bodies were there, but their beings were somewhere else. Those who came late, on the other hand, were more "present" than the others.

12   When I investigated further, I discovered that those who arrived "on time" had frequently stopped in the middle of something they were doing in order to arrive at the meeting on the dot. Those who "came late," however, were often late because they had taken the

time to complete a task or bring it to a comfortable resting point before coming to the meeting. When they arrived at the meeting, they were ready and able to face the business at hand.

I began a quiet experiment with the group. At the beginning of   *13*
each meeting, I asked the staff to sit quietly and focus on any anxieties or tensions they were feeling. I then asked them to relate each anxiety or tension to an unfinished task or process and write down what they needed to do in order to finish it. If someone felt especially tense or anxious, I would suggest that he or she take some action toward completing the interrupted task. For example, I frequently discovered that my major tension was related to the awareness that I had forgotten to take something out of the freezer for dinner. A quick telephone call home completed the process and freed me to focus on the meeting.

As we continued to do this exercise at the beginning of staff   *14*
meetings, we began to use our time more efficiently. While it used to take twenty minutes for the staff to get their bodies and beings together, it now took from seven to ten minutes (a significant reduction – and a very worthwhile one, considering that most meetings were scheduled to last only an hour). We took the option of using a combination of process time and clock time, and it worked for us. Had I not suggested that option, I would have continued trying to drag the entire staff into the agenda when they were not ready for it.

Neither approach to time was necessarily "right," but the fact   *15*
that we were flexible enough to explore new choices helped us to use our time better.

I once read an article in *Time* magazine about the atomic clock   *16*
at the National Bureau of Standards. (I have long been fascinated by the National Bureau of Standards and believe that it is one of the citadels of the White Male System. At one point, I used to fantasize that real people did not work there. Instead, there was an elaborate hierarchy of inchworms who measured *everything*! When I finally visited it, I discovered to my amazement that it looks like any other building and that real people do in fact work there!) It seems that the atomic clock is the most accurate time-measuring instrument in the world. It sits up on a hill dividing the passage of time into equal segments. Unfortunately, it still has to be reset annually. In spite of its incredible and meticulous accuracy, the atomic clock does not know about the universe. The universe is on process time.... It is slowing down. So the atomic clock has to be set back a few seconds every year!

Which is better – process time, or clock time? Neither. Both are   *17*
valid and useful. It is unfortunate, though, when our culture is denied information about process time because the White Male System insists that its way is the way the world is.

18   Women often find themselves in situations where process time is more efficient than clock time (for example, in childrearing and in relationships). As a result, we have learned to move back and forth between them with relative ease. Unfortunately, the White Male System often makes us feel guilty when we are "late" and implies that we are sick, bad, crazy, or stupid because we do not use time in the "right" way. It is difficult for us to communicate what we know about using time when we are constantly being made to feel insecure about ourselves and our own perceptions.

19   In the White Male System, relationships are conceived of as being either one-up or one-down. In other words, when two people come together or encounter each other, the White Male System assumption is that one of them must be superior and the other must be inferior. There are no other possibilities for interaction.

20   In working with men, especially business executives, I have found that many men do not necessarily want to be one-up. They just do not want to be one-down. But since those are the only two options in their System, they do their best to go one-up and put others one-down.

21   In the Female System, relationships are philosophically conceived of as peer until proven otherwise. (This, of course, is only true for women who feel clear and strong and have come to know and trust their own system.) In other words, each new encounter holds the promise of equality. One does not have to be one-up or one-down, superior or inferior; one can be peer.

22   A major difference between the two systems lies in these basic assumptions about what kinds of relationships are possible. If you can only conceptualize relationships as one-up, one-down, then you will behave in certain ways. If you can conceptualize relationships as either peer *or* one-up, one-down, you will approach them differently.

23   A few years ago I was living in St. Louis near Washington University and seeing a student in therapy. She was from another midwestern city where her father owned a business. When she informed him that she was seeing me, he decided to call and "check me out." He wanted to find out about my background, my credentials, my philosophy, my fees, and so on. I thought that his need to do so was both appropriate and legitimate. I was a stranger to him, I lived in a distant city, I was counseling his daughter, and he was paying the bill. If I had been in his place, I would have done the same thing.

24   When he called, I assumed that we would approach each other as peers. He, on the other hand, immediately approached me in a one-up manner. His tone and attitude were one of a superior addressing an inferior. Since I assumed peerness, I did not go one-down but instead offered him the opportunity to interact with me on the basis of equality. There was a slight pause, after which ensued what I call the "relationships shuffle."

When two persons are physically present in the same place, this *25* shuffle is very obvious. For example, let's say that a man and a woman meet and begin a discussion. The man assumes that the woman will go one-down – and when she does not, he does not know quite what to do next. He shifts from one foot to the other and actually moves his body from side to side (sort of like a gamecock). It is almost possible to see in his face what he is thinking: "Oh, my goodness, she's not going one-down! She's sup-posed to go one-down! What do I do now? *Someone* has to go one-down!" (Pause. Gulp.) "I guess it will have to be me!" At this point, his posture visibly changes. He seems to sink and get smaller, assuming a stooping position and hating every minute of it. He also hates the person who has "made" him go one-down, and this colors their conversation from that point on.

Of course, no one "made" him go one-down. He *chose* to go *26* one-down because that is the way he believes encounters and relationships have to be. If the woman will not go one-down, then he must – but he resents it!

This is more or less what happened during the conversation *27* with my client's father. When I chose to stay peer and did not go one-down, he went one-down.

I happened to be talking to him on a wall telephone. My husband *28* came into the room and started laughing. "What on earth are you doing in that funny position?" he asked. I was leaning over to the side in what must have looked like a very uncomfortable and contorted posture. In response to his question, I whispered very seriously, "Trying to stay peer with this fellow!". . . . His belief in his System prevented him from taking the opportunity to be peer with me. All he knew was that relationships had to be one-up, one-down. That was his reality; that was the way he saw the world. He could not relax into accepting a peer interaction, and trying to stay peer with him nearly gave me a backache!

The relationship shuffle is a common experience for White Male *29* System persons. Whenever one of them meets a Black or a woman (a person who is *supposed* to go one-down) who does not go one-down, his only option is to go one-down himself – and he really resents it. Women managers often complain of this. When they do not go one-down, as expected, then the men they are dealing with go one-down, resent being there, and label the women "uppity." This entire process can take place while a woman is just standing there, giving a man the chance to have a peer relationship with her. The man's belief in the White Male System is so unshakeable that he cannot accept what she is offering him.

I think that it is very important to realize how strongly white men *30* believe in their own System and its myths. They are thoroughly convinced that the White Male System is the only reality, that it is innately superior, and that it knows and understands everything. They are also sure that it is totally logical, rational, and objective. As a result, they are severely limited in their ability to take in new information and have new experiences.

31   I have a woman friend who is a well-known writer and psychotherapist. She once told me that she strongly resents the amount of time and energy she spends in trying to "stay level" with men who go one-down with her. She finds herself constantly either bending down physically or trying to "pull them up" to her level. She is now in her seventies, and it is getting more and more difficult for her to keep changing her posture in an effort to maintain equality with the men she encounters. Recently she said to me, "They will just have to think of some other way to handle this. I am too old for this stooping business!"

32   There is another major difference in the way White Male System and Female System persons perceive relationships. In the White Male System, the center of the universe is the self and the work. Everything else must go through, relate to, and be *defined by* the self and the work. Other things in life may be important (relationships, spirituality, hobbies, and so forth), but they are never of equal importance; they always occupy positions on the periphery of the man's life, on the outside circle.

33   I have heard women in workshops say, "The one thing my husband and I have in common is that we both love him!"

34   In the Female System, however, the center of the universe is relationships. Everything else must go through, relate to, and be *defined by* relationships. This may be why women have historically not achieved as much as men. We tend to subordinate ourselves and our work to our relationships.

35   I used to think that men moved into the Female System during courtship. At that time, a man seems to set aside his self and his work and put the relationship at the center of his universe. He is unable to think of anything or anyone but the woman he is courting. He talks about her at work and may even miss work in order to spend time with her. He seems totally engrossed in the relationship. As a result, the woman gets very excited and starts believing that she has finally "found one" — a man who understands the Female System! She happily tells all her friends, "This one is different! He really is!" She is certain that at last she has met a man who knows how to make their relationship the focus of his life, and she is ecstatic.

36   As soon as the relationship is "nailed down," however — as soon as the man is sure of the woman's affections, and they are either married or have settled into some other committed arrangement — he goes back to his self and his work. She looks around at how her world has suddenly shifted and says, "I've been duped!" He begins to notice that something has gone wrong and asks, "What's the matter!" and she says, "You don't love me anymore!" He is shocked. "What do you mean I don't love you anymore?" he says. "Of course I do." (You have 180 degrees of my outside circle! What more do you want?) She responds, "Our relationship isn't the center of the universe for you anymore. And that's what love is!" And he says, "I don't know what you mean."

He really *doesn't* know what she means. She knows his System   *37* and her own System, but he does not even realize that she has a System.

Some men I have worked with have discussed this with me at   *38* length. And they really do not understand it. What I hear them saying is this: "We men don't move into the Female System during courtship. We don't even know what the Female System is. The relationship is a task (work) to be accomplished, and when it is solidified and we are sure of it we go back to our self and our work and business as usual." No wonder the women feel duped!

I once worked with a couple who came into therapy because   *39* they (mostly she) were concerned that there was no love in their relationship. Both believed that there had been earlier. When we examined the relationship more closely, it became clear that following their courtship he had gone back to his focus on his self and his work. He had added the relationship to his outside circle where it did in fact occupy a large part of the energy he did not already devote to his self and his work. The relationship was significant to him, but only as it went through, was related to, and defined by his self and his work. It was not significant in its own right.

The woman felt unloved because the relationship did not seem   *40* to be central to their lives together. He assumed that the relationship would "heal" once she understood and accepted his System and its (*the*) reality. Any healing to be done, however, depended on their willingness to know and value each system and then make choices as to which was appropriate at what time....

... I have learned that women move through a number of devel-   *41* opmental stages. We first develop primary relationships with men (or actively seek them) in order to gain our identity and absolution from the Original Sin of Being Born Female. These relationships become the center of our universe. Everything else is relegated to the outside circle. We devote our lives to maintaining our relationships with men, and our work, selves, creativity, and intellectual pursuits are all seen as secondary to these relationships and defined by them.

Then, as we become more aware of ourselves and begin to grow,   *42* we move into the White Male System. We put our selves and our work at the center of our universe. We become "selfish" – something women have a great deal of difficulty hearing – and start to put our own needs first. We devote a great deal of time, energy, and money to the process of self-discovery and the realization of our creativity. We become "workaholics." We spend more and more hours on the job. Money, power, and influence become very important to us. We want to "make it," and our criteria for "making it" are those of the White Male System.

43   During this phase, relationships become less important to us. Some of our relationships may survive in spite of the fact that we spend so little time maintaining them, but others may fall apart. We are beginning to discover our own capabilities, and we say things like, "I am going to make my impact on the world." "I want to make a contribution that people will remember." "I have no time for relationships. I must focus on my self and my work," Some of us become more job-centered than men!

44   Once we have "made it," however, we sit back and say, "So what?" We look around and wonder, "Is this all there is? It looked so good from the outside, but now that I've 'made it' I'm bored!" We then begin to move back into the Female System – but because we have changed, our concept of the Female System has also changed. It is no longer defined in terms of our relationships with men. It is no longer used *in reaction* to the White Male System. It has taken on an identity all its own.

45   It seems as if we must first be successful in the White Male System before we can fully and with clarity move into the Female System. During the early stages of our development when we participate in a reactive female system, in which we are not clear about ourselves and our world, we are dependent on men for our identity. . . . After we move into the White Male System and become successful, we can then return to the Female System from a new perspective.

46   In the Female System we "come home" to, relationships are still the center of the universe. But these may or may not include primary relationships with men. They *never* include primary relationships with men that give us our identity. . . . They may include *equal* relationships with men and will almost certainly include close friendships with other women and genuine friendships with men.

47   This Female System includes a *relationship with the self* – something that was never present in our earlier concept of the female system. Self-awareness and focusing on the needs of the self are not the same as selfishness. We are still aware of and concerned for others. The essence of self-awareness is a tenderness toward and respect for the self which in turn allows one to be more tender and respectful toward others.

48   Many women never have a relationship with their selves because they have been taught that to do so is selfish. Or they never

become aware of any self except as it is other-defined. Some women do acknowledge the presence of an emergent, embryonic self, but they seldom deem it worthy of a relationship.

As women become clearer and develop a sense of self, they are   *49*
enthralled and amused by it and want to explore it further. Since we do not have much experience defining ourselves from within, others frequently see this process as taking something valuable away from them. This is not the case, however. We are not subtracting anything from those around us; we are simply drawing toward ourselves. By developing a relationship with our selves, we become more capable of meaningful relationships with others. This is a very different definition of "self-centeredness" than that which is experienced by the White Male System. When we make room for ourselves, we can make more room for others!

The Female System we reenter also involves a *relationship with*   *50*
one's work. Work becomes more than something one does to earn money; it becomes a "life work." It is what we need to do with our life. It means making a contribution which complements the other aspects of our life. It is not profit- and power-oriented; instead, it takes its meaning from creativity, bonding, humaneness, and service.

A woman reaches this stage of growth – who moves out of the   *51*
reactive female system, into the White Male System, and then back into the Female System again – also develops a *relationship with the universe*. She begins to have an understanding of how it all fits together and a feeling that life has true meaning. She sees herself and others in relation to the whole. She may say things like, "When I am lying on my deathbed, I think I will look back on the relationships I have had and the connections I have made. These will be the things I consider most important. It will not matter whether I have built a bridge, or written a book, or had a university named after me. I will cherish the lives I have touched and those persons whose lives have touched mine."

The essence of life in the Female System a woman comes home   *52*
to is relationships – not relationships that define and validate, but relationships with the self, one's work, others, and the universe that nurture and grow. Not static relationships that are neatly categorized and packaged, but relationships that evolve and change, contract and expand. A process of relationships.

Women seem to need a two-step process to reach this stage;   *53*
they move into the White Male System, and then they move back into the Female System. Men, on the other hand, have only to take one step in order to reach this level of awareness. Since they have the birthright of innate superiority, they do not have to . . . [obtain] their identity through someone else. Yet they still have great difficulty taking this single step.

I believe that this is due to the fact that the position of being   *54* innately superior and having the self and the work at the center of the universe is very seductive. If one defines everything through the self and assumes that this is the way the world is, it is hard to imagine a world that is *not* self-defined. Men simply cannot conceive of any other way to be. Women, though, seem to get bored with that position after achieving success at it and seek something else. There are, however, some men who want to and do move beyond the beliefs of the White Male System. . . .

55 Another major difference between the way White Male System and Female System persons view relationships has to do with the issue of sexuality. The White Male System sexualizes the universe. Individuals, buildings, tools are all defined and identified by their sexuality. The most important aspect of a person, whether that person is male or female, is how he or she expresses sexuality. A person is *defined* as heterosexual, homosexual, asexual, bisexual, celibate, etc. Relationships are *defined* as heterosexual, homosexual, bisexual, celibate, platonic, etc. It is assumed that sexuality is present in *every* relationship.

56 In the Female System, sexuality is not a major identifying characteristic. An awareness of sexuality may or may not enter into a relationship or a situation. If it does, it is usually during the later stages, and it is never all-important.

57 Individuals and relationships are not the only things that are defined in sexual terms by the White Male System. . . .

58 Tools are also given sexual labels by the White Male System. They are categorized as "male" or "female," depending on whether they are penetrating or receptive. In fact, the whole universe is seen in sexual terms. It was walking through the woods with a friend one fine spring day when he suddenly threw up his hands and said, "Ah, sex!" I started and asked, "Where, where?" "All around you!" he said. "The flowers, the butterflies, the grass. Everything is sex!" Somehow the scene looked different to me!

59 In the Female System, sex is seen as important, fun, and sacred. It is not used to *define* the world, individuals, or relationships, however. When sex is used to define the world, individuals, and relationships – as in the White Male System – the result is a preoccupation and phobic overemphasis on sex for its own sake. For most women, sex is only one aspect of lovemaking. For many men, sex *is* love – and love is sex.

60 The prohibitions of the church regarding sex and premarital sex are good examples of this phobic overemphasis. Sex is made into *the* most important aspect of a relationship – the one thing that must "wait" until after the marriage ceremony has been performed. This puts all of the other aspects of the relationship – some of which may be far more important – completely out of focus. Many people end up getting married solely because they think this will

guarantee them regular and legitimized sex. They soon find out that marriage means more than that!

I have long been curious about why the White Male System is so   *61* preoccupied with sex and sexuality. Frequently I make observations about "what is" and then set about trying to find out the "why." My answers usually come from very unexpected sources, as was true in this instance.

I was asked to serve on a panel with a priest and a minister. The   *62* topic of discussion was an exploration of sexuality and sexual freedom, or the lack of it, in our culture. The priest had prepared a lengthy "pro-sex" paper. His basic thesis was that transcendence is an essential state for the human organism and that orgasm is the one time when individuals consistently transcend themselves. Thus, he implied, sex is not only important but necessary.

Suddenly I understood the meaning of some of my observations.   *63* (I started getting the answers to some of the "whys.") If one has the self and the work as the center of his (or her) universe, then one is in a constant state of self-absorption. But if one has relationships as the center of her (or his) universe, then one is constantly focusing on others and, hence, is in a state of transcending the self. Sex may be a vehicle for transcendence; it is not *the* vehicle. Focusing on relationships can be a vehicle of transcendence. That is why it is not necessary for Female System persons to sexualize the universe in order to achieve transcendence.

The important thing to remember in all of this is that both   *64* systems have some internal consistency regarding sex and sexuality. Neither perspective is "right." Unfortunately, women are more frequently damaged in the area of sexuality than in any other area. Because of the importance that men put on sexuality, the communication between the sexes in this area is confused and disturbing. Few women have a clear understanding of their own sexuality. We are seldom given the opportunity to learn much about it. Instead, we are called upon to support the myths and perceptions of the White Male System and meet its needs. We are told that our own beliefs and perceptions are not valid, and we are exploited and dominated. When sex and transcendence are used to serve the self, this obviates the need for love and affiliation.

Any discussion of sex and sexuality must evolve into a discus-   *65* sion of intimacy. In the White Male System, intimacy is approached physically. Men assume that in order to be really intimate with someone they must be physically close. In the Female System, intimacy is approached verbally. Women assume that real closeness involves sharing and discussing their lives.

I once saw a couple in therapy who exemplified these differ-   *66* ences. Each had a different intimacy fantasy about their reconnection after an absence from each other. He traveled a great deal in relation to his work. As he approached home, his fantasy went like this: He would come home from the airport, walk through the front door, embrace his wife, take her directly into the bedroom, and they would make love. Then they would be connected and intimate with each other. Her fantasy went like this: He would walk through the door after his business trip, she would tell him everything she had been doing and thinking during his absence, and he would respond by telling her everything he had been doing and thinking while they were apart. She would share new insights and awarenesses and *so would he*. She would then be ready to make physical love. They might, or might not, but that decision would be made together. The important thing, to her, was that their intimate connection with each other had been established through mutual sharing.

67   He experienced her words as a barrier to intimacy. She experienced his physical advances as a barrier to intimacy. When they came into therapy, they informed me that they had decided to seek help because of *her* sexual problem! Her husband had accused her of being frigid – and she had started to believe him!

68   Neither approach to intimacy is "right." But when one is the way the world is and the other is sick, bad, crazy, or stupid, there is little opportunity for two equal people to come together and explore the richness of varied approaches. Only when both persons are willing to recognize and understand each other's systems can they truly begin to relate and connect. If they are unwilling – or unable – to do this, both suffer.

69   Love is also perceived differently by White Male and Female System persons. In the White Male System, love is seen and expressed as a series of rituals. In the Female System, love is experienced as a flow of energy from solar plexus to solar plexus.

70   I frequently work with couples who are tense and confused about the concept of love. The woman often insists that she feels unloved. The man then counters with a recitation of all of the things he does for her. He brings home the money and supports her and the family. He buys her presents. He takes care of the children in the evenings so she can attend a class. Surely she must see that this is what love is all about!

71   The woman then timidly responds that she still does not "feel" love from him. At this point, he accuses her of being unrealistic and a hopeless romantic and the topic is closed. What more can he do for her? Isn't he doing his best to demonstrate his love for her? Of course! He is being the perfect White Male System lover.

72   While exploring this issue with women, I have found that their perceptions of love tend to be rather vague and tentative. During the first stages of a relationship, women will often complain about not getting flowers, not getting gifts, and not being taken out. They

will equate this lack of attention with a lack of love. Their complaints are not really accurate however; they are not at the root of what these women are experiencing.

Women have been convinced that rituals like these are the true   73
expressions of love. Rituals have no meaning, though, unless another element is present as well. That element has something to do with a flow of energy.

When I ask women to come up with a symbol which they think is   74
representative of love, many draw the sign for infinity. . . . That is because they perceive love as a back-and-forth, cyclical, continuous flow. It moves from the solar plexus of one person to the solar plexus of the other person and back again. During this process, some of the "love energy" from the first person is left behind in the second person, and some of the "love energy" from the second person is added to the flow and returned to the first person.

In addition – and this is very important – this "love energy" is   75
never a finite quantity. In "real" love between two people, new "love energy" is constantly being added to the flow. One always contributes more than one takes. The "old" is still there, but it has been increased by the addition of the "new." Rituals can emerge from this energy exchange and supplement it, but they can never supplant it.

Several blocks can spring up to inhibit this process. A person   76
can send out love energy and find that the person she is directing it to will not let it in. Or the other person can let it in and refuse to take some of it out because of feelings of unworthiness, anger, and so on. Or the other person can take some of it out but not add anything to it. Or the other person can add something to it and then not let it out again. Or the initial sender can block at any of these places when the love energy returns. If the process is blocked in any of these instances, love is not experienced.

Pieces of this process can happen, but it is necessary for contin-   77
uous back-and-forth flowing, holding, and building to occur for women to experience complete loving. Needless to say, rituals are much more efficient and far less time-consuming!

Both persons must feel somewhat good about themselves in   78
order for this flow to take place. Both persons must be allowed to express love from the modality of their own System. For example, if the man can only perform rituals for his wife and not allow time for the energy exchange, neither of them will experience love. If the woman insists on the energy flow while refusing to acknowledge or participate in loving rituals, neither of them will experience love. The relationship never achieves its full richness, and both persons never achieve their full happiness. Both feel misunderstood and unloved.

A man may indeed feel an energy exchange – but within him and   79
the confines of his own System. His love energy in this case exists

solely to serve the self at the center of his universe. He may feel as if he's a very loving person while at the same time neglecting the woman he loves and her System. She then will not experience his energy as love. This is admittedly a complicated process to explain; I am impressed by how many women describe it in similar terms with such clarity.

80   White Male System and Female System persons also differ with respect to how they view friendship. In the White Male System, a friend is someone who can be relied upon to support the "team effort." A friend is a "buddy," a "pal." In the Female System, friendship involves basic respect, trust, and knowing and being known.

81   In the Female System, the focus of friendship is verbal intimacy and mutual sharing of one's being. True friends are those who totally expose themselves to each other, sure in the knowledge that to do so is *safe*.

82   Women are often hurt in relationships with men because they totally expose their beings and do not receive respect and exposure in return. In the Female System, knowing and being known are of utmost importance to friendship. The process of developing this intimacy generates a great deal of energy and excitement. Each person wants very much to know the other. There is a balance present at all times, a sense of equality and purpose.

83   An acquaintance of mine kept telling me that she and her husband were still friends even though their marriage was in turmoil. I finally told her that it did not appear that way to me. He did not respect her; that was evident from his willingness psychologically to smother her and overwhelm her with his needs. He also had no desire to know her. According to the Female System definition, that was no friendship.

84   My acquaintance thought about this for a while before realizing that she had been conforming to his concept of friendship – the White Male System concept. As long as she upheld her part of the family's team effort, she and her husband could be friends *on his terms*. When she did not play her expected role, they could not be friends on any terms, especially not hers.

85   She often tried to sit down with him and tell him about herself, her thoughts, feelings, and insights. He would dutifully listen, but he would not seek out this sharing or participate in it himself. He expected her to give him the friendship he needed, but he would not return to her the friendship she needed.

86   He did, however, share more of himself with her than with anyone else. Many of the men I see in therapy tell me that they have no one with whom they really share themselves or no one they really know very well except for their wives. The wives, on the other hand, almost always have at least one close woman friend.

This friend fulfills their intimacy needs in ways their husbands do not.

Men's friends are usually "teammates" with whom they work or   *87*
play sports. They may not ever really know them or be close to them. They may not need to be, especially if they see their selves and their work as the center of their universe. I am not saying that this is "wrong" or that the Female System way of going about friendship is "right." I do know, however, that it is very difficult for men and women – especially spouses – to be real friends, and this is a shame.

Parenting is another type of relationship that is viewed differ-   *88*
ently by White Male System and Female System persons. In the White Male System, parenting is primarily focused on teaching the child the rules so she or he can live comfortably in the System and contribute to it. The mother is usually delegated to do the teaching, but she is expected to restrict her training efforts to White Male System values and goals. As a result, the child is overprotected and constrained from exploring other alternatives.

In the Female System, parenting means facilitating a child's   *89*
development and unfolding. The emphasis is not on *making* a child into something, but on *participating* in the child's gradual discovery of who she or he is. Parent and child are seen as working together in this process. It is assumed that the child will have to learn to live in the world and therefore develop some coping skills. If the child is overprotected, then she or he will never learn the skills necessary for survival.

The Female System emphasizes the *process* of growing and   *90*
becoming. The White Male System emphasizes the *content* of being a White Male System person.

Once, when my son was very young, I saw him running down the   *91*
street as fast as his little legs could carry him. He rushed through the double doors of our house and carefully closed both of them before he began to howl. He had cut his finger badly on a neighbor's swing, and I could see that it would need stitches.

After we had returned from the doctor and he had calmed down,   *92*
I asked him why he had not been howling *before* he had come inside the house and closed the doors. He then told me that one of his favorite neighbors, who often gave him cookies, had said that "big boys don't cry."

I was appalled at the fact that my child was already being   *93*
conditioned to be a White Male System person. I sat down with him and gently assured him that Daddy cried, Grandpa cried, and so on. I wanted him to know that pain and tears are legitimate to the process of being human, that outside definitions of "maleness" are not always those that should control who we are and become. I

knew that this was not the last time I would have such a discussion with him. It's hard to be a Female System parent in a White Male System!

94   To conclude this discussion on relationships, I would like to dwell for a moment on the issue of commitment. In the White Male System, commitment means incarceration. In the Female System, commitment means a covenant relationship.

95   I have often heard men describe permanent relationships in terms of the loss of freedom. Once they have "settled down," they feel that they no longer have the freedom to move or the freedom to make choices in their lives. To them, marriage is not a growth situation – it's a jail term! This is clear from the institution of the bachelor party, which celebrates a man's last night of "freedom" before he enters into a "life sentence."

96   In the Female System, a committed relationship is a covenant sealed by a pledge. There is no implication that one's freedom is "lost" – only strengthened. Marriage is a step toward freedom, not away from it. In order to make this step, one must be an adult who has freed herself or himself from the baggage of the White Male System. One must know oneself thoroughly to enter into a covenant relationship.

97   It is important to remember that we are discussing systems and how they define themselves and function rather than individuals. No person is completely "pure" in either the White Male System or the Female System. Some men may use some Female System approaches in their relationships and some women may use White Male System approaches in their relationships.

98   However, the fact that White Male System persons and Female System persons perceive relationships so differently often makes the success of those relationships difficult. Many unhappy marriages result. In order to change this, we must all be willing to realize that the White Male System is only a system and not reality. We must learn to value the Female System for what it has to offer us all. . . .

99   In light of the observations I have made with the help of women who have felt "safe" enough to explain their System to me, I feel that I can begin to draw some preliminary conclusions.

100   The White Male System is in general an analytical, defining system. The Female System, on the other hand, is a synthesizing, emerging system.

101   The White Male System feels the need to analyze, understand, and explain the world. It does so by taking a whole, breaking it down into its component parts, and defining each of these parts in turn. People and things are seen as being however they are defined.

The Female System sees the world as constantly growing and *102*
changing. It cannot be defined; it can only be observed as it
emerges. Understanding comes from watching, learning from, and
facilitating the process of emergence. One does not need to pick
something or someone apart. One does not need to control or
define.

Why are the White Male System and the Female System so *103*
radically different? Because differences in and of themselves are
perceived in radically opposing ways by persons in both Systems.

In the White Male System, differences are seen as threats. In the *104*
Female System, differences are seen as opportunities for growth.

When differences are labeled dangerous or harmful, it becomes *105*
essential to train everyone to think and act in similar ways. Thus,
our educational system is oriented toward the "average" child. Any
young person who is found to be "above" or "below" average must
be made to fit the mold. Anyone who insists on her (or his) right to
be different must be done away with, either literally or figuratively.

Because it refuses to see the worth and meaning inherent in *106*
differences and perceives them as threats to be overcome, the
White Male System is a closed system. It stifles creativity and
devours itself from within. It wastes and loses energy and is moving toward a state of entropy.

Because it perceives differences as opportunities for stimulation *107*
and growth, the Female System has been nearly eaten up by the
White Male System. Women have recognized the White Male System as different from their own and sought to learn from it. But our
genuine curiosity and interest – not to mention our need to
survive – has backfired. We, the subordinate and inferior people,
have embraced the System of the dominant and superior ones –
but our own System has been ignored or undermined. . . .

Often, as I share my concepts and theories with other women, *108*
they beam at my descriptions of our System. Many have said to me,
"This is the first time I have ever heard someone say aloud what I
already know!" Women rarely hear about their System, and when
they do it is usually in derogatory terms. It is important for both
women *and* men to know and admit that the Female System exists
and is good – not necessarily better, but good.

It is also important for women *and* men to see that the White *109*
Male System is just that – a system. It is not reality. It is not the
way the world is. Reality is difficult if not impossible to change, but
a system can be changed, even if it means a struggle. That gives us
hope.

QUESTIONS

Language and Style

1. In what instances does the writer use examples to open the reader's eyes?

2. What means are used to make the discussion personal?

3. What special information does the writer claim to have? What special claim to authenticity?

4. Do Schaef's examples strike you as "right"?

Organization

1. Why should Schaef not have defined "women's talk" and "peacekeeping talk"?

2. What categories does Schaef use to distinguish between the Female System and the White Male System? How do these categories help organize the discussion?

3. Identify examples, comparisons, classification, and causal analysis in the extended definition.

Content

1. Compare Schaef's discussion of sexuality and intimacy with Steinem's notion of erotica.

2. Is it clear in what sense males and females can each be said to have a "system"? In what sense could one be said to "believe" in a system?

Vocabulary

commonality	meticulous
peer	absolutions
embryonic	phobic
transcendence	entropy
obviates	modality

Arrest
Aleksandr Solzhenitsyn

The Russian author of (among other works) One Day in the Life of Ivan Desinovich *discusses what it means to be arrested in a totalitarian society. The account is full of fascinating detail, drawn in part from his own experience.*

How do people get to this clandestine Archipelago? Hour by hour planes fly there, ships steer their course there, and trains thunder off to it – but all with nary a mark on them to tell of their destination. And at ticket windows or at travel bureaus for Soviet or foreign tourists the employees would be astounded if you were to ask for a ticket to go there. They know nothing and they've never heard of the Archipelago as a whole or of any one of its innumerable islands.   *1*

Those who go to the Archipelago to administer it get there via the training schools of the Ministry of Internal Affairs.   *2*

Those who go there to be guards are conscripted via the military conscription centers.   *3*

And those who, like you and me, dear reader, go there to die, must get there solely and compulsorily via arrest.   *4*

Arrest! Need it be said that it is a breaking point in your life, a bolt of lightning which has scored a direct hit on you? That it is an unassimilable spiritual earthquake not every person can cope with, as a result of which people often slip into insanity?   *5*

The Universe has as many different centers as there are living beings in it. Each of us is a center of the Universe, and that Universe is shattered when they hiss at you: *"You are under arrest."*   *6*

If *you* are arrested, can anything else remain unshattered by this cataclysm?   *7*

But the darkened mind is incapable of embracing these displacements in our universe, and both the most sophisticated and the veriest simpleton among us, drawing on all life's experience, can gasp out only: "Me? What for?"   *8*

And this is a question which, though repeated millions and millions of times before, has yet to receive an answer.   *9*

Arrest is an instantaneous, shattering thrust, expulsion, somersault from one state into another.   *10*

We have been happily borne – or perhaps have unhappily dragged our weary way – down the long and crooked streets of our   *11* lives, past all kinds of walls and fences made of rotting wood, rammed earth, brick, concrete, iron railings. We have never given a thought to what lies behind them. We have never tried to penetrate them with our vision or our understanding. But there is where the *Gulag* country begins, right next to us, two yards away from us. In addition, we failed to notice an enormous number of closely fitted, well-disguised doors and gates in these fences. All those gates were prepared for us, every last one! And all of a sudden the fateful gate swings quickly open, and four white male hands, unaccustomed to physical labor but nonetheless strong and tenacious, grab us by the leg, arm, collar, cap, ear, and drag us in like a sack, and the gate behind us, the gate to our past life, is slammed shut once and for all.

12   That's all there is to it! You are arrested!

13   And you'll find nothing better to respond with than a lamblike bleat: "Me? What for?"

14   That's what arrest is: it's a blinding flash and a blow which shifts the present instantly into the past and the impossible into omnipotent actuality.

15   That's all. And neither for the first hour nor for the first day will you be able to grasp anything else.

16   Except that in your desperation the fake circus moon will blink at you: "It's a mistake! They'll set things right!"

17   And everything which is by now comprised in the traditional, even literary, image of an arrest will pile up and take shape, not in your own disordered memory, but in what your family and your neighbors in your apartment remember: The sharp nighttime ring or the rude knock at the door. The insolent entrance of the unwiped jackboots of the unsleeping State Security operatives. The frightened and cowed civilian witness at their backs. (And what function does this civilian witness serve? The victim doesn't even dare think about it and the operatives don't remember, but that's what the regulations call for, and so he has to sit there all night long and sign in the morning. For the witness, jerked from his bed, it is torture too — to go out night after night to help arrest his own neighbors and acquaintances.)

18   The traditional image of arrest is also trembling hands packing for the victim — a change of underwear, a piece of soap, something to eat; and no one knows what is needed, what is permitted, what clothes are best to wear; and the Security agents keep interrupting and hurrying you:

19   "You don't need anything. They'll feed you there. It's warm there." (It's all lies. They keep hurrying you to frighten you.)

20   The traditional image of arrest is also what happens afterward, when the poor victim has been taken away. It is an alien, brutal, and crushing force totally dominating the apartment for hours on end, a breaking, ripping open, pulling from the walls, emptying

things from wardrobes and desks onto the floor, shaking, dumping out, and ripping apart − piling up mountains of litter on the floor − and the crunch of things being trampled beneath jackboots. And nothing is sacred in a search! During the arrest of the locomotive engineer Inoshin, a tiny coffin stood in his room containing the body of his newly dead child. The "*jurists*" dumped the child's body out of the coffin and searched it. They shake sick people out of their sickbeds, and they unwind bandages to search beneath them.

Nothing is so stupid as to be inadmissible during a search! For *21* example, they seized from the antiquarian Chetverukhin "a certain number of pages of Tsarist decrees" − to wit, the decree on ending the war with Napoleon, on the formation of the Holy Alliance, and a proclamation of public prayers against cholera during the epidemic of 1830. From our greatest expert on Tibet, Vostrikov, they confiscated ancient Tibetan manuscripts of great value; and it took the pupils of the deceased scholar thirty years to wrest them from the KGB! When the Orientalist Nevsky was arrested, they grabbed Tangut manuscripts − and twenty-five years later the deceased victim was posthumously awarded a Lenin Prize for deciphering them. From Karger they took his archive of the Yenisei Ostyaks and vetoed the alphabet and vocabulary he had developed for this people −and a small nationality was thereby left without any written language. It would take a long time to describe all this in educated speech, but there's a folk saying about the search which covers the subject: *They are looking for something which was never put there.* They carry off whatever they have seized, but sometimes they compel the arrested individual to carry it. Thus Nina Aleksandrovna Palchinskaya hauled over her shoulder a bag filled with the papers and letters of her eternally busy and active husband, the late great Russian engineer, carrying it into *their* maw − once and for all, forever.

For those left behind after the arrest there is the long tail end of *22* a wrecked and devastated life. And the attempts to go and deliver food parcels. But from all the windows the answer comes in barking voices: "Nobody here by that name!" "Never heard of him!" Yes, and in the worst days in Leningrad it took five days of standing in crowded lines just to get to that window. And it may be only after half a year or a year that the arrested person responds at all. Or else the answer is tossed out: "Deprived of the right to correspond." And that means once and for all. "No right to correspondence" − and that almost for certain means: "Has been shot."

That's how we picture arrest to ourselves. *23*

The kind of night arrest described is, in fact, a favorite, because *24* it has important advantages. Everyone living in the apartment is thrown into a state of terror by the first knock at the door. The arrested person is torn from the warmth of his bed. He is in a daze, half-asleep, helpless, and his judgment is befogged. In a night arrest the State Security men have a superiority in numbers: there are many of them, armed, against one person who hasn't even finished buttoning his trousers. During the arrest and search it is highly improbable that a crowd of potential supporters will gather at the entrance. The unhurried, step-by-step visits, first to one apartment, then to another, tomorrow to a third and a fourth, provide an opportunity for the Security operations personnel to be deployed with the maximum efficiency and to imprison many more citizens of a given town than the police force itself numbers.

25   In addition, there's an advantage to night arrests in that neither the people in neighboring apartment houses nor those on the city streets can see how many have been taken away. Arrests which frighten the closest neighbors are no event at all to those farther away. It's as if they had not taken place. Along that same asphalt ribbon on which the Black Marias scurry at night, a tribe of youngsters strides by day with banners, flowers, and gay, untroubled songs.

26   But those who *take*, whose work consists solely of arrests, for whom the horror is boringly repetitive, have a much broader understanding of how arrests operate. They operate according to a large body of theory, and innocence must not lead one to ignore this. The science of arrest is an important segment of the course on general penology and has been propped up with a substantial body of social theory. Arrests are classified according to various criteria: nighttime and daytime; at home, at work, during a journey; first-time arrests and repeats; individual and group arrests. Arrests are distinguished by the degree of surprise required, the amount of resistance expected (even though in tens of millions of cases no resistance was expected and in fact there was none). Arrests are also differentiated by the thoroughness of the required serach, by instructions either to make out or not to make out an inventory of confiscated property or seal a room or apartment; to arrest the wife after the husband and send the children to an orphanage, or to send the rest of the family into exile, or to send the old folks to a labor camp too.

27   No, no: arrests vary widely in form. In 1926 Irma Mendel, a Hungarian, obtained through the Comintern two front-row tickets to the Bolshoi Theatre. Interrogator Kelgel was courting her at the time and she invited him to go with her. They sat through the show very affectionately, and when it was over he took her — straight to the Lubyanka. And if on a flowering June day in 1927 on Kuznetsky Most, the plump-cheeked, redheaded beauty Anna Skripnikova, who had just bought some navy-blue material for a dress, climbed into a hansom cab with a young man-about-town, you can be sure it wasn't a lovers' tryst at all, as the cabman understood very well and showed by his frown (he knew the *Organs* don't pay). It was an arrest. In just a moment they would turn on the Lubyanka and

enter the black maw of the gates. And if, some twenty-two springs later, Navy Captain Second Rank Boris Burkovsky, wearing a white tunic and a trace of expensive eau de cologne, was buying a cake for a young lady, do not take an oath that the cake would ever reach the young lady and not be sliced up instead by the knives of the men searching the captain and then delivered to him in his first cell. No, one certainly cannot say that daylight arrest, arrest during a journey, or arrest in the middle of a crowd has ever been neglected in our country. However, it has always been clean-cut – and, most surprising of all, the victims, in cooperation with the Security men, have conducted themselves in the noblest conceivable manner, so as to spare the living from witnessing the death of the condemned.

Not everyone can be arrested at home, with a preliminary knock   *28*
at the door (and if there is a knock, then it has to be the house manager or else the postman). And not everyone can be arrested at work either. If the person to be arrested is vicious, then it's better to seize him *outside* his ordinary milieu – away from his family and colleagues, from those who share his views, from any hiding places. It is essential that he have no chance to destroy, hide, or pass on anything to anyone. VIPs in the military or the Party were sometimes first given new assignments, ensconced in a private railway car, and then arrested en route. Some obscure, ordinary mortal, scared to death by epidemic arrests all around him and already depressed for a week by sinister glances from his chief, is suddenly summoned to the local Party committee, where he is beamingly presented with a vacation ticket to a Sochi sanatorium. The rabbit is overwhelmed and immediately concludes that his fears were groundless. After expressing his gratitude, he hurries home, triumphant, to pack his suitcase. It is only two hours till train time, and he scolds his wife for being too slow. He arrives at the station with time to spare. And there in the waiting room or at the bar he is hailed by an extraordinarily pleasant young man: "Don't you remember me, Pyotr Ivanich?" Pyotr Ivanich has difficulty remembering: "Well, not exactly, you see, although . . . " The young man, however, is overflowing with friendly concern: "Come now, how can that be? I'll have to remind you. . . . " And he bows respectfully to Pyotr Ivanich's wife: "You must forgive us. I'll keep him only *one minute*." The wife accedes, and trustingly the husband lets himself be led away by the arm – forever or for ten years!

The station is thronged – and no one notices anything. . . . Oh,   *29*
you citizens who love to travel! Do not forget that in every station there are a GPU Branch and several prison cells.

This importunity of alleged acquaintances is so abrupt that only   *30*
a person who has not had the wolfish preparation of camp life is likely to pull back from it. Do not suppose, for example, that if you are an employee of the American Embassy by the name of Alexander D. you cannot be arrested in broad daylight on Gorky Street,

right by the Central Telegraph Office. Your unfamiliar friend dashes through the press of the crowd, and opens his plundering arms to embrace you: "Saaasha!" He simply shouts at you, with no effort to be inconspicuous. "Hey, pal! Long time no see! Come on over, let's get out of the way." At that moment a Pobeda sedan draws up to the curb. . . . And several days later TASS will issue an angry statement to all the papers alleging that informed circles of the Soviet government have no information on the disappearance of Alexander D. But what's so unusual about that? Our boys have carried out such arrests in Brussels – which was where Zhora Blednov was seized – not just in Moscow.

31   One has to give the *Organs* their due: in an age when public speeches, the plays in our theaters, and women's fashions all seem to have come off assembly lines, arrests can be of the most varied kind. They take you aside in a factory corridor after you have had your pass checked – and you're arrested. They take you from a military hospital with a temperature of 102, as they did with Ans Bernshtein, and the doctor will not raise a peep about your arrest – just let him try! They'll take you right off the operating table – as they took N. M. Vorobyev, a school inspector, in 1936, in the middle of an operation for stomach ulcer – and drag you off to a cell, as they did him, half-alive and all bloody (as Karpunich recollects). Or, like Nadya Levitskaya, you try to get information about your mother's sentence, and they give it to you, but it turns out to be a confrontation – and your own arrest! In the Gastronome – the fancy food store – you are invited to the special-order department and arrested there. You are arrested by a religious pilgrim whom you have put up for the night "for the sake of Christ." You are arrested by a meterman who has come to read your electric meter. You are arrested by a bicyclist who has run into you on the street, by a railway conductor, a taxi driver, a savings bank teller, the manager of a movie theater. Anyone of them can arrest you, and you notice the concealed maroon-colored identification card only when it is too late.

32   Sometimes arrests even seem to be a game – there is so much superfluous imagination, so much well-fed energy, invested in them. After all, the victim would not resist anyway. Is it that the Security agents want to justify their employment and their numbers? After, all, it would seem enough to send notices to all the rabbits marked for arrest, and they would show up obediently at the designated hour and minute at the iron gates of State Security with a bundle in their hands – ready to occupy a piece of floor in the cell for which they were intended. And, in fact, that's the way collective farmers are arrested. Who wants to go all the way to a hut at night, with no roads to travel on? They are summoned to the village soviet – and arrested there. Manual workers are called into the office.

33   Of course, every machine has a point at which it is overloaded,

beyond which it cannot function. In the strained and overloaded years of 1945 and 1946, when trainload after trainload poured in from Europe, to be swallowed up immediately and sent off to *Gulag*, all that excessive theatricality went out the window, and the whole theory suffered greatly. All the fuss and feathers of ritual went flying in every direction, and the arrest of tens of thousands took on the appearance of a squalid roll call: they stood there with lists, read off the names of those on one train, loaded them onto another, and that was the whole arrest.

For several decades political arrests were distinguished in our *34* country precisely by the fact that people were arrested who were guilty of nothing and were therefore unprepared to put up any resistance whatsoever. There was a general feeling of being destined for destruction, a sense of having nowhere to escape from the GPU-NKVD (which, incidentally, given our internal passport system, was quite accurate). And even in the fever of epidemic arrests, when people leaving for work said farewell to their families every day, because they could not be certain they would return at night, even then almost no one tried to run away and only in rare cases did people commit suicide. And that was exactly what was required. A submissive sheep is a find for a wolf.

This submissiveness was also due to ignorance of the mechanics *35* of epidemic arrests. By and large, the *Organs* had no profound reasons for their choice of whom to arrest and whom not to arrest. They merely had over-all assignments, quotas for a specific number of arrests. These quotas might be filled on an orderly basis or wholly arbitrarily. In 1937 a woman came to the reception room of the Novocherkassk NKVD to ask what she should do about the unfed unweaned infant of a neighbor who had been arrested. They said: "Sit down, we'll find out." She sat there for two hours – whereupon they took her and tossed her into a cell. They had a total plan which had to be fulfilled in a hurry, and there was no one available to send out into the city – and here was this woman already in their hands!

On the other hand, the NKVD did come to get the Latvian Andrei *36* Pavel near Orsha. But he didn't open the door; he jumped out the window, escaped, and shot straight to Siberia. And even though he lived under his own name, and it was clear from his documents that he had come from Orsha, he was *never* arrested, nor summoned to the Organs, nor subjected to any suspicion whatsoever. After all, search for wanted persons falls into three categories: All-Union, republican, and provincial. And the pursuit of nearly half of those arrested in those epidemics would have been confined to the provinces. A person marked for arrest by virtue of chance circumstances, such as a neighbor's denunciation, could be easily replaced by another neighbor. Others, like Andrei Pavel, who found themselves in a trap or an ambushed apartment by accident, and who were bold enough to escape immediately, before they could be questioned, were never caught and never charged; while those who stayed behind to await justice got a term in prison. And the overwhelming majority – almost all – behaved just like that: without any spirit, helplessly, with a sense of doom.

37   It is true, of course, that the NKVD, in the absence of the person it wanted, would make his relatives guarantee not to leave the area. And, of course, it was easy enough *to cook up* a case against those who stayed behind to replace the one who had fled.

38   Universal innocence also gave rise to the universal failure to act. Maybe they *won't take* you? Maybe it will blow over? A. I. Ladyzhensky was the chief teacher in a school in remote Kologriv. In 1937 a peasant approached him in an open market and passed him a message from a third person: "Aleksandr Ivanich, get out of town, *you are on the list!*" But he stayed: After all, the whole school rests on my shoulders, and *their own* children are pupils here. How can they arrest me? (Several days later he was arrested.) Not everyone was so fortunate as to understand at the age of fourteen, as did Vanya Levitsky: "Every honest man is sure to go to prison. Right now my papa is serving time, and when I grow up they'll put me in too." (They put him in when he was twenty-three years old.) The majority sit quietly and dare to hope. Since you aren't guilty, then how can they arrest you? *It's a mistake!* They are already dragging you along by the collar, and you still keep on exclaiming to yourself: "It's a mistake! *They'll set things straight and let me out!*" Others are being arrested en masse, and that's a bothersome fact, but in those other cases there is always some dark area: "Maybe *he* was guilty . . . ?" But as for you, you are obviously innocent! You still believe that the *Organs* are humanly logical institutions: they will set things straight and let you out.

39   Why, then, should you run away? And how can you resist right then? After all, you'll only make your situation worse; you'll make it more difficult for them to sort out the mistake. And it isn't just that you don't put up any resistance; you even walk down the stairs on tiptoe, as you are ordered to do, so your neighbors won't hear.

40   At what exact point, then, should one resist? When one's belt is taken away? When one is ordered to face into a corner? When one crosses the threshold of one's home? An arrest consists of a series of incidental irrelevancies, of a multitude of things that do not matter, and there seems no point in arguing about any one of them individually – especially at a time when the thoughts of the person arrested are wrapped tightly about the big question: "What for?" – and yet all these incidental irrelevancies taken together implacably constitute the arrest.

41   Almost anything can occupy the thoughts of a person who has just been arrested! This alone would fill volumes. There can be

feelings which we never suspected. When nineteen-year-old Yevgeniya Doyarenko was arrested in 1921 and three young Chekists were poking about her bed and through the underwear in her chest of drawers, she was not disturbed. There was nothing there, and they would find nothing. But all of a sudden they touched her personal diary, which she would not have shown even to her own mother. And these hostile young strangers reading the words she had written was more devastating to her than the whole Lubyanka with its bars and its cellars. It is true of many that the outrage inflicted by arrest on their personal feelings and attachments can be far, far stronger than their political beliefs or their fear of prison. A person who is not inwardly prepared for the use of violence against him is always weaker than the person committing the violence.

There are a few bright and daring individuals who understand   *42* instantly. Grigoryev, the Director of the Geological Institute of the Academy of Sciences, barricaded himself inside and spent two hours burning up his papers when they came to arrest him in 1948.

Sometimes the principal emotion of the person arrested is relief   *43* and even *happiness!* This is another aspect of human nature. It happened before the Revolution too: the Yekaterinodar school teacher Serdyukova, involved in the case of Aleksandr Ulyanov, felt only relief when she was arrested. But this feeling was a thousand times stronger during epidemics of arrests when all around you they were hauling in people like yourself and still had not come for you; for some reason they were taking their time. After all, that kind of exhaustion, that kind of suffering, is worse than any kind of arrest, and not only for a person of limited courage. Vasily Vlasov, a fearless Communist, whom we shall recall more than once later on, renounced the idea of escape proposed by his non-Party assistants, and pined away because the entire leadership of the Kady District was arrested in 1937, and they kept delaying and delaying his own arrest. He could only endure the blow head on. He did endure it, and then he relaxed, and during the first days after his arrest he felt marvelous. In 1934 the priest Father Irakly went to Alma-Ata to visit some believers in exile there. During his absence they came three times to his Moscow apartment to arrest him. When he returned, members of his flock met him at the station and refused to let him go home, and for eight years hid him in one apartment after another. The priest suffered so painfully from this harried life that when he was finally arrested in 1942 he sang hymns of praise to God.

In this chapter we are speaking only of the masses, the helpless   *44* rabbits arrested for no one knows what reason. But in this book we will also have to touch on those who in postrevolutionary times remained genuinely *political*. Vera Rybakova, a Social Democratic

student, *dreamed* when she was in freedom of being in the deten-
tion center in Suzdal. Only there did she hope to encounter her old
comrades – for there were none of them left in freedom. And only
there could she work out her world outlook. The Socialist Revolutionary – the SR – Yekaterina Olitskaya didn't consider herself
worthy of being imprisoned in 1924. After all, Russia's best people
had served time and she was still young and had not yet done
anything for Russia. But *freedom* itself was expelling her. And so
both of them went to prison – with pride and happiness.

45   "Resistance! Why didn't you resist?" Today those who have
continued to live on in comfort scold those who suffered.

46   Yes, resistance, should have begun right there, at the moment of
the arrest itself.

47   But it did not begin.

48   And so they are *leading* you. During a daylight arrest there is
always that brief and unique moment when they are *leading* you,
either inconspicuously, on the basis of a cowardly deal you have
made, or else quite openly, their pistols unholstered, through a
crowd of hundreds of just such doomed innocents as yourself. You
aren't gagged. You really can and you really ought to *cry out* – to
cry out that you are being arrested! That villains in disguise are
trapping people! That arrests are being made on the strength of
false denunciations! That millions are being subjected to silent
reprisals! If many such outcries had been heard all over the city in
the course of a day, would not our fellow citizens perhaps have
begun to bristle! And would arrests perhaps no longer have been
so easy?

49   In 1927, when submissiveness had not yet softened our brains to
such a degree, two Checkists tried to arrest a woman on Serpukhov
Square during the day. She grabbed hold of the stanchion of a
streetlamp and began to scream, refusing to submit. A crowd
gathered. (There had to have been that kind of woman; there had
to have been that kind of crowd too! Passers-by didn't all just close
their eyes and hurry by!) The quick young men immediately became flustered. They can't *work* in the public eye. They got into
their car and fled. (Right then and there she should have gone to a
railroad station and left! But she went home to spend the night.
And during the night they took her off to the Lubyanka.)

50   Instead, not one sound comes from *your* parched lips, and that
passing crowd naïvely believes that you and your executioners are
friends out for a stroll.

51   I myself often had the chance to *cry out*.

52   On the eleventh day after my arrest, three SMERSH bums, more
burdened by four suitcases full of war booty than by me (they had
come to rely on me in the course of the long trip), brought me to
the Byelorussian Station in Moscow. They were called a *Special
Convoy* – in other words, a special escort guard – but in actual

fact their automatic pistols only interfered with their dragging along the four terribly heavy bags of loot they and their chiefs in SMERSH counterintelligence on the Second Byelorussian Front had plundered in Germany and were now bringing to their families in the Fatherland under the pretext of convoying me. I myself lugged a fifth suitcase with no great joy since it contained my diaries and literary works, which were being used as evidence against me.

Not one of the three knew the city, and it was up to me to pick   *53*
the shortest route to the prison. I had personally to conduct them to the Lubyanka, where they had never been before (and which, in fact, I confused with the Ministry of Foreign Affairs).

I had spent one day in the counterintelligence prison at army   *54*
headquarters and three days in the counterintelligence prison at the headquarters of the front, where my cellmates had educated me in the deceptions practiced by the interrogators, their threats and beatings; in the fact that once a person was arrested he was never released; and in the inevitability of a *tenner*, a ten-year sentence; and then by a miracle I had suddenly burst out of there and for four days had traveled like a *free* person among *free* people, even though my flanks had already lain on rotten straw beside the latrine bucket, my eyes had already beheld beaten-up and sleepless men, my ears had heard the truth, and my mouth had tasted prison gruel. So why did I keep silent? Why, in my last minute out in the open, did I not attempt to enlighten the hoodwinked crowd?

I kept silent, too, in the Polish city of Brodnica — but maybe they   *55*
didn't understand Russian there. I didn't call out one word on the streets of Bialystok — but maybe it wasn't a matter that concerned the Poles. I didn't utter a sound at the Volkovysk Station — but there were very few people there. I walked along the Minsk Station platform beside those same bandits as if nothing at all were amiss — but the station was still a ruin. And now I was leading the SMERSH men through the circular upper concourse of the Byelorussian-Radial subway station on the Moscow circle line, with its white-ceilinged dome and brilliant electric lights, and opposite us two parallel escalators, thickly packed with Muscovites, rising from below. It seemed as though they were all looking at me! They kept coming in an endless ribbon from down there, from the depths of ignorance — on and on beneath the gleaming dome, reaching toward me for at least one word of truth — so why did I keep silent?

Every man always has handy a dozen glib little reasons why he is   *56*
right not to sacrifice himself.

Some still have hopes of a favorable outcome to their case and   *57*
are afraid to ruin their chances by an outcry. (For, after all, we get no news from that other world, and we do not realize that from the very moment of arrest our fate has almost certainly been decided in the worst possible sense and that we cannot make it any worse.)

Others have not yet attained the mature concepts on which a shout of protest to the crowd must be based. Indeed, only a revolutionary has slogans on his lips that are crying to be uttered aloud; and where would the uninvolved, peaceable average man come by such slogans? He simply *does not know what* to shout. And then, last of all, there is the person whose heart is too full of emotion, whose eyes have seen too much, for that whole ocean to pour forth in a few disconnected cries.

58   As for me, I kept silent for one further reason: because those Muscovites thronging the steps of the escalators were too few for me, *too few!* Here my cry would be heard by 200 or twice 200, but what about the 200 million? Vaguely, unclearly, I had a vision that someday I would cry out to the 200 million.

59   But for the time being I did not open my mouth, and the escalator dragged me implacably down into the nether world.

60   And when I got to Okhotny Ryad, I continued to keep silent.

61   Nor did I utter a cry at the Metropole Hotel.

62   Nor wave my arms on the Golgotha of Lubyanka Square.

63   Mine was, probably, the easiest imaginable kind of arrest. It did not tear me from the embrace of kith and kin, nor wrench me from a deeply cherished home life. One pallid European February it took me from our narrow salient on the Baltic Sea, where, depending on one's point of view, either we had surrounded the Germans or they had surrounded us, and it deprived me only of my familiar artillery battery and the scenes of the last three months of the war.

64   The brigade commander called me to his headquarters and asked me for my pistol; I turned it over without suspecting any evil intent, when suddenly, from a tense, immobile suite of staff officers in the corner, two counterintelligence officers stepped forward hurriedly, crossed the room in a few quick bounds, their four hands grabbed simultaneously at the star on my cap, my shoulder boards, my officer's belt, my map case, and they shouted theatrically:

65   "You are under arrest!"

66   Burning and prickling from head to toe, all I could exclaim was:

67   "Me? What for?"

68   And even though there is usually no answer to this question, surprisingly I received one! This is worth recalling, because it is so contrary to our usual custom. Hardly had the SMERSH men finished "plucking" me and taken my notes on political subjects, along with my map case, and begun to push me as quickly as possible toward the exit, urged on by the German shellfire rattling the windowpanes, than I heard myself firmly addressed — yes! Across the sheer gap separating me from those left behind, the gap created by the heavy-falling word "arrest," across that quarantine line not even a sound dared penetrate, came the unthinkable, magic words of the brigade commander:

69   "Solzhenitsyn. Come back here."

70   With a sharp turn I broke away from the hands of the SMERSH

men and stepped back to the brigade commander. I had never known him very well. He had never condescended to run-of-the-mill conversations with me. To me his face had always conveyed an order, a command, wrath. But right now it was illuminated in a thoughtful way. Was it from shame for his own involuntary part in this dirty business? Was it from an impulse to rise above the pitiful subordination of a whole lifetime? Ten days before, I had led my own reconnaissance battery almost intact out of the *fire pocket* in which the twelve heavy guns of his artillery battalion had been left, and now he had to renounce me because of a piece of paper with a seal on it?

"You have ... " he asked weightily, "a friend on the First Ukranian   71
Front?"

"It's forbidden! You have no right!" the captain and the major of   72
counterintelligence shouted at the colonel. In the corner, the suite of staff officers crowded closer to each other in fright, as if they feared to share the brigade commander's unbelievable rashness (the political officers among them already preparing to present *materials* against him). But I had already understood: I knew instantly I had been arrested because of my correspondence with a school friend, and understood from what direction to expect danger.

Zakhar Georgiyevich Travkin could have stopped right there! But   73
no! Continuing his attempt to expunge his part in this and to stand erect before his own conscience, he rose from behind his desk – he had never stood up in my presence in my former life – and reached across the quarantine line that separated us and gave me his hand, although he would never have reached out his hand to me had I remained a free man. And pressing my hand, while his whole suite stood there in mute horror, showing that warmth that may appear in an habitually severe face, he said fearlessly and precisely:

"I wish you happiness, Captain!"   74

Not only was I no longer a captain, but I had been exposed as an   75
enemy of the people (for among us every person is totally exposed from the moment of arrest). And he had wished happiness – to an enemy?

The panes rattled. The German shells tore up the earth two   76
hundred yards away, reminding one that *this* could not have happened back in the rear, under the ordinary circumstances of established existence, but only out here, under the breath of death, which was not only close by but in the face of which all were equal.

This is not going to be a volume of memoirs about my own life.   77
Therefore I am not going to recount the truly amusing details of my arrest, which was like no other. That night the SMERSH officers gave up their last hope of being able to make out where we were on the map – they never had been able to read maps anyway. So they politely handed the map to me and asked me to tell the driver how to proceed to counterintelligence at army headquarters. I, there-

fore, led them and myself to that prison, and in gratitude they immediately put me not in an ordinary cell but in a punishment cell. And I really must describe that closet in a German peasant house which served as a temporary punishment cell.

78   It was the length of one human body and wide enough for three to lie packed tightly, four at a pinch. As it happened, I was the fourth, shoved in after midnight. The three lying there blinked sleepily at me in the light of the smoky kerosene lantern and moved over, giving me enough space to lie on my side, half between them, half on top of them, until gradually, by sheer weight, I could wedge my way in. And so four overcoats lay on the crushed-straw-covered floor, with eight boots pointing at the door. They slept and I burned. The more self-assured I had been as a captain half a day before, the more painful it was to crowd onto the floor of that closet. Once or twice the other fellows woke up numb on one side, and we all turned over at the same time.

79   Toward morning they awoke, yawned, grunted, pulled up their legs, moved into various corners, and our acquaintance began.

80   "What are you in for?"

81   But a troubled little breeze of caution had already breathed on me beneath the poisoned roof of SMERSH and I pretended to be surprised:

82   "No idea. Do the bastards tell you?"

83   However, my cellmates — tankmen in soft black helmets — hid nothing. They were three honest, openhearted soldiers — people of a kind I had become attached to during the war years because I myself was more complex and worse. All three had been officers. Their shoulder boards also had been viciously torn off, and in some places the cotton batting stuck out. On their stained field shirts light patches indicated where decorations had been removed, and there were dark and red scars on their faces and arms, the results of wounds and burns. Their tank unit had, unfortunately, arrived for repairs in the village where SMERSH counterintelligence headquarters of the Forty-eighth Army was located. Still damp from the battle of the day before, yesterday they had gotten drunk, and on the outskirts of the village broke into a bath where they had noticed two raunchy broads going to bathe. The girls, half-dressed, managed to get away all right from the soldiers' staggering, drunken legs. But one of them, it turned out, was the property of the army Chief of Counterintelligence, no less.

84   Yes! For three weeks the war had been going on inside Germany, and all of us knew very well that if the girls were German they could be raped and then shot. This was almost a combat distinction. Had they been Polish girls or our own displaced Russian girls, they could have been chased naked around the garden and slapped on the behind — an amusement, no more. But just because this one

was the "campaign wife" of the Chief of Counterintelligence, right off some deep-in-the-rear sergeant had viciously torn from three front-line officers the shoulder boards awarded them by the front headquarters and had taken off the decorations conferred upon them by the Presidium of the Supreme Soviet. And now these warriors, who had gone through the whole war and who had no doubt crushed more than one line of enemy trenches, were waiting for a court-martial, whose members, had it not been for their tank, could have come nowhere near the village.

We put out the kerosene lamp, which had already used up all the air there was to breathe. A *Judas hole* the size of a postage stamp had been cut in the door and through it came indirect light from the corridor. Then, as if afraid that with the coming of daylight we would have too much room in the punishment cell, they *tossed in* a fifth person. He stepped in wearing a newish Red Army tunic and a cap that was also new, and when he stopped opposite the peephole we could see a fresh face with a turned-up nose and red cheeks. *85*

"Where are you from, brother? Who are you?" *86*

"From the *other* side," he answered briskly. "A shhpy." *87*

"You're kidding!" We were astounded. (To be a spy and to admit it – Sheinin and the brothers Tur had never written that kind of spy story!) *88*

"What is there to kid about in wartime?" the young fellow sighed reasonably. "And just how else can you get back home from being a POW? Well, you tell me!" *89*

He had barely begun to tell us how, some days back, the Germans had led him through the front lines so that he could play the spy and blow up bridges, whereupon he had gone immediately to the nearest battalion headquarters to turn himself in; but the weary, sleep-starved battalion commander hadn't believed his story about being a spy and had sent him off to the nurse to get a pill. And at that moment new impressions burst upon us: *90*

"Out for toilet call! Hands behind your backs!" hollered a master sergeant *hardhead* as the door sprang open; he was just built for swinging the tail of a 122-millimeter cannon. *91*

A circle of machine gunners had been strung around the peasant courtyard, guarding the path which was pointed out to us and which went behind the barn. I was bursting with indignation that some ignoramus of a master sergeant dared to give orders to us officers: "Hands behind your backs!" But the tank officers put their hands behind them and I followed suit. *92*

Back of the barn was a small square area in which the snow had been all trampled down but had not yet melted. It was soiled all over with human feces, so densely scattered over the whole square that it was difficult to find a spot to place one's two feet and squat. However, we spread ourselves about and the five of us did squat *93* down. Two machine gunners grimly pointed their machine pistols at us as we squatted, and before a minute had passed the master sergeant brusquely urged us on:

94   "Come on, hurry it up! With us they do it quickly!"

95   Not far from me squatted one of the tankmen, a native of Rostov, a tall, melancholy senior lieutenant. His face was blackened by a thin film of metallic dust or smoke, but the big red scar stretching across his cheek stood out nonetheless.

96   "What do you mean, *with us*?" he asked quietly, indicating no intention of hurrying back to the punishment cell that still stank of kerosene.

97   "In SMERSH counterintelligence!" the master sergeant shot back proudly and more resonantly than was called for. (The counterintelligence men used to love that tastelessly concocted word "SMERSH," manufactured from the initial syllables of the words for "death to spies." They felt it intimidated people.)

98   "And *with us* we do it slowly," replied the senior lieutenant thoughtfully. His helmet was pulled back, uncovering his still untrimmed hair. His oaken, battle-hardened rear end was lifted toward the pleasant coolish breeze.

99   "Where do you mean, *with us*?" the master sergeant barked at him more loudly than he needed to.

100   "In the Red Army," the senior lieutenant replied very quietly from his heels, measuring with his look the cannon-tailer that never was.

101   Such were my first gulps of prison air.

QUESTIONS

Language and Style

1. How would you characterize the writer's tone? Identify some instances of "speech-making." Despite the subject there is some humour here. Cite some examples and explain the origin of the humour.

2. Who is the "you" frequently addressed in the essay?

3. How does the writer characterize the officials who carry out the arrests? Those who are arrested?

Organization

1. Notice the exploratory nature of the discussion. What personal experiences are included? What historical ones?

2. What, more particularly, is the apparent purpose of the discussion?

3. Locate instances of classification, examples, narration, process, and causality in the discussion.

4. What aspects of arrest are dealt with in Solzhenitsyn's essay?

Vocabulary

archipelago	conscripted
unassimilable	cataclysm
Gulag	omnipotent
maw	penology
Comintern	Bolshoi
Lubyanka	ensconced
implacable	nether
Golgotha	pallid
condescended	suite
clandestine	antiquarian
cholera	

WRITING EXTENDED DEFINITIONS

An extended definition gives a writer the opportunity to explore the implications of an idea. Some ideas are worth the trouble, and the investigation yields a worthwhile result. The ideas which prove worthwhile are usually the "bigger" ideas people use daily and easily without paying much attention to their contents.

"Poison" is such an idea. Ordinarily the term is used to refer to a substance which causes illness or death upon being ingested. People are accustomed to this meaning and avoid harmful substances like prussic acid and strychnine and are careful about the mushrooms they eat. But dictionary definitions reveal only this much. What is it about a substance which makes it poisonous? A careful exploration of the idea will remind people that under some conditions substances ordinarily considered necessary and beneficial to health, such as salt, are poisonous, while other substances usually thought poisonous save lives. Exploring the idea of "poison" reveals the importance of balanced eating and drinking and suggests something about our place in the world.

There are no settled patterns of development which extended

definitions must follow, but, even though there are no formulas or rules for proceeding, the writer is constrained by an attitude appropriate to exploration. The writer does not know what will be discovered until it is uncovered. The writer should not explore in order to "find" an implication which, it is assumed, is already there. The writer should have no "axe to grind." The process of exploring an idea should work to open up its contents and is marked by curiosity rather than special pleading.

Almost any expository technique can be used to describe and organize the exploration: the types and kinds and varieties of poisons may be considered, examples may be examined, the way in which a poison works described. The writer can use any appropriate tool, but with this freedom comes the responsibility to report the findings honestly.

SUGGESTIONS FOR WRITING

Here are some ideas which are worth exploring:

1. Winter
2. Courage
3. Friendship
4. Maturity
5. Honesty
6. Common sense
7. Freedom
8. Self-control
9. Pornography
10. Feminism
11. Electricity
12. Intelligence
13. Fear
14. Adult
15. Food
16. Work
17. Terrorism
18. Prejudice
19. House
20. Efficiency.

Authors and Sources

Tiny Bennett. A long-time Canadian writer on fishing, Tiny Bennett is the author of *The Art of Angling*, from which "A Day's Fishing" has been excerpted. His book has recently been issued in a new edition.

Debra Black. Debra Black is a free-lance writer from Toronto. She has recently published articles in *Equinox, Executive, Saturday Night*, and *Canadian Business*, where "A Place in the Sun" first appeared.

Michael Bliss. Michael Bliss is a professor of history at the University of Toronto. He has published an account of the discovery of insulin (*Banting and Best*) and, more recently, a history of Canadian business (*Northern Enterprise*). He occasionally acts as commentator and political analyst for CBC television. "The Next Depression" originally appeared in *Saturday Night*.

Emily Carr. A Canadian painter and writer, Emily Carr's genius was long unrecognized. Only late in her life did her striking paintings of West Coast subjects gain notice. Her published work, as vivid in its way as her painting, includes the memoirs and recollections of *The Book of Small*, Hundreds and Thousands, and *Klee Wyck*, from which "Sophie" is excerpted.

Joseph Conrad. In 1889 this Polish-born English novelist and short-story writer gave up his career as a merchant mariner and began a career in writing. His works, a dozen books, include *Lord Jim*, from which "The Pqtna at Sea" is drawn, and *Heart of Darkness* – a story on which the movie *Apocalypse Now* is closely modelled.

Irving Copi. Irving Copi was a professor of philosophy at the Universities of Michigan and Hawaii and the author of a standard text on logic and reason, *Introduction to Logic*, from which the excerpt "Deduction and Induction" is taken.

Bergen and Cornelia Evans. The Evanses are the authors of several informal commentaries on the English language, including *A Dictionary of Contemporary American Usage*. "The Meaning of Cliché" is borrowed from that book.

Kenneth Grahame. Grahame was an Edinburgh banker who first told the "Toad" stories to his young son. The stories became *The Wind in the Willows*, from which comes the excerpt "Mr. Toad." Other books include *The Golden Age* and *Dream Days*.

Calvin S. Hall and Gardiner Lindzey. Hall and Lindzey have taught psychology at the Universities of California and Texas, respectively. Their review of personality theory, *Theories of Personality*, is the source of "Sheldon's Scale of Temperament."

Edward T. Hall. An American anthropologist and at one time an important foreign-aid official, Hall's books include *The Silent Language* and *The Hidden Dimension.* "Distance in Man" is drawn from the latter book, which explores how people from different cultures interpret the meaning of space.

Michael Harris. For some time Harris, as the Atlantic correspondent for *The Globe and Mail*, wrote a regional column of news and observations. "Signs of Spring in the Valley?" is one of those columns.

S.I. Hayakawa. A former U.S. Senator (from California), Hayakawa was born in British Columbia and made his early career as a teacher and advocate of semantics, a theory that seeks to understand human problems as problems of language. "Giving Things Names" is from his book *Language in Thought and Action.*

Samuel Hearne. Hearne was one of the earliest explorers of Canada's Arctic, which he investigated on foot and by canoe for his employer, the Hudson's Bay Company. Hearne's personal journals have been edited for the modern reader by Farley Mowat, author of many works relating to the North, including *Never Cry Wolf.*

James Herriot. Still a practising veterinary surgeon in England's Yorkshire, Herriot recalled the area's people and (no less) animals in *All Things Bright and Beautiful*, and *All Creatures Great and Small*. This was the basis of the popular television series seen on Canadian and American public television.

George C. Hodge. George C. Hodge served with the U.S. Army Air Corps during the Second World War. The excerpt is from his war diary.

Pauline Kael. Pauline Kael is the principal movie reviewer for *The New Yorker* magazine. Her reviews and essays on the movies have been published in several collections, including *I Lost It at the Movies*, from which "Why Are Movies So Bad?" is reprinted

John Kyle. John Kyle is an economist with Imperial Oil. The article "Profits" originally appeared in that company's publication, *The Review.*

Barry Lopez. Lopez has written several books on natural history – including *Of Wolves and Men* and *Winter Count*. "Ice and Light" is excerpted from his most recent book, *Arctic Dreams.*

Michael Maccoby. Michael Maccoby's essay originally appeared in *The Spectrum*, the official publication of the Institute of Electrical and Electronics Engineers.

Hugh MacLennan. Hugh MacLennan's long, distinguished career as a writer and teacher (at McGill University) has produced several novels – *Two Solitudes, The Watch that Ends the Night*, and *Barometer Rising*, from which "The Halifax Explosion" is borrowed.

Kirk Makin. Makin reports for *The Globe and Mail.* His work has also appeared in *Saturday Night.*

Nellie McClung. An early campaigner for women's suffrage in Canada, McClung also campaigned for decent, humane working conditions, as the excerpt "A Gentleman of the Old School" makes clear. It originally appeared in her book of recollections, *The Stream Runs Fast.*

Rod McQueen. Rod McQueen's work has been published in *Maclean's, Canadian Business, The Financial Post Magazine,* and *Saturday Night,* where "The Painful Realities of the New Technology" first appeared.

Peter C. Newman. Newman has written extensively on Canadian history, politics, and business. Formerly the Editor-in-Chief of *Maclean's,* his books include *Company of Adventurers* (a history of the Hudson's Bay Company), *Renegade in Power* (an account of the rise and fall of John Diefenbaker), and *The Canadian Establishment,* from which "The Acquisitors' Roost" is reprinted.

Anaïs Nin. An American novelist and essayist, Nin began her diaries as letters to her father. They were eventually published in a collection of seven volumes. "Morocco" is an excerpt from those diaries.

Mark Orkin. Books by Mark Orkin, a lawyer, include *Legal Ethics, The Law of Costs,* and *Speaking Canadian English,* an informal account of the language. The excerpt presented here is from the latter.

George Orwell. This English novelist and essayist is best known for *Animal Farm* (a political fable) and the novel *1984.* Orwell served with the Indian Police in Burma and fought briefly in The Spanish Civil War. "Marrakech" is reprinted from Orwell's collected letters and essays.

Laurence J. Peter. Peter's book, *The Peter Principle,* from which this excerpt has been borrowed, is a humorous (but perfectly serious) analysis of organizational behaviour. A more recent work examines organizations in a similar way – *Why Things Go Wrong.*

Robert Pirsig. Robert Pirsig's autobiographical book, *Zen and the Art of Motorcycle Maintenance,* from which the excerpt comes, is an account of a cross-country motorcycle trip undertaken as an anodyne to an emotional crisis and is, therefore, about an internal journey as well.

Paul Roberts. Roberts's book *Understanding English,* from which "The Oxford English Dictionary" has been borrowed, is his best-known work.

Susan Sargent. Susan Sargent is a free-lance writer. "How to Weave a Basket" first appeared in *Country Journal,* a magazine devoted to rural subjects.

Anne Wilson Schaef. A clinical psychologist, Anne Wilson Schaef's most recent book is *When Society Becomes an Addict* – an examination of addiction in Western society. "The Female System" is borrowed from her first book, *Women's Reality*.

Leonard Schifrin. Shifrin's article, "Canada's Forgotten Poor," originally appeared in *Maclean's.*

Aleksandr Solzhenitsyn. Solzhenitsyn, a dissident Soviet artillery officer during the Second World War, was arrested and imprisoned by "the authorities." His best-known works are *A Day in the Life of Ivan Denisovich*, (a novel of prison life which was later made into a movie) and *The Gulag Archipelago* (an account of the vast system of Soviet prison camps), from which "Arrest" is excerpted. Solzhenitsyn now lives in Vermont.

Robert Sommer. Robert Sommer has written many articles on the effects of physical setting on people's behaviour. "The Ladies Converse" originally appeared in his book *Personal Space.*

Gloria Steinem. Steinem, co-founder and editor of *Ms.* magazine, advances progressive political and social causes in her writing. A collection of her work, *Outrageous Acts and Everyday Rebellions*, includes "Erotica vs. Pornography," which is excerpted here.

Paul Theroux. A novelist and travel writer, Theroux's work includes *The Mosquito Coast* (a novel and successful movie) and *The Kingdom by the Sea* (an unusual travel book). "Being a Man" appeared in *Sunrise with Seamonsters*, a collection of Theroux's shorter pieces.

James Thurber. Thurber was a famous American humourist, playwright and cartoonist. His work appears in several books, among them *My Life and Hard Times*, *My World and Welcome to It*, and *The Thurber Carnival.*

Harry Thurston. Harry Thurston is a writer who lives in Nova Scotia. He has contributed articles to *Harrowsmith*, *Atlantic Insight*, and *Equinox*, from which "The Basque Connection" is reprinted.

J. L. Welch. Welch is a free-lance writer who lives in Vermont. "Secrets of the Squash King" originally appeared in *Harrowsmith* magazine.

Virginia Woolf. An English novelist and essayist, Woolf's best-known works include *To the Lighthouse* (an experimental novel), *A Room of One's Own*, and *The Death of the Moth and Other Essays*, where the essay presented here was first published.

Wayne S. Wooden. Wayne S. Wooden is an American psychologist. "The Flames of Youth" originally appeared in *Psychology Today.*